ARCHITECTURE AND THE FACE OF COAL

COAL

MINING AND MODERN BRITAIN

ARCHITECTURE AND THE FACE OF

COAL

MINING AND MODERN BRITAIN

LUND HUMPHRIES

GARY A BOYD

First published in 2023 by Lund Humphries

Lund Humphries
Huckletree Shoreditch
Alphabeta Building
18 Finsbury Square
London EC2A 1AH
UK

www.lundhumphries.com

Architecture and the Face of Coal: Mining and Modern Britain
© Gary A. Boyd, 2023

All rights reserved

ISBN: 978–1–84822–356–1

A Cataloguing-in-Publication record for this book is available from the British Library.

All rights reserved. No part of this publication may be reproduced, stored in a retrieval system or transmitted in any form or by any means, electrical, mechanical or otherwise, without first seeking the permission of the copyright owners and publishers. Every effort has been made to seek permission to reproduce the images in this book. Any omissions are entirely unintentional, and details should be addressed to the publishers.

Gary A. Boyd has asserted his right under the Copyright, Designs and Patent Act, 1988, to be identified as the Author of this Work.

Copy edited by Jacqui Cornish
Printed in Estonia

The publishers gratefully acknowledge the support of the Leverhulme Trust

LEVERHULME TRUST

The author and publisher gratefully acknowledge the support of the Paul Mellon Centre for Studies in British Art

CONTENTS

- 7 *Acknowledgements*
- 9 Introduction: An Architecture of Disappearance

PART I: PITHEAD BATHS AND THE ARCHITECTURE OF WELFARE

- 14 Pithead Baths, Modernism and Modernity
- 23 John Henry Forshaw
- 29 Miners' Welfare Committee Architects' Department and 'Official' Architecture
- 38 The Social Context of Coal Between the Wars
- 39 The Sankey Commission
- 42 The Beginning of the Miners' Welfare Fund
- 46 British and European Precedents of Pithead Baths
- 52 Landscapes of Bathing
- 56 Architecture and the Pithead Baths Movement
- 60 The Samuel Commission and the Development of the Pithead Baths Programme
- 63 Dudok, Morality and Modern Aesthetics
- 67 The Lessons of Dudok's Schools
- 73 Modernist Technological Developments in the Pithead Baths Programme
- 80 The Experimental Baths
- 84 The Modern Interior
- 90 The Evolution of Form and Representation: The Search for Expression
- 103 Exploiting the L-shape
- 114 Linear Forms
- 121 The Block
- 125 Other Iterations
- 130 Smaller Pithead Baths
- 133 Prefabrications and Mass Production

PART II: SETTLEMENT

- 142 Welfare Beyond the Pithead Baths
- 146 Traditional Mining Settlements
- 155 Morality, Mining Companies and Model Towns
- 164 Unwin and Coal Mining
- 177 Doncaster and the East Kent Coalfields: Patrick Abercrombie
- 186 The Refinement of a Coalfield Type: The Industrial Housing Association and 'The Building of Twelve Thousand Houses'

PART III: ARCHITECTURE, PUBLICITY AND THE PLAN FOR COAL

- 200 Introduction
- 201 The Reid Report and Technical Transformations
- 206 Comrie and Other Architectural Paradigms
- 216 Communicating the Nationalised Industry
- 226 Planning and Underground Architecture
- 232 Inter-colliery Architecture
- 240 Reconstructed Collieries and Superpits
- 256 Rothes and Scotland
- 267 Coda: Coal and the New Towns

- 277 Notes
- 282 Bibliography
- 292 Index

ACKNOWLEDGEMENTS

A large number of people have contributed to the production of this volume and I owe them a great deal of thanks. First of all, I would like to sincerely thank the Leverhulme Trust for giving me the opportunity to carry out this research through the award of a Major Research Fellowship (as well as a costed extension due to the pandemic). I am particularly grateful to Nicola Thorp for her administrative guidance throughout.

I am indebted to my colleagues in Architecture, School of Natural and Built Environment at Queen's University Belfast without whose support this project would not have been possible. I am especially grateful to fellow academics Greg Keeffe, Sarah Lappin and Mark M. Campbell for their help, advice and patience, and also to the professional support staff, especially Karen Rice, Maria Bennett, Roslyn Barnes and Nuala Wilson. I am also extremely appreciative of the help I received from the university's Research and Research Finance Offices.

During the course of the research for this book, I engaged with a series of archives, libraries, museums and sites which I have listed in the references section of the book. I am very grateful to the unfailing professionalism, politeness and help I received from their staff.

I would like to thank: Stefan Berger for hosting me at the Institute for Social Movements at the University of the Ruhr, Bochum; Derek Charlton, for allowing me to see inside the pithead baths at Lynemouth; Coco Whittaker for sharing her insights and knowledge of the pithead baths programme, especially in the north-east; John Cruwys for sharing information on Lea Hall Colliery and Staffordshire mining; and the panel of the session on coal I chaired at the Society of Architectural Historians (SAH) Annual Meeting in Glasgow in 2017. Their collective erudition and enthusiasm convinced me of the value of further research in this field. Denis Linehan deserves special thanks for his immense kindness in sharing his knowledge and previously culled resources on mining with me.

I would also like to thank Murray Fraser for his ongoing generosity and support, Kathleen James-Chakraborty whose generosity and insights have helped widen my perspectives on coal mining and architecture, and Hugh Campbell for his longstanding seeding of ideas. Sections of the book have benefitted from the comments and observations of Brian Ward and, of course, the whole volume is indebted to the knowledge, care and expertise of my commissioning editor Valerie Rose, at Lund Humphries, as well as the talents of the production team, especially Sarah Thorowgood and Jacqui Cornish. Any mistakes or omissions, however, are evidently completely my own.

I am also deeply grateful to the Paul Mellon Centre for Studies in British Art for the award of a publication grant which has greatly enhanced the book's production quality.

Finally, I need to thank my friends and family, especially John McLaughlin for the encouraging phone calls; and my brother Blair for drawing my attention to the overlap between mining and Junior Football teams in Scotland. My children Elizabeth, James and Judith also deserve thanks for their forbearance – 'it really is the pits, Dad' – but above all I would like to thank my wife Anna for all her love, support and kindness.

INTRODUCTION: AN ARCHITECTURE OF DISAPPEARANCE

That the combustion of coal was – and is – deleterious to our planet hardly needs to be stated. The findings of COP21 in Paris (2015) and COP26 in Glasgow (2021) have reiterated coal's negatives and confirmed its unacceptable presence as an anachronistic source of energy mired in the irresponsibility and dirt and danger of the past. Yet, there was once another side to coal mining, one which was often as socially progressive as it has been underacknowledged. While coal's establishment as the dominant prime-mover within the industrial 19th century – eclipsing all other sources of energy (Mitchell 2013; Johnson 2014; Malm 2016) – is well known, less is understood about coal mining's contributions to modern 20th-century societies, especially within the United Kingdom.

This was not just about the eventual freedoms and rise in living standards enjoyed through the post-war consumption of, for example, coal-generated electricity, but concerns other forms of environmental impact. These began within the immediate contexts of the coalfields but whose impact and influences became far more widely experienced. If coal was pivotal to the development and modernisation of 20th-century Britain, it follows that the coal miner was too. Coal mining, especially before the Second World War, was extremely labour-intensive and the sheer number of workers involved in the industry was highly significant. The capacities of the miner, collectively and individually, to work and produce coal was of critical strategic importance to the nation. Thus, the lives, health and reproduction of miners and their dependents within the spheres of work, to begin with, and latterly rest and pleasure, emerged as a site of acute interest to a series of agencies, not least the colliers themselves.

This book explores how architecture and space became a critical mode of response to the particular conditions experienced in coal mining and its communities. It is divided into three parts. 'Part I: Pithead Baths and the Architecture of Welfare' investigates the contexts, ambition, and activities of the Miners' Welfare Committee (MWC) to improve the lives of miners, especially through its nationwide pithead baths programme. Here architecture, as well as fulfilling functional requirements, was ultimately designed to be simultaneously beautiful, celebratory and modernist in its visual expression – a transmitter for a new type of deal for mineworkers. 'Part II: Settlement' considers the development of miners' settlements and housing. These aspects had remained outside the remit of the MWC but evidently were of critical importance. Housing miners exercised some key thinkers and practitioners whose projects and concepts ultimately proliferated far beyond the coalfields. Indeed, in both cases, the book proposes causal links and connections between this architecture, borne out of coal mining between the wars, and the wider development of the architecture and space of the post-war welfare state. 'Part III: Architecture, Publicity and the Plan for Coal' explores the modernisation of the industry during this last period arguing that – like the MWC projects – architectural design and representation became critical to the functional and symbolic requirements of the newly nationalised entity and its position within – and singular contribution to – post-war society.

Regardless of the many complex and often contradictory motives involved in the creation of this architecture – control, munificence, paternalism, bottom-up worker or union pressure, ameliorative capitalism, the democratic redistribution of wealth, feminist agitation, and so on – it can be described as an architecture of *labour*, of the working class. It is especially regretful, therefore, that so much of it in the United Kingdom has so emphatically disappeared. At many times during field research for this book, I would struggle to either find or imagine the presence and forms of the huge coal complex that I knew had stood in a particular location and had defined the working life, culture and society there. In 2019, at the site of Comrie Colliery, near Dunfermline in Fife – an influential model mine which, as will be discussed below, was used in the 1930s and 1940s to define a modern vision of the future of mining – I found one or two remaining buildings but none of the project's most architecturally conspicuous elements. Meanwhile, a crew of bulldozers and trucks were removing the extensive spoil heap which had lain untouched since the colliery's closure in the 1980s.

Signs of extinguished collieries can sometimes be discerned on Google Earth in the darkening grey of the ground, usually connected to, or close by the linear remnants, or extant forms of a railway. Occasionally, buildings like pithead baths can be found, sometimes in ruins but more often converted – usually unself-consciously and abruptly – to other uses. A cross-examination of the coordinates via the Ordnance Survey website and the historical overlays it provides, often reveal large, eclipsed expanses of sophisticated workings: acres of railway sidings, washeries and preparation plants, baths, canteens, cycle sheds, administrative offices, the positions of the shafts and winding gear, and finally car parks, and other latter-day functions – reminders that the disappearance of the architecture of coal is comparatively recent. As discussed below, despite the reach, scope and influence of such architecture, its physical absence is often echoed within architectural history. Yet this was not always the case.

The map of the extent of the British coalfields reveals that you do not have to go far across the country before stumbling across some site of the industry (FIG.1).[1] During the 20th century, head-gear towers of pits were visible in the landscape from as far north as Brora in Sutherland to Kent – the garden of England and on the doorstep of the capital – in the extreme south-east. There were pits in forests, in farmland, in valleys, by rivers and the sea, and on moors.

1
Map of the mid-twentieth-century British coalfields, as depicted in the National Coal Board's Annual Report for 1946.

There were pits in villages and towns, and in cities. Yet, more than just its geographical dispersal, coal was viscerally present – especially before the Second World War – in daily life.

Not only did it power industry and the railways – the primary mode of transport – but it was also in virtually every home. People who had nothing to do with the industry handled it every day. They were often familiar with its price; knew when and the method of its delivery; had a space within their homes to keep it in; and were intimately aware of some of the consequences of its consumption: the residual ashes that had to be taken out, the possibility of smoke in the house – pollution and smog in the city. Then there was the spatial culture of the fireplace, the centre of an often-uneven distribution of heat throughout the dwelling. While the figure of a miner may not have been immediately visible, their presence within the solid, dirty lumps of fuel that sustained the home was inescapable.

This was enhanced in regular depictions within the media, often concerning aspects of enduring or periodic controversy within the industry: accidents, fatalities, strikes, poverty, unemployment, squalid living conditions and so on. However, there were also periods, most notably following the Second World War, of concerted efforts to acknowledge and valorise this workforce and its contributions. But while industrial architecture is particularly vulnerable to obsolescence and demolition, the divisiveness of what could be described as the last great controversy of the industry – the Miners' Strike of 1984–5 – may also be partly to blame for the wholesale clearance of the spaces of British mining and ignorance of its architectural and spatial contributions.

The transition to an oil-burning economy in the second half of the 20th century, and the onset of the electricity grid, irrevocably changed the relationship between the population and its source of power and heat. A visible, indigenous workforce was replaced by a much smaller and invisible overseas one, and the limitations and consequence of solid coal by the permissive liquidity of oil – and natural gas, whose use was apparently free from the burden of labour – was seemingly going to be without consequences.

Despite its own evident destructive environmental record, this book argues that the uniqueness of the socio-spatial footprint of coal, and in particular the conspicuous presence of labour and how it was accommodated within architecture and space, represented a more holistic and socially sustainable response to the production of energy. This is not to say that coal mining is in any way now acceptable, but to provoke a reconsideration in how we view its social, spatial, and architectural legacies and remnants. For all the profligacies of coal, we, as a society, did immediately understand – often on an immediate, experiential level – where it came from and, to some degree, the social cost and spatial consequences of its production. A heightened awareness of origins and consequences is a defining factor in the environment movement, and is of critical importance as we transition once again and, hopefully, finally, from a fossil-based economy.

Few would argue for the retention of spoil heaps such as those formerly found at the site of Comrie Colliery. Indeed, even the MWC, in the 1930s and 1940s, made considerable efforts to remove them. But they do remain indicative of a labour force which often faced immediate danger – as well as the prospect of longer-term respiratory and other ailments specific to mineworkers – as they provided daily the energy to generate the conditions of modernity.

PART I

PITHEAD BATHS AND THE ARCHITECTURE OF WELFARE

PITHEAD BATHS, MODERNISM AND MODERNITY

For the influential art and architectural critic Anthony Bertram, the hundreds of pithead baths realised in the 1920s and 1930s represented nothing less than 'a colossal social experiment taking architectural form'. Designed by the architects of the Miners' Welfare Committee (MWC), and uniquely underpinned by State-legislated levies on coal production and profits, this unprecedented series of buildings catered for the washing – on a daily basis – of hundreds of thousands of individual workers.[1] Their effects beyond the workplace in the homes of miners would benefit and transform the lives of many more. Writing in 1938 in his book *Design* – published cheaply in the popular Pelican Special series by Penguin – Bertram described how they performed this task in a highly considered architectural manner: a modernist reconciliation of function with expression, to adorn the often bleak and isolated environments associated with the country's coalfields in FIG.1.

> The outward form has grown from the purpose of the baths. It is not an architectural character stuck on to them. The characteristic outsides of these baths are the direct reflection of their insides, and those are directly dictated by their function. This is a perfect example of architecture being a skin fitted round a social activity.
>
> (Bertram 1938: p.43)

But this was not all. He suggested the architects who designed the baths conceived of them as something much bigger than 'a mere utilitarian building … They wanted to provide, as it were, a spiritual bath as well, so that the beauty of the buildings is in fact part of their function'. Ultimately, for Bertram, the pithead baths represented the finest example he knew of 'a building that serves mankind, which is the supreme function of architecture' (Bertram 1938 42–3).

He was not alone in his assessment and appraisal of these buildings. Published in 1935 the book *Industrial Architecture* placed the British pithead baths within a global context of a type of architecture that was itself designed both as an industrial product and 'A power for good … [whose] light, space, cleanliness and planning in relation to the surrounding country or town, are all the more essential in what becomes a demand upon the social conscience' (Holme 1935: p.9) (FIG.2). Conspicuously, within this international modernist panoply of factories and warehouses, power plants, tunnel works, garages, research stations, markets, railway works, water towers, and miscellaneous architectures 'expressive of a great civilisation' (ibid.: p.13) – whose forms 'eliminate the unessential' and whose plans 'allow smooth, unhampered and expeditious progress' (ibid.: p.16) – the British pithead baths were the sole representatives in the section dedicated to welfare works.

2
Polkemmet pithead baths, alongside other examples of British and European modernism in Anthony Bertram's book, *Design*, 1938

3
Bestwood Colliery pithead baths in the context of European modernist examples in *Industrial Architecture*, 1935

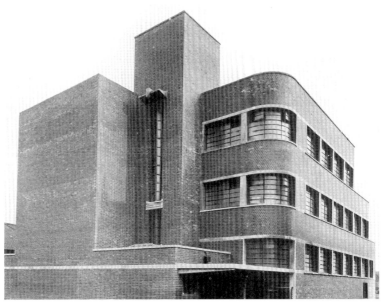

Nikolaus Pevsner also noted the significance of pithead baths in his 'Buildings of England' series. In *Northumberland* published in 1957, he juxtaposes an image of the sleek and thin horizontality of North Walbottle Colliery baths (FIG.4), designed by Frederick G. Frizzell in 1939, with a photograph on the same page of the ponderous rustications of Norman Shaw's Chesters (at Humshaugh) from 1891. The meaning is clear, the new, 20th-century phenomena of the pithead baths occupy an equally important position within the canon of architectural history as the venerated staples of the more distant past such as manor houses, cathedrals and palaces. In *County Durham* (1953), Pevsner cites the architectural interest of other examples by Frizzell at Dawdon

(Dalton-le-Dale) (1932), Elemore (1933) and Blackhall (1939). He describes their brick-built materiality and form, as characterised by 'the dominant group of chimney and water tank, boldly and squarely displayed', a typology whose early iterations were 'clearly influenced by the Dutch style of Dudok'. He also noted that there had been many other baths constructed in the county but many of them had already been demolished as their collieries closed down (Pevsner 1953: p.49).

Other subsequent writers have sought to revaluate the contribution to modern Britain of this landscape of pithead bath buildings which, as surmised by Pevsner, was essentially transitory. Their destruction, paralleling the rationalisation of the coal industry, accelerated to an almost complete disappearance by the final two decades of the 20th century. For some, pithead baths and other buildings realised through the Miners' Welfare Fund – exemplified by the baths designed for Cardowan Colliery, Lanarkshire, by Jack Dempster in 1943 (FIG.5), or the swimming pool for Sherwood Colliery by Alfred J. Saise in 1934 (FIG.6) – were key vectors in the dissemination of modernist ideas to the regions of Britain (Buckley 2007). Others have suggested parallels in scale, scope, importance and design quality – as well as some elements of architectural form in channelling the ideas of the influential Dutch architect Willem Marinus Dudok – between the pithead baths programme effected by the Miners' Welfare Committee, and the redesigning and development of the London Underground and Transport system under the leadership of Frank Pick in the 1920s and 1930s (Benton 1979a: 305).

And yet, despite the attentions of the authors above – and the numerous articles on its activities and products in architectural journals throughout the 1930s and 1940s – in comparison with the buildings produced, for example by Charles Holden for the London Underground, or other recognisable examples from what has become the modernist canon, the buildings of the Miners' Welfare Committee remain only a minor footnote within histories of

4
North Walbottle pithead baths by Frederick G. Frizzell and Chesters by Norman Shaw in Pevsner and Richmond's *Northumberland*, 1957

20th-century architecture in Britain, and sometimes not even that (see, for example, Bradbury 2018; Wilk 2006; Powers, 2005; and Feaver et al. 1979).

There are perhaps a number of reasons for this. First of all, there is their disappearance. The London Underground, while undergoing endless modernisations and developments since the time of Pick, is still extant as a system, as a series of places, and as an identifiable brand. Alongside its histories in print, film and other media, it is experienced by millions of passengers every day and recognised as absolutely critical to the functioning of the metropolis. Its heritage has also been carefully curated, its brands, insignia, iconography and even its typefaces transformed into innumerable items of memorabilia. Its key designers such as Charles Holden as well as others such as Harry Beck and Enid Marx – designers of the underground map and iconic moquette seat coverings respectively – if not exactly household names then are certainly well known and celebrated (see, for example, Green 2013; or Barman 1979). The contribution of British coal mining, on the other hand, has for decades no longer been of significant importance to the British economy and way of life. While it shared this transitory quality with many other industries, the mining of coal was especially prone to, and historically articulated by, the temporariness of its sites of production. Closures and geographical redeployments were regular and continual throughout its 19th- and 20th-century history, caused by a number of reasons including mineral exhaustion, unexpected geological conditions underground, mechanisation, economic non-feasibility and industrial unrest. By the time of the coal-mining industry's final eclipsing in the 1990s, many of the pithead baths, as noted by Pevsner, had already been quietly demolished decades previously, as part of a process of perpetual rationalisation. Indeed, it is of significance that the baths, designed not only as functional, but also – as described by Bertram – conspicuously beautiful entities, were also designed from the outset as essentially temporary buildings, conceived of and realised in full knowledge of the patterns of inevitable obsolescence that would characterise their use and life-span as a part of the changefulness of industrial development.

Another possible factor in the overlooking of the architectural significance of the pithead baths programme concerns the dispersed geography of the buildings and the types of locations they occupied. The architecture of coal mining was intimately connected on the surface to the specific geology of the seams below. While mining could take place in either urban or rural settings, it often erupted in locations far from other industries and settlements – farmland, forests, valleys, mountainsides. Accordingly, pithead baths appeared across Britain – from Argyll to Kent, from South Wales and Gloucestershire to Northumberland and Fife – over and over again in isolated settlements whose social and economic lives were dependent on the local colliery which was often the only source of employment. The character of the archetypical mining village will be discussed elsewhere in this volume. But especially towards the end of the pithead baths programme in the 1940s and 1950s, the provision of

5
Pithead baths, Cardowan Colliery by Jack Dempster

6
Swimming pool (with pithead baths behind) at Sherwood Colliery, by Alfred J. Saise

buildings in such places was often at a very small scale, sometimes – as at Tillicoultry in Clackmannanshire 1938 (FIG.7) – for as little as 70 miners. Unlike the pervasiveness of a metropolitan transport system, few people outside mining and certainly not those living in London experienced at firsthand what a pithead bath looked like or how it operated. But evidently a lack of first-hand experience of a building is not the only reason why a piece of architecture is celebrated or ignored.

Another aspect is perhaps the consequences of a reductive functionalist orthodoxy perceived as emerging within the cognoscenti of architectural modernism within the 1930s (Powers 2007: p.92; see also St John Wilson 2007). The valorisation of this landscape of white render, planar forms and cubic volumes – derived in part from the works of European protagonists such as Walter Gropius and Le Corbusier – was translated to subsequent historiographies. Against this, the pitheads baths – whose architecture embodied a different set of formal paradigms, drawing on Dudok, his connections to a broader Dutch school and from this to the work of Frank Lloyd Wright – were conspicuously different. As is well known, Wright's architecture was excluded from the *International Style* exhibition curated by Henry-Russell Hitchcock and Philip Johnson in 1932 which did much to codify the modernist movement into a set of formal or compositional principles. Within the contemporary media of black and white photographs, while the apparently stark white buildings seem to speak of a revolutionary new functionalist aesthetic language, the architectural forms of the pithead baths and their composition of juxtaposed horizontal and vertical volumes in brick, look more like examples of an incremental, rather than radical, approach. Under this conjecture they are perhaps not iconic enough nor sufficiently rhetorical in expressing their modernity. Arguably, the architecture of London Transport under Pick – also realised chiefly through the use of brick, often seen as a tradition rather than explicitly modern material, as its primary aesthetic – has also been understood in this way.

The modernist project has been described as continuing a definition of architecture first proposed in antiquity by the Augustan architectural scholar Vitruvius (see, for example, Frampton 1980/2020). Here modernism is a conscious response to conditions caused by the processes of modernisation and industrialisation which emerged in the 19th century. Accordingly, it involved shifts in Vitruvius's delineation of architecture as having three constituent parts: aesthetics (*venustas*), structure (*firmitas*) and function or use (*utilitas*). The latter, as invoked by Bertram above, came to mean a response to the social conditions experienced by the population – the unsanitary living and working environments caused by rapid urbanisation and factory production – and a search to define new forms for how it lived, worked, played and reproduced itself through health and education. This meant the extension of architecture and the attention of what would become professionally trained architects to sections of society previously untouched by its qualities or their expertise. While the pithead baths may not appear radically modern in their outward aesthetic, in terms of a social agenda they acutely embodied this seismic shift. As a comparison, the first modernist house built in Britain is frequently cited as 'High and Over' in Amersham, Buckinghamshire, designed by the New Zealand emigre architect Amyas Connell in 1928–9. As expected, it is white, replete with cubic forms and articulated by cantilevered planar balconies and floating roof canopies. Inside, however, is a traditional arrangement of rooms designed for a well-off client and which presupposes not the utopian view of a new society, expressed perhaps by its exterior, but the continuing

7
Tillicoultry pithead baths, 1938

availability of a serving class expressed through maids' quarters and a tradesmen's entrance (see Jackson 1970: p.22).

This observation of a modernist contradiction between the appearance of progress expressed through new architectural forms and the continued observance of conservative social relations through a building's programme and organisation can be – and has been – frequently extended to other early modernist projects such as Le Corbusier's villas from the 1920s. These, like Connell's first house, were designed for well-off members of the bourgeoisie. Yet by this point in the late 1920s and early 1930s the pithead baths programme – even before it reached a self-conscious aesthetic maturity in its absorption and refinement of its precedents in Dudok and others – had already begun to provide tens of thousands of miners with previously unavailable access to sanitary facilities at work. It has been suggested that the promotion of health through the creation of architectures of light, air and openness was central to the development of modernist architecture and, moreover, that many of the forms and organisation associated with the modern movement – the detachment from the ground and elevation of living spaces, and the proliferation of roof gardens, deck balconies and balconies as spaces to sunbathe – derived from a sincere, if erroneous attempt to cure, treat or prevent disease, specifically tuberculosis, through the creation of a new architecture (see Overy 2008; and Colomina 1997: pp 60–71). Other writers have proposed that white – traditionally an extremely difficult colour to maintain – also emerged not only as a symbol of modernity, but also as an expression of a new cleanliness made possible through modernisation in general and electrification in particular.

White ultimately introduces a new hygienic regime into the domestic realm and other spaces through the fact that it shows up staining and discolouration in an immediate, conspicuous visual way, one that is pervasive and experienced on a daily basis (Forty 1986). And yet, the pithead baths programme – an architecture purposed explicitly for cleanliness – did not achieve its aims of providing sanitation for workers through a formal expressive language of light, air or openness, or indeed any predominance of the colour white. Rather, the programme was realised through a measured approach to a complex series of circumstances which drew upon and embodied precedents, theories and research concerning hygiene and the provision of workplace baths and their desirability over proceeding decades. This involved the careful application of mass-produced technical elements, the development of a typological approach capable of adapting to the varying site and social circumstances, and negotiations with a multi-headed hydra of different client bodies involved in the production of the baths – the miners' representatives, mine owners and the extra-governmental agency of the Miners' Welfare Committee itself.

Another significant aspect is that the pithead baths were essentially iterative industrial products. As pieces of architecture, this also distinguishes them from many of their more celebrated British modernist architectural contemporaries – which were more often singular, one-off buildings – such as, for example, Lawn Road (Isokon) Flats by Wells Coates (1933–4); the De La Warr pavilion by Erich Mendelsohn with Serge Chermayeff (1934–5); or, to include an industrial example, the Boots buildings by Sir Owen Williams (1930–38). By the end of 1945, the architects' department of the Miners' Welfare Committee had completed 348 pithead baths across all the coalfields. Augmented by another 16 baths which had been built privately through other agencies, these provided daily washing facilities for 439,107 miners, an average of 1,261 per building (MWC 1946: p.11). Also available on site and incorporated within the same buildings, were a series of canteens serving meals on an industrial scale – hundreds of thousands of snacks, hot drinks and full meals delivered daily on a round-the-clock basis to accommodate working shift patterns. The canteen programme was accelerated during the war partly as a means of consolidating existing services, while the resources necessary for new building were limited and constrained by the rationing of material and labour shortages. Post-war and post-nationalisation in 1946, the newly created National Coal Board put in place plans to increase the yearly production of pithead baths from a pre-war average of 30 per year to, '60, 120, 120 and 130 in the years 1947 to 1950 respectively'. These were to be constructed using advanced techniques of pre-fabrication and the mass production of elements. Aspects of this, in the form of standardisation of plans and other design elements, had been trialled within bath projects produced by MWC architects since the consolidation of the building programme in the mid-1920s. Combined with the 31 contracts signed for in 1946 and a forecast of a further 50 pithead baths in 1951, this makes an estimated proposed total of 872 buildings scattered throughout all the coalfields of Britain (ibid.: 12). These, moreover, were allocated according to a system of determining need – initially through the determinants of size (the larger the more urgent) and prospective lifespan of pit – collated and organised democratically through the MWC's district and regional committees which themselves were constituted from both workers and mine owners.

The reach, scope and impact of building the pithead baths, then, was huge. What is revealed by, and reflected within, this architectural programme is not only the centrality of the coal industry to the economic and social life of Britain, but also the social significance of architecture within it. If one of the tenets of 20th-century architectural modernism, and especially in the 1930s, was a conscious and stated desire to respond to and improve social conditions, then the pithead baths achieved this at a scale and through a quality of architecture that was unprecedented. While the modernising developments of the London Underground achieved a similar reach, the pithead baths were conspicuous because they brought the benefits of high-quality architectural design and the ideas associated with modernity and modernism not only to the regions, but also candidly, exclusively, and without ambiguity, to a specific section of the working class, the miner – the 'archetypical proletarian' (Ewald 2002: pp 117–35) who, as George Orwell aptly and poetically suggested in *The Road to Wigan Pier*, was 'the grimy caryatid upon whose shoulders nearly everything that is *not* grimy is supported' (Orwell 1937/77: p.19).

The history of the pithead baths programme is complicated and sometimes contradictory. While emerging from distinct, identifiable moments encapsulated in specific pieces of legislation, its origins lie in the enduring, dangerous and unique conditions of coal mining. How these affected a labour-intensive industry with a huge workforce was, as Orwell suggests, of critical importance not just to the circulation of one city or region, but to the fundamental functioning and organisation of a whole nation. In terms of coal-mining labour alone, by 1913, over a million miners worked the seams of the United Kingdom, the vast majority of whom still used hand labour and other techniques first developed in the late 18th century (Supple 1987: pp 26–35; see also Coombes 1939). Together with their families and dependents a total of five million people can be estimated as being directly engaged in, or affected by, coal mining. This represented approximately one tenth of the total population. As suggested above, the buildings themselves drew together and embodied a series of international theories, techniques and thinking on the social, scientific, medical benefits of hygiene, bathing and the development of industrial and workplace baths. They also embraced an interpretation and deployment of a modern, emerging meaning of welfare. In terms of architectural authorship – and again unlike the other, more recognised, examples of 1920s and 1930s architecture – the baths were designed not so much by individuals but, as befits their industrial and typological qualities, by a national body which was centralised but organised into regional teams of mostly young architects. Their iterative output efficiently absorbed and incorporated both developing technologies and the latest international precedents and practices from both the disciplines of architecture *and* planning. This included a close and direct relationship with Patrick Abercrombie – who served on the Miners' Welfare Committee – and a more abstract, but equally fruitful, engagement with the ideas and forms of the 20th-century's socially and socialist orientated architecture of the Netherlands and the cooperative movement in Sweden in general, and the forms, organisation and aesthetics of the buildings of Dudok in particular.

JOHN HENRY FORSHAW

8
John Henry Forshaw in 1941

From 1925 until 1939, in what can perhaps be termed the period of most intense architectural innovation in the pithead baths programme – when the tenets of design quality were established, consolidated and ultimately delivered – the architects' department of the MWC was organised, overseen, recruited into and directed by a chief architect: John Henry Forshaw (FIG.8). Forshaw's professional life – both before and after his time with the MWC – seems to parallel some of the social developments which underpinned not only the pithead baths programme, but also larger ascendent ideas on how society and the built environment might be conceived of, managed and planned through the intervention of architectural form and the intercession of state bodies. Born in 1895 to a reasonably wealthy farming background and brought up near the then mining village of Skelmersdale in Lancashire, Forshaw was educated in the grammar school at Ormskirk before being articled to Thomas Myddleton Shallcross, a small architectural practitioner in Liverpool (Anon. 1973: p.92). In the First World War he served as adjutant (senior captain) of the 55th (West Lancashire) Division's Royal Engineers (*The Recorder*, 1 December 1945) and won a Military Cross at the Third Battle of Ypres (Passchendaele) in 1917. After the war he chose to continue his architectural education at the school of architecture in Liverpool under the headship of Charles Herbert Reilly, taking advantage of this first architecture programme to be incorporated within a university system. Developed and consolidated by Reilly, this initiative had been designed in part to extend the opportunity of studying architecture to a broader strata of society than hitherto possible. Of significance was the idea, embedded at Liverpool, of the necessity of resituating architecture and its complexities from a position within an apprenticeship system – with its associations of craft – to an appropriate and necessary object of and vehicle for academic, scholarly and intellectual enquiry. In Forshaw's case, this is evinced in the thesis he prepared for the award of his B.Arch degree which examined the issues surrounding the construction and zoning of high buildings in New York (1922). As well as the evident trans-Atlantic and architectural connections between Liverpool and New York in general, Reilly displayed a particular interest in American architectural culture. Consequently, both the content and curriculum of the school of architecture reflected an American bias expressed through the influence of the works of practitioners amongst whom 'Charles Follen McKim, Hornbostel, Cass Gilbert, and Van Buren Magonigle [were] the chief favourites' (cited in Stamp 1997: p.347).

It is understandable, therefore, that following his degree Forshaw – like many other students of the school of architecture at Liverpool – sailed west to spend some time working in New York. In fact, it is likely that this was instigated by the school through Reilly's own connections with large practices in New York, and elsewhere in North America. Such placements were apparently reserved for the best architecture students and Forshaw followed the example set by a list of talented antecedents.[2] One of the first of these was Herbert J. Rowse who would ultimately design a series of significant public buildings back in Liverpool including the Philharmonic Hall (1936–9) – effected in brick, and drawing upon the influence of Dudok – and the George's Dock Building, clad in Portland Stone and which ascribed to the style of Monumental Classicism endorsed by Reilly and the Liverpool school. Rowse's time in New York was spent in the practice of Frank Worthington Simon working on the neo-classical Manitoba Legislative Building (1912–20). Another temporary emigre was Maxwell Fry who was involved in the design of Long Island mansions for the Beaux Arts-influenced practice of Carrère and Hastings (Sharples 1996: p.29) which also designed the New York Public Library (1897–1911). As is well known, Fry – whose time at university in the early 1920s overlapped with Forshaw's – would subsequently denounce the historicist classical forms and language associated with his education at Liverpool, and adopt a modernist architecture idiom to become one of its foremost and renowned British practitioners.

Forshaw's post-degree embarkation into private practice began in New York in the summer of 1920 with a brief period in the practise of Flagg and Chambers, designers of a series of conspicuous and technologically advanced public buildings in the United States. These included the steel-framed Singer Building in New York begun in 1897 and briefly, on the completion of its tower in 1908, the tallest building in the world. Educated at the *École des Beaux Arts* in Paris, Ernest Flagg also wrote about and influenced the zoning issues and regulations surrounding skyscrapers in New York which may explain the subject of Forshaw's subsequent B.Arch degree thesis, written on his return to the United Kingdom. But perhaps more significant was Flagg's reputation as both an architect *and* a social reformer intent on realising improved buildings and environmental conditions for the working classes. Emerging from a wider sense of reformatory interest and investigation into working class conditions in New York in the late 19th century and early 20th century – perhaps exemplified by the documentary works of Jacob Riis – Flagg was instrumental to the design and construction of a new prototype to replace the city's unsanitary and environmentally problematic tenements. Based on his own critical study and appraisal of the existing, unsatisfactory condition of narrow frontages and deep light wells, he proposed to increase the penetration of, and access to, light and air, by expanding building frontages to generate larger courtyards without significantly diminishing the density of occupation. By the late 1910s, in addition to this proposal for the spatial reconfiguration of the tenement on health and sanitary grounds, he had also developed a type of system-built housing consisting of stone-faced, concrete-walled cottages. These were designed to be quickly erected by unskilled labour and provide affordable dwellings to address working class housing shortages in the wake of the First World War. His book *Flagg's Small Houses: Their Economic Design and Construction* was first published in 1922 and it is likely that this was being written and prepared while Forshaw was with the practice in New York. With its high-rise projects, strategic interventions into the design of tenements, and proposals for the rapid production of houses, what Forshaw experienced – albeit briefly – in Flagg's practice was a confluence of modern technological thinking on the structure and construction of buildings with a developed idea of architecture as a socially responsive, responsible and useful activity, one which was aimed towards improving conditions for the less privileged sections of the population. Of final significance is Forshaw's own suggestion – written later as Chief Architect to the MWC – that the organisation of its architecture department and division into project-based teams was derived at least in part from his own experience of large American offices (Forshaw 1938: p.462).

On his return to England, Forshaw worked for the Birmingham practice of Harrison and Cox who designed a clutch of civic and municipal buildings including the quite flamboyant, Mannerist swimming baths at Nechells (1910), and some housing projects. Following his marriage in 1923, he found an opportunity to deepen his relationship with the social aims of architecture by taking up his first position in public practice, in the Architectural Section of the Liverpool Corporation Land Steward and Surveyor's Office. Forshaw was to remain in public practice for the rest of his working life. His tenure at Liverpool Corporation from 1924 to 1926 meant he served under Albert D. Jenkins as surveyor (1914–38), but was sandwiched between two more prolific and important figures within the municipality's history of architectural production: Thomas Shelmerdine and Lancelot Keay. These individuals provide further context for Forshaw's own public practice. As well as overseeing slum clearances and designing new housing for the city, Shelmerdine (surveyor 1871–1914) also designed a series of public buildings – schools, libraries, offices, swimming pools and hospitals – in a Mannerist classical style. This series of works and the public services they provided, embodied a precise architectural example of a late 19th- and early 20th-century iteration of municipal socialism. Keay joined the corporation in 1925 – while Forshaw was still there – before succeeding as chief architect (the name was changed from surveyor at this point) from Jenkins in 1938. Under his leadership the corporation would produce a series of innovative multi-storey, deck access social housing schemes, such as St. Andrew's Gardens (mid-1930s), and Gerrard Gardens (1939) designed by Liverpool University graduate John Hughes as chief architect (Sharples 2004). As well as incorporating formal elements and details from Dudok, these projects drew on European modernist precedents such as the so-called *grosshäuser* in Vienna, including Karl Ehn's Karl Marx-Hof, and Bruno Taut's Hufeisensiedlung at Britz in Berlin.

In addition to broadening the franchise of prospective architectural students, the Liverpool school of architecture under Reilly also pioneered other innovations including a closer alignment between architecture and the emerging discipline of urban planning. Coinciding with the first Housing and Town Planning Act, Reilly initiated the first Department of Civic Design in 1909, realised with the support of the industrialist William Hesketh Lever, 1st Viscount Leverhulme. In 1888, Lever had instigated and supervised the construction of the renowned and influential Port Sunlight as a philanthropic and paternalistic model community and example of improved and reformed housing for his soap workers. Reilly appointed Stanley D. Adshead as the first Professor of Civic Design in 1912. After Adshead left to become Professor of Town Planning at University College, London in 1915, he was replaced by another incumbent member of the staff: Leslie Patrick Abercrombie. It was Abercrombie who became Forshaw's tutor when the latter decided to take the opportunity offered by the university to augment his employment in the Liverpool Corporation with the preparation, on a part-time basis, of a Master's Degree in Civic Design. Forshaw would go on to win the Lever Prize for Town Planning in 1924 (*Architect and Building News*, April 1941: p.2) for his project 'An Ornamental Park, Heswell, Cheshire'. Effected in a Beaux-Arts style, it was replete with bilateral symmetries and cross and radial axes. Significantly, this was a design for a piece of landscape devoted to public leisure and recreation, of parterres, and formal and informal settings for walks, as well as spaces for organised games such as tennis and bowling. Forshaw would be involved in shaping similar places in the coalfields as part of his remit within the MWC. Also in 1924, and under the supervision of Abercrombie (who was then the consultant on a series of regional planning proposals), Forshaw was invited by the Joint Town Planning Committee to prepare a regional plan for Lancaster and Morecambe (FIG.9). His report, published with a foreword by Abercrombie in 1927, made a series of recommendations – some of which were implemented – concerning communications and land-use within the two towns and the connections between them (Forshaw 1927; see also Clark 2020: p.34).

9
Forshaw's *Lancaster and Morecambe Regional Scheme*, general view of the region, 1924

These moments represented the beginnings of a long association between Forshaw and Abercrombie. A member of the MWC between 1935 and 1939, Abercrombie seems to have also had an advisory role to the Committee before this in the mid-1920s, possibly proposing the centralised structure that would define its architects' department, as well as having some involvement in Forshaw's appointment as its architect (Allison 1994; Saint 2013; Rich 2003). Most famously, however, their working relationship would realise the *County of London Plan*, produced in collaboration and published in 1943. By then, Forshaw had left the MWC and was Architect to London County Council (LCC) and Superintending Architect of Metropolitan Buildings. He assumed this position in 1941 after serving as deputy for the two previous years. During the war he also led the London Heavy Rescue Service and subsequently directed the War Debris Organisation (London Civil Defence Region) which was responsible for the removal of building material displaced and damaged by the air raids. He left the LCC in 1946. This followed some internal disagreements within the council on how the enormous task of rehousing the huge population uprooted by the destruction of the conflict should proceed. According to Arthur Ling, who was working as an architect at the LCC at the time, Forshaw saw the future of housing as his remit as chief architect and to be conducted within the framework set out by his and Abercrombie's *Plan*. The council, however, tasked the valuer's office with the responsibility for the design of housing and Forshaw apparently resigned in protest, stepping down on the exact day the transfer of responsibilities was effected, and alluding to it in his resignation speech (Arthur Ling 1951, cited in Gold 2013: p.221; Forshaw 1946; see also Saint 2013).

In 1946, he took up his final post as Chief Architect and Housing Consultant to the Ministry of Health, serving under Aneurin Bevan in the heady beginnings of implementing of the National Health Service project.[3] He remained – as the ministry shifted firstly to the Ministry of Local Government and subsequently to the Ministry of Housing – until his retirement in 1959 'making no personal mark on the great housing drive of the post-war decade but presiding over it with reticent efficiency' (Saint 2013). Forshaw's practice, writings and biographical material – contained in his personal papers in the University of Liverpool – portray him as part of a new breed of modern architect. Firstly, while having been articled himself, he was freed, like others of his generation, from both the social and intellectual limitations of apprenticeship. He was also equipped with a new set of skills with which to confront and contribute to an emerging definition of architecture that was both broad, self-consciously rooted in social purpose and that acknowledged complexity. A fellow of the Royal Institute of British Architects, an Associate Member of the Royal Town Planning Institute, and a Fellow of the Institute of Landscape Architects, Forshaw's breadth and depth of expertise is confirmed by the building projects he involved himself in, the range of articles he wrote, the talks he gave and the positions he held. His thesis investigating the contexts surrounding the planning and zoning for highrise New York, the regional plans for Lancaster and Morecambe, and the *Plan for London* were augmented by an enduring interest in mass production and

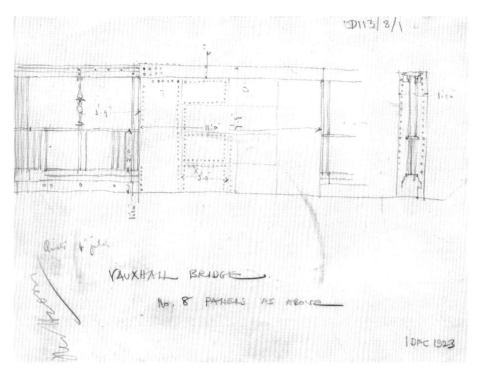

10
Sketch by Forshaw of detail at Vauxhall Bridge, London, dated 1923

11
Model of proposed urban design and housing at Stepney by London County Council Architects, discussed in a Chadwick Public Lecture by Forshaw given in London, November 1943

12
Comrie Model Colliery, mid-1930s

modularity (Forshaw 1954); the relationship between sanitation and health, and architecture and town planning (Forshaw 1943); and the design of housing and its services, including ideas concerning heating (Forshaw 1948, 1951, 1954; Forshaw and Bevan 1956, and so on).[4] In other words, his interests and activities overlapped with many of the contemporary issues exercising not only architecture, but also wider political and social discourse. As has been made clear elsewhere, in its response to social issues, modernist architecture frequently established a polemical position. What is also clear from his personal papers was that Forshaw was also comfortable in operating across a series of scales – the *Plan for London* evidently represents proposals at the scale of mass settlement and infrastructure designed for millions of people, yet the papers also contain sketches and descriptions of detailed built moments – like the drawings made in 1923 of the riveting patterns and section of the steel structure of London's Vauxhall Bridge (FIG.10). And while Forshaw's identity as an architectural author/designer within the projects he worked on is never unambiguously clear (Saint 2013), these attributes suggest he had the capacity and desire to exert a level of control over them from their strategic conception to finished details.

His training, however, arguably equipped him most precisely for the middle scale of urban design, working within or leading a team of architects and other contributors. This can be seen specifically in the housing projects of Woodberry Down Estate, Stoke Newington and the Ocean Spray Estate, Stepney, designed for London County Council in the early 1940s (Forshaw 1943), but not yet on

site when he left; or in the plan prepared in the mid-1930s for the much publicised model colliery at Comrie in Fife, which is discussed elsewhere in this volume below (FIGS 11 and 12). More generally and perhaps most successfully, however, is the urban design intent evident in the design of the pithead baths. While incorporating elements of mass production within the services and other aspects of the building, the baths simultaneously had to negotiate a diverse series of site conditions and incorporate the processes involved in the particularities of coal mining. Often – and conjoined with the use of landscape – these buildings acted as larger, ordering elements within the chaotic milieu of production, preparation and the circulation of goods and men generated by a colliery and its contexts (Forshaw 1935: p.1080).

MINERS' WELFARE COMMITTEE ARCHITECTS' DEPARTMENT AND 'OFFICIAL' ARCHITECTURE

For the development of the *Plan for London*, Forshaw and Abercrombie engaged a series of young architects and planners (many of which came from the school in Liverpool) to contribute to the project and its background research. If anything, however, the MWC was more conspicuous and radical in its use of the team of young talent that Forshaw assembled, giving a rare opportunity for relatively inexperienced architects to design significant buildings (see Manning 1938: p.63) and – even more unusually – crediting them individually as having done so (Benton and Benton 1979b: p.51). Thus the names of Jack Dempster, Cecil George Kemp, Frederick G. Frizzell, J. E. Webster, Alfred J. Saise, and Donald Denoon Jack are cited in many of the contemporary publications (including Pevsner's guides) which described and celebrated the buildings. Consequently, their names are as often attached to the baths programme as that of Forshaw's. It is tempting to view this as evidence of a flattened, democratic structure within the architects' department, one which paralleled the processes found elsewhere within the social organisation of the MWC as a whole, and indeed its origins within a proto-socialist redistribution of coal royalties and profits into services for miners.

In fact, while Forshaw stated that the organisation of the MWC architects' department was influenced by the task or regional-focused 'teams' or 'firms' structure, found within large North American practices, he also suggested that: 'in our method of approach to the work and in the continuity of development, it is perhaps more in parallel with the now famous architects' office of the Swedish Cooperative Society' (Forshaw 1938: p.426). The latter – to give it its full name, the Swedish Cooperative Wholesale Society's Architects' Office – was established in 1924 to provide a public interface between the cooperative movement's mission of providing 'foodstuffs and other necessities in the best and cheapest way' (Anon. 1935: p.5), for its members and buying public through the design of shops and other spaces of: *consumption*, like bakeries and cafeterias; *production*, in the form of abattoirs and factories for commodities, such as crisp bread and perhaps, most famously, at Luma for lightbulbs; and *distribution*, in grain silos and warehouses.

Like the MWC and the London Underground, it realised a pervasive, dispersed architecture which touched the lives of, and was experienced by, millions of people across a large geographical territory. And like the MWC and the London Underground, it made use of standardised methods of design and an approach which responded to criteria of efficiency, functionality and the display of goods which was precise and economic in its choice and use of materials. It was also, however, about the realisation of a recognisable brand. As will be described below, this was also a key factor in the pithead baths programme. In Sweden, the architectural forms created and situated in rural, suburban and urban settings alike across the country – all equipped with accompanying signage in a unifying typography – were instantly recognisable. The designs were also reproduced in contemporary publications further highlighting and advertising the cooperative's architecture and design of clean lines and fitness for purpose which penetrated everything: from its presentation of arrays of fresh and preserved foodstuffs; minimalist yet light-filled cafeterias; shoe shops with chrome chairs and associated canted stools for the trying on of shoes; to the provision of the housing and apartment buildings which, for operational purposes, sometimes accompanied rural shops or provided accommodation for factory and other workers. Also of significance, however, is that the stated premise of a particular ethos within the organisation at large, was replicated within the organisation of its architects: 'The Office in its work practices the principle of the fellowship of labour [which] constitutes a collective group of architects' (Anon. 1935: p.8) (FIG.13).

13
Test room, the Luma Factory, Stockholm by the Swedish Cooperative Wholesale Society's Architect's Office, 1930

Test-room.

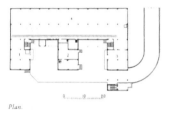

Plan.

THE LUMA FACTORY STOCKHOLM

By the time Forshaw was writing an appraisal of the architectural work of the MWC in 1938, the collective of architectural workers he had instigated and managed was divided into two groups, each with a chief architect and a team of other architects with technological support – North Group: Dempster with Frizzell, Jack, O. Parry and H. Smith; and South Group: Saise with W. Traylor, W. A. Woodland, J. H. Bourne and J. W. M. Dudding. A quantity surveyors' section was organised by a Chief Quantity Surveyor, H. J. Rayner. A. M. Turner provided engineering oversight and inputs, while Captain J. D. O'Kelly was responsible for the layout of recreational grounds (Forshaw 1938: p.431). On Forshaw's departure in 1939 his place as Chief Architect was taken by his deputy Kemp. By 1940, while he was still acting in his new role, Kemp authored an article in *Architecture Design and Construction* which listed a more granular breakdown in responsibilities, listed as a series of coalfield regions: Northern Division, Senior Architect, Dempster; Architects, Frizzell (Northumberland, Durham), Jack (Fife, the Lothians, Part of Lanarkshire), Parry (South Yorkshire,

West Yorkshire), Smith (Part of Lanarkshire, Ayrshire, Cumberland); Southern Division, Senior Architect, Saise; Architects, Traylor (Forest of Dean, Somerset, Bristol, South Wales), Woodland (South Derbyshire, North Staffordshire, Cannock Chase, South Staffordshire, Leicestershire, Warwickshire, Shropshire), Bourne (Lancashire, North Wales), Dudding (Nottinghamshire, Derbyshire, Kent) (Kemp 1940: p.156). This was likely to be the structure inherited from Forshaw's tenure rather than any new initiative undertaken by Kemp as acting Chief Architect. Writing a testimonial for Forshaw's job application to the LCC in 1939, the chairman of the MWC Sir Frederick Sykes described his 12-year contribution to its architectural production as overseeing the construction of over 300 baths buildings, with an expenditure of £5½ million through the supervision of a department comprising of 114 architects, draughtsmen and other technical staff including surveyors, engineers and clerks of works (Sykes 1939). Another document, also contained in the Forshaw papers, undated but presumably produced in 1936 and titled 'Architects' Department', shows a total number of 45 architects being supported by 29 architectural assistants (Forshaw n.d.). In spite of the geographical spread of the works carried out by the MWC architects and its division into regional teams, the department itself was centralised within premises in London. Firstly, in Romney House in Westminster then, during the war they were evacuated to the suburbs of Ashtead in Surrey, before returning to central London in 1946, to a premises in Old Queen Street, again in Westminster (MWC 1946: p.7).

In May 1939, two months before he left for the LCC, in the face of criticisms concerning apparently elevated costs and a call for its decentralisation, Forshaw felt compelled to write a memo justifying the continuing existence of the MWC architects' department as a centralised entity. He did this in uncompromisingly modernist terms, citing the reason for establishing a single, national architectural office staffed by experts on decisions (taken by previous committees in the 1920s) based on: 'Economy, Uniformity, Intimate control of the work, leading to Speed and Efficiency' [caps original] (Forshaw 1939a: p.2). He intimated that the welfare of miners was a national concern, one that had required a unified national response to transcend local caprices and interests, and ensure both a common understanding of the universal needs of miners, as well as a parity of quality in their provision across all the constituent coalfield regions. On an immediate, operational level, and echoing the 'fellowship of labour' of the Swedish Cooperative architectural office, Forshaw wrote that: 'One of the great values in the central architect's [sic] office has been its spirit or tone. Team work has been possible in all its valuable associations' [and, as a result, it had become] 'a "magnet" in drawing keen young men [sic] to it.'[5]

In a vote of thanks following his presentation on the work of the architects' department of the MWC to the Royal Institute of British Architects, Forshaw was described as being 'clearly a very modest man, because he has praised all the different architects who have contributed to these buildings and has said nothing about his own share in them' (H. M. Fletcher in Forshaw 1938: p.429).

The vote of thanks was seconded by Abercrombie who praised the efficiency of the organisation, its absorption of the 'spirit of planning' in the beneficial effect a pithead bath could have on the general arrangement of an entire colliery, its use of standardised units and its centralised structure. The latter, he surmised, allowed 'the pooling of ideas, individual interests' and a collective response to rising prices, yet still effected 'decentralisation in actual design and execution'. Perhaps most astutely and presciently, however, was Abercrombie's, at first, quite curious description of the pithead baths as being 'one of the best examples in this country of *official* [my emphasis] architecture' (Abercrombie in Forshaw 1938: p.430).

It is under this definition that Forshaw, as an architect, can perhaps be considered as being at his most modern. As intimated above, his career represented a particular confluence of many new social, cultural and technological factors which affected the production and indeed conception of architecture in general during the early years of the 20th century. As cited by Abercrombie, these included the influence of town planning and the development of standardised forms of design both at the level of the mass production of material components, and in the reuse and adaptation of entire building layouts or sections of them.

Both of these tenets, however, must be understood within the broader context of an awareness of architecture's responsibility and capacity to intervene positively in the daily lives of wider sections of the population and, in particular, the working classes. In his resignation speech from the LCC, Forshaw described himself, like Flagg, as a 'reformer'.[6] But while Forshaw's career overlapped directly with the reformatory zeal displayed by the likes of Flagg in New York, it was also shaped more indirectly by the theories on the agency of architecture and space expressed by luminaries such as William Morris in the previous century, and more recently by William R. Lethaby as well as Richard Barry Parker and Raymond Unwin – who, incidentally, also had intimate connections to coal mining – in their translation of these principles into new planned settlements.

At the same time, there was the growing conception that such interventions could not and should not be left to the caprices of private enterprise, or paternalistic experiments conducted by philanthropists such as Lever. In the United Kingdom as elsewhere, the First World War and the Russian Revolution had punctured many previously held beliefs in the social landscape and ushered in new political realities of growing working class movements and new acceptance of socialist values. The conflict's aftermath began to generate a broadly held consensus that the complexities of industrialisation and its social and urban consequences and legacies nascent in the 19th century were such that they required a new, *official* response at the level of the state (see Swenarton 1981). Aspects of this predated the war. The Hampstead Garden Suburb Act (1906) – designed and drafted by Unwin – set in motion official environmental observances to ensure access to fresh air and light in part through limiting densities and setting minimum street widths. While limited in scope, the first Town Planning Act – which passed through parliament three years later in 1909 – outlawed the construction of unsanitary back-to-back housing and compelled local authorities to construct plans for their future urban development. Benefits of state-sponsored intersessions into the environmental conditions of everyday working-class life through physical building had already been evinced by the examples of housing projects produced in Amsterdam and the Netherlands during the First War World War (see Steiber 1998) and would be conspicuously developed throughout the 1920s in the Weimar Republic and Austria. The British government's own Homes for Heroes project was launched in 1918 (albeit with a limited application) along with the Parliament-commissioned Tudor Walters Report on domestic space standards (see Swenarton 1981; and Part II below).

In the documentary film *The Proud City: A Plan for London* – made in 1946 to publicise Forshaw and Abercrombie's vision for the city – the two principle designers appear briefly as protagonists (FIG.14). It is very possibly the only surviving recording of Forshaw on film. The two are seen in a genteel domestic setting, complete with volumes of leather-bound books and a fireplace with a handsome mantle clock above it. Despite his background in Lancashire, the by-now greying, middle-aged Forshaw talks with Received Pronunciation, explaining aspects of the *Plan* in a stilted, clipped manner. Abercrombie, while more charismatic, is perhaps even more of a cliché of a remote, upper-class figure. Clad in a natty pinstripe three-piece suit, replete with bow tie and intoning in a similar drawl, at one point in the film he removes his famous monocle to polish it emphatically as the camera cuts away. To the present-day viewer, their appearance and attitudes as architect-planners appear both anachronistic and conservative. It is an perhaps an unfortunate depiction of the pair behind which the radicality and modernity of both is obscured.

It has been argued that the school of architecture in Liverpool, with a curriculum and pedagogy based partly on ideas of corporatism and Reilly's stated aim to curb excess individuality in architects (see Sharples 1996: p.34), produced a generation of architects that were themselves quasi-industrial, standardised products. Instead of the vagaries of apprenticeship, they were born from and within the strictures, parameters and more even keel of an institution. For some, this was potentially a negative. It has been suggested, for example, that the school's premium student prize, the Prix de Rome had a stultifying effect on many of its winners. And, with the exception perhaps of Maxwell Fry, the school did not create the type of creative architect normally celebrated within canonical historiographies. Instead, it tended to produce what have rather disparagingly been called 'administrators and committee-men' (Powers 1996: p.13). Many of these architects like Forshaw, or Stirrat Johnson-Marshall – who became architect to the Ministry of Education – and others entered public service in the 1950s filling, for example, the positions of city architect for Birmingham, Manchester, Newcastle upon Tyne and Southampton (Sharples 1996: p.34).

14
Forshaw and Abercrombie in *The Proud City: A Plan for London* film, 1946

Forshaw's career intersects with an exponential growth in the development and importance of public or, to use Abercrombie's term, *official* architecture. This would come to dominate the middle decades of the century and especially the construction of the post-Second World War welfare state project. His role in this epitomises the emergence of another type of modern or modernist architect for the 20th century, a state civil servant architect, the architect as bureaucrat, an administrator, an assembler of teams, a curator and deployer of other architects' talents and skills – an architect capable of operating within and negotiating ways through a growing realm of officialdom, to deliver a large volume of architectural services to large bodies of people. For some, this represents a much-neglected aspect of architectural production where 'the truly seminal structure being built at this time [lay] not in the material manifestation of architecture but in the invisible systems constructed for their conception and delivery' (Lang 2014: p.32). Others have commented on the scope, ambition and influence of the *County of London Plan* and the *Survey of London* which proceeded it and set its terms of reference (FIG.15). The latter, which embodied the research approach first espoused by Patrick Geddes, involved the analysis and synthesis of a complex series of social, spatial and logistical criteria which underpinned the idea of the *Plan* as 'a catalyst for legislation' (Lang 2014: p.33) and would involve urban rehabilitation and conservation as well as more comprehensive redevelopment and infrastructural improvement. While the *County of London Plan* was never fully implemented, both it and its preliminary *Survey* would become extremely influential, not only in the development of London, but also as a paradigm for planning strategies in other, global cities over the coming decades (Dix 1981: p.116). At the same time, London was producing another influential exemplar

in the development and restructuring of the LCC's architecture department. By 1952–3, this had grown to become one of the largest in the world, capable of operating at a series of scales from large-scale planning, to the commissioning and designing of components and furniture. Forshaw had been the author-architect of this restructuring and his interventions into its operational capacities were not only designed to deliver the programmes of works associated with and emerging from the *Plan*, but also, as has been surmised, 'mirrored on a corporate scale the restructuring philosophy he had proposed' in the *Plan*. This involved the deployment of an essentially non-hierarchical series of 'teams' of architects cast into divisions and overseen by the chief architect (Lang 2014: p.33). It is a structure which clearly resembles the one that Forshaw had developed much earlier for the MWC. It was here that his expertise, professional disposition, and apparently self-effacing and modest demeanour (Fletcher in Forshaw 1938: p.429) had coincided with a context which would be critical to the development of public architecture in the United Kingdom – the exceptionalism of the coal mining industry.

Central to the idea of architecture as public service for the good of many, is the presupposition of not only the acceptance and desirability of state intervention in public and private life, but also the role of architecture in determining and shaping this. An evident tenet of modernism, the development and acceptance

15
County of London Plan by Forshaw and Abercrombie, Social and Functional Analysis 1943

of both these facets has a far longer history, one which has intimate connections to the history of coal mining. The concentration of energy found in coal meant that coal mining and its workforce were of pivotal importance to the ongoing industrial development, economic growth and security of the nation. Coal mining was the engine of modernity. Bertram's description of the pithead baths as 'a colossal social experiment taking architectural form' was a project born out of necessity (Bertram 1938 pp 42–3). As described in more detail below, the architecture produced under the MWC was the result of an often uneasy but essential social contract between the miners, the mine owners and the government, brought about through a series of historic grievances, Royal Commissions of Inquiry, associated legislation and a series of examples of industrial conflicts leading up to, and including, the General Strike of 1926. These formed moments within more enduring controversies associated with coal mining and its labour force – the constant danger and presence of accidents, the low wages, cyclical unemployment of its workers and their dependents' resultant poverty.

In fact, the pithead baths programme – while the largest and most architecturally conspicuous – was just one of a series of measures implemented for mineworkers by the MWC under the aegis of government legislation. These offered other ways of ameliorating the conditions faced by miners and their families in their daily lives once again through the creation of architectural space and landscape: educational buildings; reading rooms; holiday camps; welfare institutes; medical centres and hospitals; sports grounds; swimming pools; children's playgrounds; convalescent homes; hospices; libraries; and other sanitary facilities and equipment. These often resulted from extensive research into physical diseases, conditions and ailments specific to mining. With the exception of housing, which was outside the remit of the MWC, the deployment here of architecture – as a conscious, reflective, designed and planned response to improve miners' living and working conditions realised through a social redistribution of wealth – would seem to represent, in embryo, many of the facilities and services that would ultimately be translated to other sections of the population after the conclusion of the Second World War, in the social and physical reconstruction of the United Kingdom.

THE SOCIAL CONTEXT OF COAL BETWEEN THE WARS

For Lewis Mumford, the noted historian, sociologist and architectural critic, mining was a particularly grievous occupation. In *Technics and Civilisation* written in 1934, he described the space of the mine as the first completely 'manufactured terrain', an unnatural, inorganic antithesis of the ideal pastoral arcadia. It was, he argued, the archetypical site where earth and land were reconceived as being no longer just about growing food, but as something more instrumental, something that could be acted or operated upon, exploited. For its inhabitants, moreover: 'Apart from the lure of prospecting, no one entered a mine in civilised states until relatively modern times except as a prisoner of war, a criminal, a slave. Mining was not regarded as a humane art: it was a form of punishment: it combined the terrors of the dungeon with the physical exacerbation of the galley' (Mumford 1934/2010: p.67).

The controversies surrounding mining in the 19th century were such that they precipitated some of the earliest state interventions into workplace environments in the United Kingdom and, indeed, anywhere. The Mines and Collieries Acts (1842), which banned women and girls from going underground, was ushered in in the wake of the public furore surrounding the Huskar Colliery disaster of 1838, in South Yorkshire, where 26 children had been killed by flooding. The evidence placed before parliament had considered not just aspects of health and safety underground, but also broader social and environmental conditions not only within the industry, but also how its workforce lived and conducted itself. In the 138 years between 1801 and 1939, the coal industry was visited by an unrivalled plethora of Bills of Parliament, Parliamentary Acts, and reports of commissions and select and departmental committees. The bills alone addressed a broad range of subjects including: the *protection of private property* – to prevent fraud (1801); to punish persons behaving riotously (1816); *social security* – for its workers, to compensate families of persons killed by accidents (1845); the payment of compensation for disability or death owing to fibroid phthisis or silicosis (1918); the allocation of Welfare Fund to aged miners (1929–30); *health and safety* – to compel the use of safety lamps (1851); the abolition of wheelless tubs (1927); *regulation* – to amend the working hours in mines to eight hours (1896); to prescribe minimum rates of pay (1918); *restructuring* – the establishment of a Ministry of Mines (1920); to make provision for the better organisation of the coal mining industry (1926); to nationalise mines and minerals (1936–7). Between 1939 and 1973, the mining industry experienced another 161 parliamentary bills including those which finally began the realisation of its long-discussed nationalisation in 1946 (Benson, Neville and Thompson 1981: pp 180–295).

While inevitably influenced by broader conditions and pressures, the Miners' Welfare Fund and the instigation of the pithead baths programme can be seen as emerging from three specific pieces of parliamentary legislation: the Coal Mines Act of 1911; and the Mining Industry Acts of 1920 and 1926. All of these, in turn, were the result of Royal Commissions set up under differing imperatives to inquire into the coal industry in the United Kingdom and make recommendations for improvements to its operation and the lives of those who experienced it. Reflecting both episodic and enduring controversies, the remits of these inquiries overlapped in their investigations of the health and safety of the workforce and its welfare. The first of these, the Royal Commission of 1906, was set up following the infamous Courrières disaster at Lens in Pas-de-Calais, in northern France, which had killed more than 1,500 workers. Amongst its recommendations, which became law under the 1911 Act, was the compulsory establishment of rescue stations within ten miles of any mine containing 100 or more employees. Section 77 of the same Act, however, made the first, if ultimately unsuccessful, proposal for the widespread introduction of pithead baths.

Its failure to induce a single pithead bath to be constructed under the act was an economic one. Requiring a two-thirds majority of the workforce to request the provision of washing facilities from the owner of the mine, the condition that collieries could not be compelled to provide baths if the cost of maintenance exceeded threepence per week per man, rendered the proposal initially 'impracticable'. It subsequently became increasingly impossible due to the rising costs caused by the First World War. The Act did, however, 'attract the attention of social reformers to the desirability of colliery bathing' (Chappell and Lovat-Fraser 1920 p.28). It also empowered a Departmental Committee on Washing and Drying Accommodation to inspect British and foreign precedents of bathing facilities and relay their findings to the Home Office. Reporting in 1913, these would ultimately contribute to the development of the pithead baths as a building type over the subsequent decades.

If the Coal Commission of 1906 followed the tragedy of the Courrières disaster and sought to instigate the provision of pithead baths, the two subsequent Royal Commissions, which effected a profound influence on miners' welfare in general, can be contextualised within other specific mining controversies: strikes or the threat of strikes. Commonly known after the respective names of their chairmen, the Sankey and Samuel Commissions of 1919 and 1925–6 respectively took place against the backdrop of particularly intense periods of labour unrest and industrial conflict which ultimately compelled the government to act as an interlocutor between the mining labour force and the owners of the mines.

THE SANKEY COMMISSION

The Coal Industry Commission Act (1919), which set up the commission led by Justice John Sankey, may have emerged out of the social upheavals of the First World War but – like the Homes for Heroes initiative and the Tudor Walters report on working-class housing – its origins lay well before this. If the global conflagration had created an increased expectation of improved housing standards for returning combatants and their families, for the miners and other interested parties the war had afforded a glimpse of another kind of working future for mining coal: of minimum wages and guaranteed employment. During the First World War, recognising the unambiguous centrality of coal to industrial production and thereby the war effort, the government had been obliged to assume control of coal mines to ensure regular and continuous supply. This began in the Welsh coalfields in December 1916 and was extended to all the country's mines three months later. 'Control' of the mines had meant a retreat from the laissez-faire economics that had dominated the industry from its beginnings. Amongst other things, it gradually implemented the fixing of prices, an effective subsidising of unprofitable pits, and offered workers wages and other concessions such as limiting the length of the working day. While necessitated by the conflict, the desirability of aspects of this quasi and temporary nationalisation had been discussed before the war, in recognition of the shortcomings of a perceptively outmoded industry much of whose technology, work practices and industrial relations had remained firmly rooted in the 19th century. Afforded a wide remit of method and scope of investigation as well as extensive powers including the ability to call witnesses and secure official information (Supple 1987: p.124), the Sankey Commission – which overlapped with the end of 'control' – was designed to scope out possible post-war futures for a highly labour-intensive industry recognised as being in much need of modernisation and restructuring, and whose traditional markets were becoming increasingly open to foreign competition.

If these circumstances were enduring and widely acknowledged, the immediate trigger for the commission was the formal claim – made to the Minister of Labour, the President of the Board of Trade and the Home Secretary – by the principal miners' union (the Miners' Federation of Great Britain [MFGB]) in January 1919, for a reduction in the working day of a miner, from eight to six hours, and an agreement from the government that the industry be permanently nationalised. Following recent scarcities in the supply of coal due to labour shortages, the claim was backed by the threat of a national strike. In the context of other serious social and industrial unrest being experienced in other industrial sectors and within British cities (such as Glasgow), this threatened to conflate into an unprecedented social crisis. The Sankey Commission's membership would be made up of representatives: of coal owners; those appointed by the MFGB; those agreed upon between the government and the MFGB; and those nominated by the government. With the miners agreeing to defer strike action for its duration, the commission represented a convenient solution to an immediate threat (Supple 1987: pp 123–4; Page Arnot 1953: p.189).

The Sankey Commission is significant for many reasons. If its initiation confirmed the strategic importance of coal and its miners as 'the basis of modern industrial civilisation' (Watkins 1934: p.25), the inquiry also revealed and communicated to a wide public audience the conditions under which its workers and their families laboured. Reported on daily by *The Times* and other newspapers, it has been termed a public trial of capitalism itself (Page Arnot 1953). Taking place in the King's Robing Room of the House of Lords, the individuals involved in the commissions had been arranged physically to resemble not so much an inquiry as an adversarial court, placing the miners' representatives opposite those of the mine-owners as if in confrontation (Supple 1987: p.126). Witnesses were called from a wide range of interested parties including: the mine owners and representatives of the union, mineral royalty owners, medical inspectors, representatives from other workingmen's unions and cognate industries, mining engineers, colliery managers, university lecturers, Inland Revenue valuers, surveyors, owners' agents and trustees, and finally miners, ex-miners and miners' wives. It has been described as an emotional propaganda victory for the miners where, for example, owners' barely answered allegations of war-time profiteering contrasted with eyewitnesses' stark accounts of an impecunious workforce experiencing dangerous working and struggling under poor living conditions. On the latter, the commission's chairman Sir John Sankey summarised in the interim report in March 1919 that: 'There are houses in some districts which are a reproach to our civilisation. No judicial language is sufficiently strong or sufficiently severe to apply to their condemnation' (Sankey 1919a: p.ix).

While the Sankey Commission's recommendations for wage increases – based around the concept of a social or living wage, rather than one derived from market pressures – and a reduction of the length of the working day were accepted and passed into law, other more far-reaching aspects of the inquiry concerning the comprehensive restructuring or nationalisation of the industry remained unimplemented. Inefficient and wasteful work-practices identified within the report would continue and questions surrounding the provision of housing for miners would also be unresolved. But the Commission's suggestion that a welfare fund designed to address a variety of aspects of miners' social well-being (but excluding housing) realised through a levy on production was also passed into law in the Mining Industry Act (1920) (Supple 1987: p.145). It was accompanied by a proposal to extend the period of 'control' until the end of August 1921 and the instigation of a new intermediary governmental agency designed to advise and oversee the complexities of the industry: the Mines Department located within the Board of Trade. It was to the latter that the committee, set up to administer the Miners' Welfare Fund, would be answerable.

The first annual report of the Miners' Welfare Committee (1921–2) was published in 1923.[7] By this time, an international slump or 'economic paralysis' (Page Arnot 1953: p.226) had meant a sudden drop in the demand for coal. This had precipitated a hastening by the government to end 'control' and its guarantees of fixed prices and wages. These circumstances – the prospect of large wage reductions in the face of a continued desire to enable a national wage agreement, supported by a national pool of coal-mining revenue, combined with a festering ill-feeling amongst mineworkers regarding the lack of resolution of the industry's restructuring, and the firm rejection of the nationalisation – tacitly recommended by Sankey – led to the MFGB's declaration of a national coal strike.[8] The coal strike began on the day 'control' was ended, the 1st of April 1921. By July the strike was broken and the miners had returned to work. They returned in the straitened circumstances of much-reduced wages and a lengthened working day, to an industry which had not only missed an opportunity to modernise, but whose traditional markets were becoming flooded with cheaper foreign coal – much of it from Germany, as part of its war reparation payments. All this coincided with a period of extreme economic turbulence and accelerated boom and bust cycles that would not stabilise until the late 1930s. The hardships endured by the miners during this time would help form the context for the subsequent Samuel Commission in 1925–6, and foment the General Strike which occurred just after its report was published in 1926.

THE BEGINNING OF THE MINERS' WELFARE FUND

It was into these particular circumstances that the Miners' Welfare Committee began and executed most of its architectural and other work. It would eventually be disbanded in 1946 as part of the long-anticipated nationalisation of the industry. Its first central committee contained five members, made up of two workers' representatives from the MFGB, two selected by the owners' Mining Association of Great Britain (MAGB), and a physician, Professor Edgar Leigh Collis. Collis, an expert on industrial hygiene and the health of coal miners, had been Medical Inspector of Factories between 1908 and 1918, and Chair of Public Health at the University of Wales since the end of the war (Waldron 2017: p.157). By the end of January 1921, the committee's first Chairman, Ronald Barnes, Lord Gorell, had been replaced by Frederic Thesiger, Lord Chelmsford, who had been Viceroy of India from 1916 to 1921. In the first report, and pre-empting Bertram's later description (see above), they collectively described the fund 'as great social experiment' whose intention 'is to provide happier surrounding for the mining community *as a whole* [emphasis original] and that our first care should be for those whose need is greatest' (MWC 1923: pp 8–9).

Under the recommendations of the Sankey Commission and in accordance with the Act, the fund was supplied by a levy of 1 pence per ton of output from every coal mine to serve 'such purposes connected with the social well-being, recreation, and conditions of living of workers in or about coal mines, and with mining education and research' (1920, cited in MWC 1923: p.6). Four fifths of the monies, called 'Districts Funds', were required to be allocated to the areas within which the money had been sourced. There were 25 districts – from north to south: Fife and Clackmannan, the Lothians, Lanarkshire, Ayrshire, Northumberland, Durham, Cumberland, Lancashire and Cheshire, North Wales, South Yorkshire, West Yorkshire, Nottinghamshire, Derbyshire, South Derbyshire, North Staffordshire, Cannock Chase, South Staffordshire, Leicestershire, Warwickshire, Shropshire, Forest of Dean, Somerset, Bristol, South Wales and Kent. Allocations to these had to follow consultations with District Welfare Committees to determine need. These committees had been set up by the end of 1921, again in accordance with the Act. Paralleling the central committee, they were constituted of both the coal owners and working men. The other fifth of the money, termed 'General Funds' had no restrictions applied to its allocation and was directly administered by the central committee. By the end of 1922, applications for the General Fund had fallen under two main categories: i) research concerning health and safety in coal mining; and ii) education (MWC 1923: p.7). Significantly, the Miners' Welfare Funds were to be explicitly for capital expenditure and the provision of *new* facilities with preference – to begin with at least – given to larger applications that would benefit the greatest number of miners and their respective communities. This 'great social experiment' was undoubtedly innovative, radical and ahead of its time. Involving a structure of cooperation between management, labour and the intercession of government, it was designed to administer a fund which redistributed profits to effect environmental and other improvements according to the demand of the greatest need and greatest number. The beginnings of its architectural programme, however, were more hesitant in embodying these ambitions.

By the end of December 1922, just over a million pounds had been collected from the levy for District Schemes and just over half a million had been allocated. The majority of this (just over £300,000, funding a total of 125 projects) was being spent on recreation and sports grounds which ranged in size 'from the single bowling green to the large "community scheme"' (MWC 1923: p.12). The design and layout for these had been provided pro bono by the Industrial Welfare Society, one of a series of agencies used as consultants for the fund. The next biggest allocation was for cultural facilities – miners' institutes, clubs, libraries, and so on – and incorporated a range of projects from the design and construction of entire buildings, to the purchase of books and other materials.

One of the larger grants awarded was in Nottinghamshire for the realisation of the East Kirby Miners' Institute, a pre-existing typology of building within coalfield communities. One of the first buildings designed under the Miners' Welfare Fund, its architecture – a hotchpotch of classical elements and other motifs, including curious dormer windows arranged within a U-shaped plan with two projecting ranges – represented an inauspicious aesthetic and formal beginning (FIGS 16 and 17). Neither its architectural language nor quality convey the sense of a new beginning, or represent the radical nature and political contexts surrounding the generation of the Fund itself. Rather it resembles

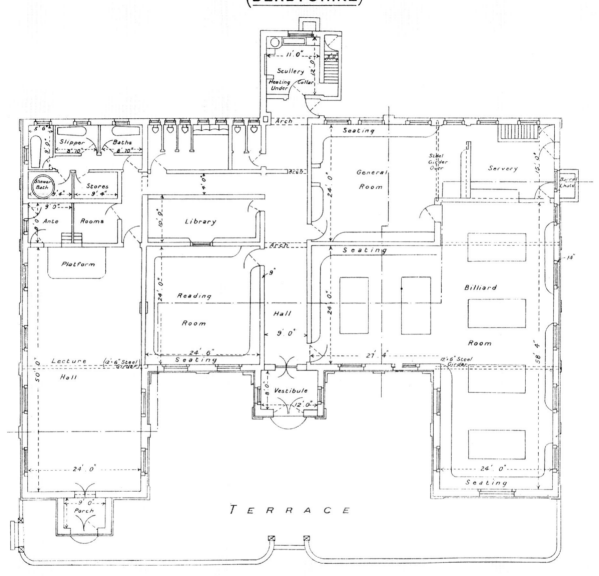

GROUND PLAN OF INSTITUTE.

previous institutes produced for miners under other circumstances and through other means. Inside it contained a range of functions: a lecture hall with a stage, a library and reading room, a general room with bar or servery, and an extensive billiards room. Miners' institutes, often supported by workers and owners alike, had been seen as a civilising force within the coalfields in the late 19th and early 20th centuries, often as one of a series of measures in mining communities – such as 'Goth' public houses selling alcohol but not

16
Ground floor plan of East Kirby Miners' Institute

17
Front elevation of East Kirby Miners' Institute photographed under construction, 1923

spirits in austere surroundings – which facilitated socialising while attempting to temper possible unruly behaviours and channel activities into acceptable and edifying forms. A moralising overtone remained within the description of the institute typology offered by the central committee in the first annual report which suggested that the programme for such buildings be designed 'to attract all the best elements of the community' and that 'the provision of reading and writing rooms is quite as necessary as is that of billiard and card-rooms' (MWC 1923: p.12). This is significant, as accusations of paternalism with regards to cleanliness and hygiene for miners, would articulate the discussion and initial controversies surrounding the provision of pithead baths, and, ultimately, would have an effect on the development of their form and aesthetic.

Of all the projects illustrated within the MWC's first report, the one which perhaps conveyed its new political context most potently, was paradoxically the oldest. The costliest and most ambitious project for the District Funds during this first period of activity was the development of a convalescent home for injured miners in Ayrshire. Financed partly by the Fund and partly by an additional levy on the local miners themselves, the initial capital had been advanced by the coal owners. The scheme involved the acquisition and refurbishment of a 19th-century Scots Baronial-style stately home, Kirkmichael House, and its pleasure gardens and grounds (FIG.18). Symbolically at least, it represented the reconfiguration and opening up of a private country estate built for a single upper-class family and its retainers, into a facility designed to rehabilitate the industrial injuries of what was, throughout the 1920s and 1930s,

18
Ayrshire District Miners'
Convalescent Home
(Kirkmichael House)

one of the most deprived sections of working-class society. Huge, new edifices for miners' rehabilitation and convalescence would soon follow, congregating on the seashores of Skegness, Blackpool and other conspicuous sites. For the origins of the physical form and organisation of the MWC's pithead bath buildings, however, it is necessary to return to before the Fund actually existed, to the Coal Mines Act of 1911, its Section 77, and the enabling of a Home Office reporting committee to enquire into British and European build precedents.

BRITISH AND EUROPEAN PRECEDENTS OF PITHEAD BATHS

The Home Office Departmental Committee on Washing and Drying Accommodation (Home Office Committee [1913]) consisted of the Secretary of Mines and a representative each from the mine owners and mineworkers.[9] Its terms of reference concerned defining: (i) 'sufficient and suitable facilities'; (ii) whether it was necessary to differentiate potential provision according to different classes and descriptions of mines; and (iii) the proposal of procedures for how the bathhouses might be managed (Home Office Report 1913: p.1). Following the findings of a previous committee's appraisal of continental facilities produced under the Royal Commission of 1906–09, the committee made visits to British examples at Wharncliffe Silkstone Colliery near Barnsley, and to Winnington, Northwich (which was not a colliery but by the chemical factory owned by Brunner, Mond and Co.) as well as a series of baths within the Belgian, French and German coalfields.[10] While its European excursions confirmed a far more widespread provision of pithead baths than in Britain, the report also described variations from country to country and indeed even within the different states of Germany, where there were differing levels of legislative compulsion for collieries to provide them, or for men to use them. In Westphalia, for example, where the baths were described as 'luxurious and having had no expense spared', their provision *and* use by the miners were both obligatory (Home Office Report 1913: p.3). In France and Belgium, meanwhile, new legislation was about to be introduced to require facilities to be provided at all collieries, but whether to wash in them or not was up the miners.

There were also distinctions within the design of the actual baths themselves. Different types of both bathing systems and equipment were used. Early pithead bathing experiments in Germany, for example, had included the use of large pool-like baths where miners bathed collectively. This was discontinued after it was found to encourage the spread of ancylostomiasis, a disease of the intestine caused by hookworm, common amongst miners at the time. Instead, shower, spray or douche baths were adopted (Chappell and Lovat-Fraser 1920: p.31). The logistics of a pithead bath involves the flow of a great deal of men, as well as water. Larger collieries in the early to mid-20th century often had thousands of workers, and smaller mines had workforces of some hundreds. These were generally organised around three shifts across a 24-hour working period. It was also necessary to store and separate clean clothes from dirty clothes. The system adopted in Germany, and widely utilised elsewhere, deployed a pulley system where miners' clothes were hauled up and suspended by a chain above the main changing area, either for the duration of the individual miner's shift (clean clothes), or for the period when he was at home (dirty clothes). Suspended above the miners' heads within a space constantly heated, as far as possible, to a temperature of approximately 70° Fahrenheit, the arrangement was designed to dry the clothes when they were not being worn. The miners themselves were expected to take their pit clothes home once a week to have them washed.

As can be seen from examples at Gewerkschaft Gottessegen on the Ruhr or the Société des Mines de Lens (No.11 pit) this often resulted in voluminous, almost cathedral-like changing areas replete with high-level or clerestory windows and articulated by a series of vertical suspending chains holding bundles attached to pew-like structures beneath, where the men could let down and access their change of clothes (FIGS 19 and 20). A plan of the baths facility at Monceau-Fontaines (No.8 Forgies Pit) near Charleroi in Belgium from the early 1920s, shows the organisation typical of these pithead bath typologies and the sequence and process of bathing in more detail (FIG.21). At the

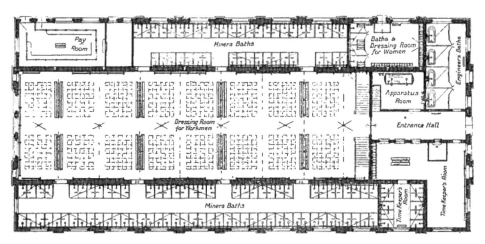

19
Gewerkschaft Gottessegen, main clothes hall

20
The shower area of the Société des Mines de Lens (No.11 pit). Miners' clothes hanging in the main hall can be seen on the upper left

21
Plan of Monceau-Fontaine Baths (No.8 Forgies pit)

22
The interior of baths at Pit No.3 of the Compagnie des mines de Bruay

end of a shift when the miners were in dirty pit clothes, they would file through the main entrance to the central space and undress on the benches below their clean clothes suspended above. These are denoted by the areas marked as grids on the plan. They would then hoist their dirty clothes upwards. From the central changing area miners could access the shower baths located on the perimeters of the building by a number of entrances. On returning to the main space they would retrieve their clean clothes from above and change into them before leaving the baths for home, using the same entrance through which they had arrived at the end of their shift. This last point is of interest as it will become a focus of criticism in the developments made by later British pithead baths. Also significant is the separate women's baths and dressing-room area, and the 'slipper' baths reserved for the colliery's more highly qualified and far fewer engineers who, presumably, could take more time to bathe. The building also contained other functions unrelated to bathing. A time-keeper's office is present adjacent to the entrance, perhaps confirming the obligatory usage by men of the facilities which, as mentioned above, was demanded in some but not all of the continental baths. The final space in this large building was reserved for the pay room where the miners would present themselves to receive their wages. Other examples of continental baths also often contained functions necessary to the operation of the colliery but not necessarily concerned with bathing.

Given the numbers of men involved, to ensure everyone was able to wash, large collieries such as Monceau-Fontaines would often operate a strict system – regulated by the baths' attendants – to limit the time the miners could spend in the showers. This would be designed to synchronise with the winding time, the time taken to dispatch the workforce in the lift cages from the pit bottom to the surface, and take the oncoming shift back down again. With each of the three shifts representing hundreds of men, winding time could be up to an hour. This meant that, with careful organisation, the first men up would be cleaned, changed and exited before the cages delivered the next batch of miners who had been waiting below. It also meant that a ratio of baths per men could be defined. Accordingly, while all miners' clothes had to the be stored and dried in the large central main changing or dressing space, the numbers of shower baths provided could be far less and still accommodate the needs of the men. The Home Office Committee (1913) estimated an average washing time of ten minutes and recommended the provision of one shower bath per six workers, so that all could be bathed within a period of about 60 minutes. Other British visitors to continental baths commented that while the facility at Monceau-Fontaines in Belgium, for instance, was very well organised and equipped, in general those provided by German collieries were consistently of higher quality when compared to Belgian and French models. This criticism, however, may also concern the use of a slightly different alternative typology used more often outside Germany and seen in baths such as those provided by the Compagnie des mines de Bruay (No.3 pit) in Northern France (FIG.22). This type allowed each miner a locker to hold his clothes rather than the

23
The basilica form of the pitheads at Bruay (No.6 pit)

suspension systems favoured in Germany. The image of the baths at Bruay show a central changing area of a similar voluminous space to that of the suspension system and facilitating a similar sequence of washing and changing. But instead of bundles of clothes hanging from chains, it contains rows of lockers. At the top of each locker can be seen a vent to encourage the drying of the clothes contained within. The Home Office Committee voiced scepticism that this arrangement was adequate to dry clothes, as well as concern that dirty pit dress would leave residues and odours within the lockers, which in turn could potentially spoil the clean clothes while storing them. For this reason, they favoured the adoption of the suspension system as a model for British pithead baths.

Also significant at Bruay and seen at Monceau-Fontaines is the provision of individual cubicles. This differed from German baths which facilitated a norm of communal washing, albeit with the segregation of younger, under-18 miners from their older colleagues. The idea of communal bathing – deemed more acceptable to foreign workers because of compulsory military service – was considered a problematic affront to the perceived modesty of the British miner. As a result, cubicles became a necessary aspect of future British pithead baths development and became part of a prototypical design commissioned by the Home Office Committee in 1913. Despite the fact that it was equipped with lockers and, therefore had no apparent reason for a lofty hall, the baths at Bruay – in common with those at Monceau-Fontaines and Gewerkschaft Gottessegen – took the form of a historical architectural precedent: the early-Christian basilica. This consists of a high central nave, flanked by lower aisles which allow the admission of clerestory lighting, as well as windows within the two gables to illuminate deep within the plan. This quasi-ecclesiastical form can be seen clearly on the exterior view of another Bruay bath facility (No.6 pit), albeit rhythmically articulated by chimneys (FIG.23). What is also conspicuous about Bruay (No.3), however, is that it is very much a mass-produced industrial object. Realised through a series of steel portal frames, its interior evokes a functionalist approach measured in hard surfaces – floor tiles and what seems like pressed metal in the construction of the lockers and bath cubicles. Nothing here is extraneous, and nothing is present that would seem to offer anything beyond a mechanistic approach to the precisely and instrumentally defined requirements of serial human bathing within an industrial workplace. This treatment of the bathing of workers as a strictly industrial process is perhaps understandable and is confirmed in the reports of another German facility which actively recycled the coal dust from the water in which miners had washed and reused it within the colliery (Chappell and Lovat-Fraser 1920). Despite the apparent pretentions of, or more likely the convenient form of the basilica, the aesthetic produced is generic. The discomforting architecture seen particularly in the interior of Bruay – which because of the locker system lacks even the softening presence offered by the bundles of hoisted clothes – but also elsewhere, could simply be a shed, an abattoir, or any other type of cheap, prefabricated agricultural or industrial structure from the 1910s and 1920s.

In fact, the Home Office Committee – perhaps overly taking cognisance of the bald description 'sufficient' in their terms of reference – proposed an even simpler version as a prototype for prospective British pithead baths: 'The type of baths and general arrangements we saw at the Lens No.5 Pit appeared to us to be the most likely to meet the conditions existing in the mines in the United Kingdom and, at the same time, to be the most economical in first cost, and in maintenance' (Home Office report 1913: p.6).

The drawings of Lens No.5 that accompanied the report reveal not even a basilica-type plan, but instead a still more basic steel-framed gabled shed with tilting high-level windows for ventilation, a floor sloped to channel runoff water and a draught lobby to attempt to keep the interior at the even temperature recommended (FIG.24). The structure was based on the suspension system but with individual cubicles, and was clad in corrugated iron rather than brick or any other more expensive material. These austere features formed the basis of the approach made to two British foundries – Carron Iron Works of Falkirk (who were specialists in cast iron components such as roll-top slipper baths

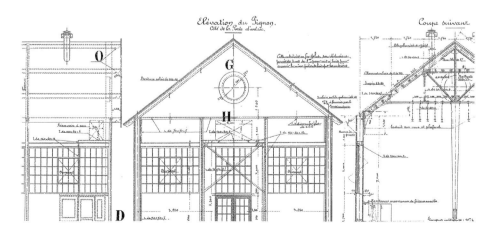

24
Drawings of baths at Lens (No.5) contained in the report of the Home Office Departmental Committee on Washing and Drying Accommodation, 1913

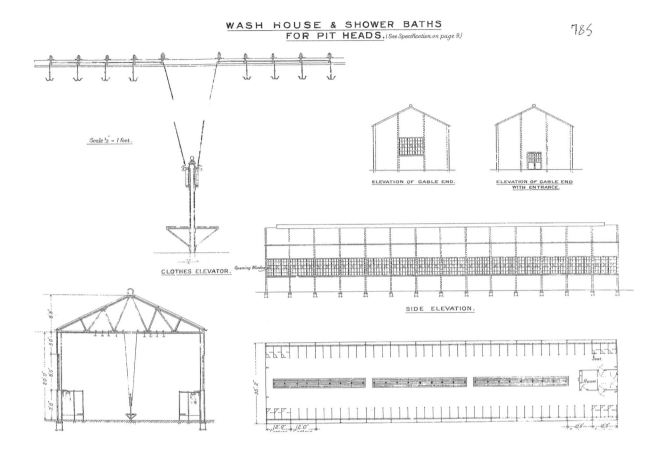

and post-boxes) and Messrs John Lysaght and Co. of Bristol – to scope out a specification for, and to deliver, an entire building. This was to be a cheap, non-site specific, repeatable model which could quickly and economically respond to what had by now been recognised as an urgent need to provide bathing facilities for British miners. The models, proposed and illustrated in the Home Office report, confirm a preconception of pithead baths as a technical problem to be resolved in as efficient a manner as possible, and to provide no more than what had been defined as a minimalist 'sufficient' response (FIG.25). There were, however, other emergent criteria which would ultimately compel this narrow functionalism to develop into more sophisticated approaches and forms for these buildings.

LANDSCAPES OF BATHING

As noted above, the Sankey report of 1919 provided revelations of the living and working conditions of miners to a wider public audience. Amongst the numerous witnesses and experts called were miners' wives. They effectively put forward the case for the social need of pithead baths, simply by describing their own domestic situations, and the daily chores and consequences of

25
Wash house and shower baths for pitheads, Home Office Committee prototypical design 1913

having to deal with the washing of miners and their clothes in their own homes. Mrs Elizabeth Hart of Wigan, for instance, gave the following vivid description:

> Imagine a house with one living room which serves as a kitchen for cooking and as a dining room. A family of two to six sons, along with the father, come home from work. After they have had their meal, they take off their pit clothes and wash. There are no facilities such as hot water laid on. The usual procedure is a small pan heated on the fire; each has to wash in his turn and sometimes before the water is ready, some of them have gone to sleep they are so tired … The shifts are so uncertain that the housewife has to be up early and late … The houses are back to back and it entails a very great strain on the women, because they have no washing boilers and they have to carry heavy pans, and that is responsible for a great deal of the internal complaints of women … And then there is the drying of clothes in the houses … in winter they have to dry all the clothes in the house. The steam comes from them … Now the women are unanimously in favour of pithead baths, because they recognise that it would take a lot of dirt out of their houses. When a woman has to have a lot of men coming home and she has no facilities whatever in the shape of water or anything like that laid on, and the children are playing in and out of the house while the men are coming in … they feel that if they could have all this dust and dirt left at the pithead it would save them a lot of work, and there would be a lot more comfort in their home life.
>
> (Sankey 1919b: 1016)

The accommodation in terms of meals and washing for multiple male miners on different shifts within the same household was not uncommon, and it was recognised that whereas a mineworker would be occupied at the pit for a set period, his wife's working day was almost always considerably longer. In a normal situation of fathers and sons working in the colliery on different shifts, this would involve a rolling programme of preparing meals and boiling water for hot baths for each of the men as they returned from the mine, followed by the daily drying and weekly washing of their pit clothes. Evidence from medical and health experts confirmed other consequences. A midwife working in the Rhondda Valley suggested that most premature births and miscarriages, as well as other 'extreme female ailments', was – as Elizabeth Hart also suggested – due to physical strain of lifting heavy tubs and boilers in their homes. For Mr Roberts-Jones, a South Wales coroner, the presence of large open baths filled with very hot water was a safety hazard, especially to young children. He had 'no hesitation in saying that hundreds of children have lost their lives duringthe past ten years through scalds at home' (Chappell and Lovat-Fraser 1920: pp 12–13). Elsewhere in the Sankey report, it is proposed that elevated levels of infant mortality were linked – especially in extreme cases like the single-apartment houses found in mining communities in Scotland – to domestic environments where, for example, if children were ill with fever, they were still compelled to 'breathe the fumes from the drying of the pit clothes' (Sankey 1919: p.526).

The Sankey commission sought to consider an enormously wide range of factors and conditions shaping the coal industry, from its economic structures to the collective and individual experiences of its workforce. Like other commissions and reports before it, such as the accounts of Hugh Seymour Tremenheere, the first Inspector of Mines in 1844, it confirmed the ongoing inadequacy of miners' housing. By the early 1910s, the socialist politician, journalist, and novelist Katharine Bruce Glasier – corresponding for the Women's Labour League – had issued a series of pamphlets to launch what they described as a 'New Crusade' to end the presence of industrial dirt within homes and deliver 'womenfolk from the hard, disagreeable and usually ill-equipped toil which the present system involves' (Glasier and Richardson 1912: p.1; see also Evans and Jones 1994). As well as contributing to the well-being of (what in the Sankey report were quantified as) over one million actual pit workers through the provision of washing facilities, and by ensuring that miners had dry clothes in which to both begin and leave their shifts, the development of a pithead baths programme was also designed to effect – if not exactly a 'domestic revolution' – then a significant shift in the circumstances at home of not only the miners, but especially their dependents.

In discussions of the pithead baths programme, it is easy to remain focused on its visible architectural achievements in the collection of buildings that, in time, would adorn pits across the United Kingdom's coalfields. Equally important, however, was the offer, through the provision of a new infrastructure outside the home, of a pragmatic approach to a housing problem that, in the political climate of the 1920s and 1930s – and especially within the complexities of private enterprise, tied housing and other forms of tenure within the mining industry – was possibly otherwise intractable. Wholesale, comprehensive improvements and redevelopment of miners' housing, while experienced in fragments throughout the early decades of the 20th century, would not be carried out until after the Second World War and the generation of the welfare state.

The benefits to this largely invisible domestic landscape of pithead baths were, as suggested by Elizabeth Hart of Wigan, initially appreciated most acutely within the coalfields by its women. From their practical, experiential perspective, however, they were joined both by the views of the Miners' Federation of Great Britain and the recommendations of a series of medical and health experts from both within and outside the industry, and a slew of reports and publications beginning in the 19th century and testifying to the hygienic, medical and moral advantages of workplace baths in general. Following on from Edwin Chadwick's seminal *Report on the Sanitary Condition of the Labouring Population of Great Britain* of 1843, these formed part of a wider backdrop of interest in the hygienic circumstances of society in general and the working classes in particular. In time, an international movement developed – which included the Women's Labour League cited above – to advocate for workplace and, indeed, public baths. For the architect Robert Owen Allsop, writing in 1894, 'the importance of public baths and wash-houses cannot be over-estimated, either on the grounds of public well-being or political economy'. The public bath was, he suggested, 'an instrument of the most powerful order for elevating the masses and stimulating a desire of self-improvement'. For the author, this concerned more than just the idea of physical cleanliness: '[t]o make an habitually dirty man clean, is to create in his inmost soul – even if but temporality – a desire to rise out of the squalor and filth with which he may be ordinarily encompassed' (Allsop 1894: p.1).

Despite its evidently moralistic overtones, Allsop's book *Public Baths and Wash-Houses* offered only a brief social history of baths within Great Britain. Concentrating instead on architectural perspectives, it became one of several publications offering technical guidance on the practicalities of constructing facilities. The first public baths in Britain, the George's Pier Head Baths in Liverpool were opened in 1828, closely followed by facilities in London – in Glasshouse Yards near the docks, and Goulston Square in Whitechapel – in the 1840s. By 1846, the Baths and Washhouses Act, designed to encourage municipalities to establish public facilities, had been passed into law by Parliament putting into motion, according to Allsop, 'a powerful lever for humanising the physically, mentally and morally debased' (ibid.: p.3).

Later publications, such as Alfred William Stephens Cross's *Public Baths and Wash-Houses* (1906) and William Paul Gerhard's *Modern Baths and Bath Houses* (1908) toned down such rhetoric and were more successful in establishing a technically focused appraisal of the state of the art of bathing and its necessary mechanics of water supply and pressures, heating systems, and different components and apparatus. After establishing the origins of bathing in the ancient world, the different purposes of washing and a description of different types of baths and settings – the tub, the slipper, the 'wave' bath (both portable and mechanical), the swimming bath, and so on – Gerhard alights on what, by the time of publication, had already been established in continental and especially German pithead baths: that the shower, or what he calls the 'rain bath', was the most advanced, highly developed and efficient form of bathing in terms of time, space and water use. He suggests that, historically, the shower was a relatively recent arrival, tracing its origins to the hygienic discipline of a French military barracks in 1857. From here it gradually proliferated in Germany following a pamphlet published by a Prussian Army surgeon who advocated its use in all public institutions, including barracks, prisons, hospitals and factories (Gerhard 1908: p.34). Perhaps significantly – given the industrial manufacturer Krupp's intimate relationship to coal-mining enterprises throughout the Ruhr area – the latter category included an early installation in its steel works in Essen.

For all the ancient origins and continuities of bathing practices, the shower represented a modern, industrial object which, since its emergence, had already undergone considered refinements to its design and ergonomic relationship with its user. Itself evidently mass produced, its efficiencies made it ideal for the application of rapid multiple or mass, simultaneous bathing. Gerhard comments upon the precise ergonomic evolution of the design of the spray head component and its positioning not above but angled from the side, so that the water does not strike the head of the user which 'to many persons is disagreeable [but only] strikes the body from the neck downwards, and the head is not wetted' except when purposefully desired. Finally, he describes the shower as a type of 'tepid' bath, one whose temperature could be easily attained by harnessing the waste or exhaust steam from a manufactory or other industrial site (ibid.: p.32). Describing its list of attributes, he also explains how the shower had been emancipated from a previous connection with a tub to create a more subtle and considered manipulation of the ground under foot, a dissolution of the boundaries between the inside and outside of the bathing area, which facilitated an efficient and rapid turnover of bathers. This boundary is reduced to a slight change in level, a small upstand, or even an articulated floor that is simply laid in slopes to drain away water. Aside from the communal showers of German pithead baths – which took this eschewing of separation to its open plan limits – showers could be rendered private for individual bathing simply by the presence of a vertical enclosure or partition. Most often doorless, these partitions could be made in galvanised corrugated iron, finished in enamel paint, or glazed brick or tile, or even wood, if it was maintained properly (ibid.: p.41). If combined with a frame structure, the partition wall need not touch the ground or the perimeter wall of the building – and indeed should not – to permit easier cleaning. Both this partition arrangement and the articulated floor can be seen in the sectional drawing of prototype pithead baths proposed by Carron Iron Works (FIG.25).

ARCHITECTURE AND THE PITHEAD BATHS MOVEMENT

The refined precision of the baths as described by Gerhard in 1908 contrasts acutely with the deficiencies of washing facilities in miners' homes as explained by the likes of Elizabeth Hart more than a decade later in 1919. However, it is also significant that, in contrast with other industries especially in Great Britain, mining in the 1920s, and indeed the 1930s, was not highly mechanised. Often miners still operated with the same hand tools and basic equipment and techniques that had been introduced decades, if not centuries, before. The labour-intensive nature of mining is one explanation for the large size of the workforce which reached its peak in 1913, the same year that the Home Office was assembling and then published their report. The arrival of a precisely defined, industrial mass-produced product as an instrument for bathing or indeed for anything else was, therefore, often outside the direct experience of miners within their domestic or working environments. The shower bath would provide an intimate introduction to modernity. And while the women of the coalfields supported its introduction, and experts and miners' unions agreed on its desirability, to begin with, for a variety of reasons, many of the miners themselves were deeply reluctant to accept it.

By the time Edgar L. Chappell and J. A. Lovat-Fraser's book *Pithead and Factory Baths* was published in 1920 the arguments for the creation of pithead facilities were well established and had been given a further boost by the findings and recommendations of the Sankey report. Indeed, *Pithead and Factory Baths* dedicates a whole chapter to what the authors described as the 'pithead baths movement', incorporating some of the social and economic arguments in favour of them, as well as discussion of their proliferation on the continent, and descriptions of the handful of facilities that had been built in Great Britain. Of further significance was the introduction provided by two of the miners' most prominent trade union representatives, Frank Hodges and Robert Smillie, General Secretary and Vice-President of the MFGB respectively. Among other things, they describe the potential of pithead baths to 'cause a domestic revolution of the mining communities of Great Britain' (Chappell and Lovat-Fraser 1920: p.vii). However, the book also gives over a chapter to list the 'principal objections and difficulties raised by the miners to the provision and use of colliery bathing installations' (ibid.: p.66). These ranged from concerns about privacy; that the baths would spread skin disease; about the temperature of the water; that pithead baths are not suited to the British climate; about the potential for the thieving of clothes and other items; about the effectiveness of the proposed clothes-drying facilities; about owners making profits out of the baths or using them to accommodate blacklegs during strikes; about miners having to get up earlier to use the baths and/or retiring to the public house after a shift, instead of going home to wash; about the cost of the baths to the men in deductions from their wages; and about the old superstition, still held in some mining areas, that the wetting of the back causes weakness in it. While Chappell and Lovat-Fraser responded to each concern in turn, elsewhere in the book they also stressed that, in the face of both reasonable and irrational concerns, there was an acute need for measures of propaganda to convince miners that the pithead baths were beneficial to both them and their communities.[11] And while pamphlets and lectures within the coalfields, and other publications such as their own book may be somewhat effective, they argued that the most potent means to generate acceptance of pitheads was not only the testimonies of those miners who had had an opportunity to use them, but also, and significantly, the buildings and spaces of bathing themselves (ibid.: p.29).

This resonated with Alfred William Stephens Cross's earlier book of 1906 which had added another dimension to the discussion of public baths. As giving it its full title – *Public Baths and Wash-Houses: A Treatise on Their Planning, Design, Arrangement, and Fitting, Having Special Regards to the Acts Arranging for Their*

Provision, With Chapters on Turkish, Russian, and Other Special Baths, Public Laundries, Engineering, Heating, Water Supply, Etc. – would suggest, Cross's publication represented a practical guide towards the erection, fitting out and operation of a comprehensive range of bathing types and facilities. But alongside all the usual details about filtration systems, high-pressure mains, and so on, the author steered the discussion towards architectural form and, conspicuously, the qualities and value of aesthetics within the design, realisation and experience of buildings. As opposed to the skeletal, diagrammatic kit-building proposed under the rubrics of economic and efficiency in the Home Office Committee Report of 1913, Cross argued for the form of public baths not to emerge so much from narrow functional criteria, but rather be conceived of and realised as pieces of civic architecture. In support of his proposition for a baths architecture of substance and monumentality, he cited John Ruskin from *The Seven Lamps of Architecture*: '[W]hen we build let us think that we build forever. Let it not be for the present nor for present alone, let it be such work as our descendants will thank us for' (Cross 1906: p.4).

26
Haggerston Baths, Hackney, 1904, by Alfred William Stephens Cross

While Cross considered many of the buildings erected after the Baths and Washhouses Act of 1846 to have been of low standard and poor quality, *Public Baths and Washhouses* is punctuated with drawings of the exteriors of municipal bath buildings which he deemed to be exemplary models. Among these paradigms – most of which had been built within about a decade prior to his publication and mainly located in London – he included his own designs for Haggerston Baths, Hackney (1904) and Clapham Public Baths (1905). Both of these were effected in brick and Portland stone in an Edwardian Baroque style (FIG.26). In addition, he included other equally elaborate baths, either recently completed or proposed as projects by several different architects for sites in, for example, Bethnal Green, Camberwell, Chelsea, Stratford and Tottenham. These, together with the many other examples of public baths and facilities built throughout the United Kingdom, formed part of a sanitary and hygienic strand within the landscape of municipal socialism that had emerged in the second half of the 19th century, in response to the environmental and social issues accompanying industrialisation and its accelerated forms of urbanisation. While providing part of a new sanitary infrastructure freely accessible to all, these buildings also participated within a landscape of ideas. Like the paternalistic overtones associated with philanthropic building, they sought to instil a new spirit of civility through hygiene among the working classes, while demonstrating the collective munificence of local authorities. The language of the architecture, its form, style and aesthetics – and often magnificence – therefore, formed part of a strategy of persuasion concerning the inculcation of new types of behaviour and attitudes to approach the type of new improved morality cited by Robert Owen Allsop in his 1894 publication. In this, arguably they reiterate one of the Victorian period's most often repeated tropes about the moral and spiritual benefits of cleanliness.

Writing just under 20 years later, however, Katharine Glasier proposed a similar vision, one which expressed even more explicitly a faith in the ideological leverage of architectural form: 'Already I can see the Bath House rising – white shining Temples of Health – in every mining village, and beside all the great glass and steel chemical works of our land. With a gymnasium added, as in many of the German mining establishments, they would be a more powerful influence against the Public House than a thousand Temperance lectures' (Glasier and Richardson 1912: p.4).

Glasier's vision would become prescient in the generation of aesthetically matured and technologically refined pithead baths that emerged in the late 1920s and especially in the 1930s. Designed by Forshaw and his team of architects at the Miners' Welfare Committee, they negotiated the confluence of hygiene and morality often found within the architecture of municipal socialism and other earlier ideologies, and translated it into contemporary modernist architectural forms.

THE SAMUEL COMMISSION AND THE DEVELOPMENT OF THE PITHEAD BATHS PROGRAMME

The pithead baths programme would ultimately expand in the wake of the second of the Royal Commissions inquiring into mining in this period: the Samuel Commission of 1925–6. Chaired by Herbert Samuel, the former High Commissioner of Palestine, once again its initiation and progress was surrounded by particularly intense levels of miners' hardships and industrial turmoil. The Commission and the legislation which followed its recommendations formed part of the backdrop to the General Strike of 1926. Among these recommendations, the Samuel Commission proposed another levy, this time on coal royalties (the money due to the owners of the land under which the coal was situated), at a rate of one shilling in the pound (MWC 1927: p.40). This was to be used specifically and exclusively for the construction of pithead baths. In the immediate aftermath of the Sankey Commission in 1919, however, these developments were still firmly in the future. While Sankey would generate the creation of a welfare fund for miners and a general acceptance of its desirability, the progress of a comprehensive pithead baths programme – whose architectural form would emerge from a complex mix of social pressures and technological and aesthetic appraisals – was still very much in its infancy in the early 1920s.

As described above, the conditions attached to the provision of pithead baths prescribed in Section 77 of the Coal Mines Act of 1911 were such that no facilities were in fact built under this legislation. However, there had been some pre-existing examples of pithead baths built at the turn of century and set up largely on the initiative of progressive mine owners, such as at Butterly Colliery in Yorkshire, or Hucknall Torkyard Colliery in Nottinghamshire. But these

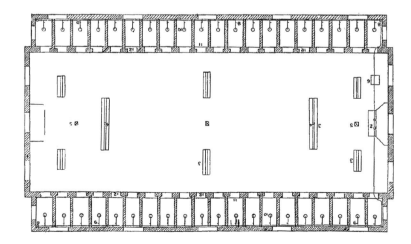

27
Plan of baths at Arley Mine, Atherton

28
View of the baths at Ocean Colliery, Treharris

29
Plan of the baths at Ocean Colliery, Treharris

 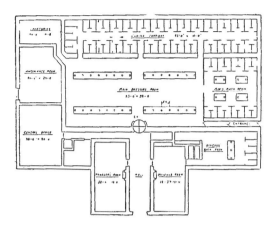

experiments – the latter involving a single plunge-pool system – described as 'crude and imperfect', had subsequently fallen into disuse (Chappell and Lovat-Fraser 1920: p.21). The earliest British baths that had adopted the general arrangement and shower systems seen in continental baths were set up in 1898 in Wharncliffe Silkstone Colliery, but again were considered inferior. Along with the baths erected at the chemical factory of Brunner, Mond and Co. (cited above), which had also impressed Katharine Glasier and the Women's Labour League, the first baths deemed an appropriate paradigm for future development by Chappell and Lovat-Fraser were installed in mines in the village of Atherton (Lancashire) and at the Ocean Colliery, Treharris (South Wales). Along with one or two other facilities – including the baths at Wemyss Colliery in Fife – these installations, according to Chappell and Lovat-Fraser, had 'done more to popularise pithead baths than all other forms of propaganda' (Chappell and Lovat-Fraser 1920: p.29).

Both Atherton and Treharris were based on the hoist and pulley suspension system for storing clothes. Arley Mine in Atherton was the first of the two to be built and opened on the 15th of September 1913.[12] Its plan is a more straightforward version of the building at Monceau-Fontaines described above and based upon the same principles (FIG.27). The men enter through a lobby in the short end of the building into a main changing and dressing room which stores their clothes above them. From here they can access a series of cubicles directly. Chappell and Lovat-Fraser commented on the aesthetic of the building, which appears in the form of a large red-brick shed, deeming it as 'handsome'. They also described a generosity in the materiality and environment of the interior: 'The walls on the inside are lined with glazed bricks to a height of six feet, bordered by a green dado, and the upper part is of white plaster. The floor of the dressing room is made of red Ruabon tiles. The [heated] room is light and airy, ventilation being effected by means of large windows and twelve ventilating cowls in the roof. The building is illuminated at night by electricity' (ibid.: p.56).

This obviously represented a building of far greater permanence, solidity and gravitas than the prototypes proposed by the Home Office Committee Report published in 1913 – coincidentally the same year that the baths at Arley mine were opened. If anything, this is even more true of the facilities at Treharris which were described by Chappell and Lovat-Fraser as a 'massive stone building' (ibid.: p.57) (FIG.28). Here, the plan is more elaborate, and the simplicity represented at Arley is disrupted by the addition of other functions (FIG.29). The main changing/dressing space again occupies the centre of the building, but this time it is wrapped by two L-shaped forms in plan – the actual shower baths to the top and right, and a range of other accommodation including lavatories, an ambulance room, offices and officials' bathroom to the left and bottom. The miners enter and leave on the long side using an entrance/exit squeezed between two spaces of authority: the manager's office and the officials' room. From here they access the principal space via a revolving door designed to maintain the air temperature inside – as constant as possible to the ideal of 70° Fahrenheit – provided by a system of pipes and radiators. Of interest is the arrangement of pairs of cubicles accessed by a small, shared outer space, where privacy is provided not by doors but by the careful placement of walls and manipulation of wall planes. These, like the cubicle walls at Atherton (and indeed at Monceau-Fontaines) are finished in glazed brick and provide a variation or development of the system at Brunner, Mond and Co., which combined a zigzag arrangement with curtains for privacy (Glasier and Richardson 1912: p.2).

Despite the asymmetry of the plan, the building's exterior presented itself in the basilica form – seen at the baths at Bruay, Monceau-Fontaines and Gewerkschaft Gottessegen – of a high, central, nave-like space flanked by lower aisle spaces. If the building itself, as revealed in contemporary photographs, does not yet appear to be the 'white shining Temple of Health' envisioned by Katharine Glasier, it managed to be both monumental and civic while responding to the existing industrial landscape in which it found itself. This was made easier by the enormous engine house, also made in stone, which dominated the site immediately behind it and, replete with neo-classical, round-headed windows, professed its own architectural pretensions. That both of these buildings at Atherton and Treharris – while located within the unprepossessing, non-civic and usually dirty and chaotic contexts of a coal mine – engendered and sought to offer something more architectural than a bald response to the functional criteria of washing industrial workers, is significant. They were among the first, it can be argued, to lend a dignity to – and a built acknowledgement of – the importance of the acts which they contained and facilitated and, thereby, to the men who used them. This function of aesthetics and its extension into an instrument of propaganda would become a central aspect of the aesthetic of the pithead baths programme as it was developed, designed and executed under the architects' department of the Miners' Welfare Committee.

DUDOK, MORALITY AND MODERN AESTHETICS

To understand why such importance began to attach itself to the physical appearance of pithead baths, it is perhaps necessary to consider the wider perception of the miner within civil society. As cited above, due to the geological dispersal of coal seams below ground, mining on the surface often erupted in isolated rural areas, far from other forms of industrial development and centres of population. Despite their pivotal position with respect to the progress of industrial development and the economy in general – as was made clear in the revelatory process of the Sankey enquiry – miners and their communities often occupied a position of some invisibility within public perception. 'To the rest of society his daily life was a matter of mystique and ignorance' and, 'even to his own family, a mineworker could appear like "'a disturbing spirit from the underworld"' (Supple, and Scott-James, respectively in Supple 1987: p.425). In addition to the uncanniness and darkness of the underground there was, obviously, the inevitable, conspicuous and constant presence of dirt within the miners' physical presence, as well as their working and domestic lives. As evinced in the 19th- and early 20th-century programme of constructing public baths in cities, and its distribution of opportunities to bathe to a wider cohort of the population, dirt was associated not only with disease, but also with poverty and – by extension – with the working classes. In the physical appearance of miners these connotations were intensified: visibly, miners were the dirtiest of workers.

Equating cleanliness with ideas of morality did not just exercise sanitary reformers, other hygiene or public health experts, or advocates for bathhouses. As has been discussed above, in the 1920s and 1930s, concerns for cleanliness occupied a crucial position in the discussions surrounding the design and development of modern architecture. Again, also of importance here was the continuing acknowledgement of the concept that the built environment – the aesthetics, space and form of architecture – had a significant effect on people's behaviour and ideas and thus could be or should be shaped accordingly. The translation of this into practice is exemplified by Bruno Taut in his exhortation that new forms of modernist architecture would be instrumental in the production of a 'new mental attitude, more, flexible, simpler and more joyful' (cited in Rowe 1995: p.131). While Taut imagined at this point that this could be achieved through the harnessing of new mechanised and mass-produced components and systems – and the aesthetics they would generate – the idea that architecture exercised a power over the psychology of the individual and the potential civility of a population continued another related concept, one he had proposed sometime earlier: the idea of the *Stadtkrone*. As a modernist architect practicing and writing in the 1910s and 1920s, before modernism had formed any strict and rigid orthodoxies, Taut was not unusual in pursuing apparently contradictory considerations on its properties and uses. Both related to a critique of the chaos, dirt and perceived iniquities of the 19th-century city. But, simply put, whereas one suggested an ordered development of the forces of mechanisation to achieve a more harmonious society and built environment, the other – which related more to the ideas espoused by the likes of Ruskin and William Morris – suggested a rejection of these forces and a return to quasi-mediaeval methods of production to achieve a similar state. Both were essentially utopian.

Taut's vision of the *Stadtkrone* (in English literally a 'City Crown') produced in an eponymous publication in 1919, occupied a space somewhere in between these positions. He proposed the design and construction of an elaborate quasi-religious, conspicuously visible civic building in the centre of large urban settlements which otherwise had been designed to have the properties of Garden Cities. Vague on the technology required to build it, Taut emphasised the more ephemeral qualities of a social and socialising structure imagined as a type of modern, highly glazed, secular cathedral akin to those precedents whose soaring presence dominated mediaeval cities. This *Stadtkrone*, like the cathedral, was designed to exert a moral or moralising influence on the population clustered beneath and around it, whom would be compelled to visit it on a regular basis for civic, ceremonial and commercial reasons. Taut's thinking on the idea of the *Stadtkrone* became very influential and – along with the architecture of other luminaries such as Hans Poelzig and Erich Mendelsohn of what became known as German expressionism – found parallels in the Netherlands in a Dutch expressionist school whose ideas in the late 1910s and early 1920s were publicised and disseminated through the journal *Wendingen*.

As has been well recorded, a 20th-century commitment to planning and social housing began early in the Netherlands, taking advantage of the county's neutrality during the First World War, and the parliamentary influence of the left-wing Social Democratic Workers Party (SDAP) to channel the National Housing Act (*Woningwet*) of 1902 into innovative new forms of housing (see Stieber 1998; and Searing 1978). These tendencies are perhaps exemplified by the buildings realised by Michel de Klerk in Amsterdam (part of the so-called Amsterdam School), including his project for the housing association *Eigen Haard* (Our Hearth) at Spaarndammerburt (1915–18) (see Casciato 1996). Encapsulating the words of the housing reformer Arie Keppler – who called on the architects of Amsterdam to become involved 'in the struggle of the working class' by creating beautiful workers' dwellings as 'monuments to that struggle' – at Spaarndammerburt De Klerk produced an architecture whose physical, visible presence within an otherwise nondescript industrial and suburban milieu was designed to evoke an acute emotive response in passers-by, and instil a sense of pride in those who inhabited it. Its expressive qualities were realised entirely in brick used in innovative ways. At a detailed level it appeared sometimes as if made of folding fabric, but zooming out it assumed other figurative meanings – famously evoking the mechanised objects of a steam ship or train at one end of the scheme, while conveying a mediaeval village at the other. Despite the relative conservatism of its interiors, the identification of the building not only with the industrial objects that many of the residents engaged with in their working lives – the project was sandwiched by railway lines and docks – but also in its emphasis on and celebration of the collective nature of their existence, has meant that Spaarndammerburt has been described not only as social, but also socialist housing (Searing 1978).

Some of De Klerk's Amsterdam housing projects were published in the 1919 edition of *Wendingen*. This was followed just over two years later by a special edition dedicated to Frank Lloyd Wright in 1922, and three years beyond this in 1925, with an issue on the Town Hall in Hilversum and other works by Willem Marinus Dudok. Dudok has been described as having subscribed to no particular style but rather, in works such as his magnum opus, the Town Hall at Hilversum, as negotiating and blending a series of precedents and influences including: Wright, Hendrik Petrus Berlage, expressionism and the Amsterdam School; the more planar orientations of De Stijl; and, finally, elements of Dutch vernacular architecture (Langmead 1996: pp 23–6). He was appointed Director of Public Works in the rapidly urbanising Dutch municipality of Hilversum in 1915. Immediately he commenced designs for the Town Hall which eventually went on site in 1923 and was completed in 1931. During this time, Hilversum had grown from a population of 35,000 in 1915, to just over 100,000 in 1934. As a consequence, between 1916 and 1930, Dudok designed 13 housing estates and about the same number of schools, as well as other projects including parks, an abattoir, pumping stations, a bathing house, and other structures for public utilities (ibid.: pp 18–29). Constructed in buff brick with oversized horizontal and diminished vertical joints to emphasis a horizontality within the detail of its walls, Hilversum Town Hall – which today seems overly large and sumptuous for what is still, in size, a modest provincial town – bears a strong resemblance to the idea of the *Stadtkrone* (FIG.30). It is an intensely elaborate, civic and cultural centre, a public building denoting a collective, and whose physical and media presence continues even now to dominate the identity of the municipality. If its concept, scale and exuberance owes something to the emotive principals of expressionism, then in its layout and control of site – including its relationship to the pond which on a still day mirrors its front elevation and casts reflections upwards into its interiors and canopies – the asymmetry of its entrance, the play of planar volumes, and horizontal and vertical elements (including its hovering canopies and tower) are indebted to Wright, and especially his Prairie Houses. Other elements within the plan also echo these precedents. While the centre of the building orientates itself around a small square courtyard, this closed form is never allowed to dominate. Instead, the outside edges of the building reach outwards to suggest and form a closer formal relationship with the immediate landscape, or are disconnected entirely from each other to articulate the flow of the generous, at times ceremonial-sized circulation. This happens both in the main entrance approach but also in the corridor spaces of the interior. While there are individual windows cut autonomously into walls where required, the horizontality emphasised through the brickwork is supported through the repeated motif of the strips of

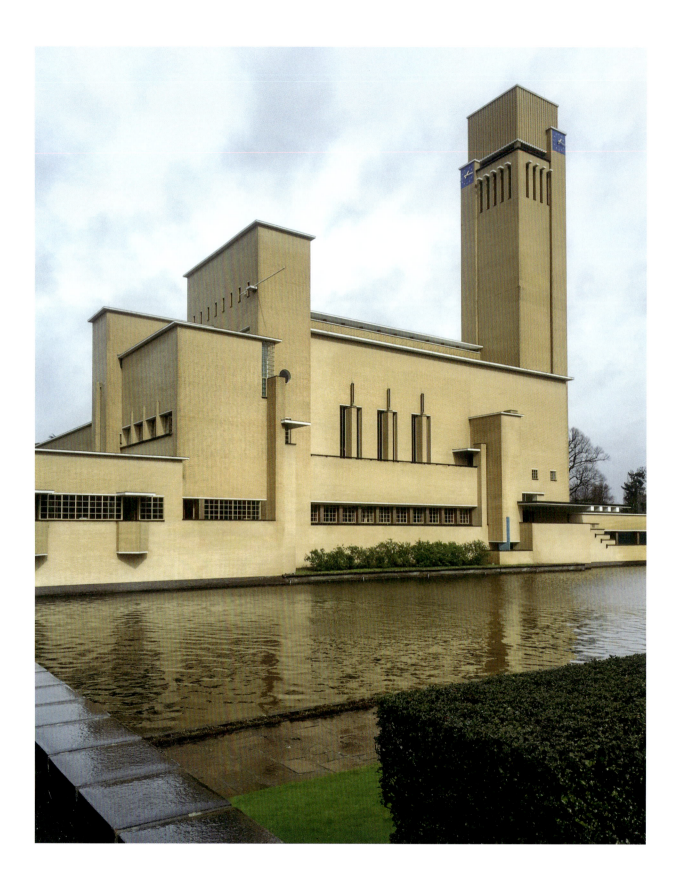

window openings that occupy the gaps created – and again owing something to Wright's motif of separating such elements – between vertical planes.

THE LESSONS OF DUDOK'S SCHOOLS

If the Town Hall can be considered as a type of *Stadtkrone* for the municipality of Hilversum, then the schools that Dudok also designed between 1917 and 1932 offered similarly emotive and conspicuous architectural moments within the smaller neighbourhoods they individually served. They did this through a similar, yet evolving architectural vocabulary of organisational strategies, formal elements, relationships between inside and outside, and details seen in the Town Hall. Collectively and individually, this vocabulary exerted a significant influence on the aesthetics and planning of the pithead baths buildings produced by the Miners' Welfare Committee architects. Along with the Town Hall and Dudok's own Badhuis baths building from 1921, the schools formed a critical precedent for how the British pitheads programme would eventually transcend the functionally orientated structures proposed by the Home Office report, to become pieces of architecture that were not only civic in their appearance, but also – and through the medium of a modernist architecture – expressive of a shared mining identity and culture.

The expression of meaning beyond apparent functionality in Dudok's work meant that, within the context of what would become the more dominant orthodoxies in modernist architecture and discourse, it appeared idiosyncratic. Henry-Russell Hitchcock, co-curator of the seminal *International Style* exhibition in 1932, labelled Dudok a 'traditionalist', while Nikolaus Pevsner termed the expressionism of the Amsterdam School in general '"an aberration" inhibiting the mainstream of modernism in Holland' (Langmead 1996: p.31 and p.9 respectively). Yet, as evinced at the time in the extensive coverage in international architectural media especially in the United Kingdom, Dudok's influence between the wars was widespread. By 1935, the same year that the Royal Institute of British Architects awarded him its Gold Medal, details of his work in Hilversum and elsewhere had been translated globally into 12 languages. While the squat ziggurat form of the Rembrandtschool (1917–20) conjures a brick monumentalism that seems historicist (as does, perhaps to a lesser degree, the pitched-roof Oranjeschool [1921–3]), the stepping planes, juxtapositions of vertical and horizontal volumes, and bands of horizontal windows combined with a flat roof at the Bavinckschool (1921) evoked a new modern language and signalled a mature style for Dudok (FIG.31). The thin, articulated, cranking forms – here formed into a Z-shape (FIG.32) – would become a pragmatic planning motif in many of his subsequent schools and indeed British pithead baths. This idea of an asymmetrical, pinwheeling plan combining with devices such as extending walls or the definitions of routes to establish or imply enclosures and intimacies with the surrounding landscape, was central to the development of Frank Lloyd Wright's Prairie Houses. It

30
Hilversum Town Hall, 1917–32, by W. M. Dudok

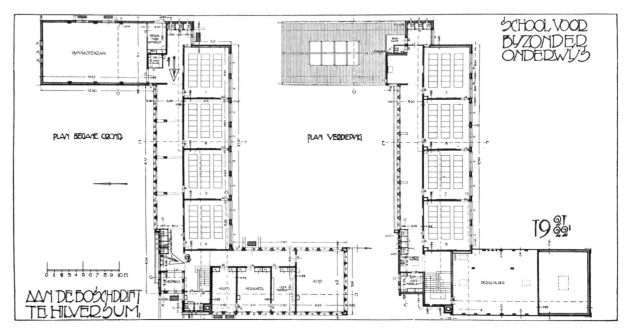

would also become an enduring motif in the plans of other modernist buildings including Mies van der Rohe's Brick Country House project (1923–4) or Walter Gropius's Bauhaus building (1925–6) – and again, pithead baths. At the Julianaschool en Catharina van Renesschool (1925–7) the device was used to negotiate an asymmetrical pentagonal site surrounded by roads and create a series of some four outside courtyards or areas bounded by either flat- or pitched-roofed ranges. This school also includes elements of eclectic and almost whimsical details – appropriate perhaps for the fairy tales of children – including slit windows (sometimes with tiny expressed canopies projecting from the wall above), curious tower elements (at least one of which was evidently indebted to De Klerk) and – most significantly for the pithead baths

31
Bavinckschool, Hilversum, 1921, by W. M. Dudok

32
Bavinckschool, plan

33
Oriel window at the Julianaschool en Catharina van Renesschool

– a series of three semicircular volumes, all apparent on the plan projecting outwards from their respective facades on the building's outer perimeter. Each of these was treated slightly differently, but some of the characteristics of the largest one – akin to an oriel window located near the school's entrance which gave an almost militaristic visual engagement with the street (FIG.33) – would become a familiar element in pithead baths and, especially, as part of their ancillary canteens. While the Fabritiusschool (1925–6) with its heavy hovering thatched roofs, and the Jan van der Heijdenschool (1925–6) with its curious relationship between walls and a similarly emphatic roof pitch, are both highly evocative pieces of architecture, the singularity of these elements would not translate into an appropriate paradigm for the Miners' Welfare Fund's programme. But the tower elements clustered around the entrance canopy to the otherwise pitched-roofed Minckelerschool (1927), and displayed elsewhere in some of the other schools such as the Nassauschool (1928), provided opportunities for the vertical disposition of the water tanks so critical to pithead baths. Meanwhile, the flat-roofed structures of the Johannes Calvijnschool (1929), Vondelschool (1929), Nienke van Hichtumschool (1929), Lorentzschool (1929–30); the Marnixschool (1930,) Valeriusschool (1930) and finally the Snelliusschool (1930–32) would provide a closer approximation of the comprehensive approach to form that would be adopted by Forshaw and his team (FIG.34).

Also of significance is that these buildings both shared and evolved mutual characteristics. The prototypical oriel window seen at the Julianaschool en Catharina van Renesschool became, in the Lorentzschool and Nienke van Hichtumschool, a much more refined object (FIG.35). Gone are the heavy brick piers and the militaristic aspect, to be replaced by thin metal frames which allow for a less circumspect and more thoroughgoing modernist exposure of the building's interior to its exterior and vice versa – redolent of Gropius's groundbreaking stairwell in his model factory for the Deutscher Werkbund in Cologne in 1914. This modernist characteristic of the dissolving of boundaries between inside and out can be seen as one strategy within the window treatments within these buildings. In the Johannes Calvijnschool, the strip windows seen in Bavinckschool have, like their oriel siblings, been relieved of their masonry structure to become, on one facade, two fully continuous strips running one above the other across its full length. At the Snelliusschool light pours into a double-height volume through a double-height window strip which again stretches across most of the which. Also seen at Snelliusschool and elsewhere, was a separation, perhaps predicated on issues of privacy, of the requirements of light from those of view in the provision of clerestory windows, again in the form of thin strips. Compositionally, these glazed strips also effected a separation of elements so that – as in another which on the Johannes Calvijnschool – vertical planes of brick, or horizontal canopies picked out in white painted timber or render, appear to float weightlessly above the elements beneath them (FIG.36).

34
Snelliusschool

35
Oriel window Nienke van Hichtumschool

This later generation of Dudok's schools – with an established and shared vocabulary of forms, organisation strategies and elements – represents an iterative architecture, refined, honed and shorn of some of its earlier idiosyncrasies. If the Snelliusschool, for example, is expressive of anything it is perhaps of a sleek industrial form which to a degree, in its re-use of repeated elements including a huge half-cylindrical vertical 'oriel' window partially glazed in glass bricks, it was. There is then some apparent rapprochement between this concept – along with the quality of apparent weightlessness in elements and the way these buildings open up at certain moments to dissolve inside/outside junctures and capture different lighting conditions – with other, what might be called purer, strands of modernism. But in the end Dudok's schools, regardless of whatever structure supports them, always form architecture which is subject to the discipline of walls – to be precise brick walls – rather than the

THE LESSONS OF DUDOK'S SCHOOLS 71

36
Johannes Calvijnschool

37
Vondelschool

permissiveness of the frame. Thus, the vertical planes that are made to float by the intervention of strip windows are brick planes. And the windows themselves are always held within or between walls. The vast double-height window at the Snelliusschool, cited above, is ultimately still just a window within a wall rather than a non-load-bearing curtain wall connected to a structural frame, like that innovated by Gropius at the Dessau Bauhaus four years earlier in 1926 or, closer to Hilversum, in Brinkman and Van der Vlugt's Van Nelle Factory in Rotterdam, begun in 1925. The closest example of this in Dudok's school is perhaps at the Vondelschool (1929) whose central vertical element contains a fully glazed stair core and a wing. But this is limited to just these two forms. The rest of the building follows Dudok's established orthodoxy of elements described above including, in this case, a semicircular headed main entrance drawn from Louis Sullivan via Wright, which provides a vertical echo of the oriel motif marking the end point of another cranking plan of thin ranges (FIG.37). In contrast to the overt and explicit aspiration for 'light, air and openness' (Overy 2008) – seen, for example, in the Netherlands in a pedagogical context at the near contemporaneous Openluchtschool in Amsterdam (1930) or, in an even more immediate location, within the context of health at the Sanatorium Zonnestraal in Hilversum (1931), both by Jan Duiker – Dudok's schools are more circumspect in their acknowledgement of transparency and their deployment of enclosure, and more strategic and nuanced in their admission of light and response to functional requirements. And yet, these modernist concerns are still obviously central to these buildings' conception, design and the experience of their users. Eliel Saarinen described Dudok as infusing 'enchanting friendliness in his design' (cited in Langmead 1996: p.25), while elsewhere the popularity of his work was considered – somewhat reductively – as emerging from a '"middle-of-the-road position" between traditionalism and modernism' (Hans van Dijk cited in Langmead 1996: p.31). In fact, in his admission of symbolism and meaning, Dudok not only absorbed and represented aspects of expressionism, but also pre-empted a subsequent shift in modernism from the apparently functionalist aesthetic of New Objectivity/International Style architecture to the post-Second World War appreciation of a desirability for a continuing presence of monumentality within a community and its cultures.[13]

This sense of monumentality and an inherent negotiation between traditional and modern forms of architecture is also apparent within Dudok's Badhuis (bathhouse) at Bosdrift, again in Hilversum and dating from 1921. This provided a further paradigm for the MWC's pithead baths programme. While the Hilversum's schools were often surrounded by – and conspicuous within

38
Badhuis at Bosdrift

– backdrops of housing often designed by Dudok himself, at Bosdrift an urbanistic intent is made ever more explicit. Once more constructed in brick, symmetrical in form about a central chimney and wedge-shaped in plan, the baths sit within a triangular site giving on to a tapering green open space which forms an endpoint to an urban vista, where one road diverges into two (FIG.38). This relates to a larger triangular site behind the baths whose rear responds to a designed landscape consisting of housing as well as the Bavinckschool discussed above. The baths building itself is internally divided up into four sections: the front public side for male and female; and the rear side, facing the housing, and again split into male and female. This arrangement was designed to simultaneously accommodate school children who could access the premises through a discrete back lane leading directly from their school. While the influence of the massing of the building will be seen in some of the pithead baths (especially those designed by Frederick G. Frizzell), it is perhaps its urbanism, as well as the precise division of the building into sections including a series of separate entrances and exits, that would provide more enduring principles.

The Bosdrift Badhuis and the Hilversum schools afforded an architecture which combined tenets of modernism and the addressing of functional criteria – hygiene, pedagogy – with a conscious and deliberate use of building as a means of conveying identity, meaning, and provoking emotion in its beholder or user. The schools especially, provided an incremental rather than revolutionary modernism one which was potentially palatable to conservative publics, such as British mining communities. In their repeated and repeatable quasi-modular elements and forms, Dudok simultaneously created a pragmatic almost systematic approach to architecture which could be economical, adaptable to varying site conditions and – in the leap from pedagogy to pithead baths – different functional criteria. Interlinking with the social pressures instigated by controversies, legislative measures and the other precedents and writings on civic bathing and hygiene cited above, these buildings provided some of the final architectural principles and forms necessary for the execution of the pithead baths programme. But this coalescence would not occur immediately.

MODERNIST TECHNOLOGICAL DEVELOPMENTS IN THE PITHEAD BATHS PROGRAMME

The mature and iconic forms of the pithead baths, accompanied by a series of further technical and organisational refinements that would ultimately supersede the continental prototypes, would only gradually emerge in the wake of the Samuel Commission and the Mining Industry Act of 1926 and its pledge of structural finances of a shilling per ton explicitly and exclusively for their provision.[14] Until then, bath provision under the Miners' Welfare Fund remained a piecemeal affair carried out under the auspices of individual collieries. Increasingly, however, these initiatives were allowed access, through the Fund, to expert advice in the form of design services offered by the Industrial

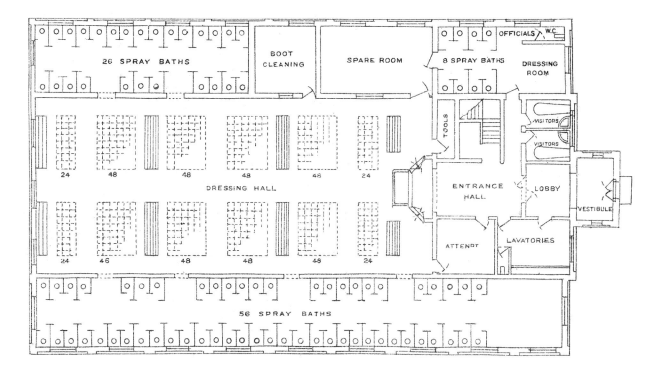

39
Plan of the baths at Linton and Ellington

40
View of the baths at Linton and Ellington

Welfare Society (IWS) which also provided guidance on the layout of recreational facilities. Emerging in 1918 as the Boys' Welfare Association and changing its name just a year later in 1919, the Industrial Welfare Society was one of a series of agencies and individuals interested in humanising the processes of industry and manufacturing for the labour force through interventions into its working spatial environments. These measures included the provision of gardens at factories and attempts to evoke an atmosphere of domesticity and the home within the industrial workplace. Again, originating out of 19th-century criticisms of industrialisation voiced by the likes of Ruskin and Morris, these provisions, partly designed to stimulate workers' creativity, still had paternalistic overtones – or were thought of, at least, as a means of contributing to increased productivity and defraying industrial conflicts (Long 2011: pp 434–5). The Industrial Welfare Society – especially through the figure of Commander Bernard Trotter Coote, a retired Royal Navy officer who had been in charge of the navy's Physical Training School from 1917 to 1919 (National Archives ADM 196/45/180) – would establish a long-standing and influential relationship with the Miners' Welfare Committee and the development of its baths schemes.

The beginning of this was a technical advisory centre, set up as an experiment with £2000 from the General Funds. If desired, the centre could offer advice to Local and District Committees on their individual proposals. Established in central London at 82 Victoria Street, SW1, in March 1923, this sub-organisation became the kernel from which the architectural department of the Miners' Welfare Committee would grow. By 1925, in the face of burgeoning demands, the advisory board would be absorbed directly into the MWC's central administration and the first appointment of an individual with architectural qualifications made. Although unnamed in the annual report for that year, this individual was presumably Forshaw (MWC 1926: 7–8).[15] By this time, 17 bath schemes had been initiated under the Fund: nine in Yorkshire, six in Northumberland and one apiece in Durham, Nottingham and Kent.[16] At a cost of £20,000, one of the largest of these was for the Linton and Ellington Collieries in Northumberland. This building – the only one described in any detail in the MWC annual report for 1923 (MWC 1924) – did not stray from the convention established by continental models and exhibited a plan almost identical to that of the baths at Monceau-Fontaines (FIG.39). In its adoption of the suspension system, it inevitably consisted of the characteristic high, central dressing hall, flanked by lower aisles containing the shower baths. Consequently, in exterior form, as at Atherton, it resembled a solid brick basilica, one which contained some attempts at decorative interest including shallow-arched clerestory windows on its long sides, and a roundel, a Serlian window and a stepping brick motif on its gable (FIG.40).

Also contained in the report for 1923, however, was notice of an innovation for the design of pithead baths – a new typology conceived in embryo by the IWS in collaboration with Messrs Dolby and Williamson, consulting engineers.

Along with the subsequent adoption of a modernist architectural language, this piece of ingenuity would form a central, unique characteristic of the British baths programme in the coming years. And while the new aesthetic when deployed, would be adapted, and interpreted by different MWC architects for and in different sites and different locations, the principle introduced in 'The Pithead Bath Scheme' would remain unaltered and irreducible. Although impossible to implement at the time of its publication under the legislation and guidelines of the Coal Mines Act of 1911, the proposal sought to depart from

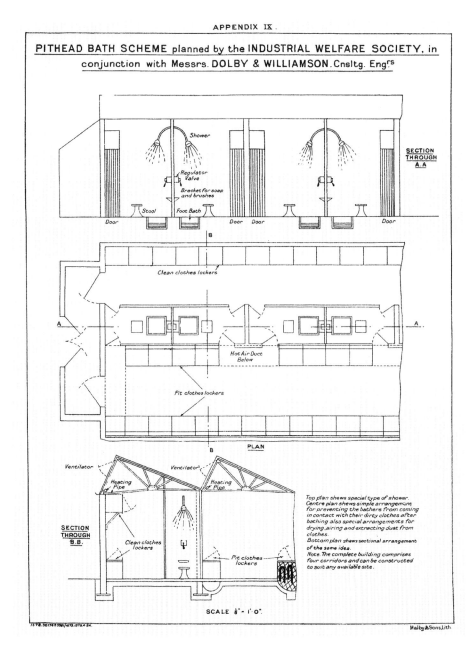

41
Pithead bath scheme by the Industrial Welfare Society

and improve the accepted norm of the continental paradigm that had so preoccupied the Home Office Committee and previous thinking on the design of pithead baths. Firstly, it offered heated lockers instead of the hoist and pulley suspension system for storing clothes. But the real advance – represented by a plan and a cross-section of a small and modest single storey, saw-tooth-roofed building (FIG.41) – was the introduction of the simple principle that dirty and clean, in both men and clothes, should be kept separate. The sequence it prescribed would, in time, come to underpin the planning of all of the MWC British pithead baths, no matter how simple and small – or complex and large. Miners coming from the pit would change from their dirty clothes and leave them in a locker in one 'pit' dressing room, before passing through a shower and cleaning themselves to retrieve and dress in their home clothes in another; this time, a 'clean' dressing room. Arranged down in the middle of the plan, the showers became an obligatory filter through which each miner would have to pass between the two zones and their respective states of cleanliness.

Following the report of the Samuel Commission, the Mining Industry Act of 1926 – which established the funding mechanism that would accelerate the production and proliferation of pithead baths – also relieved the MWC of the obligation to proceed with the hoist and pulley suspension system recommended by the Home Office Committee's Report. The first fleshing out of the diagrammatic form for a new organisational strategy for pithead baths introduced by the Industrial Welfare Society into a larger more realistic building proposal, was published in the MWC's annual report for the same year. It began with a list of critiques of the suspension system: the height necessary for the building makes them expensive; clean and dirty clothing are not sufficiently isolated from each other; dust falls from the hoisted clothes onto bathers and clean clothing beneath; bathers have to push past bundles of dirty clothing to dress, get their feet dirty and have to handle dirty clothes after washing; dirt accumulates in places where it cannot be removed; the dressing hall is often overcrowded and inadequate in seating; there is constant expense in the replacing of worn-out fittings both in cubicles and in the hook and chain fittings due to the pressures placed upon them; and so on (MWC 1927: p.41).

Instead, the 'Specimen Design for Experimental Installation' – a proposal for a long, rectangular building in plan with 100 shower baths designed for approximately 600 men offered – like the IWS prototype, three separate zones: dirty, bathing and clean (FIG.42). After a shift, miners would enter the 'pit locker' through a lobby in one of the short ends, deposit their clothes there, proceed to the showers and, from there, to the 'clean' locker room. From here, they would exit – clean and ready for home – at the opposite end of the building from where they had entered – in a filthy state – a specified and short time before. The lockers, constructed out of pressed metal in both locker spaces, would be heated and vented to 'fumigate' both sets of clothes as they were being stored. Each miner would have a guaranteed changing space in front of his own locker, and ventilation and lighting would be provided by a glazed roof.

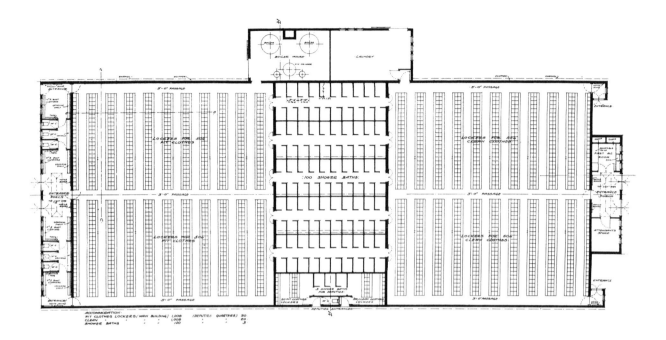

In addition to these spaces and the provision of lavatories, the proposal also specified additional accommodation including a first-aid room, boot-cleaning and greasing facilities, a space to fill water bottles for drinking underground, and the possibility of accommodating a canteen, a laundry, and a boot and clothing repair workroom if required in the future. All this, it was estimated, would come at a price considerably less than the existing suspension system baths per unit of accommodation (MWC 1927: p.42).

However, for all the criticisms of the original proposals and prototypes commissioned by the Home Office report in 1913, none were directed at issues of aesthetics. So, while it represented a recalibration of how such buildings could be organised, the 'Specimen Design' – conceived of as a steel frame with a 'wall filled in with material to blend in with existing colliery buildings', and an interior designed to be 'as nearly dirt proof as possible' (MWC 1927: p.42) – was still limited by a narrow utilitarian understanding of what such buildings could be in terms of civic presence. The only visual depiction provided was the diagrammatic abstraction of a plan which, evidently, gave little sense of what the building would look or feel like. In fact, the linear sequence and arrangement of exit and entry points, and total separation of dirty and clean orchestrated by the plan is redolent, in its economy and efficiency, of the flow of a Taylorised factory production line. By the 1920s, partly because of its successful adoption by Henry Ford, the scientific management of time, motion and activity had become widespread in American factories, transforming productive processes. But if it had begun tentatively to inform some sectors of European and British industries, the complications of coal mining – with its general lack of investment in innovation and ongoing use of traditional practices – meant that this modernising force was practically unheard of within British collieries

42
'Specimen Design for Experimental Installation'

at that time. Its comprehensive adoption would not be implemented – and often in the face of workers' resistance – until after the Second World War coinciding with and part of the instigation of wholesale mechanisation executed under the nationalisation of the entire industry. It is interesting, then, that the first widespread application of Taylorist principles seems to have been 20 years before this, and within what could have been described as a peripheral productive process in collieries – the washing of men. This was also, however, prescient within architectural culture.

If in America the deployment of Frederick W. Taylor's techniques of time and motion had become a pragmatic reality, in 1920s and 1930s Europe – perhaps because of its relative absence in industry – it was still venerated as an idea and occupied a central place in the imagination of progressive European thinkers and architects (Boyd 2012: pp 73–4). Included in the latter was Alexander Klein, who translated its methods to the domestic sphere in his renowned 'Functional House for Frictionless Living', published in 1928, two years after the MWC's 'Specimen Design for Experimental Installation' prototypical bath building. Klein's house is redefined as a system of flows where defined tasks could be conducted without interruption or diversion. Klein described the diagrams he produced to depict his proposal in medical terms as X-rays capable of seeing beyond conventional plans to expose hidden or skeletal relationships between objects, individuals and activities. The separation and isolation of different activities within systems of movement also underpinned aspects of modernist urbanistic thinking, exemplified in Ludwig Hilbersheimer's *Hochhausstadt* (High Rise City) (1924) and the Congrés Internationaux d'Architecture Moderne's (CIAM) *Athens Charter* (1933). The latter famously recalibrated the city, partly on hygienic grounds, according to the prescriptive and discrete zoning of functions: living, working, recreation, circulation. Yet both these examples were, at the time of their publication, realised as theoretical proposals rather than practical applications of Taylor's principles. Elsewhere it has been suggested that modernist architects and architecture adopted the rhetoric of scientific management within their form and appearance, while there was little evidence of its application – much like the modernist adoption of a machine aesthetic in buildings that had not actually been mass produced (Guillen 2006). And yet in the MWC's 'Specimen Design for Experimental Installation' we have the reverse. The hygienically predicated application of scientific management in the layout of the baths, the sequential and timed flow through spaces, an ergonomic concern for the design of the showers, and the absolute separation of disparate elements and activities. While evidently critiquing and adapting continental models and other precedents, all this was conceived and designed from the inside out, prior to and apparently without consideration of the aesthetic of the building. It is a modernist architecture without rhetoric. Moreover, while the principles underpinning it were essentially fixed – although there would be designed refinements to come – the form of the plan itself was described as essentially provisional: 'For the sake of simplicity the three sections of the building are here shown in line; other relative positions can be adopted according to the nature of the site, and square or L-shaped arrangements may be planned on one floor; it would also be possible to build the two lockers sections one above the other, with the cubicle section in the centre' (MWC 1927: p.80).

The building could adopt any plan arrangement necessary to fit a variety of site conditions as long as the basic diagram sequencing its spaces was adhered to. In its initial translation into built form, however, it failed to find a language appropriate to the modernity of its organisation. Nor did it necessarily reflect the functional requirements of architectural form and appearance as a type of propaganda, as espoused by Chappell and Lovat-Fraser, or embodied in another context, in the architecture of the *Stadtkrone* and expressionism, and its translations by Dudok. In fact, the series of 'experimental or demonstration installations of the new type' (MWC 1928: p.23), proposed at the end of 1926 and built during 1927 evinced only a tentative exploration of the possibilities offered by the diagram.

THE EXPERIMENTAL BATHS

Initially there were plans to build these prototypical baths at Pooley Hall in Warwickshire, Mainsforth in Durham, and Letham in Scotland. As befits their stated purpose as demonstration installations – serving at least partly the interest of 'propaganda' – it would seem that these schemes were to be located in easily accessible sites and within as wide a geographical spread as possible across the principle coalfields. Letham Colliery at Airth near Falkirk in central Scotland, for example, formed a centre point between the coalfields of Lanarkshire and Ayrshire on the west and Fife and the Lothians on the east. This proposed site, as well as the one at Llwynypia in Tonypandy, however, were ultimately considered inappropriate. The latter, interestingly, because: 'the only site available was found on investigation to render the construction of a typical building impracticable; *demonstration* [my emphasis] being the essence of the scheme, it was not desirable to erect a specially adapted building with unusual features' (MWC 1928: p.24).

Instead it was decided to replace these two with prototypes at: Dalzell and Broomside Colliery at Motherwell in Lanarkshire, to the south east of Glasgow in Scotland; and Park Pit, Treorchy, located in the centre of the valleys of South Wales. For various reasons, of all the proposed experimental baths, those at Pooley Hall, and Dalzell and Broomside, were the first to be completed, in March and June 1927 respectively (FIGS.43 and 44). Following the reasoning behind the rejection of the proposed scheme at Llwynypia, both are faithful to their prototypical antecedent's prescription of a rectangular plan, albeit with some minor modifications. Accordingly, they display a characteristic tripartite arrangement with the two sets of locker spaces – one clean, one dirty – flanking a battery of showers occupying the middle. In cross-section, a kind of inverse of the basilica typologies seen in the continental and earlier British baths is effected. The central space accommodating the showers is low and equipped with (presumably continuous) glazing lanterns within an otherwise flat roof, while the locker areas on the outside edges of the building are higher, pitched roofed, and lit by a series of portrait windows along their long walls, as well as in the gables that terminate them. The short elevations in both show signs of a designed, if formal and conventional, aesthetic consideration. Both are symmetrical: with receding brick planes and a harmonising of horizontal architraves and sills and coping at Pooley; and a similar horizontal emphasis, interrupted by two round-headed windows, illuminating the lockers room at Broomside. In both cases the presence of the pitch of the gable, realised in the inside with a steel truss, is diminished within the treatment of the elevation. Both buildings accordingly appear low slung and horizontal in emphasis – in Broomside this is apparent despite the negotiation of a significant slope across its short side.

There are, however, differences between the two. Most significant perhaps is that whereas the sequence of entry, washing and exit at Pooley took place along the long length of the building, as described in the original 'Specimen Design', at Broomside miners moved across the short side of the plan. Entering in from the clean entrance midway on one of the long sides, they exited for work in their pit clothes via an accretion on the opposite side, which also contained lavatories, boot-cleaning and greasing facilities, a space to fill water bottles, and a room containing the calorifier which heated up the water. These accretions represent an external addition to the original Specimen Design plan. At Pooley they are disciplined into two spaces, both located at the short ends, one containing the main clean entrance/exit, lavatories and boot-cleaning/greasing stands; and the other on the opposite end, containing the 'pit' exit and part of the canteen space. All other ancillary functions – the attendants' and first-aid rooms, a 'drying chamber', and heating and calorifier rooms are contained within the central section of the plan in line with the blocks of showers.[17] Also significant is the connection from the entrance to the adjacent building – containing lamp collection and deposit and other facilities – by means of a covered walkway which leads beyond this to the pithead itself. Broomside's accretions, including the one described above and indeed its plan in general are, on first view, less resolved. There is one on the long side to form the entrance, and one proposed on the lower short side for a canteen in a space approximate to the location of the canteen at Pooley. The final accretion at the top of the plan, however, represents another innovation: the first female washing facilities to be provided within a British colliery.[18] This partly explains the different entry arrangements. The women at Broomside, in fact, entered where the principal clean entrance/exit was located at the Pooley scheme. In addition to their showers, two sets of locker rooms and lavatories, the women were also provided with a rest room.

The plans, cross-sections and short elevation of these buildings were published in 1928 in the *Sixth Report* of the Miners' Welfare Committee. The seventh

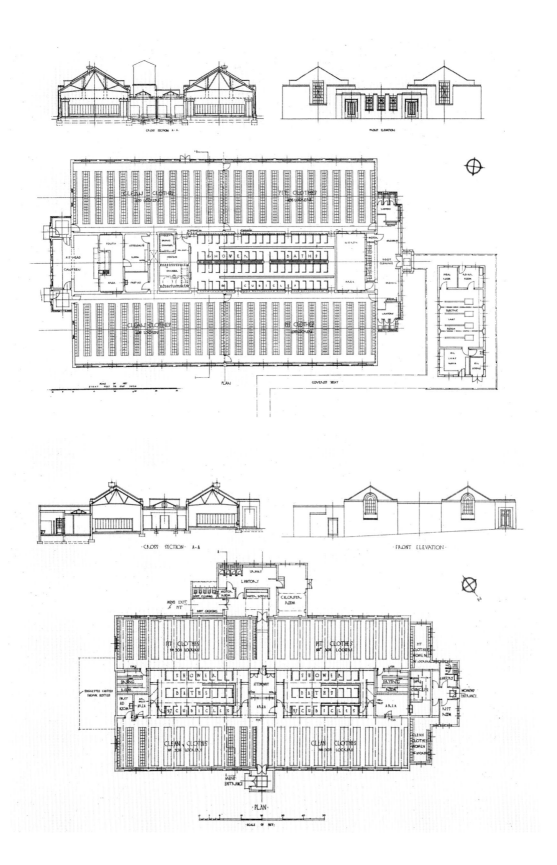

annual report, published the following year, contained similar sets of drawings describing the remaining experimental baths at Park and Mainsforth Collieries. They are almost identical in plan and cross-section to the two preceding schemes and display similar architectural treatment in their short elevations – symmetry encompassing formal windows and doors. Unlike Broomside, however, in not having to provide women's facilities, both follow the orthodoxy of entering in one of the short sides. As at Pooley, the miners would move through a space containing boot facilities and lavatories to proceed the full length of the building and emerge at the other end adjacent to – at Park Colliery, but not at Mainsforth – a canteen. Also of interest is the appearance of a high, centrally located volume which appears on the cross section and elevation of Park Colliery – but curiously not on any of the other drawings. This represents an acknowledgement of the necessity of a water tank in an elevated position to supply an appropriate pressure to the showers.

The seventh annual report also contains a photograph of what appears – by the raw state of the adjacent ground – to be the newly completed facilities at Broomside (FIG.45). Notwithstanding the complications of this particular building because of its additional accommodation of female colliery workers, it is rather unprepossessing. It is a collection of bits, of industrially-derived components within its pitched roofscape clumsily married with attempts at a formal language in the elevation – the latter unconvincingly wrought in a mixture of white render and brick. Any coherency is further compromised by the accretion on the left-hand side described above. Yet, while this last appendage is patently irreconciled to its parent building in its materiality of white render and asymmetrical composition of planar volumes – including the raised volume necessary for water storage and pressure which was omitted in the original drawings – it seems, not only to adopt a recognisably modernist language, but also to point to the future for the design of British pithead baths. Also conspicuous, however, is the crudeness of the photograph itself. Taken

43
Pooley Hall experimental baths

44
Dalzell and Broomside experimental baths

45
View of Broomside pithead baths

from a height – presumably from the headgear that would have dominated the colliery (and indeed the surrounding area) – it diminishes whatever aesthetic attributes the building may have had in its conception and drawings and, instead, serves to highlight the building's unresolved, eclectic combination of forms, and the staid and isolated manner in which it occupies its site. As the pithead baths architecture began to evolve into more mature and consistent compositions, how it was represented – evidently a key element in the production of propaganda – in both drawings and photography would also begin to assume a more considered and aesthetically driven approach.

THE MODERN INTERIOR

On the same page of the report immediately below the photograph of Broomside, was the first published image of another designed element which would become a central and enduring aspect of the baths programme's evolution: the MWC pithead bath locker (FIG.46). If, at this moment the architecture of the baths – while technically, organisationally and in terms of servicing extremely advanced – had still to achieve an aesthetic maturity, then the locker – although it would continue to undergo modifications and refinements – appeared to emerge almost fully fledged in its reconciliation of use with a modernist appearance. The locker's role in the baths programme cannot be overestimated. It represented another irreducible, non-negotiable element, one that corresponded precisely with the number of users for any given baths building, a figure which could be as large as 3,000 mineworkers. Beginning in the later experimental baths at Treorchy and Mainsforth, it was commonly arranged into free-standing double decker batteries, or 'locker nests' of 30 (15 above 15) to become, along with the showers and their cubicles, an endlessly repeatable component, a building block within the design itself and immediately recognisable on the plan of any baths building.

46
View of lockers, 1928

It was perhaps because of earlier criticism of the locker system – for example, in the Home Office Committee Report of 1913 – that considerable effort was made with their design. In September 1927, Commander Coote and John Forshaw were sent abroad to undertake another appraisal of continental bathing facilities for miners. Contained in their report are further critiques of the hoist system in favour of lockers – arguing in terms of cleanliness, that lockers were more 'humane', and of the benefits of the ingress of light unhindered by hanging clothes. On the latter, the authors stated that lockers combined with roof lights 'is very desirable ... bringing light directly over the miner and his locker' (MWC 1929: p.56). In summary, citing – but ultimately disagreeing with – the Home Committee Report's findings, they argued that the previous problem with lockers was not in the principle of their being used, but was rather a design issue. According to Coote and Forshaw, the concerns associated with them and identified in earlier reports had arisen because how they responded to their purported function through form and materiality had simply not been given enough thought. As mentioned above, the MWC pithead lockers were designed to dry and ventilate the separated clean and dirty clothes as they contained them. They did this by being connected initially to a supply of steam which was pumped into them before being exhausted into the room via louvres in the lockers themselves. Ultimately, after a period of refinement, the steam was replaced by heated air supplied via an overhead concrete plenum which would also provide heating to the room, as well as an extract for stale air (FIG.47).

The appearance of the lockers in the experimental baths of 1926 and 1927 was virtually identical to those being installed decades later when the final generation of pithead baths were being built in the 1950s. Made from flattened galvanised steel sheets – which were also used to cover the armoured plywood doors – to allow for ease of cleaning and ventilation, they were raised clear of the floor on rows of angled steel legs.[19] Each locker was designed with a minimum of flat surfaces to throw off any dirt that might accumulate. On the 'home' or clean locker side, where the men were apt 'to sit after bathing for a longer period', a continuous bench was provided in teak, while on the pit side, the corresponding bench was made, like the lockers themselves, from galvanised steel. Under the benches was a continuous shoe rack while above, for miners accessing the upper lockers, there was a continuous handrail on which in later iterations, hooks would be provided for hanging clothes while dressing. For identification purposes each door had an ivorine number plate, while every sixth door was equipped with a mirror – one to six being the general ratio of showers per men. This ratio also meant that men could be allocated a locker according to their shift to ensure an even time-based spread of miners throughout the locker rooms to avoid congestion (FIGS 48 and 49). Inside the lockers, miners would find a 'four-prong coat-hook attached to its soffit, [a] single hook fixed to its side and ... a detachable galvanised wire soap-container' (ibid.: pp 61–2).

47
Locker plenum system

48
'Clean' Lockers, 1930s

49
Locker allocation diagram

An agency called Vernon Industries was involved in the development and testing of locker refinements two decades later in or around 1949, partly through the process of making full-scale mock-ups at their works in either Birkenhead or Kirby (FIG.50). However, Forshaw and the other technical staff of the MWC must have been involved at some level in their design, presumably in collaboration with external consultants. Coote and the Industrial Welfare Society may have also played a part. As Sigfried Giedion (2014) suggested was often the case with mass-produced objects as opposed to buildings, it is not clear who the original designers were of these refined, robust, essentially modernist and iconic objects. This is equally true of some of other components generic to the pithead bath programme, such as the white tiled shower stall cubicles. Like the lockers, these evolved over the duration of the baths programme, but the most advanced version had sides which, like the lockers, were elevated on *pilotis* and similarly detached from their perpendicular walls for ease of cleaning. The edge of these closest to the passage that the men used to access the showers, tapered outward in plan to form a Y-shape (FIG.51). This was topped by another carefully considered mass-produced device consisting of two protrusions: one to hang the individual miner's towel on, the other for his locker key. Perhaps taking cognisance of the stated desire for light within pithead baths, the showers themselves were made of pipes with, it seems, as narrow a bore as possible. The mixer pipes were bent into an elegant semi-circle ending in the nozzle about 18 inches above the partition height, and often held in place by a long bar holding each run of shower heads in suspension from the ceiling. The effect was a matrix of straight and curving thin forms through which light could penetrate or be reflected in their shiny metal, hovering above the solid, glazed and also light-reflective forms of the cubicles below. The showers were, like the lockers, also equipped with a perforated soap dish designed to hang from a metal bracket between the mixer piper and either the hot or the cold feed (FIG.52). These were designed to accommodate special pithead baths soap, manufactured specifically for the purpose in units that would run into the millions, all with the letters P.H.B. impressed into them.[20]

Along with other features such as the water filling station and the boot cleaners and greasers, these objects represented a sub-building scale of architectural intervention that became common to all British pithead bath buildings, regardless of their location or region or whom the building's architect was. As such they formed an intimate and daily experience for the hundreds of thousands of miners who used them. Like the lockers, these objects also transcended time, still present in the final baths produced in much the same forms as they had emerged decades before.

Of significance is the apparent harmony that existed between these generic forms and the bespoke, yet systemic buildings within which they found themselves. Arguably, this represents a reconciliation of two strands of modernist thinking. What might be called the interior 'equipment' – itself absolutely necessary and irreducible – had been designed with respect to ergonomic and

THE MODERN INTERIOR 89

50
Locker sample in workshop, 1949

51
Showerheads above cubicles with towel and key hooks

52
MWC pithead baths soap tray

hygienic criteria through conditions of mass production both influenced by, and responding to, Taylorist methods of organisation. Accordingly it represented what Gottfried Semper and Hermann Muthesius had delineated as 'the product object', refined and honed over time and through use (Frampton 2020: p.121). This landscape of generic, yet highly refined equipment on the inside would in time be allied with an external form which, while iterative, was designed to be expressive of specific meaning and provoke a more emotive response. This is all the more potent if we imagine one of the daily circumstances in which the building was used and perceived: the end of the shift. Emerging in a filthy state from the underground, from a realm where they had experienced nothing natural or wholesome, just darkness, dirt, noise and often wetness – either from the condition of the mine or their own sweat – miners were confronted with a building designed to be filled with light, a building which was continually kept at a temperature precisely aligned to their bodily comfort, a building where – in both a modern and an efficient, yet also an almost ritualistic, ahistorical manner – they were cleansed. Later they were also provided with nutrition in the addition of canteens. It can be argued, then, that the pithead baths approached a *Gesamtkunstwerk* [total work of art], whose overall form and organisation and interior appliances combined to operate across a series of spheres and range of scales, from the physical intimate folds of skin on the miner's body, to the realm of the psychological and emotional – his and his community's sense of well-being and, ultimately, identity. This in addition to the invisible but simultaneously profound impact that the buildings had on the lives of female partners of the miners and their domestic circumstances. Finally, within the collective of pithead baths distributed throughout the coalfields, there was an expression of a civil pact between the miners and a government or state that somehow – however it had been initially provoked or excited – was responding, through the medium of architecture, to their welfare.

THE EVOLUTION OF FORM AND REPRESENTATION: THE SEARCH FOR EXPRESSION

By 1930, the initial programme of experimental installations had been completed, and the technologies and new organisational diagram separating dirty from clean tested and confirmed in over 50 schemes that were either finished or in progress. These provided 'accommodation for 60,190 men and 62 women' (MWC 1931: p.21). Yet a mature coherent and consistent architectural language, one that concerned itself with conveying or expressing the modernity and radical new nature of the pithead baths initiative was still elusive. Instead, installations such as the National Colliery Pithead Baths in Wattstown, South Wales (FIG.53) for 1,200 men, still showed fidelity to the staid rectangular form of centrally located showers, flanked by locker rooms, and an eclectic

53
Pithead baths in Wattstown

marriage of industrial forms with formal architectural motifs found in the likes of the earlier Mainsforth or Park Collieries. There were, however, the beginnings of some variations in the planning of pithead baths based on particularities within their siting in often cramped and congested colliery yards. Harrington Colliery, for example, accommodated just over 900 men in a two storey building which also negotiated a sharp change in level. The result was an arrangement of two sets of both clean and dirty lockers, which abutted each other linearly across from the showers, an arrangement which was repeated on the storey above. The showers were stacked above the empty space made by the change in level which was filled by a cycle store and the calorifiers (which heated the water), and so on. Whitburn Colliery baths in Northumberland, meanwhile, followed the plan of the experiment installation, but the pit and clean locker rooms were both entered into from above, via a bridge which straddled the main road separating the building from the rest of the colliery site. At Fortissat in North Lanarkshire, there was a scheme for a much smaller installation. This was based somewhat on a Belgian precedent at Font Piquette near Liège while maintaining the double-locker-room system established under the MWC. The men entered through the clean locker room at one end of the plan and accessed the showers – in the middle – which were flanked by the pit clothes lockers. They exited via the boot greaser and bottle-filling room at the other end. This building formed a simple, near symmetrical, barn-like, pitched-roof structure with two flat-roofed appendages at either end. Light came through a series of strips of glazing in the roof or else through a small number of portrait-orientated windows puncturing the wall. Ventilation, as in all of these buildings, was provided through the roof by generic industrial cowls common to many factory buildings.

The first real evidence of a comprehensive aesthetic breakthrough appears in the drawings describing Dawdon Colliery Pithead Baths in Durham for 2,500 men, published as one of the indicative or significant projects of 1930. Presented alongside photographs of the prosaic Roslin Colliery Pithead Baths (Lothian), and the more formal but historicist Llay Main Colliery baths (North Wales), Dawdon baths signal the beginnings of a new stylistic departure while still building within the paradigmatic plan offered by the experimental installations (FIG.54). Accordingly, the men enter the clean lockers midway on the long side of the rectangular plan through, significantly, a tower element which also contains lavatories and vertical circulation. Two ranges of showers, perpendicular to the front elevation, run between the clean and dirty locker room. The showers in turn flank open courtyards (called 'areas') between which sits the calorifier room in the centre of the plan. The pit entrance/exit occupies the middle of the opposite elevation from its clean equivalent and is contained with an articulated accretion that also holds a staircase, bottle-filling facilities, lavatories and the boot-cleaning and greasing rooms. An upper storey contains a similar but smaller arrangement of the lockers and baths below. The space above the calorifier is specified in the plan as the plenum chamber indicating the presence of the newer system of heating both the building and its lockers.

The real revelation, however, is in the treatment of the exterior. For the first time, is the successful interplay of vertical and horizontal elements that would become a characteristic feature within the pithead bath programme.

54
Dawdon Colliery bath plans, elevations and sections

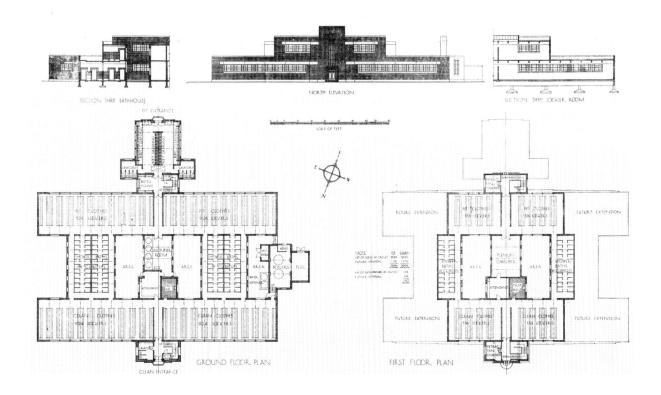

A horizontal emphasis is achieved in a number of ways. Firstly, it is in the long, low-slung nature of the building which, for the first time for a pithead baths, has been represented in its long elevation. Presumably proposed as a brick building, further horizontality is expressed by the three bands running across this principal elevation – at the ground level, above the windows on the ground floor, and again above the windows on the upper storey. These windows are also arranged into horizontal strips within which the panes are arranged in landscape rather that portrait orientation. Finally, the building is entirely flat roofed giving a crisp and definite separation between the roof and wall planes. The rising parapet above the roof also serves to conceal the rooflights, which illuminate some of the upper spaces. Unlike the generic industrial components seen on the exterior of previous pithead baths, Dawdon Colliery in County Durham is more circumspect in revealing exactly how it is lit on the inside or indeed, how it is ventilated. These aspects of function are smoothly incorporated, absorbed or hidden within its overall architectural expression – far less is left to chance or the vagaries of ill-considered responses to functional requirements.

A vertical balance is provided by the tower. This forms the clean entrance on the public side of the building which contains elements of vertical circulation and, presumably, also the water tank, reconciling it for the first time into a considered composition. Notwithstanding the symmetrical emphasis about its central access, a pithead baths building has finally achieved a modern aesthetic refinement and presents itself as a civic building of the 20th century. As the baths programme progressed, this new civic language developed. The bilateral symmetry seen both here, and in the experimental installations, would break down. New ways of configuring the plan, while adhering to the principles of separation would be explored, as alternative, less compositionally rigid precedents – such as those provided by Dudok – were appropriated where desired. Such developments would allow the integration of other elements such as the chimney stack, left – with one or two other elements – rather forlornly out of Dawdon's otherwise rigorous symmetry. New methods of representing this new architecture would also be experimented with.

Writing in retrospective on the eve of his departure from the Miners' Welfare Committee's architects department in 1938, Forshaw acknowledged that the baths programme had produced buildings that while 'designed for health and pleasure' were essentially 'civic in their social requirements' (Forshaw 1938: p.422). Yet, it is unclear what the exact impetus was ten years earlier, in the late 1920s, for the architecture embarkation signalled by Dawdon and its new modern language. While Commander Coote had written in 1931 about the ongoing necessity for propaganda to convince recalcitrant miners of the benefits of pithead baths, there was no specific suggestion that an elaboration in architectural form could represent a method of achieving this (MWC 1931: p.50). The mere fact of the existence alone of a pithead bath within a district had previously been thought by the likes of Chappell and Lovat-Fraser to be sufficient to coax miners into washing at their place of work. Moreover, the report by Coote and Forshaw – published in the MWC's seventh annual report for 1928 – which examined continental facilities, had continued to concentrate on the spatial organisation of those baths and their technical equipment and accoutrements, rather than discussing their form and appearance. Nor was there any mention of visits to anywhere else of specifically architectural interest, including, for example, Hilversum.

The design and construction of Dawdon in 1929, however, closely followed the employment by the Miners' Welfare Committee of the young architects who, along with Forshaw, would come to be associated with its most conspicuous buildings: Kemp (1928); Saise (1928); Traylor (1929); Frizzell (as draughtsman [1927] and assistant architect [1929]); Woodland (as draughtsman [1928] and assistant architect [1929]) and Jack (as draughtsman [1928]) (see Forshaw n.d.). These appointments represented the creative nucleus of the pithead baths programme as it would develop and flourish over the next ten years and beyond. It also, presumably, represented the development of an architectural culture of ideas and references that Forshaw – who had been working for the MWC since 1926 without architectural colleagues – had previously lacked (FIG.50).[21] If the division of this architectural group into regions had, in fact, occurred by this stage, then the architect for Dawdon may have been Frederick G. Frizzell, who would have had responsibility for Northumberland and Durham under the direction of John Austin 'Jack' Dempster, as Northern Division chief architect.

The overall development of a civic architectural expression for the pithead baths, however, continued to proceed unevenly for some time. The tenth

55
Menu card (signed by Forshaw) for the annual dinner of the MWC architects – indicative, perhaps of a shared sense of culture, creativity (and fun)

annual report for 1931 contains images of modern, aesthetically considered pieces of architecture such as at Wearmouth Colliery (Durham) and Bradford Colliery (Lancashire) (FIGS 56 and 57). But alongside these, were buildings which still embodied the more utilitarian collection of parts seen in the experiment installations: Baggeridge Colliery (South Staffordshire); Sneyd Colliery (North Staffordshire); Cannop Colliery (Forest of Dean); Rose Heyworth and Cwmcarn Collieries (both in South Wales). Two other buildings, both erected in Scotland at Devon (Fife) and Viewpark (Lanark) Collieries, and whose strip windows and unbroken eaves line emphasise streamlined horizontality, perhaps occupy a middle ground (FIG.58). Given its location in County Durham and thereby the sharing of an architect who was likely to be Frizzell, Wearmouth understandably echoes Dawdon. They both exhibit overall symmetry, flat roofs and the use of a central, vertical element containing both an entrance and the water tank. Unlike at Dawdon, however, at Wearmouth the windows of the two storeys flanking wings – in a motif perhaps borrowed from the principles of Louis Sullivan, but also deployed more recently in Britain by the likes of Thomas S. Tait – are combined vertically in bands of relief, pushed into a wall whose materiality otherwise gives a horizontal emphasis. In what will often become a characteristic of Frizzell's work the building, while evidently modern, simultaneously has a robust, almost archaic muscularity, a quality reminiscent of Dudok's Rembrandtschool (1920).

Dudok's influence is also clear in the pithead baths at Bradford Colliery which, if we are again to accept the regional division of architects by this time, was likely to have been designed by Alfred John Saise (or possibly a Mr Bourne who, however, was still a draughtsman in 1930 (Forshaw n.d.). In the photograph shown in the tenth annual report – which may or may not be of a public face of the building – the corner closest to the camera is a vertical element of a squat tower which almost certainly contains the water tank behind the thin vertical brick panels at its zenith. These panels resonate with the attenuated forms of the windows below, which sit above the entrance. Both window and entrance are set with a large flat expanse of soldier course bricks, which step inwards to form the surrounding to the entrance door. This careful and studied treatment of the effects of brick relief is repeated, this time to emphasise horizontality, in the other part of the building seen in the photograph. The horizontal strips of windows, whose vertical masonry subdivisions are finished in light-coloured render – are set within bands of receded brickwork. Again, this is picked up elsewhere in the facade, in the thin horizontal bands of alternate receded and pronounced bricks, visible under the lowermost windows. Finally, and perhaps less successfully, the building makes some visible concessions to its functionality in a series of ventilation holes punched rhythmically across the facade.

What is conspicuous here, as well as at Dawdon and Wearmouth, is an attention to detail with regards the aesthetic expression of the building that is every bit as rigorous in consistency and coherency as that which had been applied to

56
Wearmouth Colliery baths

57
Bradford Colliery baths

58
Viewpark Colliery baths

the more scientific determination of the prototypical pithead baths plan and its equipment. Indeed, it is significant that from this point on with some exceptions – such as the proposed installation for women workers at Parsonage Colliery (Lancashire) – the commonest form of depicting pithead baths in the annual reports will no longer be the plan drawing. The technological and organisational principles for the latter were by now essentially fixed. Consequently, and appropriately for a publication designed to publicise and propagandise pithead baths (as well as other activities of the Miners' Welfare Committee), in this new phase of architectural self-consciousness the representational focus shifted to more pictorial and less abstract forms which highlighted exterior appearances and enhanced and celebrated their civic properties.

Among other things, this shift can be seen quite clearly in how the buildings were photographed. The crudeness of the photograph of Broomside described above would become rarer. For example, while the architecture of the Scottish baths at Devon and Viewpark was arguably still under-resolved aesthetically, how these two buildings were photographed is very precise and considered. Their horizontality and the apparent similarity of their form is accentuated by the eye-level viewpoint of the camera, which situates the leading corner of the building compositionally at about a third into the space of the frame. The result is a dynamic, perspectival depiction of a largely prosaic, symmetrical facade. This application of the rule of thirds is also seen in the photographic depictions of Bradford and Wearmouth, as well in the images of the less prepossessing architecture seen at Rose Heyworth, Baggeridge, and so on. That these systematic pieces of iterative architecture should be represented by a formulaic approach to their photographing is apt. The photographic literacy present in these images was further developed later in the 1930s when it became usual for the MWC to commission professional commercial and industrial photographers – such as W. Ralston or Stewart Bale in Lancashire, or Chas. R. H. Pickard in West Yorkshire – to depict the baths completed in the various regions (see images below). These images, often by now no longer tied to the basic rule of thirds, provided careful studies of these buildings and must have contributed significantly to their broader public reception. Taken generally from an eye-level point of view, they capture crisp architectural forms often in long dynamic perspectives bathed in light or shadow. The baths themselves are usually completely new and in pristine condition, even if on occasion their immediate surrounding landscape still appears to be raw. Significantly, conspicuously and almost without exception, the depictions of these pieces of architecture are free from the smoke that was emitted from the furnaces necessary – either within the building itself or else adjacently from the 'waste steam' of the colliery boilers – to heat the building and its water for the miners. Paradoxically, and despite occasional evidence of soot staining, it was when the buildings were switched off that they presented the most acceptable image of architectural cleanliness (FIG.59).

The coming together of the funding following the Samuel Commission, the defining of the separate dirty and clean system of organisation of baths buildings, the building of an architecturally trained team under Forshaw – as well as a team of surveyors – and the apotheosis of a mature modern aesthetic which seamlessly incorporated mass-produced elements in the buildings, all contributed to an acceleration in their production. In 1929, the baths built by the MWC had accommodated less than 10,000 mineworkers. In 1930, they built enough washing facilities for over 4,000 more; in 1931, enough for just under 8,500 more; and in 1932, pithead baths for just under 12,000 more colliers. In 1933, this figure leapt again to 17,000, increasing 20,000 in 1934, just under 22,000 in 1935, and just below 24,000 thousand in 1936. By the end of 1936, the tenders for the following year had been issued for 46 buildings which would accommodate 51,000 workers (MWC 1937: pp 66–7). But this acceleration in production was also a result of an equally exponential increase in demand which, in turn, was due to the efforts made through a number of agencies – including the form, appearance and representation of the buildings themselves – to communicate the benefits of pithead baths to mineworkers. That these statistics were themselves conveyed through a precise, elegant and easily understood pictogram within the annual report for 1936, gives another perspective on the importance given to communication and the role of aesthetics within it (FIG.60). While the buildings were increasingly designed, to quote Forshaw, to be 'civic in their social requirements' through a language of modernism, other methods of communication were also being updated.

Coinciding with these developments in architecture and its representation, the annual reports – the main organ of publicity and dissemination for the Miners' Welfare Committee's activities – also received a modernistic makeover. Published by His Majesty's Stationery Office, for the first ten years of the reports had been presented in the staid and stuffy manner of an official publication. For 1934, however, at the same time as a new aesthetic maturity for the baths was consolidating, the format changed. The recently designed modernist font of Gill Sans was introduced in a new graphic format that allowed full page and other images to bleed to the edges (FIG.61). There was also a more considered layout between text and the increasing number of photographs and other forms of representation incorporated into its pages. For 1935, the cover had dispensed with HMSO's official royal coat of arms, and replaced it with a green duo-tone drawing of a coalfield scene taken from a viewpoint high above the ground but below the zenith of the head and winding gear depicted in lattice steel. Below this was a series of sharp modernist buildings with flat roofs beside the tracks of a railway line which snake into the distance (FIG.62). On the rear, and part of the same drawing, is a generic pithead baths complete with tower and oriel window, behind which can be seen a mining community endowed with recreational and sports facilities, and cottage-style and terraced houses. The drawing speaks of a harmonious reconciliation of modernism, mining and a pleasant life. The report for 1937 – whose front cover was a beautiful black, red and blue rendering of the position of the coalfields in Great Britain – also contained on the rear inside cover an equally beautiful graphic icon of a pit's headgear, whose winding wheel resonated with the roundness of the sun whose rays are shining down. Subtitled by the words Miners Welfare

59
Hafod Colliery baths as photographed by Stewart Bale, 1938

60
Pictogram of the MWC pithead baths programme, 1936–37

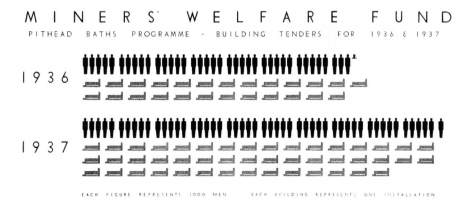

61
MWC *Annual Report* for 1934, with new layout and font

62
Cover MWC *Annual Report* for 1935

[*sic*], it can be interpreted in many ways but the presence of the sunlight, whose yellow coats the industrial form it interacts with, seems like a potent symbolism of the bringing of light, cleanliness, health, and so on, to the adverse conditions and life associated with mining. While in subsequent issues there were further alterations – the Gill Sans font was unfortunately abandoned by 1936 – the publication would retain and develop its new graphic consistency until its final episode, the report for 1939, published in 1940. Interrupted by the

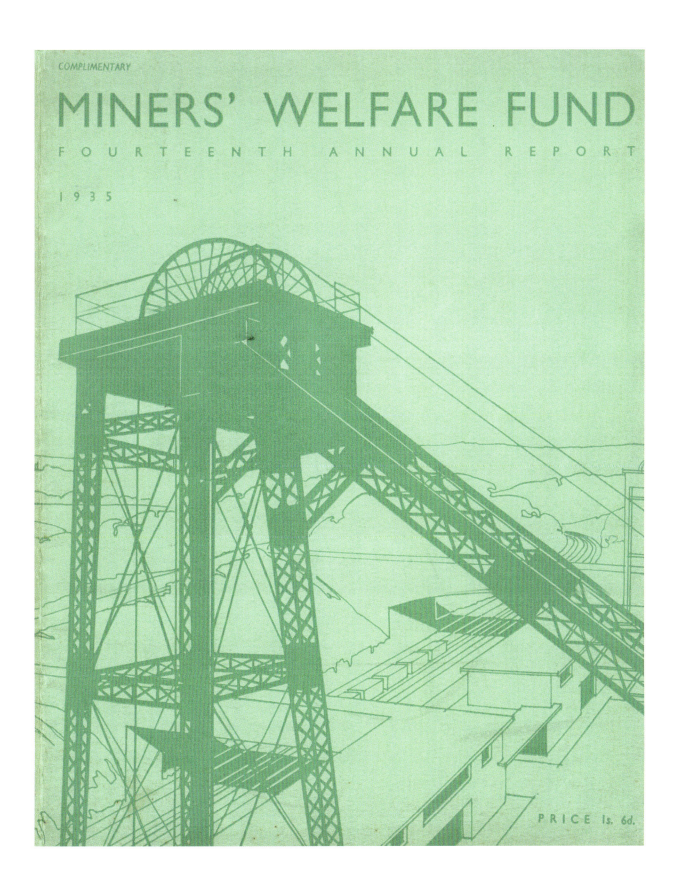

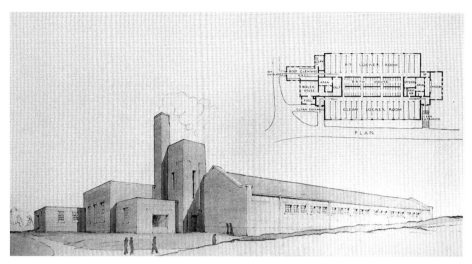

63
Shirebrook Colliery baths

64
Thorne Colliery baths, perspective drawing with ground floor plan

war, a somewhat more prosaic omnibus edition was published in 1947 covering the previous six and a half years.[22]

As mentioned above, the uses of photography also continued to develop. The representations made by commercial photographers for the MWC often emphasised a viewpoint which focused on the corners of the buildings. Redolent of the non-axial approach through which ancient Greek temples – arguably the progenitors of civic buildings – were designed to be experienced and seen, emphasis on the corner became a recurring motif not only within other types of visual depictions produced – such as drawings – but also and consistently, within the form of the architecture itself. For example, the plan of the proposed Shirebrook Colliery pithead baths (Derbyshire) from 1931, suggests a relatively straightforward building that has not strayed too far from the rectangular diagram of the early experimental installations. However, in highlighting the coming together of horizontal and vertical forms at the corner and depicting them from a viewpoint slightly lower than the building itself, the accompanying perspective drawing renders the baths heroic, commanding the hill on which it sits, like a modest industrial acropolis (FIG.63). A similar romantic vision is achieved in the rendering of the facilities at Thorne Colliery (South Yorkshire). When compared to Shirebook and Dawdon, this building is also conspicuous as one of the first to explore more fully the possibilities of variation within the plan, while still adhering to the sequencing of spaces necessary to its functioning. Its plan drawing reveals the emphatic breaking of the more static, box-like forms seen in earlier iterations, to embrace the lessons of centrifugal or pinwheeling planning, common in Dudok's schools and elsewhere within modernism. On a flat site and denied the dramatic possibilities of a hilltop, the perspective depicts its articulated, L-shape plan from a viewpoint looking at its principal re-entrant corner, catching a crisp series of planar volumes cast in either shadow or light. Within this the form of the water tower resonates with some of the other colliery buildings visible in the background (FIG.64).

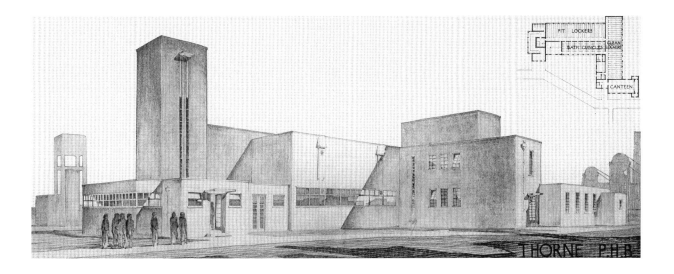

EXPLOITING THE L-SHAPE

The principal constituent components in pithead baths – the two sets of locker rooms, the showers and the water tower – formed building blocks that could be assembled and combined in an almost endless variety of ways. The manipulation and depiction of these aggregate forms, used in a series of strategies and responding to differing site conditions, was central to the range of expressions achieved in many of the baths produced in the 1930s. Certain principal approaches or types can be identified: firstly, the linear composition, often deployed because of tight sites bounded by infrastructural or topological elements such as railway lines; secondly, the block – again often used in tight or sloping sites; and thirdly, the L-shape and its numerous variants (see Allison 1994; and Buckley 1984). The latter were often used with a more urbanistic intent. As exemplified by Dudok's schools and Town Hall, thin cranking forms could be used to enclose or define external space or link with other buildings. With the support of accompanying pieces of designed landscape, this type could be used on sites where there were fewer limits on space, and to reorder or compose a chaotic colliery yard.

Consequently, the L-shape plan in its many possible iterations, elaborations and derivatives (including the Z-shape and, occasionally, the U-shape), became the most common form, establishing itself as a key characteristic regardless of the region within which the pithead baths found themselves, the architect who designed them, the materials used to construct them, whether they were single or multi-storey, or the dates when they were designed and built. Over 20 different variants of this plan type have been identified in the MWC pithead baths in Scotland alone (Allison 1994: p.61) with over 50 further examples from all regions being published in the 1930s in the annual reports.[23] Like other reiterated, serial aspects such as the lockers, the L-shape represented an enduring element, an efficient, repeatable organisational device which – in addition to fulfilling its function as a bath building – would continue to be used as an appropriate form to articulate and order wider aspects of colliery spaces and environments when the final baths were being built in the 1950s. In addition, as highlighted in any number of pithead baths buildings, the L-shape had the potential to allow an accumulation of forms that were both dramatic and photogenic, simultaneously mass produced and romantically picturesque.

Pragmatically, the L-shape and its variations could also be easily added to without compromising the overall form, offering possibilities for flexibility and future expansion. For example, before the outbreak of the Second World War, the provision of on-site colliery canteens tended not to be supported by the Miners' Welfare Fund. During this period, the urgency to provide as many pits as possible with washing facilities was considered greater than the need to provide a hot meal. When this changed – partly to do with the conflict and partly to do with the success of the baths programme – canteens were often slotted into spaces which had already been defined for this purpose at the design stage, and easily accommodated as additions to buildings which were already conceived of and composed as additive forms.

Within the basic L-shape itself there was also the possibility of playing with the angle to make it more or less obtuse according to site conditions or other requirements. Among the most striking example of this were the pithead baths designed for the 1,500 mineworkers at Polkemmet Colliery in Lanarkshire by Jack Dempster and completed by 1937 (FIG.65). Responding to a triangular site in plan, the building forms a fat, nearly symmetrical wedge shape (FIG.66). A zone of two sets each of clean and pit changing rooms occupy the rear of the building, cranking to form a flattened U-shape with protruding wings, rather than an L-shape. The space between these wings is taken up, as was necessary, by the block containing the shower cubicles. Because all of these elements are single or one and a half stories in height, the building manifests itself on its principal elevation as a long, low-slung, stepping composition arranged on either side of what appears perhaps, in strict terms of its functionality, to be an oversized tower element. Thus in contemporary photographs, the building exerts a considerable presence over its surroundings. This is made even more conspicuous by its finishing in white or cream render, as well as the tall, elegant bow window, complete with a nautical ladder staircase, which articulated the tower and presumably acted as a lighted beacon for the building in the long darkness of Scottish winters. Similar compositions, also in cream or white, and also presumably by Dempster, could be seen at Fleet Colliery in the Lothians (completed by 1937), and Michael Colliery in Fife. Another, Frances Colliery in Dysart, just along the coast from Michael, delivered another conspicuous white tower enlivened by a shallow bow window with a series of curving fin-like elements. Collectively, this set of buildings, and how they were depicted and photographed for the annual reports and contemporary journals, does not feel particularly industrial.[24] They could just as easily be accommodating a leisure function, perhaps in a coastal resort. It is a celebratory architecture which, perhaps more than any other pithead baths, fulfils those wishes expressed by Katharine Glasier for 'white shining Temples of Health'. In this and its Art Deco styling, it seems to presage the type of festival architecture – designed both to display and be displayed – that would be constructed, for example, at the Empire Exhibition in the wide expanses of Glasgow's Bellahouston Park in 1938.

At the same time, however, the interior of Polkemmet reveals a rigorous, clinical and yet humane hygienic functionalism wrought in glazed and gleaming surfaces flooded with light which, in areas of privacy, most often comes from above, through long roof lanterns or clerestory windows. Writing in 1936, its

65
Pithead baths at Polkemmet Colliery

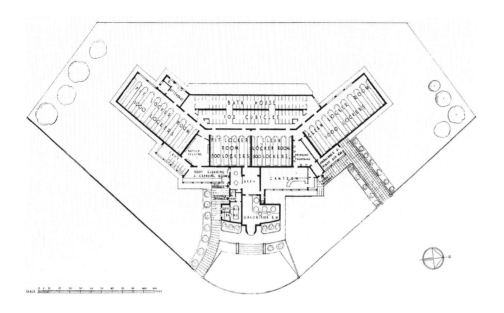

architect Dempster outlined an underlying philosophy of efficiency in modernism seen in the baths:

> We, as architects, do not feel justified in allowing expenditure in ornament and decoration in such buildings, and strive to achieve results of architectural worth through the use of line, with well-proportioned surfaces and fenestration. Economic building need not be mean, but building solely for cheapness, without regard to design, would be unworthy. The Miners' Welfare Committee aims to effect, from the external appearance of a building, a distinctive note of design …
>
> (Jack Dempster 1936, cited in McKean 1987: p.117)

This is embodied within another example, also from Scotland and also by Dempster, which shows how the L-shape could be varied to achieve more subdued and subtle, yet still civic forms of architecture. The pithead baths at Cardowan Colliery in Lanarkshire, just outside Glasgow, opened in March 1935 (FIG.67). Originally for 792 men, made out of brick, built over two storeys and complete with a tower, and formal garden with pool, it has been described as 'a miniature echo of the Town Hall in Hilversum' (McKean 1987: p.117). The sets of locker rooms form a right angle within which, on the re-entrant side, sit the shower blocks (FIG.68). Because of the requirements of two separate entrances and exits, these are located quite discretely at an extremity of each of the two ranges of the L. Consequently, and in common with many of the L-shaped pithead baths, there is what could be described as a discord between function and expression. In a conventional civic building, the main entrance or a principal public space would be expected to coincide with the focus of visual interest – the coming together of forms around the outside corner and the

66
Polkemmet Colliery baths, ground floor plan

67
Cardowan baths

68
Ground floor plan of Cardowan pithead baths

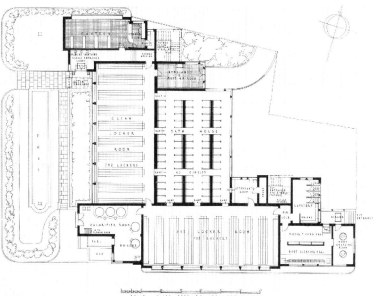

tower. Yet at Cardowan, this space is occupied by the decidedly non-public boilers, calorifiers, a fuel store and ash repository. Above all sits the plenum and above this again, the water tank. A second storey, equipped for an additional – but smaller – number of 432 men was added later. Requiring less area it stepped inwards from the building line below. This was made clear in a contemporary axonometric drawing which shows a series of planar volumes stacked on top of and around each other (Forshaw 1935: p.1080). The building also contained typical ancillary services including an ambulance bay and a canteen whose huge window addressed the railway line. Its 'walls, flooring and counter are finished in tiles, the predominant shade light primrose with flame coloured tiles to sill seat and door architrave … the counter and table tops are finished in self-coloured grey linoleum' (MWC 1937: p.36). Photographs of the exterior again confirm a horizontal emphasis, evoked through the low

form of the ranges, the ribbon windows and thin cantilevered canopies, counterpointed by the vertical massing of the elements at the corner.

The pithead baths in the new colliery of Betteshanger represented the use of the L-shape at the other end of the country (FIG.69). Designed by Cecil George Kemp, and opened in 1934 in the emergent and developing coalfield of Kent, Betteshanger's baths were included (along with those at Polkemmet) in the 1939 *Architects' Journal* poll of the most popular buildings of Britain (cited in Allison 1994: p.57). Built over two storeys, faced with local Deal bricks and accommodating 2,520 men, the L is formed as usual by the perpendicular abutting of the clean and pit locker blocks. The showers, equally accessible to both, occupy the angle between them. The rest of the accommodation, the lavatories, boot-cleaning facilities, and the brightly lit and gleaming canteen (complete with 'a small stage' for concerts [Forshaw 1935: p.1088]), and so on, occupy the extremities in single storey forms. The apparent solecism between the function and expression of the tower element seen at Cardowan has been resolved by removing the tower from the angle, and placing it instead at the end of one of the two storey ranges where, more appropriately, it

69
Betteshanger baths (photographed by L. H. Felton, courtesy of RIBApix)

accommodates the 'pit' entrance and exit. The 'clean' entrance and exit is located close to the canteen. Betteshanger appears to eschew the tendency to emphasise the horizontal seen elsewhere. The tower is highly articulated with glass bricks on a least one of its sides and its verticality is echoed in other elements such as the stacks of windows over the 'pit' and 'clean' entrances and exits.

In the west – opening in October 1938 and designed by W. M. Traylor to accommodate 2,040 men (Salway 1998: p.16) – the L-shape form of the pithead baths at Penallta Colliery near Ystrad Mynach, was configured to negotiate the typical valley topography found in the South Wales coalfields (FIG.70). Located at the edge of the colliery, the building was set back from the public road by a rectangle of landscape bordered by a low wall and railings. Its public front consisted of two sets of clean lockers, one atop the other, and a canteen which reached forward in a semicircular motif, once again borrowed from Dudok. This indicated the presence of the 'clean' entrance/exit and clean stairs underneath the adjacent squat tower. The pit locker rooms formed part of the perpendicular range, which occupied the change in level caused by the slope from the public road to the colliery yard. In between these two ranges the showers zigzagged in two blocks leaving an open atrium space, called 'the area', in the centre of the building – an attendant's room and a disability ward on the ground floor, and an attendant's and first aid room above looked into this. The basement floor beneath the 'dirty' lockers contained the boot-greasing and cleaning facilities, and next to this, beneath one of the shower blocks, were the lavatories, calorifiers and the plenum room. The pit stairs leading downwards to the pit entrance/exit was neatly located at the bottom end of this range.

The lower clean and dirty locker rooms were lit by a familiar ribbon of horizontal clerestory windows and the upper ones, which presented only a blank brick wall in elevation, were lit by long rooflights running down their centres. Once again, as photographed in the annual report for 1938, a sense of horizontality is achieved by a combination of harmonising elements at a series of scales: the building's long, low forms on its public front, the strip windows, and the sill, parapet, lintel and string course details picked out in a light-coloured or painted concrete (FIG.71). The latter's contribution is exemplified by the parapet, which wraps the top of the curving form of the canteen to merge its line with that of the lintel of the lower, clean locker's windows.

Lancashire – like Scotland and Cumbria – was unusual in the continuing presence of female colliery workers carrying out surface tasks like coal grading in its collieries. Sometimes, like in the Scottish experimental baths at Broomside discussed earlier, facilities for female washing were located as part of the main pithead baths. Elsewhere, such as at the Clock Face Colliery, opened in 1939 and designed by Alfred J. Saise for 1,600 men and 40 women, female colliery workers were afforded a discrete building. The pithead baths at Clock Face were also conspicuous as one of a series of projects – including, for example, the slightly later project at Calverton in Nottinghamshire – where the landscape possibilities of the L-shape were deployed to their full potential (FIG.72). Here, the familiar plan form is bounded by a busy road which separates the pithead bath building from its parent colliery. The outside area in between is extensively landscaped with planters (next to the building), and grass and trees, as well as containing an access road and turning circle for vehicles. The 'clean' entrance and exit is located just off the main road at the end of the clean locker range, which runs at right angles to it. Near the entrance, the canteen is formed partly by another Dudokian semicircular oriel motif. The 'pit' locker range runs parallel to the road and ends in a slender and elegant tower displaying towards the zenith of its facade, a panel of glazed bricks, representing, perhaps, a clock face (FIG.73). The use of glass brick is also found elsewhere in the complex and, combined with the use of light-coloured render

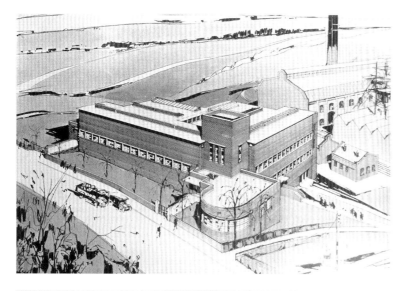

70
Bird's eye perspective of Penallta Colliery baths

71
Penallta Colliery baths from the public roadway

72
Clock Face Colliery, pithead baths and canteen ground-floor plan

rather than brick, these features give the building – especially when depicted photographically from the point of view of the road – a machine-like, almost vehicular aesthetic. The overall engagement with the road is also interesting. Located between the male and female baths is another block (containing the lamp room and offices, and so on), with a dynamically expressed outside staircase. This links to a substantial bridge that takes the miners back and forth, to and from the pit. This block, which completes a U-shape form with the male baths, merges at the same time to form a piece of infrastructure, one that seems to predict the development, 20 years later, of such arrangements in motorway service stations. In their report on continental baths from 1928, Coote and Forshaw had identified the linear, covered walkway in precedents such as at *Zeche de Wendel*, Germany – which allowed miners to access the baths sheltered from the elements – as a great benefit especially when combined with the 'systemic grouping' of other colliery elements to make a coordinated overall plan (MWC 1929: p.60). This combination of elements is present at Clock Face which, rather than a building or a collection of buildings, appears to have been conceived and executed as a coherent complex. Although couched in a different aesthetic, it contains in its multiple identities similarities to Michel de Klerk's Het Ship project in Amsterdam. Simultaneously resembling a machine and a civic centre, Clock Face's tower announces its presence as a significant industrial site across a flat and otherwise agricultural landscape to the urban settlements, just visible in the distance.

It is also a piece of infrastructure interacting intimately with another piece of infrastructure. And, when seen in the aerial photograph – taken presumably from the pit's headgear – the linearity of the tower resonates with that of the bridge, so that the former also feels both infrastructural *and* civic which, of course, it is (FIG.74). The entire scene, captured from above, and beset with these linear, functional yet civic elements – sharp, flat-roofed architectures

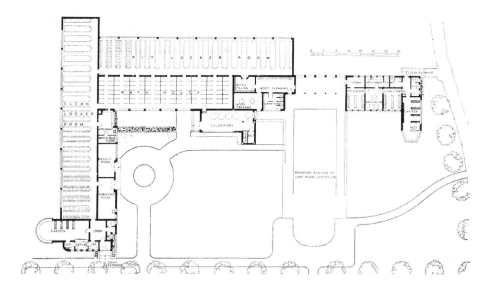

73
Clock Face Colliery pithead baths

74
Clock Face Colliery pithead baths from the winding tower

75
Women's washing facilities at Chisnall Hall Colliery, Lancashire

76
Newton Colliery, Lancashire, women's rest room

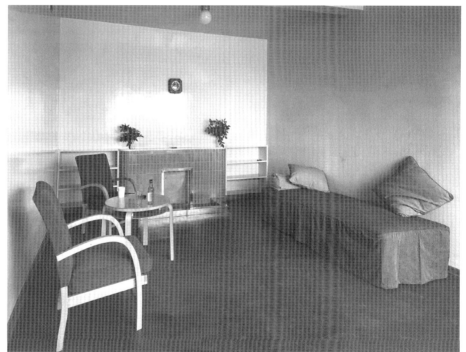

and distant housing – is redolent in real space and form, of those visions of the ideal mining settlement depicted on the covers of the MWC's annual reports a few years earlier, in 1936 and 1937 respectively. The harmonious quality of all this is perhaps confirmed by the female baths – which can be seen in the ground-floor plan – located discretely on the other side of the central bridge block, and linked to the rest of the complex by a pergola. Home not only to the usual facilities, in miniature, of separate 'clean' and 'pit' locker rooms, it also has its own separate canteen. Located at the end of this, occupying a spacious bay window, is a women's 'rest area'. This type of facility, often equipped with soft furnishings and sometime even a day bed, was quite commonly provided in pithead baths in Lancashire and Scotland, ensuring that where women still worked on the production of coal, even if in quite small numbers, that provision for their hygiene and comfort was equal to – or even surpassed – that provided for male workers (FIGS 75 and 76).

LINEAR FORMS

At Coventry Colliery in Warwickshire, some of the more bucolic landscape intentions seen at Clock Face Colliery's pithead baths were effected by a linear rather than L-shape form. Sited in 'a typical piece of English landscape, rather flat but well-wooded and very delightful' (Forshaw 1938: p.434) at a colliery which was just over 20 years old, the building was designed by W. A. Woodland and opened in 1935. Forming part of a side of a large triangular expanse given over to landscape, and provided with walks and other leisure amenities, it was also aligned along a new entrance road (FIG.77). This was provided with a turning circle to allow buses to drop off miners at a small, landscaped, civic-type space positioned between the main baths building and a smaller one containing cycle stores and two cottages (one each for the baths' superintendent and the plant watchman). This led on to an outside semicircular area which – rather like the similarly shaped elements at Ernst May's suburban settlement of Römerstadt Siedlung on the outskirts of Frankfurt (1927–8) or, more likely, Frank Lloyd Wright's Barnsdall 'Hollyhock House' (1921) – provided a place from which to view and, in this case, access the landscape amenity beyond. Bounded by hedges, its shape echoed the familiar curving oriel form of the adjacent canteen. The 'clean' entrance and exit was located here, slipped between the canteen and an ambulance room. Inside, the 'clean' and 'pit' locker rooms,

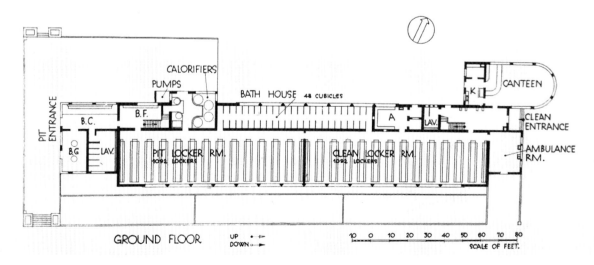

77

77
Pithead baths at Coventry Colliery, ground-floor plan

78
Coventry Colliery, axonometric drawing showing pithead baths and landscape

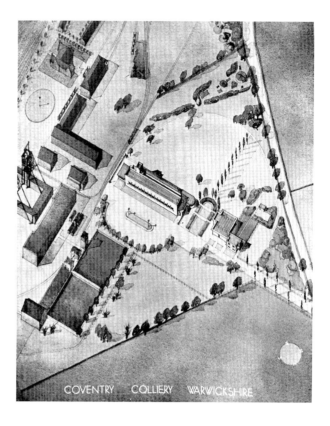

designed to accommodate 1,890 miners, were placed back to back. The showers – part of a neatly designed linear zone which included both entrances and exits – sat parallel to them, overlapping with each. There was a similar arrangement on the second storey which contained two more locker rooms and showers, as well as the plenum. As at Penallta and numerous other examples elsewhere, the lower locker rooms were lit by a continuous strip of clerestory windows, and the upper ones by a continuous strip of rooflights of similar dimensions. Finished in a light-coloured render, the curious vertical details springing from the strip window uprights on an otherwise unadorned wall also make the front facade redolent of Wright's Barnsdall House. But these details aside, it is the synthesis between building and landscape at Coventry baths – along with how the composition also attempted to stitch into an existing colliery plan, which was not 'as satisfactory as it might have been' (Forshaw 1938: p.434) – that is most indicative of the architects' ambition. All these aspects were expressed in the axonometric drawing of the project, published in the annual report for 1934 (FIG.78).[25]

As mentioned above, linear forms were often used on restricted sites where the expansive possibilities of the L were not possible. Designed by Traylor for 988 men, and opened on the 28th March 1936, the pithead baths at Hafodyrynys in Monmouthshire were squeezed between a set of railway sidings and a steep hill, a location and site quite typical of coal-mining valleys in South Wales

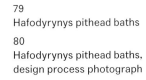

79
Hafodyrynys pithead baths

80
Hafodyrynys pithead baths, design process photograph

(FIG.79). Not typical, however, was the continuing presence of dense forestation. According to Forshaw, the Welsh valleys tended to have been stripped of their trees. Hence he suggested that the building had been designed as a long, low, thin form at least partly to allow the preservation of the view of the wooded hillside behind it (ibid.: p.436).

The pursuit of this ambition gives an insight to some of the design processes and methods used in the production of pithead baths. Photographic surveys of potential locations for the baths were routinely carried out by the architectural staff of the Miners' Welfare Committee, who used either white stakes driven into the ground before taking the photograph, or else drew on the photograph itself to define the exact site for a proposed building. One of the photographs of Hafodyrynys, however, shows the white outline of the building ghosted, as it were, into the frame. It is not clear at what point in the design process this composite drawing/photograph was made, but it seems to have been intended to test the building's form and its potential impact on the view of the forest (FIG.80). Taken from a viewpoint on the railway tracks slightly below the floor level of the proposed building, it evokes a sleek, yet heroic, form in a perspective whose main visual interest, once again, lies in the vertical massing and the curving element of the canteen located at the nearest extremity. In the finished-building – which negotiates a slope along its length rather than, as you might expect across its breadth – these elements enhance an aesthetic which once again tends to the machinic and vehicular: like a boat or a train, honed, strea lined and moored to both hillside and railway line. The site condition was also unusual in that the subsoil was 'deeply made ground', resulting in piling works which, again according to Forshaw, 'logically' led to a concrete frame supe structure which was filled in with brick finished in a white render (Forshaw 1935: p.1079). The plan is a version of that seen at Coventry. The two sets of lockers are placed in series with the showers – parallel to and overlapping with them – forming part of a linear zone of services which contains the boots facilities, calorifiers, plenum and boilers, but which ultimately ends in the oriel window of the canteen and the views it creates down the valley. The 'clean' entrance is at the rear of the canteen. Both are at a lower level to the rest of the building, which is accessed by a small dog-leg stair located in the entrance lobby. The pit entrance is found at the far end of the building, facing the railway. The high level of similarity in the planning of Coventry and Hafodyrynys is again indicative of the iterative nature of the pithead baths. In the case of the linear form type, which could offer less potential for large-scale variations, this was especially pronounced.

But the similarities did not stop in just the layout of the plan. Elements seen in both Coventry and Hafodyrynys, for example, are also present in the earlier Blackhall Colliery pithead baths in Durham. Designed by Frizzell and opened on 11th August 1934 for 2,496 men, the latter occupied a constrained site bordered by a railway line on one side, and a main road on the other. An aerial perspective published in 1935 (FIG.81), depicts the building aesthetically as a close relation of Hafodyrynys, a long linear form terminating in a cluster of sculptural curving elements and apparently finished in white render. Meanwhile, the two storeys of the main block are occupied, as at Coventry, with a similar arrangement of the two sets of lockers and showers. Again the lower locker rooms are lit with clerestory windows and the upper ones by two sets each of long rooflights. But there is variation in detail. In opposition to Hafodyrynys, the forms that focus interest in the perspective contain not the canteen and the clean entrance, but the pit entrance and the boot-cleaning and greasing facilities. In addition, the clean, sleek machine-like form that seems to draw upon the adjacent, functional lines of the railway and road captured in the perspective, is

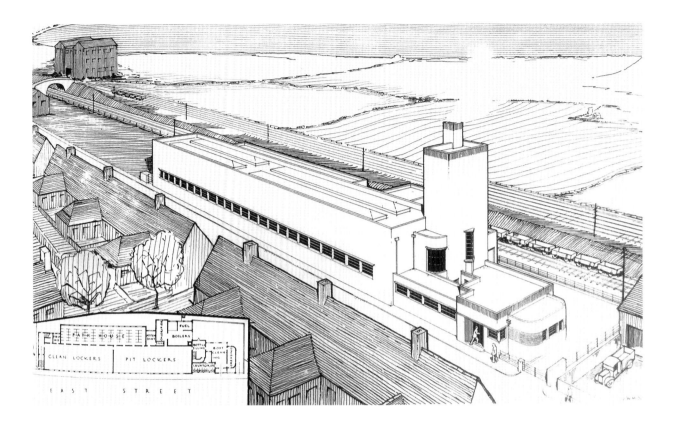

challenged by that fact that the building was actually built and finished in brick. In the photograph taken from the roadway – in other words, from a point of view of how it might actually have been experienced – it looks less like a heroic machine and more like a more modest, if still conspicuous, civic institution.

Other close relatives within the linear form type include Wyndham or Wellesley Collieries, both of which exhibit the norm of combining generic forms and organisations with particular elements or details. In both we can assume the basic arrangement of locker rooms with showers, seen in the schemes discussed earlier. Positioned on a sloping site, just off a main road, the white, abstract and machinic Wyndham Colliery pithead baths for 1,288 men in South Wales, topped and tailed its generic block of lockers and showers with a tower on one end and a glazed semicircular staircase protruding from the other. Its photograph in the annual report for 1938 positions its roof line as a horizontal datum, more or less exactly according to the rules of thirds. As the only truly horizontal element in the photograph, it throws the building into a sharp and harmonious contrast with the chaotic and sublime industrial and natural landscape beyond it (FIG.82).

Wellesley Colliery at Buckhaven in Fife, was conspicuous in that it had been one of the few collieries to provide washing facilities for miners – using the suspension system – before the Samuel Commission and the development of the MWC

81
Blackhall Colliery pithead baths, aerial perspective with plan

82
Wyndam pithead baths in landscape

programme. The new pithead baths building for the pit was designed by Jack Dempster and Donald Denoon Jack to occupy a narrow sloping site next to the railway line, which separated it from the main colliery. Opening on the 6th April 1940, the construction photographs reveal an extensive concrete substructure with retaining walls, which would support the building's brick finished upper forms. Again, the building can be thought of as containing two different parts, the generic and formulaic locker rooms and the shower section, accompanied by more bespoke endpieces which were often called upon to knit into local and specific contexts, while providing visual interest at the buildings' termini.

Like Blackhall and Coventry, the locker and shower block was two storeys with the upper one lit by rooflights. Once again, this meant an elevation articulated by a strip of clerestory windows (lighting the lower lockers), with a large expanse of uninterrupted wall plane above which – in this case – was brick. In the photograph taken from the bridge crossing the railway to the pit, this part of the building presents a dynamic form that resonates both with the linear site and its infrastructural context; the treatment of the strip window, including the thinness of its lintel and sills, for example, is made to echo the rhythm of the sleepers and even the gleam of the lines of the railway tracks (FIG.83). This part terminated in the upright of the water tower with attached chimney. From here the rest of the building adopted a more civic language, including a quasi-pergola motif made from thin rectangular concrete columns. In fact, like

at Blackhall, Wellesley baths had a public face. This had to address an existing urban setting of the town, as well as accommodating the change in level, to allow miners access to the locker rooms and so on. Thus at Wellesley, the bespoke part of the building performed the role of attaching the town to the more generic parts. As the plans of this building remain elusive, it is difficult to discern the exact entry and exit sequences. The Ordnance Survey map (revised 1948, published 1952; NT 3698), however, shows a pathway leading to the other end of the building. This was presumably the clean entrance and, if so, the pit entrance then would have had an incongruously close and intimate relationship with the town. But it was also immediately adjacent to the main pedestrian entrance to the pit: the bridge over the railway to the colliery. Dirty miners must then have appeared on a daily basis in Buckhaven, coming back from their shifts across the bridge to enter the baths. In any case, Wellesley was one of the largest pits in Scotland and, as the map suggests, its visual presence in the town would have already been conspicuous and significant.

Like the selection of L-shape buildings and its variants, this small sample of the linear-form type of pithead baths building is drawn from across most of the British coalfields, and features a range of different architects responding to different conditions, in different sizes of buildings, for different numbers of miners. And while the relationship between clean and pit locker rooms and their showers was more or less systematic, fixed and essentially unalterable within the constraints of the building's form, what is conspicuous is the similarity in the arrangement of some of the components, features and elements which could be have been changed. This emerges even at the level of sometimes quite eclectic detailing. The decorative vertical elements springing from the strip window uprights in the baths finished in white render and designed by Woodland at Coventry in Warwickshire, for example, also showed up in Scotland in the brick baths designed for Aitken Colliery by Dempster in 1934 (FIG.84). The form of the latter, if anything, appear even more indebted to Frank Lloyd Wright's Hollyhock House and its adobe antecedents. As discussed earlier, the MWC architects and their respective teams of senior and junior assistants, despite having different regional responsibilities, all operated out of the same office in London. While the district architect and his assistant tended to remain responsible for the same district, junior staff moved between teams according to the burden of work (Myles-Wright 1954: p.47). For R. D. Manning writing in the *Architects' Journal* in 1938, there was 'an obvious connection between the procedure followed and the atmosphere prevailing in this office … a freshness and vigour in the design … and a quality of *logical* [my emphasis] excellence' (Manning 1938: p.63).[26]

THE BLOCK

Manning also suggested that the opportunities given to younger members of the architectural staff 'when their faculties are at their liveliest' (ibid.: p.64),

83
Pithead baths at Wellesley Colliery

84
Aitken Colliery pithead baths

contributed significantly to the quality of the architecture produced. This was particularly in the case of Frederick G. Frizzell. Born in 1902, and employed as an MWC draughtsman in 1927, he became assistant architect and presumptive author of the aesthetic breakthrough of Dawdon pithead baths when he was only 27 years old. Frizzell was arguably one of the most talented and esoteric of the MWC architects in terms of his use of reference and development of form. And while equally at home in designing both the L-shape and linear plan types of pithead baths – seen, for example, in the elegant project for Lynemouth Colliery (1938, and still extant but in ruins) or at Blackhall discussed above – it is in the final principal type of baths, the *block*, that his work is perhaps at its most compelling.

Although the Elemore Colliery at Easington Lane in County Durham closed in 1974, its pithead baths building – designed by Frizzell and opened in December 1933 – is, remarkably, still extant.[27] Located 'on the crest of a hill and … seen prominently' across the countryside, the building – which accommodated 1,670 men – occupies a small, approximately square site (MWC 1934: p.54). The photograph published in the annual report for 1933 (FIG.85) shows the clean entrance, which allows access to the clean stairs behind, addressing the street. To its left are the gable walls of the clean locker rooms with the range in front of and beneath the tower containing the shower cubicles. The pit locker rooms are hidden in the rear. Of far more significance, however, is the overall form which – as much as it draws on the massing of Dudok's Rembrandtschool (1917–20) – also evokes the forms of a temple, a ziggurat or some other form of pre-Christian religious structure. In the context of an otherwise ordinary village, its looming muscular presence must have been – and indeed still is – striking. Because of this juxtaposing relationship to the village and partly just due to the fact that it is still there, it seems to epitomise, as much as any other and more perhaps than most, the spirit and ambition of the pithead baths programme. Simultaneously modern and archaic it presents a quasi-religious architecture this is visible from afar across the landscape, is by far the most impressive building in the locality, and was designed not only to allow an underground proletariat to wash, but also to celebrate both this achievement and their working-class identity. Close up, the quality of the building materials used, and the consideration given to their use in details such as the horizontal banding of protruding and receding brickwork or in the tiny circular windows, and the evident care taken in the now ruined landscaping, confirms these qualities (FIG.86).

At Ryhope Colliery, also in Durham, what could be termed Frizzell's more expressionist tendencies took advantage of a steeply sloping site to realise a synthesis of landscape and building across a series of levels, which ultimately included the later insertion of a canteen into a void in the building's substructure (MWC 1937: p.75). Opening in March 1936 and serving 1,850 men, the baths were arranged in a symmetrical front of projecting brick forms clustered around a central tower with a chimney in a manner not dissimilar to Dudok's

85
Elemore pithead baths

86
Elemore pithead baths, 2019

87
Ryhope Colliery pithead baths

composition for his Badhuis in Hilversum. At Ryhope, this was articulated with a series of details which interweaved concrete and brick elements in curving, protruding and recessing forms, as well as in the curious T-shaped corner-window details which combined vertical and horizontal emphases (FIG.87).

At Easington, one of County Durham's biggest mines, Frizzell was confronted with another constrained site between the colliery's cooling ponds and a road. Originally designed as a two-storey building but with the option to be extended to include a third, by 1935 the building for 2,240 men was under construction (MWC 1936: unpaginated). The full three-storey edifice, accommodating a total of 3,360 miners, was opened on the 10th February 1937. As at Ryhope, it interweaved a principal material of brick with linear concrete elements of sills, lintels and canopies, but this time into a series of curving and billowing forms at a series of scales. At the larger scale, these included a single storey semicircular form – of the kind seen often in the canteens at other pithead baths – and the entire end of the three-storey locker range which turned the corner to the shower house, both in curving brick and the curving glass of windows. Beneath this in scale were the sinuous, engaged columns which ran along the length of the lockers block and were somewhat incongruously interrupted by the thin and narrow fin-like canopies protruding from the facade which turned two corners to become lintel details for the shower rooms' windows (FIG.88). The photographs of this building help portray it, unusually for a pithead baths, as a dark, sombre, brooding edifice, full of shadow, almost like a German expressionist film set. Its apparent uncanniness is heightened by the eccentricities of the tower with its attenuated corner window, and an interior photograph taken looking up into the void of a board-marked in-situ, unfinished concrete stair. To the left of this latter image, standing on the incomplete ramp of the stairs in front of the tiling that will finish the walls, is the ghostly figure of a young man in glasses dressed quite informally in a short-sleeved shirt. Holding something – perhaps a sketch or notepad, perhaps a camera – the figure is possibly that of the architect Frizzell himself (FIG.89).

OTHER ITERATIONS

If sometimes Frizzell's work appeared to incorporate alternative precedents – or different interpretations of precedents that could, in turn, suggest new aesthetic readings of his pithead bath designs – other architects and buildings in the MWC's programme also occasionally offered idiosyncratic responses to site and brief conditions. Like Frizzell's more expressionistic efforts, these buildings were often executed by architects who otherwise produced buildings which sat more comfortably within what might be described as the programme's more mainstream planar modernist idioms.

While an element in the experimental and early baths of the series, the appearance of pitched roofs within the programme's mature modernist aesthetic

88
Easington Colliery pithead baths

89
Stairwell at Easington colliery pithead baths, possibly showing the architect Frederick G. Frizzell

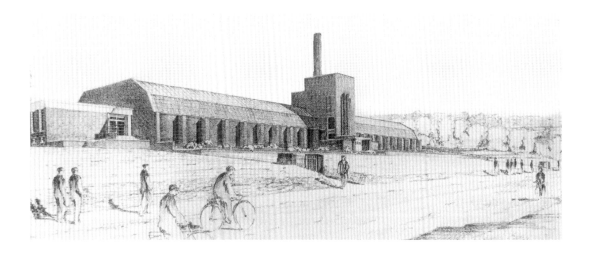

happened often enough for it to be termed a sub-genre. For example, at Madeley Colliery in North Staffordshire designed for 800 men, which opened in December 1934, Woodland produced an L-shaped building complete with an oriel window canteen, a tower and shower blocks all with a flat roof, yet furnished the two locker ranges with a gambrel (double-pitched) roof constructed in what appears to be a lightweight corrugated metal material punctuated with portrait rather than linear rooflights. A gambrel roof (this time with linear rooflights) was also seen in the barn-like locker blocks arranged symmetrically around a central tower by Saise for the Newstead Colliery pithead baths in Nottinghamshire for 1,680 men, which opened in January 1935. Like Woodland at Madeley, Saise also used a combination of flat and pitched roofs at Newstead. At Silverwood, one of the biggest collieries in South Yorkshire, Kemp designed a similar symmetrical arrangement of two large, single-storey barn-like locker wings on either side of a flat-roofed central water tower with a chimney. Here, however, he adopted a Mansart roof through which light was presumably allowed to penetrate the locker spaces within – the walls of these spaces being left blank with no windows. Furthermore, they were beefed up with a row of muscular buttress-like elements which rhythmically articulated the front and rear facades (FIG.90). Frizzell was also involved in creating pitched-roofed pithead baths such as at Morrison Busty Colliery, designed for 1,000 men and opening in June 1936. Here, he created two parallel locker ranges each with the similar profile of the gambrel roof seen in the other examples. Again, this was a single-storey building. The gambrel roof also appears at Morton Colliery in Derbyshire, designed by Dudding or Woodland and completed before 1937.

There are other examples, but what is not clear is exactly why pitched roofs were chosen for these buildings. There were no specific site conditions in these collieries which would have made these measures any more desirable than anywhere else. Nor is it clear why the gambrel-type roof seemed to be the most popular form. Like the other repeated elements within the MWC

90
Silverwood Colliery pithead baths

programme, its use was not limited to a specific region or specific architects. It may, however, have had something to do with economy – as at the earlier pitched-roofed experimental baths, the spans inside could be realised in thin steel trusses and the roofs themselves finished in lightweight materials. In terms of dates, the appearance of these roofs clustered around 1933 to 1935, so it may have been the testing of a new prototype. And while the flat roof was evidently a more acceptable form of modernism, Dudok had deployed pitched roofs in some of his schools and other buildings. Finally, there is also the possibility that the more conservative pitched-roof form may have been preferred by some local miners' welfare District or Local Committees. Made up of both mineworkers and mine owners these committees were, after all, essentially the clients for the baths.

Some of the other more idiosyncratic forms can be explained by specific site conditions and the innovative structures used to resolve them. Tirpentwys (FIG.91) in South Wales (1937) designed for 1,600 men, for example, occupied a site that sloped steeply downwards towards a railway line. The abrupt change in level was negotiated by an open concrete frame structure of rectangular and diagonal elements that formed a platform for the more conventional planar volumes above. A similar arrangement occurred at Denby Grange (Caphouse) in South Yorkshire (1938), albeit on a more modest scale, for 240 men. Here a substructure of light-coloured concrete columns – somewhat reminiscent of Le Corbusier's famous *pilotis* – held a concrete slab which supported above what was, by this date – and apart from the inclusion of a concrete open-air entrance deck – a fairly conventional MWC pithead baths building finished in brick. Like at Clock Face Colliery, at Wheldale Colliery (FIG.92) in West Yorkshire (built for 1,200 men), the baths formed part of a larger infrastructural project which include a covered walkway and footbridge which led to an elevated lamp room. Borrowing perhaps from the Prairie House vocabulary of Frank Lloyd Wright, the lamp room's cantilevered forms, which hung over the ambulance garage and other medical facilities below, provided another unusual counterpoint to the more standard MWC forms and geometries.

Of all these quirks in the conventions established elsewhere by the programme, the building designed for Arniston Colliery in Midlothian by Dempster, and opened in February 1938, was perhaps the most outlandish and spectacular. Nicknamed 'the spaceship' by local miners (Allison 1994: p.63) it was conceived and executed in a fully circular form containing a series of concentric rings which stepped up in section towards a central water tower complete with radiating fin-like elements. Built to accommodate 570 men and equipped with 52 shower cubicles (Benton 1979a: p.305), the clean and pit locker rooms occupied the outermost zone along with two interior wedge-shaped blocks of other accommodation sitting between and separating them. A larger wedge contained the toilets and calorifiers next to the clean entrance and the boot-cleaning/greasing and bottle-filling facilities adjacent to the pit entrance. A smaller one contained the attendant's room and ambulance and first-aid

91
Tirpentwys pithead baths

92
Wheldale Colliery pithead baths

services opposite (FIG.93). All these spaces were lit by a continuous band of clerestory windows which formed a ribbon around the exterior wall. The showers occupied an inner zone above which the roof stepped up to admit a further band of clerestory windows. This happened again in the innermost band immediately below the tower which contained the plenum and a staircase access to it. Again, as at the likes of Polkemmet – whose forms, by the same architect in some ways anticipate the purer forms of Arniston – these windows, while evidently letting light in, would also – of course – emit it in an even more dramatic fashion. This is made explicit in a drawing published in the

THE BLOCK   129

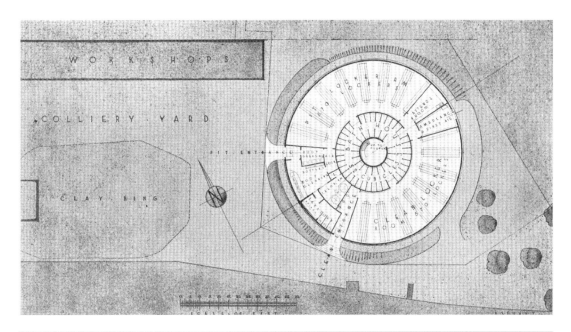

93
Plan of pithead baths at Arniston Colliery

94
Drawing of Arniston colliery pithead baths at night

annual report for 1933 which depicts a night scene with the entire baths, perhaps rather hopefully, shining forth like a floodlit beacon (FIG.94). It has been suggested that the building expressed a kinship with other circular buildings such as Charles Holden's Arnos Grove underground station completed in 1932, or even R. Buckminster Fuller's experiments with his Dymaxion House also in the 1930s (Allison 1994: p.63). But there is also a possible precedent in the light-filled half-circle with concentric zones illuminated by stepping roof elements offered by Walter Gropius's Employment Office in Dessau from slightly earlier in 1928–9.

95
Arniston Colliery pithead baths with landscaping

Unlike the brick building at Dessau, the pithead baths at Arniston was made primarily out of concrete. Photographs taken at the construction stage show the complicated use of timber formwork shuttering to achieve the pop-up roof rings. The necessity of such innovation within an already unorthodox building would undoubtedly have added to costs and delays, and helped to ensure that Arniston remained a unique, unrepeated experiment (see Allison 1994: p.63). Finished in light-coloured or white render and skirted with curving landscape features enclosed by concrete retaining walls, another photograph shows the building in its context, its pure forms and pristine condition shortly after completion. The traditional and utilitarian brick building on the left-hand side of the image demonstrates, through juxtaposition – as if this was necessary – the thoroughly radical nature of the architectural form achieved here (FIG.95).

SMALLER PITHEAD BATHS

The Coal Mines Act of 1911, while having proposed the provision of pithead baths under certain conditions, had also exempted collieries which had 100 miners or fewer and/or had a forecast of fewer than ten years of production before their deposits were exhausted. As the cost per bather increased as baths become smaller, this was predicated on economic grounds. The Miners' Welfare Committee had subsequently decided not to exclude such collieries entirely, but instead try to develop 'less substantial and costly installations than the normal' pithead baths, using 'rapid methods of construction' for short-life pits. As a result 14 installations, accommodating from 24 to 288 men each, were constructed between 1934 and 1939. These trialled 'reduced scales of accommodation, modified standards of finish', as well as alternative approaches to building including prefabrication techniques borrowed from British Army camp – or other temporary – structures, and the use of timber and steel frames with steel or asbestos cladding (MWC 1946: pp 12–13).

The scale and layout of some of these installations such as at Brora in Sutherland – the remotest outpost in the archipelago of British coalfields – was similar to those facilities for women coal workers in Lancashire or Scotland, such as at Clock Face Colliery described above. Designed in 1936 for just 24 male miners, Brora was also the smallest pithead baths. It still contained the usual two sets of lockers but with an open and communal shower room instead of the usual cubicles. All these were somewhat incongruously located under a pitched

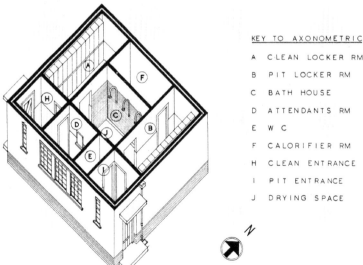

96
Perspective and axonometric of pithead baths at Brora Colliery

KEY TO AXONOMETRIC

A   CLEAN LOCKER RM
B   PIT LOCKER RM
C   BATH HOUSE
D   ATTENDANTS RM
E   WC
F   CALORIFIER RM
H   CLEAN ENTRANCE
I   PIT ENTRANCE
J   DRYING SPACE

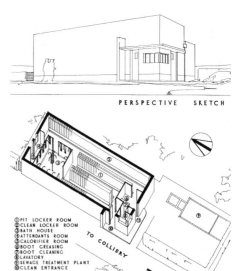

roof, with traditional Scottish crow-stepped gables. Everything else – the attendant's room, a space for the calorifier, and the toilet – were placed in an attached and moderately more modernistic volume with a flat roof and thin canopies projecting over the pit and clean entrances (FIG.96).

Small size did not mean an indifference to a modernist expression. A precursor to Brora, Grange Ash Colliery in West Yorkshire designed for 200 miners and

97 and 98
Photograph and axonometric and perspective drawings of Grange Ash Colliery pithead baths

99
Tillicoultry pithead baths

opened in August 1936, for example, was a svelte roof-lit, flat-roofed brick box. A photograph published in 1937 focuses, in a familiar way, on the nearest corner, which is articulated by the pit and clean entrances (FIG.97). These are linked by a thin concrete canopy whose line is picked up in the lintel and sill of the corner window below. These elements (along with the mysterious and possibly decorative piece towards the end of the left-hand wall) provide an economical and strategic source of visual interest in an otherwise mute form. The forms of the previously cited pithead baths at Tillicoultry, completed by 1938 for 70 men, were either more interesting or less resolved. Constructed in buff brick, a mixture of soldier course coping details on some parts of the building, and concrete parapets elsewhere, combined with other slightly curious elements – such as an inwardly curving entrance space and a glazed lean-to roof (presumably containing the showers) – to make a building of a domestic scale but with civic pretensions. The new and hopeful patch of planting and landscaping in front of it perhaps confirms the tension within these aspirations (FIG.99).

PREFABRICATIONS AND MASS PRODUCTION

Perhaps the most significant in the series of small pithead baths was Alexandra Colliery in Lancashire, for 216 men and opening in 1939. Constructed in a steel frame and clad with prefabricated double-sheeted asbestos walls, it was built as an experiment to test whether these alternative materials and methods could be of benefit 'on grounds of simplicity and speed of erection and by adaptability to unit construction on a larger scale' (MWC 1940: p.13). It is interesting to contrast this pithead baths building with the previous one at Tillicoultry which opened just a year earlier. While the latter is still explicit about its civic pretensions, Alexandra's facilities adopt another rhetoric, one which is far more candid about displaying how it was made and the components used. The walls, which appear to be prefabricated panels, are the same on both the inside and outside of the building and give a vertical rhythm to both rooms and elevations. The shallow pitched roof appears to be of a similar material and is stopped at the eaves level by a metal parapet. Like the other pithead baths, clerestory windows still illuminate those interiors where privacy is necessary, but the water tank, the usual site of a coming together of horizontal and vertical forms and the opportunity – taken even in the tiny building of Tillicoultry – for an architectural statement, is here simply perched naked on the roof (FIG.100). It is like the qualities of the mass-produced and unchanging elements found, for example, in the interior of all pithead baths – what Semper and Muthesius might have termed the 'product-objects' – which have become the expression of the architecture itself, displacing in this building at least, the need for a formal, civic language. In this way, this little building is prescient. And not just superficially in the treatment of the water tank that will be echoed in Alison

and Peter Smithson's school in Hunstanton a decade later. It anticipates another form of modernism, one that in initiatives such as the Consortium of Local Authorities Special Programme (CLASP) schools and elsewhere, would – under the aegis of the new welfare state – increasingly address some of the same social issues that had been at the centre of the MWC's architecture by means of lightweight and alternative forms of construction, standardisation, mass production, modularisation and ideas of flexibility and adaptability in buildings (see Wall 2013).

This future would be shared by developments in the pithead baths programme itself. Commencing during the war in March 1941 – when the Miners' Welfare Commission (as it had become) requested some priority over building material when they became available after the war – by 1943 the Commission had submitted plans for a building programme that would aim to provide all collieries with baths within ten years of the end of hostilities. By 1944, 'a careful overhaul of methods of organisation' had been initiated and 'every item of the standard designs of accommodation, structure, plant, fixtures, fittings and furniture' reviewed and modifications made. 'Speeding up the planning, construction, and organisation, and obviating delays' become the subject of a special study and precipitated a decision to adopt a more widespread application of mass production and standardisation as the most effective means of achieving this (MWC 1946: p.11). Between 1927 and 1940, 325 baths accommodating 407,000 men and women had been produced, an average of about 30 baths per year. The new programme was even more ambitious and meant the construction of 510 new facilities for a total of 321,000 workers. Immediately after the war, the proposed timescale for this was cut from ten to seven years. In 1946, as mentioned earlier, 31 contracts for pithead baths were issued. Consequently the programme then demanded a rapid increase to 60, 120, 120, and 130 contracts in the years 1947 to 1950, 'allowing the sixth and seventh years for completing contracts, with only 50 new ones in 1951 and 1952' (MWC 1946: p.12). In fact, by 1955 the number of baths operating had increased by 70 per cent to 622 accommodating a total of 676,000 miners and representing 90 per cent of the required facilities (Sales 1956: p.102).

This new series of buildings never attained the rarefied aesthetic functionalism presaged by the pithead baths at Alexandra. Neither, however, did they return to the heroic period between 1933 and 1939 when, according to the *Architects' Journal* 'the work of the Miners' Welfare Committee was of the greatest interest to architects' (Anon. 1954c: p.42). While the anonymous writer's observation may be true, it also misses the point. Many of the greatest significances and achievements of the pithead baths programme were hidden or denied a public view. As previously stated – and somewhat acknowledged by the MWC itself – the greatest impact was probably within the homes of mining families (FIGS 101 and 102). Furthermore, the baths buildings themselves were sequestered in often isolated locations and only a small few of those

100
Alexandra Colliery
pithead baths

whose aesthetic form or other significance made them conspicuous, made it into the public eye. Outside the annual reports and those discussed in the architectural press, there are many pithead baths buildings – including the still visible site outline of the one at South Bantaskine Pit in Falkirk, less than ten minutes' walk from where I was born and grew up – for which no apparent record exists, even in unpublished archives. We may never know exactly what they looked like although, given the consistency of the architecture programme they came from, we can form a better than rough idea. As discussed above, the attrition rate of these buildings has been devastating. Of the more than 600 buildings created, only a handful remain. Some of these, such as at Big Pit in South Wales – which allows the visitor to experience at first hand the materiality and physicality of this building type (see FIGS 103 and 104) – are in museums. Others exist only in fragments and are used for other things: as at Dullatur (FIG.105) in Lanarkshire in which a farmer stores machinery and other material; or at Highhouse Colliery in Auchinleck, which now houses light industrial workshops. Still others, whose shells at least are still complete, such as at the Grade II listed Lynemouth described by Pevsner in *Northumberland*[28] – or Penallta in South Wales, or Chatterley Whitfield in Staffordshire – are empty, stripped of their equipment and fittings, and in various stages of ruin.

It is both significant and, perhaps paradoxical, that some of the more architecturally conservative work produced under the Miners' Welfare Committee/Commission (but usually not by its architects) – such as the parks and recreational areas, including bandstands, mining institutes, hospital and health centres, swimming pools, educational facilities and other interventions – have had better survival rates. Often created within the community rather than within places of production, they have frequently remained as critical pieces of social infrastructure, even as the communities surrounding them declined and fragmented after the local pits closed. Hidden in plain sight, their origins within an industrial nation, and an enlightened approach to a particular workers' welfare, is often obscured. Of the rehabilitation centres established in historic stately homes some – such as Blair Castle near High Valleyfield on the northern bank of the River Forth in Fife – still (in 2021) house aged and injured miners. Others have reverted to other uses including returning via the property market to single family occupancy as at the aforementioned Kirkmichael House in Ayrshire.

It could be argued that the greatest design advances of the pithead baths programme took place not in the incorporation of a Dudok-inspired modern aesthetic, but rather in the less visible research into – and analysis of – European and other industrial bathing systems. Its incorporation – through the consequential reassembling of their programmes into separate clean and pit sequences complete with heated lockers in a new, basic repeatable typology for baths – produced a Ur-form whose principles were followed in all subsequent iterations. Under this conception, the utilitarian and prosaic

101
A miner's home *before* pithead baths, as portrayed by the MWC

102
A miner's home *after* pithead baths, as portrayed by the MWC

experimental installations of the late 1920s represent as much of a breakthrough as the mature aesthetic forms seen, for example, at the likes of Betteshanger or Snowdon Colliery in Kent. And yet as a source of morale and an expression of both dignity and working-class identity, the aesthetic and form of these later buildings were essential to their perception, acceptance and transmission both within and outside the coal industry.

Part of the significance of the MWC's pithead baths programme lies in the establishment of all these things simultaneously within an organisation that understood the uses and qualities of both system-built and bespoke forms of architecture, and combined them in the rapid production of iconic buildings. This architecture was produced under pressing need, in a time of economic depression and shortages, by a group of architects and other professionals who had to be in constant communication with various client bodies and committees, and responsive to shifts in legislation and policies. And while the final generation of pithead baths produced in the late 1940s and 1950s – exemplified in facilities such as at Brookhill (Nottinghamshire, 1952), Nuneaton (Warwickshire, 1954), Lady Victoria (Midlothian, 1954) and Dudley (Northumberland, 1957) – did not quite meet the wholehearted approval of, for example, the *Architects' Journal*, its architectural output, redesigned and adjusted to negotiate the new reality of both post-war constraints and opportunities, provided an even more effective and efficient provision of services. For this, Cecil George Kemp and Jack Dempster, the successors to John Henry Forshaw as chief architects, must be credited.

Kemp's tenure from 1939 to 1949 also coincided with another momentous moment, not only for the Miners' Welfare Commission, but also in the history of the coal industry and, indeed, the history of Britain – the long awaited nationalisation and the creation on the 1st January 1947 – Vesting Day – of the National Coal Board. The Coal Industry Nationalisation Act of 1946 also created the National Miners' Welfare Joint Council on which members of both the Board and Commission were represented – members of the Commission becoming automatic members of the Council. On the 1st July 1952, under the Miners' Welfare Act, the Miners' Welfare Commission was essentially dissolved and its responsibilities absorbed within other bodies. The final acts in the pithead baths programme were undertaken by an altered and decentralised structure, the Divisional Boards of the National Coal Board, Architects' Department, while other welfare buildings for miners 'as civilians' would become the responsibility of the Coal Industry Social Welfare Organisation (CISWO) (Myles-Wright 1954: pp 42–8).

By the time English architect and planner Henry Myles-Wright wrote his valedictory of the Miners' Welfare Committee architects' department in 1954 in the *Architects' Journal*, 50 per cent of the architectural profession in Britain was employed in public, or what Patrick Abercrombie had termed, 'official' practice. While describing the pithead baths buildings produced by the MWC

103
Wall finish at Big Pit

104
Locker details at Big Pit

105
Detail of rainwater hopper in the remains of Dullatur pithead baths, 2019

as 'pioneering', Myles-Wright also suggested that the modern vision they pursued had been transformative not only as described here, to the social conditions of the miners and their families, but also for the architecture profession itself in Great Britain, and a generation of young, forward-thinking architects for whom the unlikely site of coal mining 'seemed to prove the truth of their hopes and a beginning of their realizations' (ibid.: 44).

PART II

SETTLEMENT

WELFARE BEYOND THE PITHEAD BATHS

When discussing the contribution of the Miners' Welfare Committee, it is easy to become preoccupied with its production of pithead baths. But within its remit to support 'such purposes connected with the social well-being, recreation and conditions of living of workers in or about the coal fields' (Mining Industry Act 1920), the reach of MWC's other activities and strategies was enormous. It provided health facilities in the form of convalescent centres, hospitals, ambulance schemes and nursing services, and facilitated the development of therapeutic treatments such as hydrotherapy and the use of artificial solaria to counteract the lack of natural sunlight experienced by miners; educational grants and scholarships which allowed mineworkers and their children to acquire skills and pursue interests and careers both inside and outside the industry; facilities for indoor leisure largely through the construction of miners' institutes which, while varying in function individually, could host a variety of cultural and other amenities including theatres, libraries and reading rooms, dance halls, cinemas, billiards and other games rooms, child welfare clinics, gymnasia and hobbies rooms, slipper baths and swimming pools and even provided space to rent to shops, offices or banks if desired, for the convenience of mining communities. There was also, of course, the construction of outdoor leisure facilities. The majority of these, in addition to the provision of general sporting venues and playing fields, and so on, were dedicated, as a first priority, to the establishment of safe spaces where miners' children could play (FIG.106). All this, it should be noted, existed outside – and in

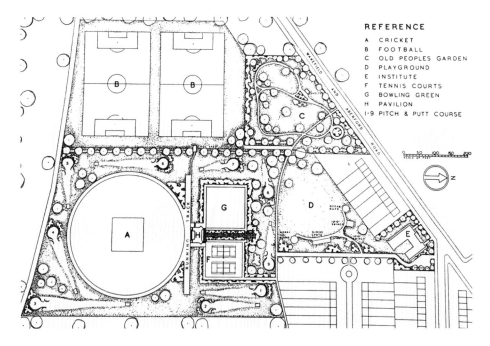

106
Recreational grounds at Hamstead Colliery, South Staffordshire, 1937

addition to – the workplace initiatives which included the pithead bath schemes and their ancillary service such as canteens (FIG.107) and bicycle storage, as well as other developments designed to improve working conditions, such as attempts in some collieries to provide a supply of fresh water underground. These, finally, were connected to the ongoing funding of research which focused not so much on developing the methods of working coal or its utilisation, but rather on the onsite health and safety of those charged with its extraction (Mines Department 1931: pp 26–59).

It has been suggested that architecture and space – in the form of 'social housing, school and universities, hospitals and health centres, leisure complexes, arts centres … nationalised industries, infrastructures' – the building of cultural, health, educational and leisure facilities were central and critical tenets in the development of the welfare state project in Europe (Swenarton, Avermaete and Van den Heuvel 2015: pp 1–2). In other words, during *les trente glorieuses* following the Second World War, these modern socio-spatial initiatives relied upon the production of architecture and space for their delivery, not only to fulfil functional criteria, but also, in terms of aesthetics and form, to transmit the idea of a welfare state ideology and its principles. Under this conception it can be argued that the buildings and other spatial and infrastructural interventions produced under the MWC some years

107
Coventry Colliery canteen

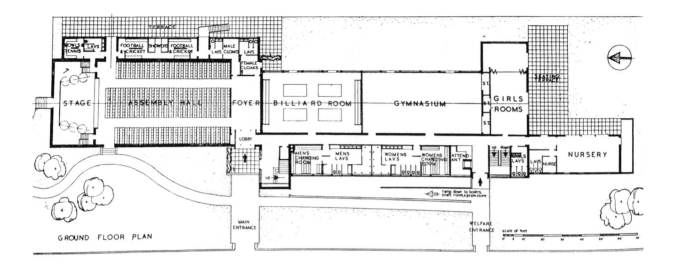

and decades earlier – created as part of a democratic redistribution of wealth – represented an early, embryonic version of this. Thus, individual buildings such as the Kells Welfare and Community Centre in Cumberland, designed for a particular mining community, can be seen as prototypes of the public, civic and state-funded infrastructure that would become translated and universalised across the general population beyond the coalfields in the years following 1945.

Perched above the town of Whitehaven overlooking both the Irish Sea and the Solway Firth, Kells Community Centre was the result of a combined contribution of funds from the National Fitness Council and the Miners' Welfare Commission. On the outside, it displayed a similar architectural language to the pithead baths: sleek, low-slung, flat-roofed brick forms with a horizontal emphasis accentuated further by ribbons of strip windows. Inside, however, the community centre accommodated a composite series of facilities for health, recreation, sport and amusement (FIG.108). Designed by J. A. Dempster and H. Smith and opening in 1938, the building took at least some inspiration from the Pioneer Health Centre in Peckham (designed by the renowned modernist engineer and architect Sir Owen Williams) which Forshaw had visited in 1936 not long after it had opened.

In his report to the MWC on his visit, Forshaw described the building as a 'vast undertaking, organised primarily to study social problems principally from the psychological and medical aspects' (Forshaw 1936: p.1). Meanwhile, an article in the *Architectural Review* written in 1935, had termed the Pioneer Health Centre 'a field experiment in applied biology'. The author celebrated the building as a positive attempt at social engineering under aspects of medical surveillance aimed at the unit of the family and effected through the active agency of architectural space and form (Richards 1935: p.7).[1] Light and cleanliness were harnessed as design elements conducive to fitness and health. As is well known, a top-lit swimming pool forms the central hub of this rectangular building whose periphery was occupied by a series of other spaces dedicated to the mixing of social, medical and health purposes: a gymnasium, a children's playground and day nursery, a lecture room on the ground floor, a lounge (which sold beer) and a lounge and cafeteria which looked into the swimming pool area on the first floor – with medical consulting rooms, spaces for a dental practice, library and rest room, and areas for study and recreation, on the second floor. All this was realised in a minimalist framed structure of splay-headed columns and glass curtain walls, adapted from Williams's own earlier works at the Boots pharmaceutical factory at Beeston, near Nottingham. Forshaw was somewhat impressed, especially with the 'maximum "open spaciousness" … and the feeling of being unconfined in room and in activity' which he surmised was reflective of the philosophy behind the building. However, and perhaps understandably given the predilection for Dudok and the brick wall in MWC's pithead baths, on the whole he felt there was 'too much glass'. He also remarked, rather sniffily, that with regards to the 'changing rooms, sprays – in cubicles – and lockers … we [the MWC] have nothing to learn from the Centre'. Finally, he was ambiguous on what he perceived as the austerity of its finishes, suggesting that a coat of distemper here and there might have relieved areas of untreated concrete (Forshaw 1936: pp 2–3).

At Kells, the central hub of the swimming pool space at the Pioneer Health Centre was replaced by a multipurpose 'assembly' hall, capable of seating 659 and which could be used as a cinema, theatre, concert hall or, with the removal of the chairs, for dancing. Instead of clustering around this space as at Peckham, the rest of the building was strung out in a linear form, taking advantage of the abundant space of a non-urban site to create a relationship with both the landscaped ground on its public roadside and the playing fields to its

108
Kells Community Centre, ground floor plan

109
Nursery, Kells Community Centre

rear. The central hall was realised as a large unfenestrated brick box which also contained the entrance space and foyer. The foyer separated this part of the building from the rest of its more specific activities which were lit by the strip windows: a billiards room, double-height gymnasium, girls' room, nursery (FIG.109), and the building's lavatories on the ground floor; and a games room, boys' room and refreshment area with a terrace on the flat roof above the nursery, on the second floor.

While the Kells Welfare and Community Centre was less candid in its enthusiasm for aspects of social engineering than the Pioneer Health Centre, it acknowledged and was emblematic of a similar perspective. This was shared in one way or another, explicitly or implicitly, by all the works of the MWC programme: the ability of architecture and the spatial environment to instil new behaviours at the level of the individual which, if repeated often enough, would contribute to a progressive and positive reshaping of larger communities. This tenet was central to the ethos of architectural modernism and also lay at the heart of the slightly older concept – shared by Forshaw and evoked in his interests in the synthesis between landscape, health and planning – of architecture and space being agents of 'reform'. But if the activities and architectures of the MWC formed paradigms for the civic and social infrastructures that would transform British society after the Second World War, there was one critical ingredient missing. While it has been argued above that the installation of pithead baths effected a revolution in domestic circumstances for mining families, from the beginning – and as was made clear in Section 20 of the Mine Industry Act of 1920 (which established the Miners' Welfare Fund) – housing was unambiguously excluded from the support and actions of the Fund.

And yet, as it emerged from its insalubrious beginnings to address the exponential growth in the coal industry and its workers during the late 19th and early 20th centuries, the housing of miners would, through a combination of factors and agents, simultaneously become a critical, formative and influential element in the making of innovative new forms of modern, 20th-century housing and the design of new types of settlement both within and beyond the coalfields. This would occur at a series of scales, both before and after the Second World War.

TRADITIONAL MINING SETTLEMENTS

Sir John Sankey's description of the conditions of miners' housing in 1919 as 'a reproach to our civilisation [where no] official language is sufficiently strong to apply to their condemnation' (Sankey 1919b: p.ix) was just one in a series of critical observations on a controversial topic that had exercised social, sanitary and medical reformers and critics for many decades. These ranged from more recent and regional examples such as Dr John C. M'Vail's *Report of the*

110
Miners' Housing in early 20th-century Scotland, from M'Vail

111
Typical arrangement of miners' housing in early 20th-century Scotland, from M'Vail

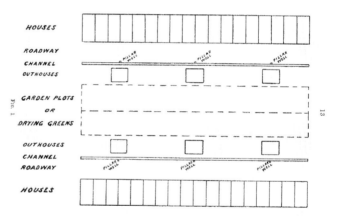

Housing of Miners in Stirling and Dunbartonshire produced under request from the Local Government Board and published in 1911, to older 19th-century accounts like Seymour Tremenheere's comprehensive and national-based inquiry into the *State of the Population in the Mining Districts* conducted under an Act of Parliament and published in 1857 (see FIGS 110 and 111). While M'Vail highlighted some improvements caused by recent acts of legislation, both authors described enduring continuities in conditions of degradation caused by poor quality construction and materials within the housing stock, issues of overcrowding and resultant problems with sanitation which, judging by Sankey's comments published following the end of the First World War, were by then still endemic. Indeed, some of the problems resulted from the reuse of old existing stock from the 19th century which, because of economic and other uncertainties surrounding this extractive industry – especially in Scotland where royalty leases were typically shorter than elsewhere – meant it often made little economic sense to construct new housing. The levels of poverty within miners' housing were the result of a combination of factors, some of which were specific to the industry. Of significance firstly was the rapid growth in coal extraction where the number of workers rose, between 1850 and 1914, from about 200,000 to 1,200,000. As mentioned in Part I, with their families this meant a total of approximately 4 million individuals directly involved in or dependent upon mining, a population almost as big as that of Scotland, and larger than every city in the United Kingdom outside London. Added to this, the precise nature of the work itself – underground, physically exhausting, frequently wet and always filthy – established, especially before the proliferation of pithead baths, specialised housing needs that were, at best, generally unsatisfied (Supple 1987: pp 458–9).

These issues were exacerbated by the particular geography of the coal industry and its tendency, because of the geological distribution of the seams below, to occupy often isolated and rural areas far from other forms of industry and available sources of labour (see, for example, Church 1986: pp 600–611; Daunton 1980: pp 143–75; and Supple 1987: pp 457–62). Many colliery companies, especially in older mining areas such as the Great Northern Coalfield of Durham and Northumbria, constructed much of their own housing settlements to attract workers. Costs associated with housing were simply accepted and factored into the initial investment calculation involved in the development of any pit – a development which, incidentally, could take many years and sometimes decades to produce a return for its original capital outlay. These conditions realised a greater proportion of 'company' or 'tied' housing than was normal in other industries. For example, it has been estimated that by the 1920s, between one quarter to one third of miners' housing was still owned by colliery companies (Supple 1987: p.457), a figure which had decreased significantly since the previous century (Church 1986: p.600). It proved to be an enduring form of tenure continuing even in the newly developed coalfields of the early 20th century, such as Nottinghamshire (Waller 1983). Accordingly on the nationalisation of the industry in 1947, in addition to taking possession of its more obvious facets – 1,500 collieries and their associated plant and equipment, 55 coking ovens, 30 manufactured fuel and briquetting plants, 85 brickworks, and so on – the newly formed National Coal Board also acquired other, more unusual inheritances from the centuries-old industry. These included 140,000 houses, 27,000 farmhouses and agricultural cottages, 233,000 acres of farmland, undeveloped lands set aside for housing and other holdings of miscellaneous land. In fact, 'some entire colliery villages were owned, and the property there included schools and villages halls' (Ashworth 1986: pp 23–4).

For obvious reasons, tied housing tended to proliferate around the more remote pits where there was no other labour supply, and in the north-east of England it was often provided rent free as an additional stimulus to attract potential workers. Such housing, especially in the early years of development in the coalfield, was often built grudgingly and solely for the sake of expediency. The mining landscape of Durham, for example, has been described as 'a sprinkling of nucleated villages within the drab undulating topography' (Daunton 1980: p.143 and passim). Usually huddled as close to the pits as possible, let for free, frequently overcrowded, and unsanitary both inside and in the open areas surrounding and between them, they exhibited little concern for quality, good planning or the provision of amenities. Not only was it not particularly within the interests of colliery companies to make improvements but also, according to a correspondent of *The Times* in 1928, despite the conditions, miners and their families who 'could often afford to pay rent for more adequate accommodation are tempted to remain where they can live for nothing and the will to progress is subtly stifled' (cited in Garside 1971: p.288). The transitory nature of mining was another factor with colliery owners still unwilling to invest any more than they had to in providing housing for pits whose lifespan may prove to be less than they had initially speculated upon. The situation, however, was not geographically homogeneous and, moreover, shifted over time. Other forms of provision and tenure coexisted or even dominated certain coalfields. Some housing was constructed by speculative builders and owned by rentiers; some, increasingly in the 20th century following governmental inducements and subsidies, was provided by local authorities; and some resulted from the activities of the miners themselves, through the establishment of cooperative societies and house-building clubs. The latter became common in South Wales where, at the same time as miners in Durham and Northumberland were occupying rent-free dwellings, patterns of loan-provision and home ownership had been established and consolidated (Daunton 1980).

Regardless of how the housing was supplied or where within the national coalfields it was located, mining communities often shared enough exceptional characteristics for commentators to attempt to define a typical settlement. The first aspect is the isolation and the resultant raw and brutish imposition of headstocks, spoil heaps and other forms of despoilation onto often otherwise bucolic landscapes and agrarian societies. In the earlier mines of the first half of the 19th century, these shock industrial forms – which, in fact, were often quite small concerns – were surrounded by mineworkers' cottages or huts, haphazardly placed, and often constructed in the traditional vernacular materials of, for example, daub walls and thatched roofs associated with poor agricultural labourers' dwellings and indistinguishable from them. Reporting to the *Children Employment Commission* in 1842, Robert Franks described the overcrowding and squalor he witnessed in a miner's hut in the east of Scotland:

> The hut itself is a wretched hovel, perhaps ten to twelve feet square, in which a family of from six to ten individual are huddled together; two bedsteads and sometimes only one, nearly destitute of covering, generally a few stools, sometimes the hanging of a chair, and some damaged crockery, fowls, occasionally a pig or a jackass, dogs, and whatever animals that they possess, share

> the room with the family and the only objects of comfort which present themselves are the port and the fire over which it invariably hangs. The almost general absence of furniture is to be attributed, as the women and men told me, to its giving no convenience in 'flitting', a term used when colliers leave their places of work and seek employment elsewhere
>
> (Franks in Great British Commissioners 1842)

By the late 19th and early 20th centuries, in part a consequence of the rapidity with which coalfields and collieries were opened up and developed over the previous decades, mining settlements were often consolidated into an austere, uniform almost barracks-like urbanism (FIG.112). The *Report of the Royal Commission on the Housing of the Industrial Population of Scotland (Rural and Urban)*, published, just before the Sankey Commission in 1918, drew upon a series of Scottish case studies to arrive at a generic description:

> The 'Miners Row' of inferior class is often a dreary and featureless place, with houses, dismal in themselves arranged in monotonous lines or in squares. The open spaces are encumbered with washhouse, privies, etc., often out of repair, and in wet weather get churned up into a morass of semi-liquid mud, with little in the way of [a] solidly constructed road or footpath – a fact which adds greatly to the burdens of the overwrought housewife.
>
> (Ballantyne 1918)

While Scotland and Durham were considered sites of particularly poor housing conditions, there were inevitable variations. In South Wales, for example, settlements often had to negotiate steep valley topologies sometimes between the pit top below and the slag heap, as demonstrated so tragically at Aberfan, located further up the valley side. Such 'featureless', terraced rows of, at best, utilitarian houses, closely clustered around pitheads attended (as identified and ultimately to some extent rectified by the MWC) by a lack of open space or other recreational opportunities outside the chapel and the public house, became a common and distinctive sight on all the coalfields in the late 19th and early 20th centuries and entered the public imagination.

Images of such villages, for example, were committed to literature by the likes of D. H. Lawrence who was born in 1885 in Eastwood in Nottinghamshire, 'a mining village of some three thousand souls' (Lawrence in Boulton 2004: p.285). In *Sons and Lovers* published in 1913, he described the clearing away of the thatched cottages of an older mining settlement, 'the notorious Hell Row', and its replacement 'to accommodate the regiments of miners … in great quadrangles of dwellings on the hillside … and the Bottoms which consisted of six blocks of miners' dwellings, two rows of three, like the dots on a blank six domino' (Lawrence 1913/2012: pp 3–4). He stressed the abstract character of these buildings as impositions and evoked the sense of coal mines as a modern

112
Typical miners' row housing around Newmoor colliery, Ashington, Northumberland in the 1930s

interloper in an older and rural Nottinghamshire geography, 'an accident in the landscape, and Robin Hood and his Merry Men were not far away' (Lawrence in Boulton 2004: p.285). A photograph of the regimented colliery rows at Lumphinnans in Fife taken in the 1930s (FIG.113) corroborates these qualities within another region. Like Lawrence's description, it captures a mining settlement within a rural setting. Washing is strung out in a long unpaved area, between terraces of mean-looking brick housing, which runs down a slope toward the range of hills in the distance. The presence of children playing amongst the washing lines suggests that this earthen area, which in winter must have been inadequate even for the purposes of washing, served simultaneously as an area of recreation. Miners' or colliers' rows emerged as an identifiable typology – almost a trope – across the coalfields with later iterations, while introducing some improvements and generally being larger in size, following the basic design principles (Griffin 1977: p.159). Photographs taken for the National Coal Board Photographic Records of the village of Denaby Main in South Yorkshire – shortly before it was demolished 1975 – for example, provide evidence of the enduring nature of these unrelenting forms, an expedient architecture of two-up two-down brick terraces, with back lanes arranged in a grid-iron pattern, traversing a hilly topography with a semi-rural setting viewed beyond (FIG.114). The similarities between Denaby Main, Lumphinnans, Lawrence's description and numerous other examples suggests, despite differences in site, location and epochs, something approaching a universality in the image and identity of such places.

It has been suggested that the particularities of the physical environment experienced by miners realised specific forms of culture and society within coalfield communities (see Supple 1987 and Church 1986 for example). Set within the French coalfield of Pas-de-Calais and based on several visits the author undertook to the area, Emile Zola's novel *Germinal* (1885) evoked the

113
Lumphinnans, Fife in the 1930s

114
Denaby Main, South Yorkshire in the 1970s

chaotic lives of a settlement of miners in the last quarter of the 19th century. While almost certainly containing elements of exaggeration, his sympathetic portrayal of a rough-and-ready community prone to disobedience, drunkenness, petty violence, casual sex and militant industrial action, reflected a broader and international public perception of miners as an unruly set of autochthones – men and women who, in as close to a literal description as possible had, in the words of Friedrich Engels and Karl Marx, been 'conjured out of the ground' by the forces of untrammelled capitalist and industrial development (Engels and Marx 1848/1978: p.477). The scenes described by Zola in northern France were echoed in often lurid and dramatic accounts of the coalfield villages in late 19th- and early 20th-century Britain. The sublime horror associated with mining underground had had one of its first mass public airings in Britain in the press and official reports following the Huskar pit disaster in 1838. This, in turn, led to the 1842 report by the Royal Commission of Inquiry into Children's Employment (Mines) which, as well as condemning the appalling conditions and dangers that children had to face, their diet and educational prospects, also managed to convey an atmosphere of potential sexual immorality taking place unseen underground – signified by the minimal dress adopted by workers in the heat and damp of the mine. Female use of trousers and decisions to work bare-breasted, for example, 'made girls unsuitable for marriage and unfit to be mothers' (Great British Commissioners 1842).

The rapidity in the opening up and growth of some of the new coalfields, and the migratory nature of the labour who arrived to work in them, led to some of the settlements – for example, in Leicestershire such as Whitwick between 1830 and 1860, South Yorkshire at Denaby Main later in 1871, as well as elsewhere in other counties and at other times, such as Coatbridge in Lanarkshire – being defined as 'frontier towns', characterised by a large predominance of men, boisterous conduct, gambling, heavy drinking and prostitution (Griffin 1977: p.163). Writing in 1928, J. R. Raynes felt compelled to detail the insalubrious scenes of the 'weekend debauch' in pit villages from the recent past in his history of disputes between capital and labour in the coalfields:

> In the drinking shops one discovered miners, miners' wives, and miners' babies, all in one clamorous babel of voices, drinking, disputing, and bawling. Where seating accommodation was not adequate, they sat on the floor, and women would sit about nursing babies, giving them an occasional sip for the sake of quietness. Moot quarrels were revived in such an atmosphere, and men came to settle matters. There were fights and screams and shouting half the night and not seldom a tragedy.
>
> (Raynes 1928: pp 44–5)

In fact, the public house often appeared in earlier mining settlements before even the building of the local church. As well as slaking the thirsts of workers with a notoriously dusty and hot occupation and offering 'relief, escape and relaxation of tensions' (Duckham 1970: p.259), the pub also often provided the sole recreational facility and the chance to socialise and pursue entertainment outside the confines of the home, such as skittles or quoits. The latter gambling game was captured by Henry Perlee Parker in the famous *Pitmen Playing Quoits* painted in 1836. Set in the north-east coalfield, it evokes miners at their leisure, gambling in the smoky half-light and shabby, insalubrious surroundings of a mine whose slag heap and head stocks loom behind the mostly sooty figures and the rough timbering of a coal yard, illuminated by a blazing torch and bounded by a drain running into a black stream.

Another critical aspect in the generation of a distinctive culture among mineworkers emerged from the highly unusual conditions of the work itself. In the dangerous, uncanny, and psychologically intense realm of being underground, safety and mutual survival was entirely dependent on collective organisation and action. The strong social bonds and sense of solidarity engendered in the pit were often reproduced above in tight-knit connections between work and community where 'life *down* the pit and life *around* the pit were indissolubly linked' (Supple 1987: p.478, emphasis original). But the idea of miners exclusively occupying archetypal, homogenous pit villages was stereotypical. Coal seams presented themselves under urban as well as rural areas, and a significant proportion of miners and their families lived in towns and cities such as Manchester or Newcastle, surrounded by other types of industrial workers and other sources of employment. And yet, their collective experience underground combined with – as recognised by campaigners for pithead baths – an often conspicuously dirty physical appearance when present in the public realm on the surface, contributed to a popular public perception of their being a breed apart. This idea of exceptionalism, which also became engrained in their own sense of identity, encompassed their work lives, their domestic and community environments and helped to engender the forms of collectivised consciousness including socialism, communism and anarchism – as well as the other more traditional religious-orientated systems (including a predominance of Methodism) – common within mining communities.

Allied to these circumstances was the crucial position of coal miners to the British economy. Recent historians have discussed the radical social and economic changes brought about by coal mining and the conditions of its production during the 19th and 20th centuries. The emergence of coal as industry's prime mover displaced earlier sources of power, such as timber or water. This process was one of concentration. The effective yield of a single coal mine – embodied in a condensed high-yield form of carbon – quickly surpassed the energy outputs of vast territories dedicated to forestry or other sources. It has been argued that the concentration of energy within the mineral ultimately found a parallel in those involved in producing, handling and distributing it – the miners and other workers in railway and other forms of workers (Johnson 2014; Malm 2016; and Mitchell 2013). Once again, as George Orwell had summarised in *The Road to Wigan Pier*,

> Our civilisation … is founded on coal, more completely than one realizes until one stops to think about it. The machines that keep us alive, and the machines that make the machines, are all directly or indirectly dependent upon coal. In the metabolism of the Western world the coal-miner is second only to the man who ploughs the soil.
>
> (Orwell 1937/1989: p.18)

These circumstances generated the potential of unprecedented political and social power within a sector of the working class which – in the national coal strike of 1921, the General Strike of 1926, and numerous other examples of stoppages throughout the 20th century – was increasingly both understood and wielded. Indeed, the two principal strikes within the 1920s were only episodes within more enduring antagonisms and discontent within the structure and operation of the coal mining industry, the conditions of its workers' lives and the levels of remuneration that had lasted for decades and would continue for decades to come. But they did serve as explicit triggers to the development and application of what has been described as the '*ameliorative capitalism*' of the Miners' Welfare Fund (Watkins 1934: p.275 cited in Supple 1987: p.477; my emphasis).

Perceptions of militancy, immorality and general lawlessness within an increasingly vital factor in the progress of industrialisation provoked a series of reactions from coal owners, reformers, and the government in 19th- and 20th-century Britain. The government legislation which banned women and children from working underground would ultimately be mirrored by, to begin with, privately funded measures designed to counteract – above ground – some of the unruliness and shock associated with new migratory workforces arriving from all over the country; and further afield – including Ireland – into previously agrarian and traditional landscapes. In time, the manipulation of architecture and the recalibration of domestic and communal space would become central to this. But if the living conditions of miners were ultimately too important to be left to the unfettered forms of expedient capitalist development then – like the execution of the baths programme – comprehensive state-sponsored intersession into the design and construction of housing and settlements for miners took some time to come to fruition, drew upon a series of precedents, practices and circumstances, and was partial and fragmented in its resolution, even in the second half of the 20th century. Within this process, two broad approaches can be discerned: firstly, one of more overt and obvious coercion, exemplified in the likes of Denaby Main; and secondly, that of a more covert and gentle persuasion involving the provision of additional services and the conscious use of aesthetics as agents of reform. The latter found an extremely influential form in the model villages of New Bolsover and Creswell. In practice, however, the two approaches often overlapped and – while the qualities of reform would ultimately proliferate in the 20th century – aspects and tactics associated with the other, more direct, approach also persisted within coalfield communities.

MORALITY, MINING COMPANIES AND MODEL TOWNS

The concept of the model town or village was evidently not exclusive to coal mining. The idea of producing quasi-utopian or ideal environments can be seen as having two facets: firstly, to improve the living conditions of the working class; and secondly, as an act of reform – to settle, educate and 'civilise' potentially boisterous proletarian workforces newly released from traditional social bonds and mores by the coming of the Industrial Revolution. This was famously demonstrated in the likes of New Lanark, developed in the late 18th century by David Dale and Robert Owen, at Titus Salt's Saltaire in West Yorkshire (1851), George Cadbury's Bournville (established in 1893) or – as discussed in Part I – William Hesketh Lever's Port Sunlight (1888). These well-known examples were echoed by many smaller settlements established from the 18th until the 20th century, spread across the British Isles and initiated within an extensive range of industries from, for example, the farming of estates and the realisation of railways, to the brewing of beer, and the making of lace. Not all of these were realised as paternalistic enterprises. Some sought to embody types of socialism. But the latter was not necessarily the experience of coal miners – at least not to begin with.

Examples of model settlements from the 19th century and created specifically for mineworkers were widely dispersed among the coalfields. These included Tudhoe Grange, a suburb of Spennymore, County Durham (1865–70) which was a series of parallel streets with semi-detached cottages in a quarter acre of gardens built by Marmaduke Salvin; Howe Bridge, a suburb of Atherton, Lancashire (1870s), a company village for Fletcher and Burrows containing brick terraces, shops, a village club, baths, a church, schools and garden and sporting facilities; Blackwood in Monmouthshire, Wales (initiated in 1820), built by John Hodder Moggridge, a colony for miners containing shops, workshops, a school and market house and which leased plots to miners to encourage them to build their own houses (it was accompanied by the nearby settlements of Ynysddu and Trelyn); and Coaltown of Wemyss, which originated as an estate village for Wemyss Castle, before becoming a miners' settlement after 1890, and included the provision of a primary school (1896–7) (Darley 2007: pp 277–320).

With reference to the latter, it has been suggested that pit villages connected to aristocratically owned estate mines often became 'pockets of paternalism' (Griffin 1977: p.161). For example, H. S. Tremenheere reported in 1845 that the Earls of Fitzwilliam, at Elsecar in South Yorkshire, provided their miners with accommodation substantially better than normal: 'four rooms and a pantry … a pig-stye … proper conveniences are attached to each six or seven houses … gardens of 500 yards of ground each … Each man can also hire an additional 300 yards for potato ground' (Tremenheere 1857: p.25). Subsequently, the Earls also supported schools, a mechanics institute and a library, as well as providing other forms of relief including pensions for aged servants. This was echoed by the actions of the Earl of Moira in Leicestershire, who in addition to larger and better built housing, provided pensions and financially supported the construction of schools, churches and other facilities (Griffin 1977: pp 161–2). There were other aristocratic owners who followed similar patterns.

These relationships are of significance as they begin to evoke issues concerning the levels of social control exercised within mining villages and settlements by coal owners. Historically this was especially true within Scotland. Here, quite remarkably, miners still experienced forms of serfdom until as late as the last quarter of the 18th century. This has been explained as another consequence of the relative remoteness of coal mines and the resultant endemic necessity to fix a labour force. In places such as County Durham it had resulted in the creation of bonds (and an annual 'binding day') which specified and fixed time periods of work to be executed by the miner at the behest of their employer. In Scotland, however, the Poor Laws of 1579 and 1597 had allowed the option of a convicted vagrant to choose servitude to 'anyone who would keep him in employment'. This had been followed by an Act in 1672 which specifically conferred the rights of coal masters to apprehend vagrants and their children and compel them, without trial, to work in their collieries. There were also other methods of ensnarement[2] and until 1st July 1775 – and the Emancipation Bill (15 Geo. III., c. 28) introduced by Sir Alexander Gilmour Lord Advocate of Scotland, had received Royal Assent – colliers in Scotland were unable to move or find other forms of employment without a testimonial from their former master. By withholding such a document, the employer could – and it has been suggested that they often did – effectively bind the miner to his service for life. In practice these forms of serfdom concerned the miners' whole family and were essentially hereditary. In Scotland and elsewhere until the legislation of 1842, while the father and his older sons hewed the coal, his wife, daughters and younger boys often worked with him underground, either as putters (hauliers) or performing other tasks in what amounted to a semi-autonomous family-centred team operating within the larger structure of the mine. Full unequivocal emancipation of the Scottish miners was only achieved in June 1799 under another Act (38 Geo. III., 56) (Ashton and Sykes 1929:pp 70–83).

Much has been written about how tenets of social control persisted into the 20th century, especially the use of the tied housing system, but also in owners' monopolisation of other services and facilities necessary to the miners within their settlements. The eviction of striking colliers and their families from their homes in Denaby Main in South Yorkshire in 1869 following a lockout dispute over the right to join a trade union, demonstrates one example of the leverage that colliery owners had, not only over the working life of miners, but also their domestic circumstances, as well as those of their dependents. Further evictions occurred in 1877, 1885 and 1902–03 (Benson and Neville 1976: pp 111–12). Moreover, despite the emancipation of the colliers–serfs in Scotland at the end of the 18th century, it has been proposed that anti-tied housing rhetoric expressed by the Scottish branch of the National Union of Mineworkers as late as the 1950s, demonstrated that Scottish miners did not feel that they had achieved absolute liberty until the widespread assumption of housing provision by local authorities and the Scottish Special Housing Association (SSHA) in the middle decades of the 20th century (Phillips 2019: p.60). On the other hand, it has also been argued that, during moments of economic crisis, tied housing offered at least some security of tenure. Miners might be temporarily laid off, but were less likely to lose their homes than those renting on the open market (Daunton 1980: p.162).

Denaby Main has been cited as an example of a planned 'company town', of a kind common in the coalfields. In the late 19th century, filled mainly with migrant workers from other regions, it consisted entirely of two-up two-down miners' cottages with no baths and only outside toilets. Except for two properties, all of the housing was owned by the colliery which had also instigated the local schools (originally called the Denaby Main Colliery Schools), built the parish church (and appointed its trustees), and owned the company shop, hotel and butchers. While the Truck Act of 1872 had severely diminished, if not entirely eliminated, earlier practices by colliery owners of making payments in kind – of goods or vouchers redeemable at company shops (Church 1986: pp 163–4) – what have been described as the 'octopus-like tentacles' of the colliery company also influenced other non-transactional aspects of daily life, such as recreation and village sport. It has been argued that this represented a 'total institution' exercising extensive control over its 'frontier' workforce. In fact, combined with the use of other strong-arm tactics exercised by the colliery owners, including the instigation and deployment of a private company police force, it gave rise to a countervailing attitude amongst its miners. Perhaps paradoxically, Denaby Main became renowned for its workers' militancy (Benson and Neville 1976: p.113, p.142).

While a planned settlement, Denaby Main was evidently not a model town or village. Its construction was not inspired by a spirit of philanthropy and the relationship between the colliery's owners and employees was, it seems clear from oral histories of the place, not one of paternal benevolence and grateful acknowledgement, but rather a more polarised, simmering class-based antagonism which periodically erupted into explicit moments of conflict (see Benson and Neville 1976). This is perhaps apparent within the expedient and mean utilitarian nature of its architecture. The images of Denaby Main from the 1970s, immediately prior to its demolition, affirm an uncompromisingly bleak grid-iron urbanism untroubled by any form of idealism. Instead, it presents a landscape ground out under the influence of the byelaw legislation of the late 19th century which governed rudimentary sanitary measures and defined the typology of regimented, double rows of identical houses facing each other which were familiar to many mining settlements. If the desire was for the control of the population, then the environment produced – which did not allow for much, if anything, above a bare-life minimal standard of existence and where contradictions often remained starkly apparent – was arguably a form of architecture and urbanism which was neither sufficient nor sophisticated enough to realise this.

Although their underlying motivations varied, it can be argued that one of the distinguishing features between model settlements such as Port Sunlight or New Bolsover and mere 'company towns' was a desire on the part of the owners to influence a territory of ideas and attitudes through the holistic use of a physical landscape, one which involved and, crucially, expressed the provision of facilities beyond those of a basic, subsistence living. This is not to say that philanthropic initiatives for model settlements for workers solely embodied the concerns of social control. Rather they can be seen as attempts to resolve certain contradictions of capitalism, including – at least in part – concerns for the improvement of workers' conditions and lives. That these concerns might also attract or create a better class of – or more compliant – workforce was doubly advantageous. Thus, the provision of welfare and the active utilisation and planning of architecture and space became agents both of reform and persuasion. By the early 20th century, earlier more direct forms of coercion were gradually – but not completely – being replaced with subtler methods of inculcation where the properties of aesthetics were conscripted as additional aspects of influence.

New Bolsover and Creswell in Derbyshire offered a bucolic contrast to the bare, grid-iron mining settlements exemplified by Denaby Main and their close cousins in the byelaw housing of industrial cities. Built at the end of the 19th century by the Bolsover Colliery Company, both new settlements were characterised by geometric layouts which arranged houses around large communal green spaces, laid out in grass, planted with shrubs and trees, and articulated by pathways. At Creswell the cultural and recreational intentions for this space were confirmed by the inclusion of a bandstand. At New Bolsover a school occupied the axial point at the limit of its U-shaped half enclosure (FIG.115).[3] The latter was built in 1891 on a gentle westward-facing slope beneath Bolsover Castle, the seat of the Duke of Portland, who owned the royalties to the coal. Consisting of 200 houses it was formed in an open double-U shape of two rows of terraced houses separated by an access road, faced by both sets of back courts. The access road was bifurcated by a tram system, which not only carried the workers to the pits, but was also used to supply coal to their homes and remove the contents of the ash pits and privies (Gaskell 1979: p.446).

This was the arrangement at the backs of the houses. The fronts of the inner houses directly addressed the recreational green space, while those of the outer ones were orientated towards the surrounding allotments, and beyond this, to the countryside. Accordingly, both inner and outer sets of houses within the U – unlike the face-to-face housing of traditional miners' rows – were accorded and enjoyed a close visual relationship with a pastoral or natural setting. This embracing of the rural or landscaped view is reminiscent, within a different architectural idiom, of the aspiration expressed at Jean-Baptiste Godin's ideal settlement Le Familistère de Guise (1859) which promised each of its industrial iron workers the opportunity 'to sit at his window and smoke his pipe or read his book in complete privacy, for all the world as if he were the owner of a villa standing in its own grounds' (Benevolo 1971). Built in 1894 three years later than New Bolsover, the 280 houses of the larger Creswell followed similar principles but within the enclosed form of a double octagon (FIG.160). In addition to the houses and landscaping, other facilities were provided: a cooperative store, an institute and a school in New Bolsover; and a similar set in Creswell. And in both, the relationship to nature and the

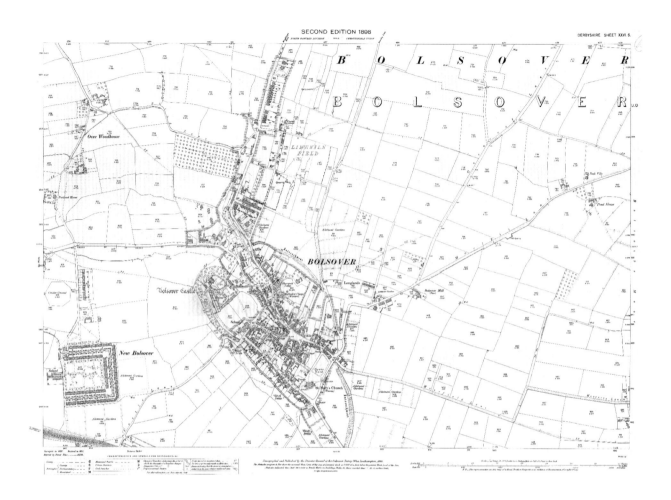

outside was further cultivated by surrounding allotments, pigstys, cricket grounds and bowling greens.

The settlements were built entirely of brick. At New Bolsover, designed by Arthur Brewill and Basil Baily, there was a combination of two- and three-storey houses which reflected, by both size and position, the hierarchy of workers and overseers within the pit itself. A further aspect of hierarchy is provided by both the location and architectural elaboration of the shared facilities of the cooperative store and institute. These formed the termini to the two northern rows of housing abutting them in a rather elegant Arts and Crafts language of arched windows, coupled with corbelled upper bay windows with timbered and infill gables on the store, and similar material and asymmetrical massing of forms on the institute opposite. They were further distinguished from the housing by roof tiles instead of slate.

If the open-ended courtyard of New Bolsover owed something in its overall form to Augustus W. N. Pugin's drawing 'Antient Residence of the Poor', published in *Contrasts* in 1836, and its origins in mediaeval monasticism and

115
Plan of New Bolsover

116
Plan of Creswell

almshouses, then at Creswell this overtly institutional motif begins to break down. This occurs not only within the softening of the overall geometry, but also in the shortening of the terraces into smaller runs and the corresponding making, here and there, of cottage-like, semi-detached dwellings. There is also a greater variety of forms in the architecture of the housing itself with the facades of the terraces and semi-detached dwellings often articulated with straight, as well as curving, Dutch gables. These are especially pronounced in the 'officials' houses' (Griffin 1977 p.165) which, along with the cooperative store and the large and symmetrical institute, signalled the axial entrances to the central green.

New Bolsover and Creswell were conceived of and constructed as prototypical model villages for the Bolsover Colliery Company under the supervision of John Plowright Houfton, its General Manager, along with Emerson Muschamp Bainbridge, its owner.[4] Both retained aspects of overt control in the forms of omissions and surveillance. There were no public houses and no more than three glasses of beer per person per day were permitted within the institutes. There was also the presence of the company policeman who oversaw the workforce and reported any misconduct to the management (Thornes 1994: p.81). However, it is in their function as ideological landscapes that the two model villages are perhaps at their most interesting and influential. In 1906, Emerson Bainbridge, the chairman of Bolsover Colliery was quoted in the *Derbyshire Times* describing the capabilities of the architecture produced to effect moral improvement:

> They thought that it was quite conceivable that if they had the right surroundings, the absence of temptation for the men, the presence of all kinds of facilities for the men to rule themselves and promote their own welfare, there was no reason why these should not be villages where these things should exist successfully – the absence of drunkenness, the absence of gambling and the absence of bad language.
>
> (Bainbridge cited in Gaskell 1979: p.446)

In addition to the evident opportunities to cultivate opinion offered by the schools,[5] institutes and churches provided or partly funded by the management, the design of both settlements – complete with their 'village greens' – counterpointed the isolated but urban-like traditional mining settlements with their repetitive serial forms, with an image of a quieter, ordered and rural-orientated life. This seemed to speak of older social bonds, of a benevolence and deference which perhaps was underpinned by an aristocratic noblesse oblige. This was certainly implied by the positioning of New Bolsover underneath the conspicuous, towering edifice of Bolsover Castle. As well as owning the castle and lands that the village was built on, and the royalties to the coal underneath, the Duke of Portland took an active involvement in dispensing welfare to its community, presiding over a calendar of annual events in a manner akin to a traditional agricultural estate village (Gaskell 1979: p.447). Dominating views from the village, the sight of the castle provided a constant reminder of his role and the miners' place. In 1900, the *Derbyshire Times* recorded the thoughts of a spokesperson for the residents on the spirit of cooperation and the idea of the social contract embedded within the villages: 'Results have proved that the kindly, considerate policy pursued by the representatives of the employers evoked a similar spirit amongst the employed and tended to be to the advantage of both' (cited in Gaskell 1979: p.44).

But if New Bolsover and Creswell purposefully or otherwise displayed the lingering presence of patronage, their embrace of the countryside and its health-giving properties of light and fresh air simultaneously gave them a modern outlook. In this echoed and embodied the criticisms of the industrial urban condition found in the writings and theories of William Morris, Augustus W. N. Pugin and John Ruskin. And while the orthogonal rows of New Bolsover, bent into a U-shape to make an enclosure, may still have been recognisable as akin to the traditional colliers' housing, the more picturesque arrangement at Creswell suggested a new departure, a transition that was equally evident within the career of the architect responsible. Percy Bond Houfton began – like his cousin John Plowright Houfton – working at the Bolsover Colliery in an engineering and managerial capacity, before founding his own architecture practice *after* he had designed Creswell. He went on to design a series of houses and housing, often for collieries, within an Arts and Crafts style. The most conspicuous of these was another model village, Woodlands. This was built over ten years after Creswell, between 1907 and 1909, on the newly developing coalfields near Doncaster for the Brodsworth colliery under the aegis of Arthur Markham, a member of a significant family of coal entrepreneurs.

Woodlands was an extensive scheme of 653 cottages on 123 acres whose houses displayed, in the use of harling, steep gables and overhanging eaves, the influence of Charles F. A. Voysey. Written about by Patrick Abercrombie before it was finished, it was divided into two sections of housing, the 'Park' containing 121 cottages and the larger 'Field' containing 532 houses (FIG.117). The two were linked by a clutch of public buildings including a school, a church and a vicarage, an institute, a building for baths and a cooperative store 'combined in a formal and regular manner with formal planting'. Abercrombie also noted the scheme's location within the historic planting and landscaping of the nearby Woodlands manor house and suggested that the 'natural characteristics' of the 'magnificent forest trees' and 'ring of shrubberies … governed the design of the village'. All the houses were arranged around the peripheries of large open green spaces with the cottages in the 'Park' enjoying additional private gardens. Notwithstanding Abercrombie's comments on the organic nature of the plan, the 'Field' was laid out in a radial form of wide tree-lined avenues with the axial Main Avenue articulated by a double row of trees. Finally, as for the scale of the individual house, he described what must have been an additional boon for miners whose working lives involved hours of work in darkness and fetid spaces: double-aspect living spaces 'lit at both ends'. These living rooms not only allowed the ingress of light from both sides, but also fresh air and cross ventilation. Significantly, Abercrombie reviewed the Woodlands project for *The Town Planning Review* under the title of 'Modern Town Planning: A Comparative Review of "Garden City" Schemes in England' (Abercrombie 1910: pp 111–28). Perhaps of equal significance was the slightly disparaging tone of the entry in *Yorkshire: West Riding* by Nikolas Pevsner for his 'Buildings of England' series written decades later in 1959, which commented on what would become the ubiquity of some of the scheme's characteristics: 'As a model estate built as early as *c*.1910 Woodlands deserves mention, although (or perhaps because) it does not look in any way different from so many council estates built on the fringes of towns between the two wars' (Pevsner 1959: p.557).

That both Abercrombie and Pevsner placed the Woodlands estate within larger contexts of theory and practice, and Pevsner located the scheme as an early manifestation of a style of later municipal estate building is noteworthy. It has been argued that the development of new model industrial settlements in the

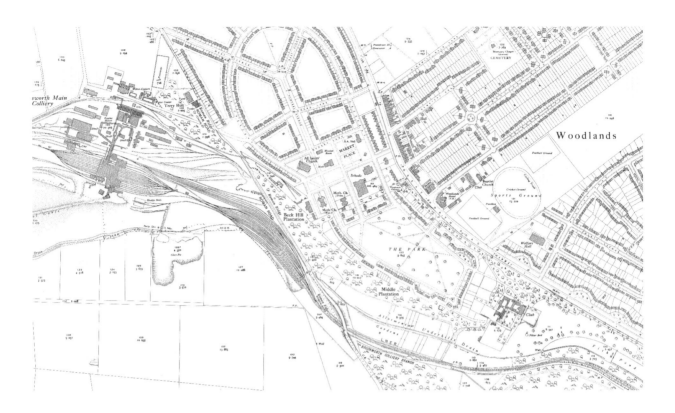

later 19th and early 20th century influenced the town planning movement in part by providing contained moments for 'practical experimentation' (Ashworth 1954; and Gaskell 1979). Certainly, the concerns for light, space, order and the valorisation of the countryside seen at New Bolsover, Creswell and latterly at Woodlands, had also been identified, appreciated and would ultimately be incorporated into the work of another architect who, like Houfton, had cut his teeth as an engineer in a northern coal mining company in the late 19th century. His name was Raymond Unwin.

UNWIN AND COAL MINING

Born in Rotherham in South Yorkshire, Unwin's pivotal influence on the development of planning and housing design in the United Kingdom and beyond has been well acknowledged (see, for example, Cherry 1981; Jackson 1985; Swenarton 1981 and 2008; Miller 1992; Ravetz 2001).[6] Through groundbreaking projects such as at Letchworth (1905) and Hampstead (1906), he was credited along with his partner Richard Barry Parker not only with pioneering the reconciliation of the principles of the Arts and Craft movement with those of the Garden City, but also with the application of this union within economically produced, working-class dwellings (Ravetz 2001: p.57). The resultant rethinking of domestic space and its mass proliferation within social and other tenures of housing between the wars has been recognised as an outcome of the influ-

117
Woodlands scheme by Percy Houfton

ence that his schemes and writings – especially the treatise *Nothing Gained by Overcrowding!* (1912) – exercised over early government planning policies in Britain and in particular, on the influential Tudor Walters Report of 1918. Stemming from a committee which included Unwin himself and chaired by Sir John Tudor Walters, many of the report's findings would become incorporated into the Housing, Town Planning Act of 1919. Not only advocating an architecture of cottage typologies allied with open space that would characterise the immediate post-First World War *Homes for Heroes* programme, the Tudor Walters Report would also define the design and space standards of social housing for more than a generation. Unwin also exerted further influence as an 'official architect', a civil servant firstly in the Local Government Board and Ministry of Munitions during the war, then in the Ministry of Health (firstly as Chief Architect and latterly Chief Technical Officer for Housing and Planning) until his retirement in 1928. After this, and amongst other activities, he became technical advisor to the Greater London Planning Committee and developed, in two reports in 1929 and 1933, ideas that he had first expressed in an essay from 1921. These proposed that 'a green belt [be] preserved around London to protect its inhabitants from disease, by providing fresh air, fresh fruit and vegetables, space for recreation'. But perhaps more significantly, this restriction on the metropolis's growth would be made possible 'by the development of satellite towns' (Unwin 1921: pp 181–2, cited in Cherry 1981: p.93). These concepts would underpin the Barlow Commission from 1940, from which – after the Second World War – the New Towns programme would emerge (see also Part III).

But while Unwin's Oxford-forged socialist beliefs and their debt to the social, spatial and architectural criticisms of modernity and industrialisation offered by the likes of Morris, John Ruskin and Edward Carpenter have been well documented, the intellectual and formative value of his experiences in the Midland coalfields has perhaps been less widely acknowledged. From 1887 to 1891, he served as an engineering apprentice, draughtsman and ultimately chief draughtsman for the Staveley Coal and Iron Company in and around the Derbyshire town of Chesterfield. During this period, his interest in, and absorption of, social and socialist theory was combined not only with a practical knowledge of the intricate workings of the coal industry both under and above ground, but also with activities as a socialist activist and organiser, first in Manchester, and then within the Derbyshire and Nottingham coalfields. In addition, his formal employment as chief draughtsman included an increasing involvement in the design of housing and settlements for rapidly expanding colliery workforces. Accordingly, he accrued an unusual and almost certainly unique set of skills, experiences and connections. This included an intimate understanding and appreciation of the particular conditions of deprivation – of air, light and open space and other environmental inadequacies – experienced by miners and their families within both their working and domestic conditions. In fact, as a designer of traditional miners' row settlements for the Staveley company he was, for a while at least, involved in their perpetuation.

But he also became aware of possible alternatives, was on personal terms with Percy Bond Houfton, and was exposed to some of the consequences of the more progressive and philanthropic ideas of the Markham family, as well as other coal owners. The cultures and environments of coal mining were evidently not the only influencing factor in the formation of Unwin's critique of and prescription for working-class housing. But it is significant that within the mining communities of the Midlands that he experienced as a young man, he found a unique microcosm of some of the preoccupations that would remain foremost in his thinking and practice, not only for the rest of his life, but would also go on to inflect the projects of countless other architects and planners. These encompassed not only the extreme spatial and environmental deprivations that defined working-class lives within the coalfields, but also some enduring paradigms within the planning and design of housing on how to respond to such conditions.

By 1860, the Staveley company had 4,000 employees and a company village with 600 cottages located in and around Chesterfield in Derbyshire. Subsequently, new colliery leases would be agreed with the landowner, the Duke of Devonshire, and the company would diversify into the production of iron (and ultimately chemicals). To begin with, as chief draughtsman, Unwin was made responsible for designing and supervising the making of mining equipment. In an article for the socialist newspaper *Commonweal*, he denounced this task in true Marxist style, as his being 'set to design machinery for the express purpose of displacing labour' (Unwin 1888: pp 108–9; and Miller 1992: p.19). Another article written in 1889 proposed – quite prophetically in the later works of the MWC in its repurposing of manor houses for miners' convalescence – the democratic or otherwise expropriation of Sutton Hall, the manorial seat of the Arkwright Family and its reconfiguration as a setting for a 'happy communal life' of integrated social classes (Unwin 1889).[7]

By 1888, the Staveley Coal and Iron Company was under the control of Charles Paxton Markham, a socialist sympathiser whose brother Arthur would later commission Houfton's scheme at Woodlands. Markham had respect and sympathy for Unwin – presumably knowing about or indulging the socialist activities that the latter sometimes worried may get him fired – and accompanied his chief draughtsman to new pits and on surveys (Miller 1992: p.19). In a relatively early text, written in 1890, again for *Commonweal* entitled 'Down a Pit', Unwin described a day spent underground. He gives a comprehensive and – while acknowledging the danger faced by the miners – a sympathetic, but largely unemotional account of the workings of a coal mine and the experiences of the miners: from boarding a 'Paddy' train with the other workers before dawn; descending in the cages; walking or 'travelling' from the pit bottom via the often very low 'roads' to the coalface; and remerging in sunshine and brightness via a different shaft, over a mile from where he had initially descended, hours later in the afternoon. Of significance is Unwin's detailed grasp of the variety of technical, social and economic aspects of the pit. He discussed the geology of the coal, how it presented itself at the face, and how it was worked – by the hewer who undercut or 'holed' the coal, which was then brought down using gravity and a wedge or a lever, to be loaded into 'tubs' by the filler and taken away. In the colliery he described, this occurred via the traditional and generic 'pillar and stall' method where a series of rooms or chambers were carved out underground with columns of coal left in between to support the roof, before these in turn were – as far as possible – removed to allow the earth – often quite dramatically and suddenly – to resettle. He remarked on the actions of 'creeping', the incremental but often constant movement of the ground above and beneath which squeezed the tunnels or roadways, deforming the timbers placed to hold it back. Alongside these more technical observations, however, he also discussed the social organisation of the coal-getting under piece-work contracts.

> A stall, i.e., a part of the face from twenty to forty yards long, is allocated to one or more coal getters, who are paid at so much per ton for all they send out. Under them will be working one or two, and sometimes three or four fillers, who will be paid by the day. The ponies and the pony drivers are generally provided and paid directly by the employers. There are a few places, however, where it is customary for a sort of contractor to take a district, comprising of several stalls, and to find men, ponies and everything. But the most usual way is for the colliery owners to provide ponies and the lads and pay them directly, while the stall men pay their filler. But here is a curious division of authority. The stall men are responsible for and have to pay their fillers; they have entire control of them while at their work; but generally, they have no power either to engage or to get rid of them.
>
> (Unwin 1890: p.178)

His description of the 'muddle' of contracting and subcontracting systems underground captured and highlighted some of the social and economic complexities and inequities involved within the mining process. Despite variances from coalfield to coalfield these, combined with the intricacies and complications of how coal output, as well other necessary but not directly extractive operations – such as timbering, heading (the making of 'roads') or ripping (raising the height of a road) – were priced, measured and paid for, were a common and ongoing source of tension between miners and their employers and would continue to be so until the second half of the 20th century. Like other commentators, Unwin suggested that health and safety within the mine could be – and often was – compromised by payment by piece rates, causing miners to feel compelled to take unnecessary risks or not perform other less lucrative tasks adequately, to increase their wages or make up for a lack of productivity. The latter could be caused by many different circumstances including the allocation of less productive or more difficult stalls. Accordingly, he welcomed recent government intervention (meaning specifically the Coal Mines Regulation Act 1887) dismissing its pejorative description as 'grandmotherly' and suggested, significantly, 'that a coal pit illustrates better than anything else the advantages and disadvantages of Government regulation [as] the most direct and effective means of carrying out any measure for the benefit of the men' (Unwin 1890: p.189). Finally, while he did not dwell upon it, and perhaps as is inevitable to any commentator who has gone down a pit, he contrasted the conditions below, barely lit by artificial means, with the wholesome natural light of the surface – both at the moment of his descent and then on his return upwards when: 'the first glimpse of daylight casts a reassuring ray on the side of the shaft … [s]lowly we emerge into the full dazzling light, and as we glance at our lamps we wonder how we can possibly have got accustomed to walk by such slender illumination' (ibid.: p.178 and p.189).

Unwin's account of the coal mine appeared on the same pages in *Commonweal* as the serialisation of another, infinitely more famous and influential critical account of society and its environments, one which also used the contrast between light and dark, and cleanliness and dirt, but rather more metaphorically: William Morris's *New from Nowhere*. Along with Edward Bellamy's contemporaneous *Looking Backwards* (1888), Morris's utopian novel has been credited with exerting a huge influence over Ebenezer Howard and his attempts to spatially define a new society in *To-morrow: A Peaceful Path to Real Reform* (1898) and its subsequent republishing as *Garden Cities of Tomorrow* (1902). Memorably, it distinguished between the grimness of contemporary industrial capitalist production and its tendency to dense insanitary urbanisms, with the possibilities of a future which drew on a mediaeval past, dis-urbanisation, or decentralisation, and the moral and hygienic salubrity of the rural village. Its visionary, idealistic depiction of a peaceful, pastoral, natural life provides an acute contrast to Unwin's matter of fact account of the artificial and mineral underground conditions of a coal mine.[8]

Perhaps flippantly, the influential urbanist, planner and writer, Peter Hall, described St Andrew's Church in Barrowhill, near Chesterfield, not only as the first building in the partnership of Parker and Unwin, but also as 'the birthplace of garden cities' (Hall 2014). Built by the Staveley Company with an endowment from the Duke of Devonshire for miners in 1895, its redbrick utilitarian exterior was designed by Unwin but with many of the interior fittings, including a mosaic reredos by Parker (Miller 1992: p.24). These were accompanied by stained-glass windows by William Morris. But perhaps of more interest is the character of the series of housing projects realised before this for the expanding colliery company, involving Unwin in at least some capacity, and located around the Chesterfield area in: Poolsbrook, Brimington, Barlborough, Markham Colliery and Warsop Vale. These mostly echoed the familiar abstract pattern of the typical miners' row housing described above, defined by terraces and back alleys with privies, an arrangement that echoed – but was not necessarily subject to – the byelaw legislation that Unwin would later rail so vehemently and successfully against. Of these settlements Poolsbrook, built between 1892 and 1893, was one of the largest and the most unrelenting in its form. Set between two railway lines in a landscape already scarred by mining, it comprised of 216 cottages in blocks of 12, arranged in a rectangle of three blocks per row across six rows and served by a school, a chapel and a public house (FIG.118).[9]

Unwin apparently threatened to resign unless the houses were supplied with hot water and baths, but his wishes were not carried out (Jackson 1985: p.25; Miller 1992: p.20).[10] His frustration was perhaps indicative of a growing awareness of the agency of space in what has been identified as a shift in his political beliefs from an early idealism – which involved, for example, an adherence to the abstentionism from the processes of parliament prescribed by William Morris and the Socialist League – to a more pragmatic position. Ultimately, this would lead to his acceptance and advocacy of State intervention not only – as he proposed in 'Down a Coal Pit' – into the working conditions of the working classes, but also their domestic and other circumstances. Like others before and after him, the change in his beliefs can superficially be described as a choice

118
Poolsbrooke miners' housing

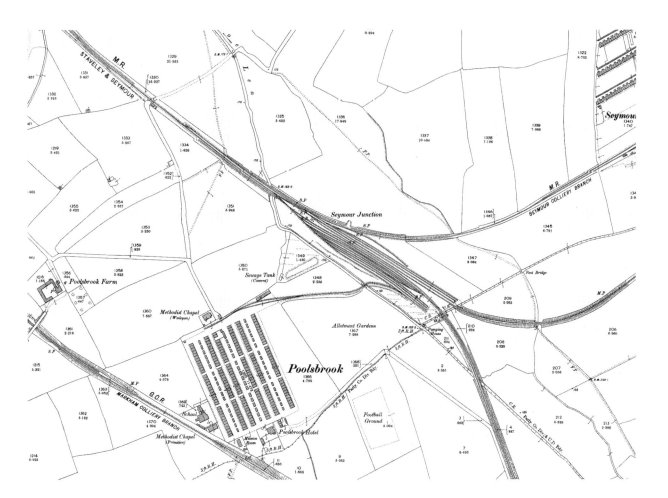

between a desire for immediate revolution and the embracing of a slower, more incremental path of reform and improvement. Mark Swenarton has argued that in Unwin's case this was at least partly the result of his direct experience within the northern socialist movement. This led him from the 'joy in labour' espoused by Ruskin to a position, influenced by the writings of Edward Carpenter and his advocacy of the 'simple life', where the consumers – the occupants or users – of buildings rather than their producers assumed a greater importance (Swenarton 2008: p.96). In the case of housing this is particularly significant as it suggests a concomitant shift in emphasis from male industrial workers to female domestic workers. It is also clear that beyond whatever ideological tenets of 'practical socialism' influenced Unwin, his unique circumstances and set of skills had allowed him to directly encounter, experience (including living, at least for a while, among them in Chesterfield), empathise with, and intimately understand a very specific section of the working classes. Indeed, even on a personal level, he was close friends with Katherine Bruce Glasier, the feminist, socialist and campaigner who would later memorably call for pithead baths as 'white shining Temples of Health' to adorn every mining village in the country (Glasier and Richardson 1912: p.4). Along with her husband John Bruce Glasier, she was a witness at his wedding in 1893.

While understanding and accepting the reasons for it and sympathetic to its existence, Unwin's criticism of the strictures and inflexibility of the byelaw housing legislation that followed the Public Health Act of 1875 is well known. In *Cottage Plans and Common Sense* (written for the Fabian Society in 1902), for example, he acknowledged its positive effects in securing 'air-space' for each house, but suggested that it failed in providing another essential prerequisite, one which it is clear was often particularly deficient within miners' lives: light. He demanded, therefore, that:

> [E]very house shall be open to a sufficiency of sunshine. Every house should at least get some sunshine into the room in which the family will live during the daytime. Into as many more rooms as possible let the sun come, but let no house be built with a sunless living room: and this condition must cease to be regarded merely as *desirable* when it can conveniently be arranged: it must be insisted upon as an absolute *essential* [emphasis original].
>
> (Unwin 1902: p.3)

He proposed a series of measures by which this could be achieved, 'that every house should turn its face to the sun, whence come light, sweetness and health', and that the orientation of streets should also be made to 'fall in with this condition'. Of equal importance was:

> [T]he consequent abolition of the backs, back yards, back alleys and other such abominations which have been too long screened by the insidious excuse of that wretched prefix *back*. For if every

house is to face the sun, very often it must also have "its front behind" [emphasis original].

(ibid.: p.3)

It is easy to see Unwin's prescriptions within the context of his intimate knowledge of the spaces of mining settlements. Indeed, they offer a means to provide the antithesis of the type of housing that he himself had been involved in laying out for the Staveley Company. Not only was the abstract, barracks-like, grid-iron plan of the Poolsbrook village, for example, beset with the usual back alleys of miners' rows, but it was also orientated expediently to follow pre-existing field patterns, on a north-north-west / south-south-east axis. Within the face-to-face terraced housing, this ensured that any light that could penetrate beyond the backlands was both compromised and unevenly distributed.

In *Cottage Plans and Common Sense*, Unwin suggested another corrective to these circumstances, one that he had already written about in *The Art of Building a Home* (1901) and that represented an enduring motif which he would continue to develop over time in a series of examples. This began tentatively at New Earswick for the confectionary manufacturer Rowntree, with more confidence in the plans for Letchworth and Hampstead, and in text in his influential tract *Nothing Gained by Overcrowding!* (1912): the gathering of dwellings around squares or quadrangles. Detailed within a section entitled 'Co-operation in Building', the adoption of the quadrangle would help curb what he described as the 'inordinate desire for individual independence' of modern times and instead, through the additional realisation of common rooms freed up by the abolition of individual parlours, evoke and encourage the collective spirit of 'an old English village'. He cited mediaeval colleges as a paradigm of this: 'What more satisfactory town buildings could one desire than some of the old colleges? Yet these consist primarily of rows of small tenements grouped round quadrangles or gardens with certain common rooms attached … Why should not cottages be grouped into quadrangles, having all the available land in a square in the centre?' (Unwin 1901).

He provided diagrams of two schemes he had designed in the 1890s – one urban, one rural – as illustrations. 'Design for Proposed Co-operative Dwellings in a Yorkshire Town' (Block Plan) shows 37 small, terraced houses. Shorn of the habitual 'backs', they are linked by an arcade and arranged around a common open space. Another, virtually identical scheme for 28 larger houses with a slight larger communal space was also depicted. These had both been conceived for a site in Bradford and may or may not have been designed for coal workers.[11] But what is perhaps more intriguing is the apparent relationship between these, Unwin's other quadrangular scheme depicted in *The Art of Building a Home*, and precedents much closer in time and space than 'old colleges' – ones whose practical application rather than theoretical position had already been established. Unwin's U-shaped open-quadrangle plan for a rural hamlet, bears a striking resemblance to the overall form of the ideal village of New Bolsover designed by Brewill and Baily, barely six miles from Chesterfield, while its stepping lines of terraced housing represent a picturesque variation on the short geometric ranges of Houfton's Creswell model village (FIG.119). The position of the common rooms at the end of the terraces in Unwin's Yorkshire Town scheme also echo the position of the store and institute in New Bolsover. Already existing within actual built miners' housing at New Bolsover and Creswell were the germs to provide an immediate alternative, not only to Unwin's own early attempts at miners' housing, but also more generic issues in contemporary housing such as the consequences of the byelaw legislation.

Unwin's theoretical project for a rural hamlet is orientated on almost the same axis as Poolsbrook, but instead of an indifferent and dense urban fabric, the open communal 'village green' actively enjoys the southerly aspect and the potential of direct unfettered sunlight – its equivalent at New Bolsover faces an equally desirable west. But one of the most conspicuous differences between Unwin's hamlet and New Bolsover and Creswell is the removal of the light-blocking 'backs' and the replacement of the double rows with a single layer of housing, all of which face the communal space. In fact, Unwin may have already had the opportunity to try out a prototype of the U-shaped collective plan in a housing scheme produced at Warsop Vale, also for the Staveley Company in the 1890s. Cranked loosely around a large open area replete with cricket

119
Unwin's design for a rural hamlet

120
Warsop Vale miners' housing

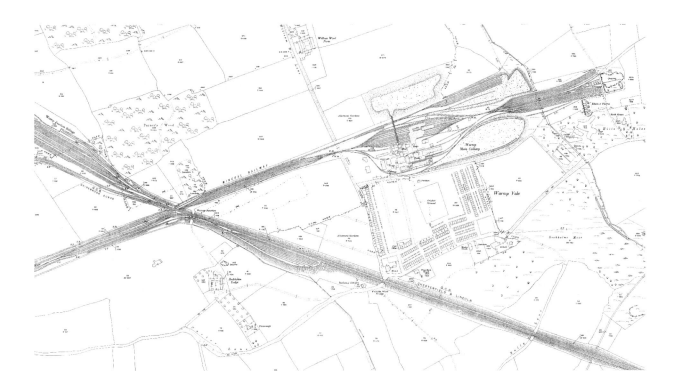

ground and pavilion, the potential recreational and collective focus of this space as a type of village green was, however, significantly compromised by the arrangement, orientation and use of the familiar typology of row housing, with back alleys and privies. Sometimes three rows deep, this meant that the central open space was most often overlooked by privies rather than the fronts of houses. Meanwhile, other facilities such as the school, institute, Mission Church and Methodist Chapel, along with a hotel, were arranged loosely around the outside periphery of the scheme (FIG.120).

Despite using what Unwin would suggest was the deeply flawed typology of row housing with backs, the schemes at New Bolsover and Creswell allow the fronts of all their houses to directly benefit from light, air and open space. Moreover, the lane and double-U shape effectively anticipates the separation of service traffic from pedestrians developed in Radburn decades later. In Unwin's hamlet, meanwhile, all access is still provided along the edges of its 'village green'. It is also significant that while Creswell, with its comprehensive adoption of enclosed green space was contemporaneous with the developments at Bournville, the latter was still defined by rows of housing, while at Port Sunlight by 1899 only a tentative adoption of the quadrangular typology had been applied. Little is known of Brewill, Baily or Percy Houfton's politics or theoretical influences. But Houfton did know both Unwin and Parker (who was born in Chesterfield) personally and has been described as a friend of theirs (Jackson 1985: p.78). And while the influence of Unwin and Parker's innovations at Letchworth and the like, on Houfton's later Woodlands scheme is clear, it appears from the earlier New Bolsover and Creswell that the exchange of ideas travelled in both directions. In fact, there was to be another influential example of this apparent cross-fertilisation.

Unwin's call for no 'house to be built with a sunless living room' in *Cottage Plans and Common Sense* implied that the deep and narrow house plots, complete with parlour and additions to the rear – and typical of speculative byelaw housing – be replaced with wide-fronted houses, without parlours and with the previous clutter of back-land services, all pulled together under the one roof. This would 'present an open and fair surface to sun and air on both its free sides' (Unwin 1902: p.3 and pp 5–6). About the same time Unwin was writing this, Houfton was designing a prototype of a double-fronted cottage. This won two important competitions, the Sheffield Corporation Competition in 1903 and the Letchworth Cheap Cottages Exhibition of 1905 (for which he was awarded £100).

The latter had been devised by Thomas Adams, the estate manager at Letchworth (and latterly the first President of the Town Planning Institute). It followed the publicising by John St Loe Strachey, the editor of *The Country Gentleman*, of the difficulties in procuring economical, affordable housing for rural labourers. The exhibition, which had over 60,000 visitors, was a type of ideas competition which the judges – who included Octavia Hill and William R. Lethaby – suggested would 'be of immense benefit toward the end of obtaining suitable cheap cottages for the country labourer and artisan' (Cheap Cottages Exhibition 1905b: p.iii). It was constructed with full-sized exhibits with a cost limit of £150 attached to each dwelling. This meant that the specifications associated with byelaw legislation had to be challenged by innovative construction methods or use of materials. Of the 130 entries built around the area of Norton Common, for example, two were built using prefabricated concrete panels. However, many of the other entries were criticised by the judges for being too autonomous, ornamental, or unrealistic for the labouring classes, with the curt statement that: '[their] designers do not appear to have realised the problem put before them' (ibid.).

The simple appearance of robust roughcast walls and a similarly modest interior in Houfton's prize-winning entry, on the other hand, satisfied the judges of its both its suitably and economy (FIG.121). The blank gable walls with chimneys and simple pitched roof, however, also made it amenable to use as a repeatable unit. While detached in its built iteration at Letchworth, in the drawings of the scheme built by the Sheffield Corporation, it presented itself, 'with its wide frontage [and] absence of projection' (Swenarton 1981: p.23) like an increment in a larger serial, linear form: either a semi-detached dwelling or, more likely, row or terraced housing (FIG.122).

It has been suggested that Houfton's scheme owed something, especially in its scale and use of white roughcast over brick walls, to the series of modest

121
Percy Houfton's cheap cottage

dwelling types including the cottages at New Earswick (1902–03) (Swenarton 1981: p.21) or the 'Inexpensive Four Room Cottages' designed by Unwin and Parker (c.1904–05) (Jackson 1985: p.78). Yet Houfton's design appears to have preceded the latter. Meanwhile the former still has its Water Closet problematically accessed via the outside of the building, a circumstance that Houfton's 'cheap cottage' had already resolved. Moreover, both of these Unwin and Parker schemes were still articulated with the gables and dormers that Houfton eschewed in favour of a simple pitched roof form with unbroken eaves. The adoption of the latter, as well as the resolution of the WC access issue, however, can be seen in Unwin and Parker's slightly later scheme for 'A Group of Inexpensive Five Room Cottages' (1906). Houfton's cottage scheme also finds an echo in the clear lines and simple pitched roof of the double-fronted cottages – disposed in semi-detached or row forms – found in Letchworth at, for example, Cromwell Green, designed once again by Unwin and Parker, from about 1905. These are the simplest and perhaps, therefore, most repeatable type in the Letchworth lexicon (ibid.: p.80).

It is difficult to say precisely who was influencing who within these schemes, but of significance is the suggestion that these projects collectively represented a stylistic departure. Their 'simplicity of design and standardisation of components … implied a very different kind of architecture from the romantic gable-ridden elevation generally associated with the garden city movement' (Swenarton 1981: p.26). This would proliferate 'a little more than a decade later, to appear as the official doctrines of state housing'. Pevsner's comments on the similarities between Houfton's Woodlands scheme and the ubiquitous aesthetic of subsequent council estates accordingly take on another layer of significance. While dressed up here and there with the addition of gable elements to terminate blocks or articulate the longer rows, the common domestic unit – the one which Abercrombie praised for its ability to admit light and air from both sides within what he described as this '"Garden City" Scheme' – is clearly a version of Houfton's cheap cottage or a close derivative of it.

But if the double-fronted serial cottage typology innovated by Houfton and Unwin and Parker would ultimately become commonplace within British social housing, its more immediate application and indeed, perhaps its origins were, as implied in its use at Woodlands, in the desire to modernise another more specific, familiar, and enduring typology: the miners' row or terrace. Houfton's prizing-winning entry 'Detached Cottage No.14' for the Cheap Cottages Exhibition at Letchworth in 1905, was commissioned by the Messrs Green Brothers of Whittington, near Chesterfield. While it is not precisely clear who the Greens were, Whittington, along with Whittington Moor and New Whittington formed part of an archipelago of coal mining communities a stone's throw away from Barrow Hill, and collectively were the site of long-running and future mineral interests of the Staveley Company. It is also perhaps of significance that the patron of the Cheap Cottages Exhibition itself was the

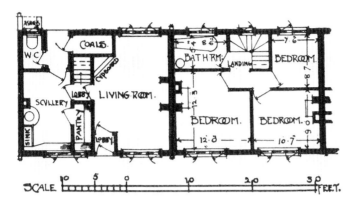

122
Houfton's double-fronted cottage at Sheffield, ground and upper floor plans

123
Ground and upper floor plans, house plan 'Type D' from the Tudor Walters report

Duke of Devonshire, who owned the land on which the Staveley Company's operations were executed.

Two-storey double-fronted cottages can be seen as a common repeatable form in Houfton's own subsequent schemes. These include the so-called 'White City' planned settlement he designed in Rainworth, Nottinghamshire around 1910 for the Staveley Company to house the pit sinkers (those who dig the initial shafts) for its new Rufford Pit. Here, the house type is used in the row formation typical of traditional mining villages whose functional expediency is affirmed in this case by the use of numbers rather than names for the streets. And yet the houses, uniformly constructed in brick, are all equipped with both front and back gardens of near equal sizes, while their broad fronts and shallow plans ensure a more than adequate supply of both light and access to fresh air. The adaptability of the type is made clear by its use both in this formation and, as seen, within the Garden City contexts of both Letchworth and Woodlands. Garden City layouts can also be seen in other housing estates that Houfton made for collieries – such as at Clipstone (again for the Staveley Company), with its elliptical central green space, or Shirebrook and Micklefield in Derbyshire; or Wharncliffe and Tinsley in South Yorkshire. In addition, he designed two settlements in South Wales for the Markhams – whose mining interests had strayed there – and finally, a series of municipal housing schemes in, for example, Chesterfield at Boythorpe, Highfield and Derby Road (Cousins 2021: p.2).[12]

Houfton's cheap cottage for Letchworth still exists. Located at No.217 Icknield Way, its austere rendered form, unbroken eaves and blank gables, pregnant with the possibility of linear, serial expansion, stands out against an otherwise mainstream suburban landscape of autonomous dwellings with roof dormers, half-timbering and bay windows. As such, it seems to present itself almost as much a harbinger of a European modernist future of *Existenzminimum* buildings by, for example, Jacobus Johannes Pieter Oud and Ernst May, as a reflection on the feudal meditations of Morris, Ruskin and the Arts and Crafts movement. Perhaps of more immediate significance, however, and one of the

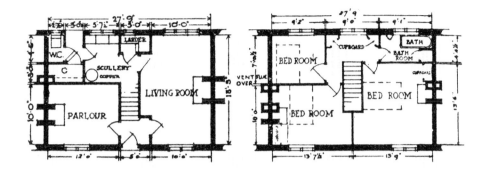

key reasons for its proliferation within the United Kingdom, was its effective enshrinement within the recommendations of the Tudor Walters Report. The prescribed house plan 'Type D'[13] which would become a widely used model for social housing bears – with its shallow front-to-back width and wide double-front with central entrance and staircase – a close resemblance to the form and layout of Houfton's cheap cottage project, albeit with the retention of a parlour and a correspondingly reduced scullery (FIG.123). Arguably then, No.217 Icknield Way represents a prototype whose simple, almost austere principles and economic use of form would help define a generation of interwar social housing and settlements generally and far beyond the limits of the coalfields, but whose roots lay in the actions of Houfton and Unwin and their respective responses to the particular domestic circumstances of mineworkers.

DONCASTER AND THE EAST KENT COALFIELDS: PATRICK ABERCROMBIE

Throughout its history, coal mining has been a migratory phenomenon. In the United Kingdom as elsewhere, extractions commonly proceeded from the easy-to-win seams to the more difficult and potentially hazardous, and in general, from exposed to concealed coalfields. While accepting the ongoing strategic importance of coal mining to an industrial economy, these movements often coincided with advances in technology or even market conditions, both of which could allow the winning of previously economically unviable deposits. Thus, since their first initiation British coalfields continually shifted over time, introducing obsolescence to older and worked-out areas, while instigating new pit developments and their associated settlements in new areas above untapped sources. Some movements inscribed a local, incremental creep. Upon reaching the feasible working limits of a mine or being faced with an untraversable geological obstacle, often the easiest thing to do was the sinking of another shaft. Accordingly, vast underground networks were realised with tunnels often passing from one working pit to another, or from working pits into previous – now worked-out – operations with all being accessed from the surface by an archipelago of shafts serviced by headgear, apparently – from the perspective of the surface – strewn haphazardly across the landscape.[14] But these smaller local moves were echoed – especially, but by no means exclusively, in the restructuring of the industry in the second half of the 20th century – by larger regional shifts from older to newer coalfields. In Scotland, for example, production fell off in the traditional mining areas of Lanarkshire and Stirlingshire, but expanded in Ayrshire, the Lothians and in Fife (see Part III). England experienced a similar pattern; the Great Northern Coalfield entered a slow decline while activities in Yorkshire, the East Midlands and Nottinghamshire and Kent increased. In the early 1920s, the two most important coalfield developments to be discovered and made operational were at Doncaster and East Kent. Both engaged the thinking of another critical theorist of 20th-century architecture and planning: Patrick Abercrombie.

On the eve of the First World War, the deep pits of the newly opened coalfields around Doncaster in South Yorkshire which were 'possibly the most favourable working conditions of any British coalfield' (Fawcett 1924: p.441) 'were among the most advanced in the world … in terms of layout and organisation' (Supple 1987: p.183). These new levels of improvement in the planning and spatial configurations of collieries, both above and below ground, began to coalesce with other considerations on the organisation of space in the coalfields at a series of scales from that of the domestic dwelling to that of entire regions. Consequently, while not without some improvement, the older coalfields generally remained the site of poorer housing and overcrowding, whereas in the new areas – often led by more progressive theories and thinking – the sinking of shafts were often followed by the construction of modern, up-to-date housing typologies and village layouts.

At Doncaster, the new coalfield lay under a low-lying swampy and almost exclusively agricultural area that stretched across a series of local authorities' boundaries. This led to new measures to reconcile the strategic needs of what was expected to metamorphosise into the site of a rapidly expanding coal mining industry with other existing and proposed criteria: the 'regional plan'. In May 1920, Abercrombie and T. H. Johnson (the Doncaster town surveyor and architect) were commissioned by a consortium of local councils, including Doncaster Corporation, to produce the Doncaster Regional Planning Scheme. This would be the first in what would become a series of such plans undertaken by Abercrombie during his lifetime (Abercrombie and Johnson 1922: p.v; Fawcett 1924: p.440). Designed to 'prevent the repetition of the sordid and haphazard growth that … characterised the development of coalfields in the past', the planning scheme repudiated, 'the idea of the unlimited expansion of Doncaster and the creation of dreary isolated pit villages' (Dix 1981: p.107). Instead, the authors proposed a network of ten or more self-sustaining communities separated from each other by a green belt consisting of some of the land most liable to flooding, and recommended that the population of these settlements be fixed at somewhere between 10,000 and 20,000, and be defined by the Garden City standard of eight houses per acres.

The proposed new settlements were to be integrated within a wider series of zoning and infrastructural propositions for the positioning of new industry and other land uses, including recreations and the preservation of landscape. These, located within the context of the inevitable exploitation of an emerging coalfield, aimed at serving both the exigencies and negotiating the consequences of the collieries, including the risk of subsidence (which was afforded an appendix of its own in the report)[15] and the reuse of slag-heap materials to raise the levels of low-lying grounds at risk of flooding. The latter was also predicated on aesthetic grounds as a measure to preserve countryside views and their potential as rural, recreational amenities. The settlements would be conveniently connected to a simultaneously revamped, metropolitan-style Doncaster which would remain 'the focal centre of the business, social, intellectual and artistic life of the surrounding towns' (Thompson 1923: pp 135–6). Abercrombie and Johnson were vehement that the latter should not be considered mere 'suburbs of Doncaster: fragments, as it were, of her suburban growth that have got separated from the parent mass':

> On the contrary, they are complete entities whose existence is in no sense the result of an overflow from Doncaster but is owing to one or other of the fundamental causes of urban birth. They should therefore be equipped with the organic formation needful for full corporate growth. While each community forms part of the Doncaster Industrial Region, in other words is a member of a well-regulated family, each individual possesses full functional powers.
>
> (Abercrombie and Johnson 1922: p.85)

Abercrombie and Johnson were, within the context of a holistic regional plan for this coalfield, suggesting the provision of prototypical New Towns. Published in 1922, their report coincided with Raymond Unwin's proposals for a similar arrangement in his essay 'Some Thoughts on the Development of London', published as part of a collection of texts edited by Sir Aston Webb in 1921. It is interesting that these early proposals for New Towns emerged from two impulses: a reconfiguration of the metropolis and a reconfiguring of the settlements and land use associated with the coalfields. These twin stimuli could still be observed in the overall picture of New Towns development following the Second World War. Of course, Abercrombie would become an active member of the Royal Commission on the Distribution of the Industrial Population (Barlow Commission) whose report published in 1939 recommended the policies of decentralising urban populations and industrial workforces which precipitated the New Towns Act of 1946. He would also reiterate and formalise proposals for a series of satellite settlements around the capital in his own Greater London Plan from 1944.

In fact, the series of 16 regional plans (and, in particular the first, Doncaster) that Abercrombie undertook between 1923 and 1935, developed ways of working – especially in their use of Patrick Geddes's method of executing extensive surveys to establish existing social, economic and physical conditions – which would lay the foundations in both scope and technique for his subsequent plans for London and other cities.[16] They also built on his calls, published in 1918, for the need to establish a survey or inventory of national resources as the basis for post-First World War reconstruction (Abercrombie 1918). The regional plans were commissioned in the context of the series of legislative acts produced from 1919 onwards (the Town Planning Acts of 1919 and 1925, and the Town and Country Planning Act of 1932) either by a local planning committee or a joint committee if, as at Doncaster, multiple local authorities were involved. Perhaps significantly, a considerable number of the plans – for example, the Wye Valley (which included the Forest of Dean), Bristol and Bath, Middlesbrough and Teesside, North Wales, East Kent, as well as the civic survey of Sheffield and the earlier South Wales Regional Survey (1921) which Abercrombie was involved in – were located within the coalfields, and the underlining seams or the mines themselves were described as both 'a force of economic development [and] a telling example of the link between development and the deep structure of the region' (Dehaene 2005: p.138).

If the Doncaster plan established certain premises on method – and along with his *Dublin of the Future* scheme from 1916 confirmed Abercrombie's reputation – then the scheme for East Kent represented another landmark (Dix 1981: p.109): 'the first coordinated attempt at industrial regional planning in this country' (Smart 1931: p.518). Like Doncaster, it was based around the inevitable exploitation of a new coalfield. But whereas Doncaster had represented an extension to an existing field, the coal deposits underneath East Kent had been previously overlooked. It was a hitherto agricultural landscape untouched by industrial development on the doorstep of London and the gateway to Europe. For Abercrombie:

> What an exciting foundation did that peaceful undulating country of East Kent rest upon, pursuing for two thousand years an agricultural and seaside existence, perturbed by nothing more agitating than an ephemeral military conquest or so! That deep peace is now permanently invaded; for, however much we may minimise the ugly effects of industrialisation, and however well-planned the new additions may be, so as to conform to the genius of the locality, a change fundamental and complete will have taken place from the peace of the country to the busy hum of men.
> (Abercrombie 1931: p.505)

Abercrombie's commission was preceded by a planning conference on the new coalfield in Canterbury in 1922, followed by a meeting in 1923 of the East Kent Joint Town Planning Committee which consisted of representatives from the 17 local councils whose boundaries contained the coalfields. Another meeting, again in 1923, was called by the Archbishop of Canterbury, hosted at Lambeth Palace, and attended by, for example, Lord Beauchamp (Lord Warden of the Cinque Ports), Lord Alfred Milner and Neville Chamberlain, who would become the Minister of Health and Housing in 1924 (Abercrombie 1931: p.507). Written in collaboration with John Archibald (a Member of the Town Planning Institute), the East Kent Regional Planning Scheme had two iterations, a preliminary report published in 1926, and a final report published in 1928. It covered an area based on the 200 square miles of workable coal seams that stretched from midway between Hythe and Folkestone in the west to near Whitstable, and from there eastward to just before Ramsgate. Written before the exact location of the series of new pitheads had been established, the scheme stated three broad aims: 'to facilitate the economic development of the region; to preserve its existing beauty as far as possible; and to safeguard the health of the future community' (Abercrombie and Archibald 1928: p.3).

The result was an attempt at an integrated strategy which while balanced by other criteria – especially the preservation of the scenic beauty of this, the 'Garden of England' (Abercrombie 1931: p.506) – was dominated by and proceeded from the requirements of coal mining (FIG.124). The future population of the area was worked out through a consideration of the amount of coal present in the seams, an estimate of the number of pits which would be required to extract it, and their annual productive capacity in tonnage. From this, the number of potential miners needed could be calculated. The precise number of new pits and the duration necessary for them to achieve full productive capacity varied between the two reports as new information emerged. The preliminary report suggested a timescale of 30 years before full production was achieved by 18 pits collectively producing 13,500,000 tons of coal per annum (Abercrombie and Archibald 1928: p.46). To service these 18 new and existing pits – which included Betteshanger, Chislet and Snowdown – the authors proposed the expansion of some existing settlements and the building of eight new ones, each of which would be located within the folds an undulating chalk Kentish landscape (FIG.125).

These assessments were revised in the final report to a period of ten years before full production was achieved, executed by 12 pits with a collective annual output of 10,000,000 tons. These 12 pits would produce a population of 12,000 each – of these 3,000 were miners and the rest their families 'on the basis that one workman being the nucleus of a population unit of four'. This made an overall predicted increase in population of approximately 150,000. It was calculated that in January 1928, 3,130 coal miners were employed in Kent collieries giving an overall total – factoring in a high current percentage of nonmarried miners – of 10,000. This population was settled either in one of a series of what Abercrombie termed 'New Towns' – Aylesham 2,000, Elvington 640 and Chislet 350, with 790 in other housing schemes surrounding Woolage, Snowdown and Betteshanger, making a total of 3,780 – or else in existing

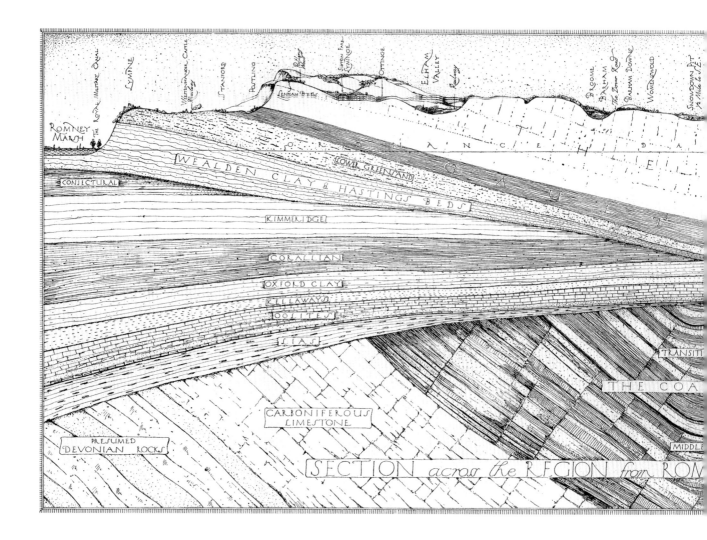

towns such as Dover, Canterbury, Deal and Slurry, with a population of 6,220. This meant that housing for a predicated population of 140,000 or, in other terms, 28,000 domestic units had to be provided within ten years (Abercrombie and Archibald 1928).

Recognising that the instances of deep coal mines within a landscape is not continuous, like factories, but rather is episodic, Abercrombie and Archibald proposed the clustering of industries and a small amount of the housing around the pitheads. The rest of the housing would be placed to potentially serve more than one pit. Despite a lack of information in the precise future siting of the new collieries, the preliminary plan had been quite definite in the location of the proposed new settlements. The final report, however, was more ambiguous and suggested their exact positioning within the landscape that would be determined by strategic criteria. In fact, there were a series of unknown factors present when the regional planning scheme was being determined. It was not known, for example, whether the coal would be for export or

124
East Kent regional plan, section by Abercrombie and Archibald showing the relationship between coal measures and surface urbanism

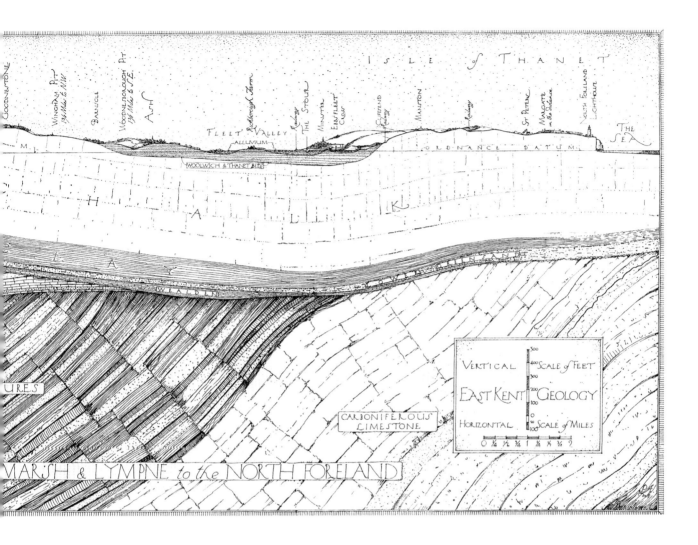

internal use; whether it could be pulverised as a fuel source, to be consumed somewhere on site to provide electricity for the metropolis or elsewhere; or whether the opening of the coalfields would, as in South Wales, lead to the creation of iron and steel works as companion industries. All these eventualities would have consequences. The scenario of steel works or coal predominantly for export, for example, would influence the disposition of infrastructural provision, with intensified transport links to the channel ports necessary. Already the authors had proposed the construction of an overhead rope railway to take coal directly from Tilmanstone Colliery to the Port of Dover. The rest of the collieries were to be linked by a mixture of private mineral railways, with lines provided by the Southern Railway company and road networks.

By 1928, only one of the proposed 'New Towns', Aylesham, had actually been located and begun. Pixhill, designed to serve the Betteshanger and Ripple Pits, had been 'temporarily' stalled and would be permanently abandoned. Chislet and Elvington, meanwhile, had been pre-existing villages, but were much expanded by new colliery housing. In a paper published later in 1931, Abercrombie discussed the merits and demerits of a decentralised approach to housing the miners versus an idea of a larger 'single New Town' designed to serve most of the collieries. With the addition of perhaps an existing historic setting – such as found possibly in Canterbury or Dover – and the consequent gathering of other interests and trades, he suggested that such an arrangement could avoid the apparent homogeneity of life in a mining settlement, 'that unhealthy pit mentality which pervades some of the Welsh mining villages, cut off by mountain ridge from the outer world'. By the time he wrote this, he was estimating a revised new population of 180,000 that would provisionally be housed in 'five or six smaller towns' (Abercrombie 1931: p.510).

In the end only Aylesham – equipped with a marketplace, schools, churches, institutions, playing fields, a railway station and central boulevard all 'planned out and ready for expansion' – fulfilled his desire for a fully functioning town, rather than a mere 'housing scheme'. The settlement took on the forms associated with a Garden City. The 'Bird's-Eye View of Architects' Original Planning' included in the East Kent Planning Scheme final report shows the central axial boulevard connecting the railway station and its generous plaza to one of the churches via the marketplace, bifurcating the settlement into two halves of approximately the same size. Other churches are located on a cross axis leading from the hemispherical marketplace. Much of the rest of the fabric consists of cottage-form housing clustered around gardens with further open space beyond to expand into via a network of roads. A sprinkling of institutions articulates the perimeter. While only partially constructed – the central boulevard terminating at one end with a grand station, for example, was dispensed with – it has been suggested that the plan form as built, with its semicircular crescents on axis and canting access avenues, contains elements of whimsy, bearing a distinct resemblance to the elevation of the pithead's winding gear (Boughton 2018a) (FIG.125).

For several reasons, Aylesham never realised the promise that Abercrombie ascribed. The working conditions of the local pit Snowdown – nicknamed 'Dante's inferno' – were extreme. The other proposed pit, Adisham never materialised. The funding was insufficient to build the houses in the 'simple Georgian, modified with a provincial touch' architecture language that the authors of the regional plan had advocated (Abercrombie and Archibald 1928: p.84). Instead, constructed using a mixture of methods – some brick, some steel and concrete structures – the houses produced were often drearily uniform and homogeneous. There were also issues with the integration of workers and their families who arrived seeking a new life, often from very deprived backgrounds in the older mining areas of, for example, Scotland, Lancashire or Durham. Realising a cohesive community in these circumstances within what, despite Abercrombie and Archibald's best intentions, had emerged as another isolated mining settlement lacking in amenities but with a high cost of living, proved difficult. Aylesham gained a reputation as a rough town; labour

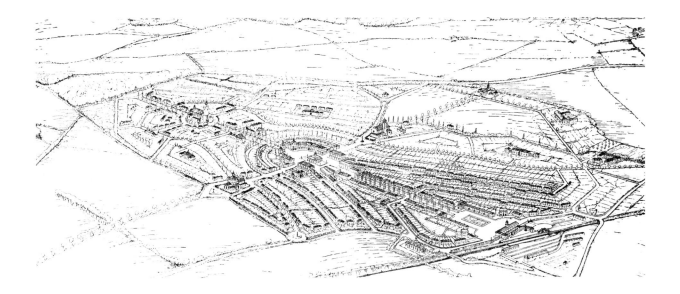

125
Bird's eye perspective of proposal for Aylesham new town by Abercrombie and Archibald

turnover at Snowdown was high, and initial and revised estimates for future populations of 10,000 or even 28,000 never materialised. Instead, throughout the 1930s a high proportion of houses remained empty – and the number of inhabitants static – until after the Second World War (Jeremiah 2000: pp 55–6; Broughton 2018b).

The wider aims of Abercrombie and Archibald's regional plan were also compromised, foundering – at least in part – on the economic circumstances of the Depression. The concerted effort required to implement the plan also dissipated, with each of the 17 local authorities originally involved ultimately prioritising their own autonomous interests (Dix 1981: p.109). And yet, in its attempt to systematically integrate the needs of the coal industry and its labour force – at this time still very much the key economic drivers of an industrial economy – with other criteria including infrastructure, communications and the preservation of amenity and rural landscape, it provided another vision of the future. Both the Doncaster and East Kent Regional Planning Schemes – along with his other regional plans – anticipated the Barlow Commission (1940) into the distribution of industrial population, and the Scott Committee (1941) into rural land use. These, along with Abercrombie's own regional plan for London, would influence the urban and rural landscape of post-war Britain. Doncaster and East Kent also provided more precise antecedents for some of the consequences of these later reports, including the post-war New Town movement and, in particular, the New Towns of Glenrothes, Peterlee, Washington and Cwmbran. As will be described in Part III, these settlements would emerge from further attempts to integrate the needs of a by-then nationalised coal industry – as evoked in the national *Plan for Coal* (1950) which included strategies for both its modernisation *and* decline – with expectations of new patterns and ways of life for the post-war population, including its miners (see Part III below).

But Abercrombie's work also had an effect more immediately within the late 1920s and especially in the vicinity of Doncaster, where his regional plan – which remained only advisory and unimplemented – overlapped with a series of new settlements which were collectively realised according to the Garden City principals that he, among many others, advocated. But unlike his own future-looking attempts at a cohesive and integrated attitude to planning, these new villages were often the result of a more conversative and fragmented approach. These were capable of embodying the same forms and language of the Garden City in both a socially progressive and retrogressive manner, across a range of scales from that of the house and garden to that of the entire settlement.

THE REFINEMENT OF A COALFIELD TYPE: THE INDUSTRIAL HOUSING ASSOCIATION AND 'THE BUILDING OF TWELVE THOUSAND HOUSES'

If Raymond Unwin's attitude towards planning and housing had been at least partly shaped by his experiences within the Derbyshire and Nottingham coalfields of the late 19th century then perhaps appropriately – and as seen at Woodlands – the principles of the Garden City movement became a defining feature in the housing settlements designed to accompany the opening and expansion of the new coalfields of the early and interwar decades of the 20th century. In 1928, the *Colliery Guardian* published a series entitled 'British Colliery Villages'. Using the latest technology of aerial photography, images of these settlements (some of which were still under construction) – such as Great Wyrley in Cannock Chase; Bloxwich in South Staffordshire; Carcroft, Maltby, Thurnscoe and Wombwell in South Yorkshire; and Lynemouth Estate, Northumberland – confirmed Unwin- and Parker-inspired, Abercrombie-endorsed credentials of radial routeways and cottage typologies, with gardens arranged around open spaces of various shapes including circles and quadrangles.

While much of this, and indeed most of the housing production in general during this period, was constructed by local authorities – colliery-owned houses fell from 171,000 to 141,000 between 1925 and 1946 (Supple 1987: p.458) – coal companies still assumed responsibility for the building of a significant number of new dwellings within planned new settlements. These took advantage of the grants and subsidies made available to local authorities, non-profit-making associations and private contractors through the Housing Acts of 1919, 1923 and 1924, and the Public Works Loans Act of 1922. Accordingly, individual collieries or colliery-owned housing associations embarked upon a range of construction programmes. These included the 1,100 houses built at Moorends in South Yorkshire by Pearse Partners Ltd, owners of Thorne Colliery; or the same number of houses at Bircotes on the border between South Yorkshire and Nottinghamshire, built by Barber Walker and Company. Meanwhile, the Bolsover Colliery Company updated their model villages at New Bolsover and Creswell with new settlements at Rufford, Clipstone and Edwinstowe in Nottinghamshire, while the Chislet Colliery Housing Society Ltd built a village of 300 houses at Hersden, as part of a government-encouraged initiative to open up the Kent coalfield (Hay and Fordham 2017: pp 30–32).

Eclipsing the scale of these efforts and the most conspicuous of all the housing associations was the Industrial Housing Association (IHA). Between 1919 and 1928, the IHA built just under 12,000 dwellings and 35 villages, almost all of which were for colliery workers. The large majority of these were in the Yorkshire and East Midlands coalfields with a scattering located in North and South Wales, and Staffordshire (FIG.126).[17] Of significance, the IHA represented a consortium of mining interests that had originally pooled technical resources to exploit the deeper 'Barnsley' or 'Top Hard' seam of the South Yorkshire and North Nottinghamshire concealed coalfield, especially around the Doncaster area. Again, as in the previous century – and indeed perennially – the tapping of the coal seam did not necessarily correspond with existing settlement patterns. In fact, the development of deep-mining techniques necessary to generate sufficient profits required 'an extensive coal reserve royalty typically amounting to between 7,000 to 10,000 acres' (Hay and Fordham 2017: p.21). Consequently, the new pit villages would generally be isolated and separated on the surface by large swathes of agricultural land.

Also of significance was the appointment of Sir John Tudor Walters to lead the construction programme via his own practice, the Housing and Town Planning Trust Ltd. He joined an influential board of coal owners which included Charles Paxton Markham and was chaired by Lord Aberconway who had interests in several coal and iron concerns in both the Midlands and Yorkshire. In 1927, towards the end of the programme, Tudor Walters published a book on the association's achievements entitled *The Building of Twelve Thousand Houses*. Here, he described the IHA as a kind of cooperative society, one that paralleled those set up for the working classes, but whose members in this case were 'large employers of labour'. Of the £6,000,000 expended in constructing these schemes, he stated that 10 per cent was provided in share capital by these members, who received no direct profit in dividends from their investment (Tudor Walters 1927: pp 14–15). He also discussed the benefits of operating in terms similar to those available to the Miners' Welfare Commission architects. As a large conglomerate, the IHA had the capability to achieve economies of scale and a rapid rate of construction that was further enhanced by standardisation within both the design and use of critical sizes and materials. The consortium was also able to deploy a flexible combination of both employing

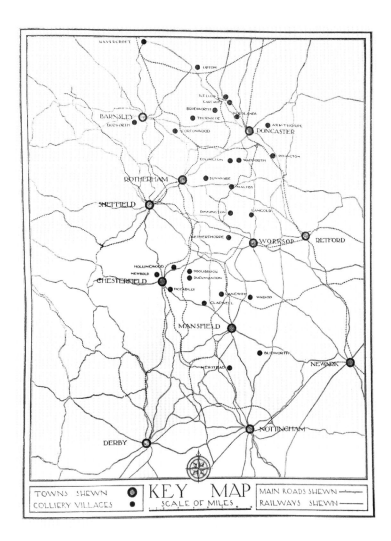

126
Map showing new Industrial Housing Association villages in the Yorkshire and East Midlands coalfields

main contractors and engaging labour directly. Understandably, the design and aesthetics of the houses closely followed Tudor Walters' eponymous report from 1919 and, thereby, the influence of Raymond Unwin: the schemes were characterised by a doctrine of good planning and settlement, being based on simple and efficient forms judiciously positioned to 'secure light and air' while creating and addressing open spaces:

> We were quite determined from the commencement that the layout and house plans should be on the most modern lines, that we would have plenty of open spaces, no monotonous lines of dreary houses, no barracks blocks, and no 'jerry' building, but that the layout of the land should in each case be carefully considered with a view to preserving any natural beauties that the site might possess, and that the frontage line should be broken up into well-designed groups of houses with plenty of variety in

the elevations. We were not prepared to spend money in striving merely for architectural effect but believed rather that it was in the grouping and proportion and harmony of the design that the best effect could be produced.

(ibid.: p.24)

At eight houses per acre, dwellings were provided with front gardens which allowed them to be set back from the roadway. To realise a unified appearance, blocks of houses were often linked by walls, which simultaneously screened 'the outbuildings, and prevent the gloomy vista of back gardens, clothes hanging out to dry etc., from the main roads which disfigure the appearance of many colliery villages' (ibid.: p.27).

Tudor Walters also acknowledged the importance of aspects of the Miners' Welfare Committee's activities, stating the necessity of providing sites for leisure, recreation and children's playing areas, as well as shops and other amenities. These are all illustrated within the plates used to depict the schemes within *The Building of Twelve Thousand Houses*. All of these are drawings rather than photographs. The plans, provided at a series of scales from the layout of entire villages to those of individual houses, collectively reaffirm the qualities of the Garden City: blocks of houses occupy the peripheries of green spaces that they both define and enjoy. But within this there is variety. At Armthorpe on the outskirts of Doncaster, for example, the core of the scheme is laid out in a semi-circle with a formal central axis which runs through a central garden and a civic or ecclesiastical building towards an existing forest, Shaw Wood. A semi-circle is also deployed at Blidworth, near Mansfield, albeit less comprehensively, terminating another central axis with a formal site for a church. Houses enclose a series of different shapes, some of which are penetrated by cul-de-sacs. Other site strategies convey how these planning ingredients could be used on sloping as well as level sites. Sunnyside village, near Rotherham, is almost entirely symmetrical, consisting of an axial central avenue which meets a circumferential crescent at one of a series of open spaces. The overall formality, however, is softened by its occupation of a gently inclined landscape. Cortonwood village outside Barnsley displays a double diamond of dwellings which surround a children's recreation ground. Three avenues radiate from this, to meet another circumferential avenue which terminates, again, in a semi-circle of housing with a small quadrangular spur of a cul-de-sac leading from it. The whole arrangement is laid across a slope descending diagonally in contour lines from the diamond to the semi-circle. Meanwhile, the formal and nearly symmetrical village of Dinnington, north-west of Worksop is given a natural bias by its position on a slope running in an approximately east–west direction across its U-shape motif. At a larger scale, the village of Langold (north of Worksop) occupies its sloping site in a series of formal and informal patterns that range from the symmetrical positioning of the two avenues that radiate from one of the principal entrances to the site, to elliptical and circular cul-de-sacs. Yet here the overall impression is of a more organic approach, with formal elements expressed most precisely in smaller more specific moments. At Langold, as well as at Hollingwood and Thurnscoe, the stated aims of Tudor Walters in *The Building of Twelve Thousand Houses* to let the natural characteristics of the site dominate – its landscape, trees, slopes and other attributes – are perhaps at their closest to realisation (FIG.127).

The circular layouts found at New Rossington provided the obverse of this. Here the IHA provided a series of extensions to a pre-existing model settlement already laid out in a configuration of concentric circles in 1913 by Maurice Deacon, the colliery owner, who was also a member of the IHA board of directors. Deacon had also been involved in another model precedent for miners, with a circular form at Maltby which was built in 1910. About the same time, another partial circular scheme, this time resolved into a teardrop shape had been designed at Oakdale in South Wales by A. F. Webb and commissioned by Arthur Markham (Hay and Fordham 2017: p.8). In fact, New Rossington was one of several schemes where the IHA added to an existing mining settlement. Its extensions occupied a series of different sites around the original circular form, the most conspicuous of which was another larger circle located to the southwest, and designed to accommodate 500 new houses. This was a much more nuanced and sophisticated layout than the earlier circle, whose limitations had been criticised by Patrick Abercrombie

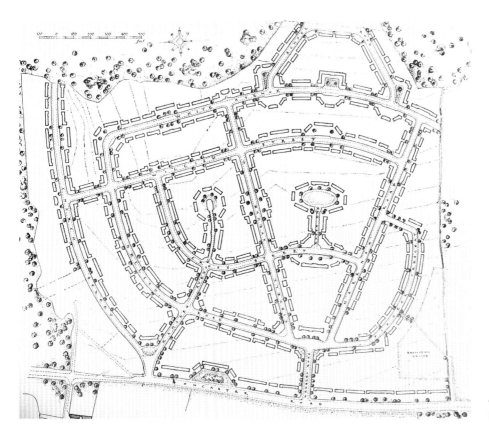

127
IHA village at Langold

(1922), and it managed to create a variety of shapes of open spaces and housing arrangements including cul-de-sacs.[18]

If the site layout plans in *The Building of Twelve Thousand Houses* confirm the influence of Unwin's thinking at the scale of the entire settlement, then the larger scale plans describe, in more detail, the relationship between domestic units and the private, semi-private and public spaces in which they find themselves. They also confirm the overwhelming preponderance and value of a unit entitled 'Non-Parlour Three-Bedroom House Type'. Once again this is a close derivative of the 'Type D House' of Tudor Walters's 1918 report for the Ministry of Health and, therefore, of Houfton's cheap cottage. Its repetition as the basic increment in almost all of these projects is presumably a result of the stated strategic design approach to realise economies of scale through 'judicious standardisation' and repetition. Yet, it is also seen to be versatile and could be arranged to crank around 45 degrees to soften or articulate corners. At intersections it could be made to 'produce the effect of a front elevation to both roads' (Tudor Walters 1927: p.27). Finally, in addition to these civic and economic attributes, drawings such as 'Sunnyside village: the Crescent West' clearly demonstrate its ability – due to the position of the central entrance and staircase which allows the front to back dual aspect of the living room – to realise an intimate connection between indoor and outdoor space and, as described

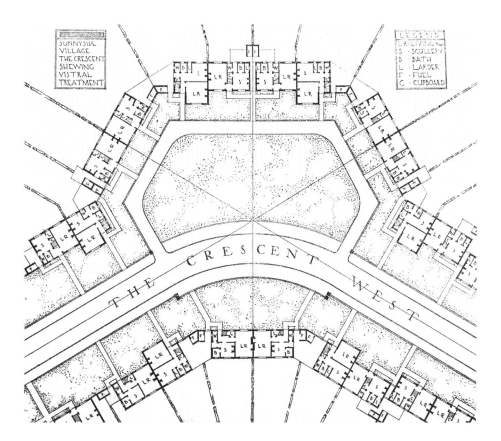

128
Sunnyside village: the Crescent West

at Woodlands by Abercrombie, an unhindered and abundant ingress of light into the interior from both sides (FIG.128).

The qualities of light, space, air and nature are also conveyed in the final set of drawings illustrating *The Building of Twelve Thousand Houses*: a series of perspectives which invoke, in a more pictorial and accessible form, the bucolic intentions of the schemes. Individual and clusters of houses are depicted adjacent to trees or other types of planting, often under big skies, populated by voluminous clouds. Often composed using the same rule of thirds – seen in the near contemporaneous photographs of the pithead baths commissioned by the Miners' Welfare Commission described in Part I – these drawings convey the antithesis of the messiness, and cramped and anarchic environment of the mine. Instead, they are dream-like, harmonious landscapes which – save for the odd intrusions of a motor car, a lorry delivering coal or, very occasionally and at a distance, the headstocks marking the tops of the mineshafts – are free not only from the overt symbols of industrial modernity, but also the presence of the other underground landscape which the villages simultaneously support and depend upon (FIG.129).

But perhaps the most conspicuous aspect of these views is that, with one or two exceptions, they are marked by an absence of men. The Mines and Collieries Act of 1842 notably forbade women to go underground, and except for a handful of coalfields, it was unusual for women to work in any capacity in collieries. The mono-industrial and isolated nature of pit villages, therefore, meant a heightened gendering of space and division of labour. Men worked in the mines, while women were compelled to accept the role of housewife and

129
Amthorpe village, Beech Road

what has been described generally as the unacknowledged labour of 'social reproduction' in the home (Fraser 2016: p.106). Thus, while male miners were either underground, sleeping due to the nature of shift work, or at unspecified leisure activities, the streets are depicted as being left, generally, to children, old people and, especially, women.[19] If women's workplaces in mining communities was emphatically and often exclusively the home, then the layout of its interior is significant, especially those spaces specifically dedicated to productive and hygienic work, rather than recreational purposes: the kitchen or scullery and the bathroom. In fact, *The Building of Twelve Thousand Houses* suggested the presence of some degree of scientific management in the layout of kitchens: 'In the planning of the houses consideration should be given to the convenience of the housewife, and the position of the pantry, cooker range, kitchen dresser, and sink in relation to the number of footsteps that have to be taken to performs the day's work' (Tudor Walters 1927: p.30)

Despite the very small number of buildings completed by the Miners' Welfare Commission when the book was published and the villages built, Tudor Walters also suggested the position of the bathroom within the house be made dependent on the local provision or otherwise of pithead baths, a statement (also echoed by Abercrombie in his *East Kent Regional Planning Scheme*) which confirmed the recognised potential of the latter's impact on domestic space.

> In the absence of pit baths in a colliery village, where the man comes home from work in his pit clothes, the downstairs bathroom with access from the back lobby enables him to get rid of his working clothes, have his baths, and dress in his ordinary attire, without carrying the pit dirt and odour into the house, and for these reasons the downstair bathroom has been chiefly adopted in the colliery villages. From the standpoint of the women and children, the upstairs bathroom is more convenient and in designing new villages attached to collieries where pithead baths are provided, the balance of the advantage would be in favour of the upstairs bathroom.
>
> (ibid.)

In the apparently most populous house type – the Non-Parlour Three-Bedroom House – the kitchen occupied a commodious square-shaped space just off the central entrance, at the front of the building. The sink was located under the window, not only to allow sufficient light, but also views of the street. Unlike the deep plan byelaw houses with their scullery spaces pushed to the rear, this arrangement placed the kitchen area in a visible public zone of the house, and connected the individual performing tasks there – most likely a woman – to the public realm outside, and the comings and goings of the street. The cooking range was adjacent to the sink and enjoyed the opportunity to survey the outside world while working. The larder was to the rear and next to this was a short passage which led past the bath and WC to the back door. This then was the proposed configuration in a village whose colliery was without the provision of pithead baths – the returning miner could easily access this washing space from the back door before, once cleansed, progressing into the rest of the house (FIG.130).

It is an arrangement with some similarities to the clean and pit entrances and exits that characterised the planning of the Miners' Welfare Commission pithead baths in their mature form of organisation. It also expressed a refinement of both Houfton's cottage in its iteration for the Sheffield Corporation Competition in 1903, which had its bathroom upstairs, and the Tudor Walters 1918 governmental report's 'Type D House', which still contained a parlour, at the expense of a more commodious and convenient scullery. For Raymond Unwin, the parlour had represented a contradiction to his ideal of a simple and functional approach to dwelling – a superfluous space whose occasional use was largely symbolic and sentimental rather than practical: 'However desirable a parlour may be, it cannot be said to be necessary to health or family life' (Unwin 1902: p.13).

Tudor Walters agreed, criticising both the extra costs involved in the building and furnishing of parlour houses, as well as the subdivision of the ground floor and loss of space that providing a parlour entailed. He also, however, specifically reiterated Unwin's comments on the extra effort that the lighting of additional fires, and so on, in the parlour added to the working day of 'an already overburdened housewife' (Tudor Walters 1927: p.30).[20] In 1919 in the Sankey report, Elizabeth Andrews, a miner's wife from South Wales, had commented – within the context of the desirability of pithead baths – on the 'drudgery work of the women' within the coalfields (Sankey 1919b: p.1020). The refinements in the plans of, for example, the Non-Parlour Three-Bedroom House – and the possible links between its layout and those of the pithead

130
A block of non-parlour three-bedroom houses

baths – suggest a typology further adapted for the specialised housing needs associated with coal mining. Within this, not only the functionality associated with the bathroom and the kitchen, but also the latter's light-filled position overseeing the public realm at the front of the house would seem to be designed in an attempt to relieve at least some of the drudgery of women workers within this very particular domestic realm.[21]

For D. H. Lawrence, writing in 1929 of the Nottinghamshire coalfields of his childhood,

> The great crime which the moneyed classes and promoters
> of industry committed in the palmy Victorian days was the
> condemning of the workers to ugliness, ugliness, ugliness:
> meanness and formless and ugly surroundings, ugly ideals,
> ugly religion, ugly hope, ugly love, ugly clothes, ugly furniture,
> ugly houses, ugly relationship between workers and employers.
> The human soul needs actual beauty even more than bread.
>
> (Lawrence 1929: p.90)

Completed contemporaneously with Lawrence's text, the bucolic imagery of the IHA settlements – of broad skies, streets lined with cranking and stepping cottages filtering into green open spaces and bestriding rolling landscapes – pulled together by an apparently enlightened group of mine owners with the services and expertise of a modern planner and architect, seemed to address, in part, some of Lawrence's social and aesthetic criticism. Indeed, more recently, it has been noted that the appearance of the interior of the 'typical non-parlour living' illustrated in *The Building of Twelve Thousand Houses* bore a 'comparability with the design ethics' of functionality and simplicity seen within international exhibits for middle-class domestic consumption, specifically in the 'breakfast room' at the Monza Exhibition of Industrial and Decorative Art, in Italy, in 1930 (Jeremiah 2000: p.71). If Unwin's early experiences within miners' housing – along with the prototype of the 'cheap cottage' – had inflected the aesthetic and design DNA of municipal housing generally between the wars, then its appearance within the zeitgeist of middle-class design provides further indication of a fitness for purpose and a broad acceptability.

And yet, for some mining communities as late as the 1920s and 1930s, the harmonious aesthetics associated with the Garden City and an austere Arts and Crafts style seen elsewhere in municipal housing generally, were being used – like the earlier model villages of New Bolsover and Creswell – as instruments in ongoing systems of social control. The picturesque new villages of Langold and Blidworth (both constructed by the IHA) cited earlier, along with other new villages at Firbeck, Ollerton, Bilsthorpe and the aforementioned Clipstone and Edwinstowe, accompanied the opening up and development of the new Eastern Sherwood Forest coalfield – the so-called 'Dukeries' – by a series of colliery companies including Bolsover between 1918 and 1928 in Nottinghamshire. While such situations may have existed elsewhere, and indeed within other IHA developments, collectively these particular settlements – situated within one of Britain's most productive and profitable coalfields between the wars – have been described specifically as 'model villages' (Waller 1983). Designed, like earlier precedents of company towns, to both attract and accommodate a varied, unknown and potentially unruly immigrant mining population arriving from elsewhere in the United Kingdom, each village was owned by a single authority – the coal company – which was also responsible for its inhabitants' employment.

In addition – and again as at Creswell and New Bolsover – the cultural life of the village was also often dominated by the coal company in its setting up and close interest in recreational facilities and organisations such as: sports, in the forms of village or colliery football or cricket teams; or music, such as brass or silver bands, or choral associations. These have been described as 'having a positive moral effect as well as [acting] as a harmless safety valve to divert men's attention from more controversial matters' (ibid.: p.195).

In 1927, an article in the *New Statesman* commented on the enhanced quality of the built environment found in the new Dukeries villages.

> New mining villages are rising all over the Dukeries … The worst canker of mining life has been eliminated. Here we have none of those huddled shanties, rotten with age and dirt, uninhabitable and uninhabited by thousands upon thousands of our coal getters in every coal district in the kingdom. Here we will have none of the ghastly rows of ill-built, insanitary houses … Here in the land of the Dukeries the narrow meanness of the owners has been discarded. They have shown a wider outlook – a realisation of the social importance of cleanliness, of the social value of comfort – which marks an almost revolutionary tendency in their class … Housing is the first of the great magnets that draw the best blood of the English mining areas to the Dukeries.
>
> (*New Statesman*, 24 December 1927, cited in ibid.: p.256)

The quotation not only again acknowledges the persistence, well into the 20th century, of slums reminiscent of those found in the 19th-century mining districts, but also highlights emergent social values in the provision of housing: 'the social importance of cleanliness', 'the social value of comfort'. Both could be considered as cohesive, unifying factors in the social construction of a new settlement, and the villages often represented a huge improvement in living conditions for incoming workers from other British coalfields. But evidently cleanliness, or the aesthetics of cleanliness, could also be a means of instilling control, order and influence over the workforce. In 1932, it was commented that at New Ollerton, the Butterley Company 'loses £1500 a year over its housing scheme, but the tranquillity and content of the employees make it a cheap investment' (Graves 1932). At New Ollerton, hot water – after being heated in the pit – was piped to individual houses. But both here and elsewhere, no pets – the keeping and racing of greyhounds and whippets was a traditional miners' cultural pastime – were allowed in the houses on sanitary grounds, noisy or 'immoral' behaviour could be punished, and the lawns which typically fronted the houses within the Garden City type layouts were compulsorily mown, at a cost of two pence weekly to the workers. Indeed, the gardens often became a particular focal point of surveillance, with untidy hedges, a lack of weeding, or even standing on one's own lawn being fineable offences in some of the Dukeries villages. Once again like at Creswell and New Bolsover decades earlier, these strictures were often enforced by company policemen. But surveillance in general was also facilitated by the nature of the spaces themselves, the harmonious layouts of wide streets and front lawns which accompanied, updated, elaborated and aestheticised some of the techniques of control over workers that had existed in the coalfield, and elsewhere, for decades. The loose, almost organic plans of grouped houses enclosing space and points of symmetry influenced by Unwin which, with variations, structured both the villages of the Dukeries and the IHA, allowed the potential of a more subtle, naturalistic orchestration of social hierarchy. At Bilsthorpe, for example, the manager's house occupied a hill overlooking the village, while houses specially designed for management – the head electrician, the head mechanical engineer and the under-managers – along with 'privileged' workers, such as chargehands (known as 'butties'), while all fully integrated into the unity of the scheme were all identifiable within the fabric of the village. At Ollerton meanwhile, the tenets of bucolic spatial harmony within the composition of the village were combined with the appropriation of traditional symbols of hierarchy. Here, the colliery manager rented the impressive, conspicuous and historic Ollerton Hall from a local aristocrat, while at Edwinstowe, the Bolsover Company acquired Edwinstowe Hall – a local historic mansion and traditional seat of aristocratic patronage.

Such symbolic acquisitions perhaps further justified the *New Statesman*'s concerns that within the landscape of benevolent paternalism and improvements to mineworkers' housing and settlements in the Dukeries, 'a new feudalism' was being established (*New Statesman*, 24 December 1927, cited in Waller 1983: pp 106–107). The journal cited the recurring and familiar issues surrounding the provision of both employment and housing (as well as other services and facilities), by a single agency: intensified relationships of worker dependency on their employers articulated through structures of reward and threat. The latter included the potential to evict families because of dismissal at work, or vice versa, where an infraction into the constructed and supervised harmony of the village could result in a worker losing his job. Consequently, the *New Statesman* suggested that the Dukeries coalfield was the site of the continuation of some regressive industrial relationships which were inherited from the 19th century and had died out elsewhere. One of these, for example, was the perseverance of the so-called 'butty' system, where a subcontractor was paid for a specific task in the mine and was then responsible for paying his own 'employees' (Supple 1987: p.36), an arrangement which was seen to add another layer of hierarchy, control and potential for abuse over the workforce. Added to this was the fact that the official mineworkers' union, the Nottingham Miners' Association (NMA) – which was associated with the national Miners' Federation of Great Britain (MFGB) – had an almost negligible presence within the Dukeries between the wars. Instead, many of the workers remained either unaffiliated, were subject to company unions controlled by the management, or connected to the 'non-political', autonomous, and controversial Nottinghamshire Miners Industrial Union (NMIU), the so-called 'Spencer' union (Griffin 1962: p.203).[22]

The use of the term 'industrial feudalism' by the *New Statesman* in describing the new Dukeries coalfield is both significant and ironic. For Unwin, drawing on the theories of Carpenter, Morris and Ruskin, a reinterpretation of a pre-industrial, non-urban landscape offered an alternative to the environmental deprivations and social inequalities associated with industrial capitalism. Yet, here such landscapes of cottages, open spaces and an architecture style – indebted, via the Arts and Crafts movement, to the reappraisal of mediaeval precedents – rather than offering potential new freedoms for workers, were used to reinforce, mask or inculcate modern industrial relationships within terms of traditional deference and obligation. Even the local manor house, which for Unwin in his polemical text 'Sutton Hall' (1889) had represented the potential for a redistribution of wealth and resources, had been harnessed to reinforce and symbolise traditional hierarchies. And yet, this physical and aesthetic landscape was elsewhere simultaneously permissive. Outside the particular social geographies of these coalfields, as has been shown in Abercrombie's Aylesham, Unwin's settlement paradigms – which responded so precisely to a critique of 19th-century miners' row housing – defined generally the experience of interwar housing in Great Britain, without necessarily facilitating the type of intense socio-spatial relationship deemed required to manage the immigrant workforce in the Dukeries. And while such a landscape may have been understandable – as at New Bolsover or Creswell – at the end of the 19th century as a reaction to the rapid and unprecedented course of industrialisation and urbanisation, it is remarkable that it would endure in the Dukeries until after 1947 – and the nationalisation of coal. Even then, the National Coal Board would acquire a significant amount of housing stock that was still tied to collieries – and it would take some time to disentangle the problems associated with the confluence of employers and landlords within a single authority.

PART III

ARCHITECTURE, PUBLICITY AND THE PLAN FOR COAL

INTRODUCTION

> Never before has it been so vital to the purpose and progress of the nation. It is the bedrock of our British wealth and welfare … coal!
>
> (Legg 1952: 00.22s)

Thus began the narration of a film released in 1952. Accompanied by stirring music and images of a variety of scenes of industrial and domestic life in Britain – from factory chimneys, coking ovens, steel works and shipbuilding, to cosy firesides – the narrator stressed the absolute centrality of coal mining to the nation's economic and social life throughout the 19th and early 20th centuries. But this was no elegy. The film was about the future. Destined for cinemas countrywide, *Plan for Coal* was designed to bring to as large a public audience as possible the rather more staidly presented findings of a government report, whose title it shared. Published by the National Coal Board two years earlier in October 1950, the document *Plan for Coal* attempted to shape the vision, scope and means to achieve the continuation of coal's hegemonic position as Britain's principal fuel source and prime mover of industry. This would involve the wholesale restructuring of British coal mining.

> The plan outlined in this document proposes a balanced programme of capital development, designed to increase output, improve productivity and reduce costs, by employing men and money where they can produce the best results. The biggest problems of the industry have been and are human problems. Of necessity the plan deals with investments, schemes, and engineering projects, yet they are only a means to an end, to breathe new life into an old industry, improve the conditions of those who work in it and help the industry to serve the country better.
>
> (NCB 1950)

The desired result was its transformation from what, in terms of its use of technology and social practices, was an often-outmoded anachronistic industry – one which in the public perception retained more than a whiff of the austerity of the 1930s, and was still closely associated with the controversies of accidents, strikes and labour militancy – into a modern, rationalised, technologically advanced and scientifically determined entity staffed by a new breed of highly skilled miners. The latter would both provide the power and become conspicuous participants in the (re)construction of the brave new post-war state, and the new forms of society and its expectations being forged there.

The modernisation of the industry evoked in the *Plan for Coal* in both its filmic and publication forms, and realised in part over the next 15 years or so, was influenced by several factors and antecedents, and emerged from a series of social, political circumstances and technical developments. The most critical of these was the nationalisation of coal mining in 1947, the first industry to be so treated. This put it in a uniquely emblematic position as the pioneer of a new means of organising industry in Britain, in the vanguard of a new relationship between a population of workers and their management. The proposed 'new deal' – seen as necessary to attract new workers into the industry – would ultimately also concern issues outside the workplace, such as the provision of housing and new settlements. But more immediately, the experimental nature of nationalisation, the problems that the new mining entity inherited, the time it would take to build up and realise coal mining's new forms, and the fact that this had to be done within what was often an indifferent or negative climate of opinion, meant that how the ideas and progress of the National Coal Board and the industry at large were communicated, both internally and externally, became increasingly important.

And while actual physical modernist architecture in the pits, other industrial sites, and in forms of settlement would ultimately become both result and icon of its transformation, other more ephemeral methods of communication – often reusing techniques (and indeed sometimes the same personnel) developed for wartime propaganda – were quicker and more efficient in conveying information. Throughout the late 1940s and 1950s films such as *Plan for Coal* were preceded and augmented by other, often state-sponsored forms of popular media, including pamphlets and broadcasts. For example, the first ever live underground transmission was conducted in late 1952 by the BBC from Tillicoultry Colliery in Central Scotland: 'a model modern mine with an OMS of 54 cwts'. The aim of the programme was 'to take the coalface to the fireside of every viewer' (Anon. 1953a: p.5). There was also a series of conspicuous exhibitions on coal which sometimes took place as part of larger national or international events (see also Linehan 2003: pp 132–50). These exhibitions, which straddled the pivotal moment of nationalisation, involved renowned modernist architects and designers. In fact, within all this media, representations of architecture and space – both above and below ground – were used as transmitters of the progress of modernisation. The transformation and simultaneous – to use a contemporary description – *rebranding* of the coal-mining industry and its workforce was, therefore, dependent on a unique and unprecedented coming together of a series of strands: social and political, technical and design. These combined to effect and legitimise the necessary changes and communicate a paradigmatic vision which encompassed not only the future of coal mining, but also, to some degree, that of the United Kingdom.

THE REID REPORT AND TECHNICAL TRANSFORMATIONS

The roots of coal-mining's modernisation from the late 1940s onwards can be seen in the report of the Sankey Commission from 1919 and its calls for a large-scale reconstruction of the mines up to, and including, their nationalisation. This suggestion had been framed by the adoption of government control over the mines during the latter stages of the First World War. In its aftermath was a growing acceptance that, due to its strategic importance, further exploration of how to assure as unbroken a supply of coal as possible was necessary for the nation's future economic, and, indeed, military security. Within this was an acknowledgement of a pressing need to ameliorate the often adverse state of labour relations between the coal owners and the miners. But as discussed earlier, many of Sankey's more far-reaching propositions, including the reorganisation and rationalisation of the industry into fewer and larger units, were not implemented. The lack of progress made by the Coal Mines Reorganisation Committee, established under Part II of the Coal Mines Act of 1930 as part of a governmental strategy to make the industry more competitive, was indicative of this. Their proposals were either abandoned or indefinitely postponed due to the pressures of the collective private interests of coal owners on one hand and, on the other, by the extremely difficult economic climate that beset most industrial nations for much of the 1920s and 1930s.

The nationalisation of the industry, however, had remained one of the key ambitions of the Miners' Federation of Great Britain which, by 1945 had reformed itself into a new unified, nationwide entity: the National Union of Mineworkers (NUM). Government control was repeated during the Second World War and the country's coal stocks and reserves were nationalised in 1942 (Court 1951: Part IV). And when the Labour Party, who had also advocated nationalisation since 1919, was elected into government in July 1945 – with the substantial support of mining voters, and including former coalfield dwellers in its cabinet, *and* armed with a treatise on the nationalism of coal written by Harold Wilson, as well as its 1945 manifesto titled *Let Us Face the Future* which called for the same[1] – the passing of the Coal Industry Nationalisation Act in 1946, 'became inevitable' (Kelf-Cohen 1973: p.19). Of course, as a longstanding socialist aspiration, the passing of the Act was at least in part politically motivated. But among the arguments made by the government in the Bill published in December 1945 by Emmanuel Shinwell (previously Secretary of Mines and now Minister of Fuel and Power)[2] were extensive references to the findings contained within a report commissioned by the previous Conservative government in September 1944: *Coal Mining: Report of the Technical Advisory Committee*. Known more popularly after the committee's chairman Charles Carlow Reid, the Reid Report was published just months before the Labour Party came to power in March 1945. Its terms of reference were: 'To examine the present technique of coal production from coalface to wagon, and to advise what technical changes are necessary in order to bring the industry to a state of full technical efficiency' (Reid 1945: p.1).

As suggested here, and within its full title, the Report focused principally on appraising and suggesting improvements for the technological aspects of mining coal in Great Britain. All seven members of its committee were ostensibly apolitical, but had been actively involved in the extraction of coal, and six of them had qualifications in mining engineering. Reid himself was Director of Production at the Ministry of Fuel and Power. Before this he had been Manager and Director of the Fife Coal Company based in Cowdenbeath, a concern that had often won its coal in difficult conditions and had been long regarded within the industry as a 'model of efficiency' (Ashworth 1986: p.123).

Yet the Report implicitly and, at times, explicitly acknowledged that a successful future for the coal-mining industry, with its huge attendant labour force, could not be achieved by technical means alone. It would also have to respond to other circumstances. These included not only the existing working and social lives of the miners and their communities, but also the psychology of both the workers and their employers. The intimate relationship between technology and labour is perhaps clarified by the unit of measurement used in the report to evaluate productivity. Measured in tons, Output per Manshift (OMS) would become the universal means of calculating performance and efficiency in coal mining over the coming decades. It was central to the methods of comparative analysis used by the Technical Advisory Committee in determining the state of British coal mining versus other coal-producing countries. While the Report provided narrative descriptions of how each of these individual countries used technology to extract their coal – Belgium; Czechoslovakia; France; Germany: Ruhr, Upper Silesia and Saar; Netherlands; Poland; and the USA – these comparisons were ultimately defined and quantified numerically using OMS statistics.

Appendix I, which presented a table synopsising these findings, made the troubling data surrounding British performance starkly clear. Using 1913, the peak of British production, as a base of 100, it showed increases in productivity as a series of indices over the years from 1925 to 1938. Within this, British mining was the worst performing country, with a score of 113 for the final year measured. Only France (excluding the Saar region) came close with 119. The rest of the countries recorded much more accelerated increases. Britain's wartime adversary Germany, for example, easily outstripped British performance – its main coal-producing regions of the Ruhr, Upper Silesia and the Saar recorded at 164, 162 and 142 respectively, in 1938. Perhaps unexpectedly the best performance came from the Netherlands with 201 for the same year (Reid 1945: p.141), but it was the results for the Ruhr that were of particular interest and importance, because mining conditions there were thought to be closest to the degree of difficulty of extraction found within most British coalfields.

The Reid Report concluded that the deficiencies in British OMS performance since 1913 had been caused by a systematic lack of sustained investment in the development and deployment of new technologies within the industry.[3] By 1947, for example, almost a fifth of the coal produced was still cut by hand and there were still over 21,000 pit ponies in operation (Hall 1981: p.92). In the combination of the finite or absolute terms of time and labour presupposed in OMS measurements, the clearest means of increasing productivity is clearly within the application of machinery. What the *Report* ultimately recommended, therefore, was effectively an underground technological revolution, one which would introduce at a comprehensive scale, the rationalised methods and systems found within other, more conventional, modern productive facilities: factories.

Central to this was the rapid deployment of mechanisation in key areas within the pit: the coalface itself, in both cutting and roof support; and haulage, in the transportation and circulation of both coal and men, vertically and horizontally. These interventions, however, would not be possible in isolation. Underground working is complex and defined by a lack of uniformity. Unlike a factory, operations within a mine take place in an environment which is essentially not fixed and where production conditions – which can happen anywhere within an 8 km radius of the pit bottom – can, and do, change almost constantly, according to both foreseen and unforeseen quirks in geological and other unique, below-ground conditions. Being an extractive process, the coalface (effectively the production line) constantly shifts and so the systems involved – especially those for coal cutting and removal – have to be moved, not merely from time to time, but on a daily basis. Meanwhile, the infrastructure of tunnels (underground roadways, and so on) which allows access to these coalface areas, and can permit the underground disposal of spoil, also has to be both constantly extended and constantly repaired (Ashworth 1986: p.62).

While the *Report* did not explicitly suggest nationalisation, the investment required for the widespread introduction of mechanisation presupposed the kind of extensive structural changes that some other previous reports – most notably Sankey – had also deemed necessary: the reorganisation of the industry, from hundreds of (often small) privately owned collieries of varying sizes, into larger operational units of both production and administration. For Reid and his colleagues this 'reorganisation of the industry needed to be undertaken on the basis of [entire] coalfields and not of individual mines' (Townshend-Rose 1951: p.36). While its roots and impetus were in the updating of underground working practices, the transformations necessary to modernise the industry and increase productivity implied, therefore, an integrated infrastructural response – vertically, above and below ground, and horizontally, across and between the coalfields. This would operate in both space and time, encompassing a series of scales from the physicality of the coalface itself, to the more ephemeral divisional, regional and national networks that would coordinate and seek to unify methods of production through the application of OMS and other systems of measurement. All this would come with social consequences.

As the industry remade itself as a rationalised, technically advanced entity, it was understood that the traditional profile of the miner as a skilled manual labourer using hand tools, would have to evolve to become that of a skilled technician, engaged in the operation of machines. But the new coal-mining industry would also require an increase of white-collar workers to orchestrate not only research, but the long- and short-term regional and national planning that the *Report* precipitated, and would – to some extent – be fulfilled in the *Plan for Coal*. Part of this would involve the surveying through boring and other methods – sometimes offshore, as at the Firth of Forth, or elsewhere in the North Sea off the Northumbrian coast – of existing and potential new coalfields to determine future supply, and the siting of a new generation of much larger pits. The latter would be designed holistically from the outset as carefully planned entities to accommodate the latest technological systems and encourage the frictionless flow of coal and men. Drawing on recommendations from Charles Carlow Reid, the modernised industry would emerge from some of the findings of the Scientific Department of the fledging National Coal Board, and the development of a Field Investigation Group which would undertake Operational Research (OR) within collieries, under the authority of Sir Charles Ellis. Writing in 1948, Ellis who had been Scientific Advisor to the Army Council during the Second World War, described his task as responding to: 'the urgent need for an objective analysis of the chain of operations from the face to the surface, to establish the cost of each link in terms of power, manpower and effort generally' (cited in Tomlinson 1971: p.3). In addition, extensive surveys of existing mines would also have to be carried out to establish whether they had the potential to be remodelled according to the new technological criteria, or whether their 'rationalisation' would be one of closure. The influx of technology into mining would produce both human obsolescence and other significant levels of social adjustment – the closure of old mines and the opening of new ones implied redundancies or migration, either locally or farther afield. The latter, however, was a familiar disruption within mineworking communities and, paradoxically perhaps, represented a degree of continuity between historic experience and this new phase of mining.[4]

The creation of the necessary new types of workers – whether culled from the existing workforce or newly entering the industry for the first time – would also require new specialised training centres to be shared between collieries or even coalfields. Increased mechanisation, meanwhile, suggested the production of standardised and uniform machines and parts, implying the creation of more shared facilities to develop, produce and test them. In addition, it had also been recognised that mechanically won coal was often of a different quality to its hand-won equivalent, and required additional treatment – screening, sizing and cleaning – before it could be taken to the marketplace. This would necessitate the production of further, and more sophisticated, coal-preparation plants – which washed the coal – to serve either individual or groups of mines. Accordingly, an entirely new series of buildings was required either within the collieries themselves, or as part of a regional and national network of coal interests and production. This remaking of space on the surface would occur at least partly within the public eye and would, therefore, have both visual consequences and opportunities. Significantly then, the Reid Report suggested that:

> Where plans are being made for a new mine or for remodelling old mines, it is desirable that the advice of an architect should be taken on the surface layout … [E]very effort should be made … to make the colliery surface attractive. [Because the] appearance of the colliery can hardly fail to affect the psychology of all those employed in the mine, and there can be no hope of creating among the workmen a pride in their place of employment unless management makes a serious attempt to create something of which to be proud.
>
> (Reid 1945: p.97)

For the Technical Advisory Committee, therefore, it was functionally necessary that the technological transformation of the industry had an appropriate visual accompaniment and aesthetic expression. Furthermore, while they acknowledged that once again European mines 'have pointed the way in this respect', they also proposed that there were in Britain: '[A]lready examples of new mines, and old mines reconstructed which could worthily serve as models for the future' (ibid.).

COMRIE AND OTHER ARCHITECTURAL PARADIGMS

The *Plan for Coal* film of 1952 had had an antecedent in another production released seven years earlier in 1945, the same year the Reid Report was published. *The New Mine*, as its title suggests, describes the working life of a recently completed colliery. It proposed that the eponymous facilities at Comrie near Dunfermline in Fife represented a vision for the future of mining. The film uses a similar range of comparative techniques of past and present that would define the later *Plan for Coal* film. Images of historic practices and traditional mining iconography are contrasted with the new conditions found at Comrie. A chaotic and filthy smoke-belching colliery, a legacy from the 19th century, juxtaposes the ordered composition of a series of clean-looking buildings complete with landscaped surroundings that include an ornamental fishpond. If not for the presence of the adjacent headgear, the industrial purposes of these buildings would not be clear. Rather they look civic, reminiscent perhaps of a provisional town hall. Underground, hand-working the seams with picks and shovels has been completely replaced by the application of coal-cutting machinery and attendant conveyor belts. These are arranged according to the longwall retreating method of mining, superseding the more traditional room and pillar process, and ventilated by a forcing (blowing) rather than the more usual extracting fan (Reid 1939).[5] Tubs full of coal pulled by diesel locomotives glide along well made and level roadway tunnels to meet the steel-caged lifts that will bring them to the surface above. There, preparation plants and washeries clean and grade the coal, before it is automatically loaded on to the waiting lines of railway wagons that are filled efficiently in series. *The New Mine* also stresses other new practices. Introduced by the narrator as 'miners', a clean-looking group of young men in sports jackets and ties occupy a classroom, attended by a teacher in a lab-coat and that most emphatic icon of the application of science, the test tube. Elsewhere, miners, fresh from a shift, cavort modestly and good naturedly for the cameras in the pithead baths, before repairing to the canteen to drink tea or enjoy a hot meal.

If this seems like an early apotheosis of at least some of the aspirations of the Reid Report, then this is perhaps because Comrie Colliery was owned and operated by the Fife Coal company, which had been under the directorship of Charles Carlow Reid himself. The architecture of this mine is also familiar. Its aesthetic and materiality borrow from Dudok, and the principal building at the centre of the U-shape layout – with its sleek horizontality expressed in form, detail, and windows, contrasting elegantly with its vertical tower – is clearly recognisable as a pithead baths. Influenced by his training in both architecture and planning, the Chief Architect of the Miners' Welfare Commission, John Henry Forshaw had advocated throughout the 1930s that pithead baths should operate as compositional devices within the surface layouts of collieries, and bring order to their often-turbulent environments (Forshaw 1935: p.1080). 'Pithead improvements' were cited in the MWC's *Fourteenth Annual Report 1935* as providing: '[a] considerable contribution to the advancement of that new outlook permeating industry today, which strives to establish the place of work as an orderly and well-planned development bringing the least disturbance to the neighbourhood in which it operates and at the same time catering for the well-being of its employees' (MWC 1936: p.17).

Partial fulfilment of this objective has been seen in many of the pithead baths projects, ranging from the mere juxtaposing of the aesthetic presence of their carefully composed forms against often dreary and utilitarian pit-surface backdrops, to a more active role in the reordering of space, such as at the likes of: Coventry Colliery (Warwickshire, 1935); Manvers Main Colliery (South Yorkshire, 1937); or Clock Face Colliery (Lancashire, 1939). Comrie, however, represented the first comprehensive and integrated expression – both above and below ground – of modern planning in a coal mine in Britain. The surface represented a collaboration between Forshaw and the MWC's architects, who designed the layout and the buildings, and the coal company's own architect who carried through the development – with the MWC team remaining throughout as consultants. The MWC's *FifteenthAnnual Report 1936* celebrated the project:

> The conception of the work as a planned [my emphasis] development, including the selection and reservation of a site

for future baths and the agreement upon lay-out and elevational treatment for all the colliery buildings in a uniformity throughout, marks an important step in industrial planning … it is evident that the undertaking will become a standard in modern colliery construction and will demonstrate once more that, with a properly thought-out scheme, it is possible to open new works without ruining the appearance of the countryside.

(MWC 1937: p.29)

Complete with a small settlement of officials' housing, it was finished by 1942, with the expectation that other new collieries seeking the architectural advice of the MWC in the mid-1940s – such as at Merry Lees (Leicestershire) and Machrihanish (on the Mull of Kintyre in Argyllshire) – would produce similar results. This aspiration was to a large extent achieved at Calverton (Nottinghamshire) which was begun in 1937, and composed with an axial approach passing under an elegantly thin concrete canopy, with a play of symmetry and asymmetry in the sleek forms of its overall layout (FIG.131). Despite being started under private enterprise this colliery would become the first pit to be opened after nationalisation. Consequently, its technical achievements, including the freezing methods necessary to drill through water-saturated ground during the sinking of its shafts, and its positive aesthetic presence – 'the countryside, around the trim pithead at Calverton, will not be spoiled, for this pit is planned on far-sighted lines' (Anon. 1950a: p.11) – were widely and positively acknowledged. Meanwhile at Chislet in Kent, the MWC architects were requested to remodel and replan the existing colliery and

131
Calverton Colliery

132
Chislet Colliery and village

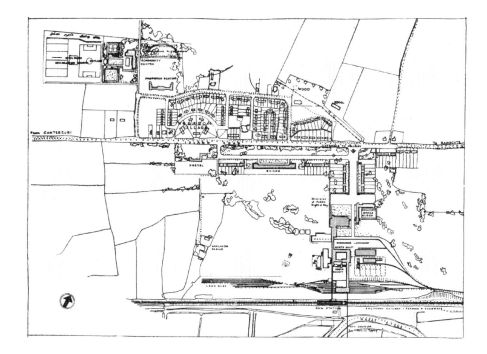

develop its range of facilities. Significantly, their scheme for additional offices, officials' houses and a new pithead baths proposed – with a new hostel and shopping centre – to integrate the colliery layout with that of the existing village: the merging of industrial with civic space (MWC 1946: p.19) (FIG132).

These then are presumably the model collieries that the Reid Report cited as potential precedents for the reconstruction of the industry. But Comrie is significant in another way, one that would also become a conspicuous feature in British coal-mining's post-war future. Once again this drew upon the lessons of the MWC pithead baths scheme generally: the use of building as an object of propaganda and publicity. Only now, the physical iconography of the modern built artefact was increasingly allied with other forms of media, including, as has been shown, the moving image. Long before *The New Mine* film was commissioned, however, a version of Comrie had already been presented to a large public audience as 'The Model Coal Mine' at the Glasgow Empire Exhibition in 1938 (FIG.133). Sponsored by the Mining Association of Great Britain (MAGB) – the coal-owners' consortium – the exhibit was a sectional model of a pit built at a scale of a quarter inch to the foot. Representing a depth of 700 feet, it was designed to give a general idea of the surface layout, and its relationship with the 'typical scenes from the underground workings of a completely electrified modern colliery employing about 1,500 men and producing 2,500 tons of coal per day' (MAGB 1938: p.1).

The model displayed a harmonious composition of the various structures above ground. Like at Comrie, the two headgear towers (one for men and one

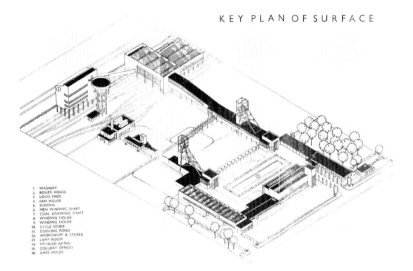

KEY PLAN OF SURFACE

1. WASHERY
2. BOILER HOUSE
3. LOCO SHED
4. FAN HOUSE
5. SCREENS
6. MEN WINDING SHAFT
7. COAL DRAWING SHAFT
8. WINDING HOUSE
9. WINDING HOUSE
10. CYCLE STORE
11. COOLING POND
12. WORKSHOPS & STORES
13. LAMP ROOM
14. PIT-HEAD BATHS
15. COLLIERY OFFICES
16. GATE HOUSE

for coal) and their respective winding houses were arranged symmetrically on opposite sides of an open space that developed into a more formal, landscaped courtyard in the presence of the pithead baths and lamp room. The latter were ranged parallel to the main public road outside the pit to form its main public front. The principal vehicular entrance, which was located between the end of the baths and the colliery offices, took the form of a tree-lined avenue on axis with the glazed front of the coal-drawing shaft's winding house. Shrubs, trees, hedges and grass were incorporated throughout. A copse screened one end of the colliery near the public road, with a hint that a similar device was present on the opposite side. Meanwhile, a neat hedge was arrayed around the rectangular pool which, as at Comrie, was used not only for cooling the machinery of winding houses, but also formed a picturesque foreground to the baths building, an arrangement deeply reminiscent of Dudok's Hilversum Town Hall. A single line of trees provided a screen between this – what could be described as a civic area – and the more industrial and utilitarian presence of the rest of the colliery. And yet, the composition of all these elements remained consistent. The articulated U-shape form of the cooling pond courtyard continued in the linear link from the coal shaft to the screening plant, and was balanced opposite in the boiler house, locomotive shed and fan house. Finally, the courtyard form was loosely completed by the screening plant and the washery. The latter, like the railway tracks beneath and around it, was parallel to the pithead baths range which provided its opposite. Within all this, the washery water tower stood like an erratic chess piece, between the railway lines, its round concrete forms giving a last sculptural quality to a layout that sought to combine landscape, civic and industrial forms to make an integrated whole.

133
The 'Model Coal Mine' at the Glasgow Empire Exhibition, 1938

134
The Miners' Welfare Fund at the Glasgow Empire Exhibition, 1938

The 'Model Coal Mine' was exhibited in the Coal Hall of the United Kingdom Government Pavilion, under a vaulted space dominated by the looming presence of a mural heroically depicting headgear and a washery tower like the one in the model. Within this space, visitors could learn not only about coal as a fuel source in the home and industry, but also its other modern uses – its carbonisation, its characteristics and possibilities as a chemical raw material, its synthesis into oil and alcohol, on so on. Alongside these scientific initiatives was information about advances made by the Safety-in-the-Mines Research Board, and finally, an exhibit explaining the work and scope of the Miners' Welfare Fund (Anon. 1938: p.112) (FIG.134). Here, some of the Fund's main achievements and activities were conveyed in a series of photographs: a children's playground, a rehabilitation centre, opportunities for education, and a series of cultural and recreational pursuits including a theatrical play and various sports. The overall form of this exhibit was derived from the curving wall and oriel-window forms seen in many of the pithead baths. Indeed, the MWC show's principal element was another model presented behind a horizontal vitrine within one of these curves. While depicting the landscapes and features of a typical coalfield community, complete with the inevitable spoil heap, the model emphasised the ameliorative measures and improvements to this environment engendered by the Fund, and orchestrated through the Committee – including the pithead baths.

While all this represented a comprehensive vision of a modernised industry and its integration of scientific, technical and social concerns, in fact the Coal Hall was only the smaller of two spaces dedicated to mining and the mineral. The other was the much larger and conspicuous Coal Pavilion, designed by Thomas S. Tait, the architect responsible for the master planning of the whole Empire Exhibition, as well as numerous other buildings within it, including its most emphatic icon – the so-called Tait's Tower. The Coal Pavilion was located in a prominent position immediately to the right of one of the grounds' main entrances – from Bellahouston Station on Mosspark Boulevard – and just south of the colossal Palace of Engineering. According to the official exhibition brochure, 'Coal is not only represented by the actual exhibits inside the pavilion, [the building] is made entirely of steel, symbolising the close relationship between the coal and iron and steel industries'. The brochure went on to catalogue the various ways in which coal contributed to the production and aesthetics of the pavilion, from its superficial use 'as the main decorative effect of the rock garden', to its more hidden role in the creation of the floodlights, the equipment of the film theatre, the paints used on the buildings, and the energy to maintain the neon signs (Anon. 1938: p.185). The latter, emblazoning two sides of the building with the lit-up legend *Coal: In Home and Industry*, confirmed a shift in emphasis between the overall message of this pavilion and the Coal Hall.

In collaboration with the Mining Association of Great Britain, the Combustion Appliance Makers Association (Solid Fuel), and the British Steelwork Association, Tait's building was commissioned by the Coal Utilisation Council (CUC). Set up in 1932 in the context of increasing competition from oil, the aspirations of the CUC concerned the research and marketing of new and further ways to use coal and increase its consumption. This would become a central aspect in the National Coal Board's activities post 1947. Accordingly, alongside exhibits concerning production – such as the models of machinery charting the progress of mechanisation in mines over the previous decades – were displays showing similar technical advances in the consumption of coal. These including demonstrations of fires whose rate of burning could be automatically controlled, and new coal-burning cookers, 'installed in a scientifically planned modern kitchen in which the necessary labour-saving equipment is arranged such that all the ordinary work can be carried out with the minimum number of steps and the least possible expenditure of [human] energy' (Anon. 1938: pp 186–7).

Alongside these domestic appliances – through which '[t]he pavilion makes just as much appeal to women as to men' – other more industrial uses and processes were displayed. These included another advent of the future, one that would become critical after the war to the marketing of coal as a fuel to the producers of electricity: the development of methods of pulverising the mineral, demonstrated by a coal crushing and pulverisation plant, 'shown in motion' (ibid.: pp 186–7).

The Empire Exhibition in Glasgow was visited by over 12 million individuals. How many viewed the Coal Hall or entered the steel-framed and steel-corrugated-clad building designed by Tait – with its shallow barrel-vaulted structure and clerestory windows, semicircular apse-like extrusions and curious, fin-like vertical elements derived, it seems, directly from Dudok's

Julianaschool en Catharina van Renesschool (1925–7) in Hilversum – remains unrecorded. Coal, however, had also had a presence at other conspicuous and large-scale exhibits in the early and middle decades of the 20th century. An exhibition more firmly focused on its productive side, for example, had featured at the previous Empire Exhibition in Wembley in London in 1924–5. This had been in the form of a full-sized colliery mock-up, complete with a series of tunnels dug to a depth of 45 feet beneath the surface. The working headgear, powered by an electric engine, was capable of dispatching 2,000 visitors per hour underground, where they could view various carefully reproduced scenes of the latest in contemporary coal production and its application of technology. A joint initiative between the coal owners and representatives of the miners (the Mining Association of Great Britain and the Miners' Federation of Great Britain respectively), and the Institute of Mining Engineers, the mine and the museum which accompanied it were reputed to have cost over £100,000.

It can be argued that the two Empire Exhibitions were essentially international trade fairs, somewhat similar in the intent to display manufactured commodities that had grounded their progenitor – that great homage to Victorian industrialism – the Great Exhibition of the Works of Industry of All Nations which had famously taken place in London's Hyde Park in 1851. Coal mining's position in mid-20th century British life, however, was affirmed by its inclusion in the, perhaps, more culturally rarefied atmosphere of the influential event designed to mark the centenary of the Great Exhibition: the Festival of Britain in 1951. Supported by and identified with the same Labour Party government that had nationalised the mines and that was developing the welfare state, the Festival of Britain has been described as a celebration of post-war reconstruction and reform, one that 'set the broad parameters of a social democratic agenda for a new and modern Britain' (Conekin 2003: p.4). While the organisation of the overall event was 'in part an early experiment' (Forty 1976: p.37) for the modernist technocracy of the coming years, coal-mining's presence within the Festival was, perhaps significantly, rather more abstract, experiential, emotive and social, than in its previous showings in the Empire Exhibitions.

In the main festival site on the South Bank of the Thames in London, exhibiting buildings were distributed across two zones: upstream, representing 'the land', and downstream, which dealt with 'the people'. Coal, evidently, was located in the former section within a building dedicated to Minerals of the Island, designed by the Architects Cooperative Partnership (ACP) and linked, by a high-level walkway, to the nearby Power and Production pavilion (designed by George Grenfell-Baines in association with H. J. Reifenberg). Its most conspicuous feature was the abstract geometry of the 'truncated tetrahedron, clad with concrete coal-faced blocks ... mounted on a grass covered podium which concealed the main entrance' (Harwood and Powers 2001: p.68). *The Times* describes the edifice as a 'coal mine turned inside out' (*The Times* 1951: p.6) – an unkinder critic might have compared it to an attenuated spoil heap. A compelling if slightly uncanny presence amongst the other

Festival buildings, the magazine *Illustrated* – publishing its appraisal in 1950 before the exhibition's actual opening – reported that the towering inverse mine was designed to be seen from inside and below, so that 'crowds will know what a miner sees at the bottom of the shaft' (*Illustrated* 1950: p.43). *Coal* magazine, which described the festival as 'the greatest show on earth', reported that near the 'bottom' was a miniature coalface, manned by five West Midlands Miners 'ready to explain the miner's life, everything from what he gets for snaps [snacks] – to how you work a Samson stripper' (Anon. 1951b: pp 12–13). Coal-mining's main presence in the Festival of Britain, however, was off the main site, in the Exhibition of Industrial Power held in the Kelvin Hall, Glasgow. This was one of a series of satellite, provincial and travelling exhibitions, which included the 'Live Architecture Exhibition' in London's East End, events concerning farming and factories in Northern Ireland, hillside farming in Wales, and HMS *Campania*, the Festival ship, a repurposed aircraft carrier which sailed from port to port around Great Britain.

The Glasgow exhibition, planned by Alistair Borthwick and coordinated by Basil Spence, chiefly concerned heavy industry.[6] Laid out in an intricately twisting

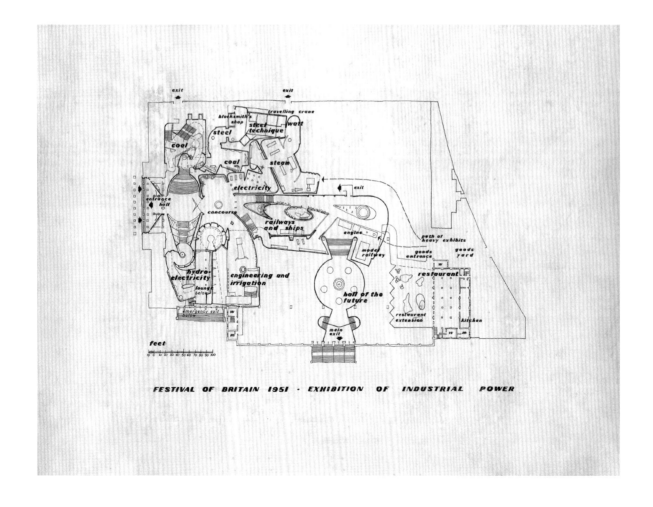

sequence, which in plan is reminiscent of some sort of combustion engine (FIG.135), it presented coal alongside hydroelectric energy as the potential and actual twin fuels of Scotland's new modern age. The responsibility for the production of the other elements shown – steel, electricity, engineering, railways and ships – lay principally with coal. The dual elemental power sources, however, were introduced together in the main entrance space within a large single icon which merged a colliery winding wheel on the left, with a water wheel on the right, to indicate their respective sections in the building. Both exhibitions were accessed by sets of stairs – hydroelectricity by a modern lightweight, riser-less transparent construction covered by a suspended glass pitched roof, designed to protect the visitor from the spray of the water jets that flanked its sides.

The entrance to the Coal Hall could not have been more different. Designed by Spence, it was accessed through a monumental and archaic, amphitheatrical space. This incorporated a wide ceremonial set of steps leading towards a concave and ponderous 'cliff' or coalface containing a sculptural mural made by Thomas Whalen (FIG.136). As they climbed the steps, visitors would catch diagonal glimpses of 'a symbolic sun created by a "stroboscopic" flash contained in a Perspex sphere', through the exhibition entrance (Conekin 2003: p.67), a smallish portal in the massive cliff. The exhibition's brochure described Whalen's sculpture as 'a black cliff hewn into forms and figures which symbolise Man's conquest and use of coal' (Anon. 1951a: p.23). This coalface crescent presented ancient tree fronds, a snail-like fossil and mythical figures (including the inevitable King Coal). But perhaps its most conspicuous and significant figure was located on the left-hand side, directly opposite the carbon monarch and upon whom he was dependent for his power: a miner (FIG.137). Somewhat stylised, this figure – swinging a pickaxe and complete with helmet, head-lamp

135
Exhibition of Industrial Power, Festival of Britain, Glasgow, 1951, floor plan

136
Model of Thomas Whalen's coal sculpture featuring King Coal, Festival of Britain, Glasgow, 1951

137
Thomas Whalen's coal sculpture, detail of a miner figure, Festival of Britain, Glasgow, 1951

and muscled bare torso at a scale of four or five times life-size – was reminiscent of Socialist Realist depictions of hero-*Stakhanovite* workers of the mid-century Soviet Union.[7] And while the rest of the Hall of Coal retained familiar iterations of the mining industry's progress through displays of the latest mechanical cutters, strippers and loaders, and so on, there were also further Socialist Realist-style depictions of over-scaled and well-built miners – sometimes viewed from below and looming over great blocks of coal – accompanying the more prosaic information on aspects of their lives and work.

Attracting a mere 280,000 visitors, the Kelvin Hall's Exhibition of Industrial Power was not considered very successful. Yet the presence of coal here, and in its tetrahedral counterpart in the Minerals of the Island pavilion on the South Bank, reiterated the message established in the earlier Empire Exhibitions – the continuing economic centrality of coal mining to Britain. In the Festival of Britain, moreover, the vicarious fun-park experience of descending to the underground of 1924, and the technophilia of 1938, had been replaced by a more sombre reflection on mining, one that also contrasted the lightweight and often whimsical architecture seen elsewhere in the 1951 celebrations. Part of this appears to be a reconsidered representation of the human figure of the miner in the production of coal and, thereby, its role in the reproduction of everyday life. And while depictions such as Whalen's tend towards the mythic – much like the caryatid figures cited by Orwell, or the miner as an autochtone hewn from the ground evoked by Emile Zola's *Germinal* – these personifications provided, within the context of the visions of a modernistic future framed by the Festival, a new cultural and visual appreciation of mining labour.

COMMUNICATING THE NATIONALISED INDUSTRY

The Festival of Britain was staged some four years after the nationalisation of coal and the instigation of the National Coal Board in 1947. Decades in the making, nationalisation had come to fruition on the 1st of January 1947, the so-called Vesting Day, with a ceremonial event staged in pits across the country. While often accompanied by the raising of an NCB flag – and sometimes the accompaniment of miners' brass or silver bands, singing, or other festivities – essentially this involved the simple erection or unveiling of a notice or plaque. Written, appropriately, in a modern sans-serif typeface, it bore the straightforward yet solemn and ultimately far-reaching testimony: 'This Colliery is now managed by the National Coal Board on behalf of the People.'

One immediate administrative aspect in the nationalisation of the industry was the new, national-scaled remapping of the island's coalfield geography. The 1,000 or so pits inherited by the NCB were allocated to 48 'Areas'. While these could range from six to 66, the average numbers of collieries per Area was 20 pits, with a collective annual output from less than 1 million to over 8 million tons of coal. In turn, these Areas were grouped into nine 'Divisions' which were based on a combination of traditionally defined coalfields and a regional system that the Ministry of Fuel and Power had initiated during the war (Townshend-Rose 1951: pp 55–6). Despite one or two variations, the Divisions also bore a resemblance to the coalfield geographies established under the Miners' Welfare Committee to facilitate its nationwide provision of facilities and services.

Scottish Division	Scottish Coalfields
Durham Division	The Durham Coalfield
Northern (Northumberland and Cumberland) Division	Coalfields of Northumberland and Cumberland
North Western Division	Lancashire and North Wales Coalfields
North Eastern Division	Yorkshire Coalfields
West Midlands Division	Black Country and Potteries Coalfields
East Midlands Division	Nottingham, Derbyshire, and Leicestershire Coalfields
South Western Division	South Wales and Coalfield of South-west England
South Eastern Division	Kent Coalfield

While Divisions enjoyed some autonomy, they were ultimately answerable to the policies of the central National Coal Board. This was based in the newly acquired Hobart House, a large and ponderous neo-classical building acquired by the NCB and located in central London's Belgravia.[8] While its structure would alter (most notably following the 1955 report of the committee chaired by Alexander Fleck on management and accountability within the NCB), the first board, constituted on the 15th of July 1946, consisted of nine full-time members. It drew from experts in coal production such as Charles Carlow Reid, trade unionists such as Ebby Edwards (former General Secretary of the MFGB), and other scientific and technical experts. It was chaired by The Lord Hyndley, who had formerly been Controller General at the Ministry of Fuel and Power, Commercial Manager of the Mines Department, Director of the Bank of England and Managing Director of Powell Duffryn Ltd, the colliery company founded in South Wales. His expertise and experience were indicative of the mixture of managerial, technical and labour-relations skills found in the rest of the board, each of whom had 'a special knowledge of a particular aspect of the industry's past activities or of an activity which was now to be developed'. Accordingly, each was given a department within the organisation to supervise: Production (Reid and T. E. B. Young); Marketing (J. C. Gridley); Finance (L. H. H. Lowe); Manpower and Welfare (Lord Citrine); Labour Relations (Eddy Edwards); and Scientific (Sir Charles Ellis) (NCB 1948: p.2).

In 1957, reflecting on ten years of the nationalised industry, Emmanuel Shinwell echoed the sentiments first expressed in the Reid Report, 'The transformation of the pits from private to public ownership was more than a technical and administrative change. It was largely *psychological* [my emphasis] in character' (Shinwell 1957, p.1).

Central to this transformation was the promotion and reiteration of the concept that the new system of organisation and administration was a collective, common and national endeavour, one where previously defined, and often antithetical, relationships between 'Boss' and 'Worker', as well as 'Sectional interests' (ibid.: p.3) had to be dissolved and replaced with a new understanding.[9] Speaking ten years earlier in 1947 at the National Union of Mineworkers' annual conference Arthur Horner, General Secretary of the NUM (and noted Communist), shared Shinwell's sentiments. Perhaps specifically to address issues of wildcat strikes and absenteeism amongst the workforce, he stressed the need for 'A new consciousness … a new morality' to be created within the industry (cited in Hall 1981: p.95).

The newly nationalised coal industry inherited a series of acute structural problems which could not be solved easily or quickly. One of the key issues with the technical solutions proposed by the Reid Report in 1945, for example, was the length of time it would take to construct new capacity in the form of new coal mines. Two diagrams produced by the NCB in 1957 – as part of a published retrospective on progress within the first ten years of its operations – communicated these timeframes. The first recorded that it took at least nine years for a mine to start producing coal, nine years during which capital and manpower was expended without any return. The other diagram showed that, of the 200 major reconstruction and new-build schemes proposed in 1947, only about 30 had been completed by 1956, and none at all before 1952 (NCB 1957a: p.10). So, while the NCB departments listed above began their operations immediately, the results of their works in reorientating the industry would remain invisible for some time to come.

As Shinwell suggested, all this took place within the context of 'the lukewarm attitude, if not implacable hostility of the opponents of nationalisation' on one hand and, 'the high expectations of the mineworkers' on the other (Shinwell 1957: p.1). The latter's potential discontent was partly based on the fact that a different type of managerial structure had been both imagined and proposed in the 1920s. This had involved much more worker involvement than had been realised in the appointment to the board – influenced by Herbert Morrison's creation of the London Passenger Transport Board – of a series of technocrats. Meanwhile, one of these technocrats, Charles Carlow Reid, conspicuously resigned within two years of nationalisation, citing that he did not believe that 'the present cumbersome and uninspired organisation will produce for the country the coal it needs for home and export purposes' (cited in Hall 1981: p.92). Not only this, but for much of its first ten years at least – during its most intensive period of new start-up works, when capital was expended in initiatives that had not yet realised the production of coal – the industry was often presented as being loss-making. Furthermore, many of the targets proposed within the *Plan for Coal* in 1950, proved over-optimistic and had to be revised in subsequent NCB publications – firstly in *Investing in Coal* (1956) and then again in the *Revised Plan for Coal* (1959). Finally, added to this was one of the most critical problems faced in the early years of nationalisation: the ongoing acute shortage of labour. Lack of sufficient manpower had already led to underproduction and instances of critical shortage. The most conspicuous of these occurred at the precise moment of the nationalised industry's birth, in the winter of 1946–7, when an unforeseen severity of weather combined with a lack of coal caused severe disruptions to everyday life nationally. These included power cuts and sections of the population being left without the means to heat their homes. This was ultimately resolved, but only temporarily. By January 1951 there remained significant enough coal shortages to be described as a 'crisis', one which Britain could still only overcome through the importation of foreign stocks (Noel-Baker 1951: pp 10–11).

All these circumstances combined with the fact that the coal industry was United Kingdom's first experiment with nationalisation. As such it was representative of the aspirations of a particular political ideology, which promoted it as both engine and icon of a new modern era. Consequently, the activities of the NCB would be continually under scrutiny and critique. Within these initial moments of uncertainty, prospective and real progress in the transformation of the industry had to be visualised and disseminated both within and outside the industry. The realisation of a coherent, homogenised industry of related parts and harmonious labour relations out of the piecemeal interventions of previous decades of private enterprise would necessitate not only inevitable physical and administrative changes, but also – and crucially to the development of a new psychology or morality – the representation and communication of what the new industry might look like. This, moreover, would have to take place not only within the industry, but also reach externally to promote a wider understanding of, and an altering in, the popular perception of coal mining – specifically to attract new labour. And while the production of new buildings and spaces would ultimately contribute to this, in the years immediately following nationalisation, the presence of the architecture associated with long-term projects had to remain, at least temporarily, within the realm of visualised conjecture. In the interim, the gap between future projections and reality in the social, technological, scientific and physical transformation of the coal industry promised by the Reid Report would partially, at least, be filled by the projections of media and public relations events.

It is not entirely clear which NCB department held the portfolio for publicity. It may have emerged from the Marketing Department which was 'responsible for formulating the Board's marketing policy and … not normally concerned with the day-to-day work of marketing the Board's products' (NCB 1948: p.64). The latter was generally devolved to Division level, often to reconcile the specificity of a region's product – for example, anthracite from South Wales – with a commercial and profitable destination for its absorption. The term 'public relations', which was linked to the term 'film' in the index of the NCB's first four years of annual reports had, however, a different meaning – one which was much farther reaching in its intention than the mere selling of products: 'Publicity, too, can help not only to remove any sense of isolation which the mining communities may still feel, but also to bridge the distance between the collier working below ground and the members of the National Coal Board responsible for the industry's policies in London' (ibid.: p.38).

Two long-term public relations initiatives were launched in the early years of nationalisation. Firstly, a coal publication titled *Coal: The NCB Magazine* (latterly *Coal: Magazine of the Mining Industry*) was produced, beginning in May 1947 initially with the assistance of the Central Office of Information (COI). The latter was the governmental marketing and communications agency which had been founded in 1946 from the wartime Ministry for Information. By the end of 1947 *Coal*, which sold for 4d, had a circulation of over 100,000 copies. It would run until 1961 when its name was changed to *Coal News*, and it became a national newspaper which would continue in circulation until the mid-1990s. The other key enterprise was *Mining Review*, a monthly film made in the idiom of a news-reel, and distributed commercially to cinemas – within the coalfields to begin with, but latterly more universally. With its iconic opening from the upward-looking perspective of the top of a pit cage ascending a shaft from the deep towards the light of the surface, *Mining Review* would become the longest-running industrial newsreel in Britain, extending to over 400 episodes over a period of 30 years, until 1983 (Cranston 2009: p.8). Like *Coal* magazine, initially the films were produced by a subsidiary of the COI – the Crown Film Unit – before being contracted to external filmmakers such as Data Film Production. Beginning in 1952, however, the NCB began to make its own in-house films through the National Coal Board Film Unit, an agency which lasted until its dissolution in 1984.

Rather like the recategorising of the geography of the coalfields into a coherent and national endeavour, *Coal* and *Mining Review* were, at least in part, designed to encourage the sense of unity between regions, and the workers and management that Shinwell had considered necessary to the survival and future of the nationalised industry. But PR strategies were also evidently about external communications. And while in a broad sense this concerned the presentation of the mining industry and its workers to a more general audience – to allow for a greater understanding of their lives and lifestyles – was also the more immediate and specific aim of attracting additional workers. In 1947, the nationalised industry had estimated a need for 100,000 new miners to increase its workforce to a desired total of 730,000 individuals (NCB 1948: p.45). This motive not only underpinned the early issues of both *Coal* and *Mining Review*, but also preoccupied other visual output from official sources during the periods immediately before and after nationalisation.

Pamphlets like *Mining People* (produced by HMSO in 1945), for example, sought to stress how much the traditional working and social lives of miners had already been transformed and modernised, chiefly due to the interventions of the Miners' Welfare Commission, and its provision of baths as well as other social, recreational and rehabilitation, research, and education facilities. Significantly, the final image in this publication showed a superimposed collage of a young miner beckoning prospective colleagues into a clean, modern, ordered industry emblematised in the background by the architecture of Comrie Colliery, photographed from an aerial perspective (MWC 1945: unpaginated) (FIG.138).

Both this and other pamphlets, such as *The Future of the Coal Miner: How Coming Changes Mean a New Deal and New Opportunities for All who Work in the Coal Industry*, drew on the clear unambiguous aesthetics of the public information publications produced throughout the Second World War.[10] Indeed, in a section titled 'We won the war … we can win the coal!', the latter publication drew comparisons between the benefits of mechanised weaponry in fighting the Germans and the necessity for similar innovations to be used in modern mining. Fronted by a headshot of a miner with helmet, *The Future of the Coal Miner* – also produced in 1945 (this time by the Ministry of Fuel and Power) – provided an explanation of the findings of the prosaic and dense Reid Report in a more accessible and visually orientated form. In its extensive use of graphics in its illustration of mechanisation, but especially in its sectional drawings of past and future pits – topped by Victorian buildings and architecture inspired by the MWC's pithead baths respectively – it would provide another precedent for some of the sequences seen later in the *Plan for Coal* film of 1952. As made clear in the title, however, the pamphlet also emphasised

138
Comrie Colliery in *Mining People*; architecture as propaganda for the modernising industry

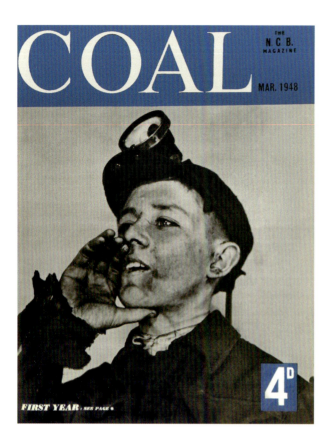

139
Cover of *Coal: The NCB Magazine*, March 1948

the beneficial changes in conditions that would come with working in a mechanised and rationalised industry. These included more secure employment and opportunities for 'proper training and promotion … among the most important of the rights to which the mine worker is entitled' (Ministry of Fuel and Power 1945: p.39).

As part of a continuation of the recruitment strategy, both *Coal* and *Mining Review* presented a mixture of articles about work in the collieries and the home and social life of the coalfield communities that surrounded them. Within this there was a tension between a propaganda-led evocation of mining – as would be presented at the later Festival of Britain – as a kind of mythologised 'calling' (akin, for example, to the sense of national duty involved in joining the army), with the proposal that mining also simply offered good terms and benefits in an increasingly normalised place of work. This can perhaps be seen clearest in some of the early cover shots in *Coal*, with their heroic depictions of sooty-faced miners – the headshot of a miner with an open hand to his face as if calling out, perhaps to potential recruits, of March 1948 is particularly redolent of a piece of Soviet propaganda (or indeed the depictions of miners seen in 1951 in Glasgow) – and how they contrast with the inside contents (FIG.139). The first issue in May 1947, for example, contained: congratulatory messages from Emmanuel Shinwell, The Lord Hyndley and Will Lawther (representing the unity of the ministry, the chair of the NCB, and the president of the National Union of Mineworkers collectively); an essay titled 'Crying for the Moon' which gave an appraisal of the significance of achieving nationalisation against naysayers; a treatise on the economic importance of coal; articles on mining machinery; a biographical note of a miner's experience in a prisoner of war camp; a short story called the 'Leaping Lad'; a letters page; and photographs taken from around the coalfields. Perhaps most indicative of the diversity of messages conveyed, however, is the juxtaposition between a critical account of the new deal for mineworkers under nationalisation written by Arthur Horner and, directly opposite, a piece by 'Our Woman Correspondent'. The latter, laid out almost like an advertisement, concerned the hidden role of coal in making a range of products for women, including the rayon for sheer stockings (nylon was originally also made with coal), and was replete with a large photograph – one of four accompanying the article – of a model showing them off.

This article had perhaps two intentions. Firstly, as indicated in the excerpt below, it reiterated the often-invisible agency of coal – and therefore coal miners (albeit expressed within mythical terms) – in the production and reproduction of many taken-for-granted objects within daily life:

> Few women, fondling a length of glowing fabric, spare a thought for the crude base of the thing of beauty that has been fashioned for them ... So, remember next time you admire a shapely stocking or cosy curtain, that the man who wins the coal not only supports, Atlas-like, the world of industry on his shoulders, he also brings beauty into being.
>
> ('Our Woman Correspondent' *Coal* 1947: p.13)

Secondly, in its discussion of concepts of feminine beauty within commodities, it acknowledged the aspirations of and – as a consequence of the potential of the new deal for miners – opportunities for the women of the coalfields to participate in the acquisition of what previously would have been considered unattainable luxuries.[11] It was, however, the first of the two intentions of the article by 'Our Woman Correspondent' that underpinned another significant exhibition on coal mining, which was held in London in September 1947. 'The Miner Comes to Town' was announced on the front cover of the September 1947 issue of *Coal* magazine, in another iconic, collaged image – a miner, dressed for underground complete with helmet and safety lamp, standing heroically huge against the backdrop of the Houses of Parliament and its world-famous clock tower. Inside, an article described the exhibition, guiding the visitor on what to look out for. It also, however, explained the rationale for its existence: the 'great chasm' of general ignorance between the population and its knowledge of coal mining and miners: 'The man in the street has a hazy idea that coal is just dug out of the ground and that miners are chaps who spend most of their time, when not in the pit poaching and boozing

– gipsy-looking chaps with silk scarves knotted around their necks and a whippet slinking at their heels' (Chaplin 1947: p.6).

The author suggested that one of the functions of the NCB was to bridge the gap in understanding, with this exhibition as one 'imaginative step towards that end'. Once again, the centrality of coal and its miners to the security of post-war, modern life was reiterated: 'without coal we will die as a nation. Without coal all the great plans of reconstruction will go awry'. The social pact between miner and state implicit within the offer of nationalisation, of better wages and conditions in return for more harmonious industrial relations – is extended, 'now that the people – that means you and me – own the coal industry' – towards the rest of the population:

> In short there is a double responsibility. We cannot afford to have the mining community isolated as it was in the bad old days. The battle for coal will be won only when both the public and the miner are aware of their responsibilities. This can be accomplished only when they meet on common ground and this is the real purpose of the Exhibition – not to provide casual visitors with a spectacular show, but to provide a meeting place for potential partners.
>
> (ibid.: p.7)

Part of this common ground or meeting place was to be underground. Or nearly. As *The Times* acknowledged on the exhibition's opening day the 11th of September 1947, 'Because it is impractical to take Londoners to see the collieries, the collieries have been brought to London' (Anon. 1947: p.3).

A section of the exhibition called 'Marble Arch Main Colliery' would take the form of a full-sized simulacrum of a mine whose tunnels of 'fibrous plastic' were constructed from casts taken from the real Rufford Colliery in Nottinghamshire. The latter's workshops also supplied the haulage rails and corrugated roofing which accompanied a collection of modern machinery, including the Meco-Moore cutter, the Joy loader, armoured flexible conveyor belt systems, as well as – perhaps incongruously in the context of modernisation – a string of pit ponies which the King gave leave to be quartered in the Royal Mews for the duration of the exhibition (ibid.: p.12). The 'mine' was managed by the assistant manager of Astley Green Colliery near Manchester, who was tasked with organising teams of guides of 45 miners from all of the country's coalfields (ibid.: p.3).[12]

'The Miner Comes to Town' was opened – with the release of homing pigeons to return to their homes in the coalfields – by the same triumvirate (joined by the Lord Mayor of London) of Shinwell, Hyndley and Lawther, who had celebrated the launch of *Coal: The NCB Magazine*. 'Marble Arch Main', however, was just one section of the larger exhibition which was held in the Central Office of Information's Exhibition Centre on Oxford Street. Perhaps inevitably, the replica mine was located within its basement. Also on show, however, was

140
'The Miner Comes to Town' exhibition: replica of a coal mine headframe in Hyde Park, London, 1947

the model of the Model Pit based on Comrie Colliery, which had been part of the Glasgow Empire Exhibition in 1938, and which, after its display here, would be transferred to the Science Museum. Meanwhile, just around the corner in Hyde Park another replica, this time of the iconic forms of a pit's headgear, was built to function as a public bandstand. Six colliery bands would play daily to a public audience until the end of the exhibition on the 25th of October. High above the bandstand/headgear and its position in central London, flew the NCB flag (FIG.140).

These snapshots of the working and cultural lives of miners were accompanied by other sections of the exhibition, realised in a more avant-garde idiom by a series of modernist designers associated with the COI. Many of these individuals would not only remain pivotal to the design of the Festival of Britain exhibition just under four years later, but would also be extremely influential generally on the course of modern British design and architecture in its mid-century iterations: Peter Moro and Robin Day – *Coal, key to economic problems of today*; Gordon Cullen – *The miner's life and his struggles for recognition*; Pauline Behr – *Surface handling and marketing of coal*; and Misha Black – *The miner at home*. Black was also the Supervising Designer, with James Holland and R. J. Harrison as Chief Designer and Chief Architect respectively.

Part of the Day and Moro section involved the by now familiar trope of exposing just how much of modern life depended on coal. This was divided into four elements 'Industry', Transport', 'Things made from Iron and Steel' and 'Home Life Enjoyment'. The latter included 'the Woman's Fair and Exhibition' which displayed a series of commodities within frames made from the mineral. One of these contained a 'shapely stocking', like the one cited earlier in *Coal*, but now filled by an isolated mannequin leg cantilevering from the wall. The 'coal-frames' were linked by lines and arrows on the wall, and by taut wires which emerged to show connections to other items and factors across the space in a three-dimensional matrix. Suspended in space within this, was a clear Perspex box decorated by a ribbon. Inside, it held a single piece of coal, a gift to the nation. The exhibition was seen by more than 160,000 people (NCB 1948: p.38).

PLANNING AND UNDERGROUND ARCHITECTURE

As well as an underlying motive to encourage recruitment into the industry (Anon. 1947: p.3), the 'Miner Comes to Town' exhibition again sought to affirm the central position of coal mining to the engine of the post-war economy. This economy would also be underpinned by the monetary state intervention advocated by John Maynard Keynes, and its society defined by the improvements in social security and welfare recommended in William Beveridge's seminal *Social Insurance and Allied Services* report (1942). As is well known, the latter was one of a series of legislative acts passed under the Labour government, such as Aneurin Bevan's National Health Service Act, which came into effect in 1948. The post-war's mixed – sometimes termed Fordist – economy would also be characterised by an accelerated production of consumer goods, often for use within the home. Embedded within this was the assumption that the increase in production would generally take place within the same industrial nation state as the commodities would be consumed in. In other words, both production and consumption within the United Kingdom, for example, would be balanced. and, to a certain extent, planned. 'Home Life Enjoyment' was then a strategic segment in an economic system conceived holistically as a series of inter-related parts in the service of the nation. While the beginnings of an insistence on planning the post-war society could be seen as early as 1941, in, for example, the *Picture Post* magazine's special issue 'Plan for Britain' – swiftly followed by a series of articles including 'Work for All', 'Plan the Home', 'A Plan for Education', 'Health for All' and 'A New Britain Must be Planned' (Kynaston 2007: p.20) – the apotheosis of this trend was perhaps George Brown's ill-fated *National Plan* published over 20 years later in 1965. Its emphasis on reducing both military and spending abroad and increasing exports would be based on a reorganisation of industry, in general, on a more technical, and thereby, efficient basis. This would be engineered socially by a common agreement between unions and employers on 'prices, productivity and incomes', as well as a programme 'to cover the human effects of industrial changes … redundancy compensation, wage-related unemployment benefits and better training', in return for an end to 'restrictive practices' (Brown 1965: p.19).

In other words, Brown's *National Plan* seemed to echo the recommendations of the Reid Report 20 years before, and its proposals that through reorganisation and the systematic adoption of technology, a similarly coherent coal-mining industry – a single system consisting of inter-related parts – could arise out of the uncoordinated accretions of the previous decades of private enterprise. The *Plan for Coal* finally established the deployment of many of the Report's technical recommendations from 1945, as well as the calls for the modernisation of existing mines, the development of new ones, and the provision of training to mineworkers that had formed some of the key objectives of the NUM's 'Miners' Charter' from 1946. The capital investment costs for the *Plan for Coal* were estimated in 1950 as being in the region of £635 million with some 250 collieries (out of the existing 900 or so) being reconstructed, a series of new pits sunk, and some 350 to 400 pits to be closed by the early 1960s.

In its explanation of these circumstances and their social consequences and opportunities, the *Plan for Coal* film drew on many of the public relations techniques that had either been developed for, or embraced by, the NCB since its inception half a decade earlier. The sectional drawings comparing the underground and surface arrangements of past and future pits shown in the Ministry of Fuel and Power's publication *The Future of the Coal Miner*, for example, were adopted and animated within the *Plan for Coal* film. The latter contrasts the previous age – where sloping tunnels followed the inclines of coal within its seams – with new methods of so-called 'horizon mining' where, rather that following undulations in the coal seam, level, underground roadways were driven from the shaft, through the coal measures, making an orthogonal relationship between horizontal and vertical excavations (FIG.141). Widely used in the coalfields of continental Europe and first trialled in Great Britain at Llanharan Colliery in South Wales in 1948 (Anon. 1948: p.5), 'horizon mining' allowed the replacement of older and compromised techniques of moving coal and men, such as endless rope railways – which were limited in the weight they could carry – with the much larger capacity of diesel or electric locomotives pulling longer trains, or the rapid movement of coal (and men) allowed by the use of conveyor belts. The new, rationalised underground would also include the use of chutes to convey coal from one level to another, where, instead of the trams or tubs systems of wagons, it could be taken to the surface in much larger and more efficient 'skips'. A more judicious and rational use of underground space would also mean that much of the spoil from the excavations could remain permanently below the surface, while new underground bunkers could also be created to store, if necessary, surplus coal temporarily before it was brought

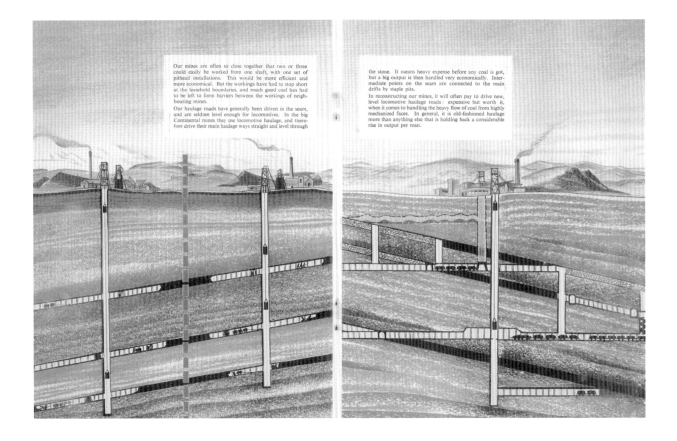

to the surface and dispatched to market. Accordingly, the two environments depicted above ground also varied significantly – the older colliery was a familiar raggle-taggle of brick buildings, with a spoil heap served by an aerial ropeway, while the modern mine – its waste retained underground – was a shining white, flat-roofed building, set within a bucolic, spoil-free landscape.

While conditions evidently varied across the coalfield and indeed often much more incrementally – adjacent pits could experience radically different mining conditions – what the *Plan for Coal* and the Reid Report before it endorsed, was the adoption, where at all possible, of a single method of mining. And while the latter had initially recommended the stall and pillar system, by the early 1950s – and embedded within the projections for the new generation of pits – the longwall method (as used in Comrie) was seen as the most advantageous means to accommodate the new technologies and techniques being developed in the three key areas of: (1) hewing coal; (2) moving it; and (3) supporting the roofs at the coalface. The longwall system, as its name implies, creates a long cutting face for extracting the coal, which can be anything up to 200 metres in length. This runs perpendicularly to the roadways, which are driven outwards from the 'pit bottom' at the base of one of a colliery's two obligatory shafts. The latter – which are not exclusive to longwall mining – separately convey the men and the coal vertically, as well as

141
Modern horizontal mining (right) compared to traditional methods

acting as the principal convectors of ventilation: the downcast shaft brings fresh air from the surface, which is extracted by the upcast shaft after circulating around the workings. This process was often aided by the construction of a 'fan drift', which was dug at an angle to intersect the upcast shaft, and, as its name suggests, accelerate the extraction of the 'pit air' from a mine.

Longwall mining contained two variants: advancing, which pushed the face outwards from the pit bottom; and retreating, which established a face at some distance from the pit bottom and worked backwards towards it. Latterly, the second system would become more widespread in NCB mines. Both variants were designed to allow the uninterrupted passage of a combined cutter-loader. This extracted the coal and pushed it onto another critical piece of equipment, the armoured flexible conveyor (AFC). By the late 1950s, the cutter-loader, the AFC and the roof supports had been refined into one combined, integrated system. As the coal was cut from the face, the hydraulically powered 'self-advancing' roof supports moved forward, carrying with them the AFC, which bent snake-like to accommodate the differences between cut and uncut planes. The AFC also provided a continuous rail for the cutter-loader to run along in its interaction with the coalface. Once extracted, the coal travelled via the latter to the end of the face, where it was transferred to another conveyer belt running at right angles. From here it was moved through the mine's roadways towards the pit bottom and its vertical journey to the surface. The entire working zone of the coalface – where the coal was cut – measured no more than two metres in width and moved continually forward along its length (FIG.142). As it did so the ground behind, no longer held by the roof-supports, simply collapsed in an area subsequently known as the 'goaf'. Apart from incremental improvements and refinements to the machinery used – including the subsequent use of computers, experiments in the late 1970s and 1980s with Remote Operated Longwall Face (ROLF) (Bryan 1976: p.51; also, Robens 1972: p.92), and the tantalising and controversial possibility of remote-controlled, miner-less mining – the basic principles of this system would remain virtually unchanged until the cessation of deep-colliery operations in Britain in the early 2000s.

The move towards uniformity in underground production and elsewhere realised other benefits. The counterpointing of a single entity National Coal Board with a unified and national miners' union in the NUM meant not only the development of national pay agreements, but also ultimately a nationwide rationalisation of the hitherto intricate and complex piece-rate price lists for the everyday tasks conducted by the miner underground. These concerned not only the cutting of the coal and its value by weight, but also the less-immediately quantifiable activities like roofing, timbering, heading, and so on, which not only allowed production to happen, but were also critical to the collective safety of the mine and its occupants. Prior to nationalisation such price agreements had been negotiated either at the level of individual mines or coal companies, and had been an ongoing source of discontent.

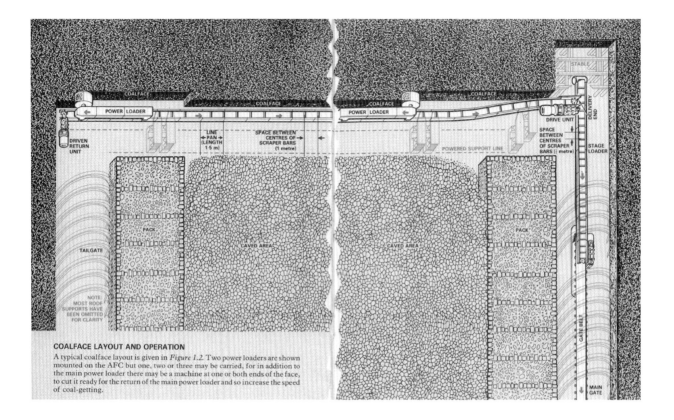

COALFACE LAYOUT AND OPERATION
A typical coalface layout is given in *Figure 1.2*. Two power loaders are shown mounted on the AFC but one, two or three may be carried, for in addition to the main power loader there may be a machine at one or both ends of the face, to cut it ready for the return of the main power loader and so increase the speed of coal-getting.

The distillation of the diverse working practices of the more than 1,000 collieries managed by over 800 different companies inherited by the NCB, into a series of limited methods for extracting and moving coal, allowed the sharing and development of expertise within a new nationwide space. This is made clear in the series of pamphlets produced by the NCB (chiefly by its Industrial Training Branch) to provide explanations – for (presumably) new miners – of some of the by-now generic methods, conditions and equipment that they were likely to face in underground space. Highly visual in their design and illustrated often with architectural-type drawings, some of these were reprinted decade after decade. *Strata Control* (first edition 1952, reprinted 1974), for example, examined the layers of rocks and seams, memorably comparing a section through the earth with a cream-filled sponge cake, before illustrating the different methods by which the ground above could be supported and how to use them. *Shaft Story*, first published in 1958 – and including beautiful and hilarious sectional drawings by William Heath Robinson caricaturing medieval mining methods (FIG.143) – explained the different components of a pit's shafts, their uses and position within the colliery, and the various techniques used to sink them – including freezing and permanent lining. *Pit Ventilation* (published in 1950 and revised in 1972 and 1981) explained the various gases that can be found in a pit and the methods by which air is brought through underground workings, including the use of doors to stop and direct the flow. Two pamphlets

PLANNING AND UNDERGROUND ARCHITECTURE   231

142
Diagram of longwall (advancing) method with self-advancing props and armoured flexible conveyor (AFC)

143
Parody of colliery shaft workings, by William Heath Robinson

were dedicated to *Transport Underground: Part 1 Moving Out the Coal*, and *Part 2 Moving Men and Supplies*. Both were published in 1976. The former provided an update on *Moving Coal Underground* (published in 1959 and reprinted in 1959 and 1962), expanding on its discussion of pony traction and endless ropeways, to include overview diagrams of how coal is moved around underground, as well as detailed drawings of conveyer systems. A specific iteration of the latter is discussed in *Armoured Flexible Conveyors* which was published in 1982 and described their uses, components and hazards, in a series of elegant diagrams and drawings, some of which explain its integration with the self-propelling supports at the coalface. Finally, in this selection, *Coal: Its Origin and Occurrence* (published in 1952, and reprinted in 1953, 1956, 1960, 1964, 1967, revised in 1970, and reprinted in 1974) provided a broad introduction to the mineral itself, its different types, as well as its vertical and horizontal distribution, not only within the coalfield strata of Great Britain, but also globally.

INTER-COLLIERY ARCHITECTURE

Given the time frame and complexities involved in sinking new pits or reconstructing existing ones, many of the first buildings to emerge above ground under NCB control in the 1950s were either smaller concerns, easier to realise, and/or part of the wider range of other facilities that the organisation had acquired on Vesting Day. And yet many of these were strategically critically important and both concerned and expressed the remaking and unifying of mining space across the country on its surface. Unlike the often hand-to-mouth operations of pre-nationalisation private collieries (many of which were extremely small), the large, singular entity of the National Coal Board had the opportunity to plan and dedicate extensive resources to the establishment of networks of centralised units and facilities at National, Divisional or Area levels. The expertise, findings and services developed in these spaces would then be devolved and used to improve, refine or simply maintain the practices and operations of individual mines.

These shared, inter-colliery spaces included, at a national level, those for research. The Coal Research Establishment, established at Stoke Orchard in Gloucestershire in 1950, for example, was designed to further efficiencies in the combustion of the mineral. Its otherwise rather nondescript industrial set of buildings and yards, located within a rolling rural landscape, were articulated by an overabundance of flues, chimneys and pipes, as well as laboratories to explore the liquefication of coal. Meanwhile, matters immediately relevant to the getting of coal – underground transport, tunnelling and drifting, strata control, and controlling and measuring atmospheric and environmental conditions – were investigated in the Mining Research Establishment located at Isleworth, near London. At Bretby in South Derbyshire, the Central Engineering Establishment was dedicated to the development of new types of mining machinery and coal preparation, and to carry out '"acceptance trials" of equipment developed within the board and outside'. By 1955, all these had come under the authority of the Research and Development Committee of the NCB, while medical and industrial relations research were orchestrated by the curiously titled Human Problems Research Committee (Jones 1957: pp 83–4).

New shared facilities at Divisional and Area level included the construction of 'central workshops and stores', like the ones built at Lugar in Ayrshire, or Shafton in Yorkshire, in 1954 and 1959 respectively. Related to the attempts to homogenise space, mining practices and machinery underground, such complexes were designed to a standardised layout plan developed by the NCB national headquarters in London, and were considered pivotal to the progress of mechanisation (Anon. 1960: p.11). By 1955, Lugar had a staff of 140 mechanics, electricians, blacksmiths, platers, erectors, welders and other tradesmen, who worked in a series of 60ft-wide bays within the building. These bays were used to undertake the regular overhaul of mobile underground equipment such as coal cutters, underground locomotives and conveyors, while also maintaining heavier and immobile equipment such as screens, washers and winders. Mobile squads of workmen could also be made available for larger scale maintenance or major installation jobs at the collieries themselves. The administration section attached to the workshops contained a manager's office; planning and progress, time and cost offices; a lecture room; a mechanical drawing office; and plant records. At Lugar, the stores containing mining equipment were held in a building measuring 60 ft wide by 300 ft long, with many of the smaller items held in 15,000 storages bins on two levels (Anon. 1955a: p.10). In the 1½ acre of storage at Shafton any item could apparently be found in less than one minute via the facility's revolving index system (Anon. 1960: p.13). Interior shots of both Lugar – which accompanied other workshops and stores in Scotland at Cowdenbeath (Fife), Shotts (Lanarkshire), Alloa (Clackmannanshire) and Newbattle (Lothians) – and Shafton show steel-framed buildings, well-lit from an abundance of both rooflights and what appears to be at times glazed curtain walling. The stores especially have the appearance of a completely ordered and scientifically managed factory floor. Of final significance, however, is perhaps the acknowledgement of the aesthetic value of the exterior of these surface buildings. In an article printed in *Coal* magazine in 1960, above a photograph of what must be described as a quite unprepossessing set of low-slung, industrial-looking, pitch-roofed and gabled structures at Shafton, is the title 'New face of the Coalfields' (ibid.: p.11). Other facilities would have more of a public presence.

Meanwhile, medical, safety and health issues, which before 1946 had fallen under the remit of the Miners' Welfare Commission, were placed at a national level within the Safety in Mines Research Establishment. This had facilities in Buxton and Sheffield, the latter containing a Dust Explosion Gallery. It is sobering to read that still in 1955, 425 miners lost their lives and another 1,889 had been injured in accidents, even if these figures represent a remarkable improvement on the 881 killed and 3,212 injured reported in 1932 (Roberts 1957: p.47). While there was the continuation of the medical rooms and services provided by the MWC within individual collieries, other shared infrastructures were constructed at Area or Divisional level. These included mobile X-ray units, designed to examine all new recruits to the industry, which trialled in the South Western Division in 1957, and latterly proliferated throughout all the coalfields. In the same year there were also at least two mobile Pneumoconiosis Field Research units dedicated to further exploration and understanding of the infamous miners' lung disease. Constructed with a van coupled to an extendable trailer, these units were equipped with tent-like structures stiffened with steel tubular skeletons to form pieces of temporary mobile architecture within the

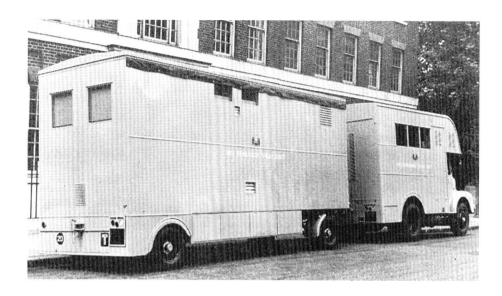

coalfields (FIG.144). Other less visibly conspicuous research was conducted on other medical conditions commonly experienced by miners. These included: beat disease (which affects the knee, elbow and wrist joints); nystagmus (a disease of the eye caused by low levels of lighting); rheumatism; dermatitis; epidermophytosis (a fungal infection of the feet); and Weil's Disease (Rogan 1957: p.99).

Meanwhile other shared initiatives at Area or Divisional level included specially created training facilities for apprentice miners such as those located at Tondu in South Wales, Sauchie in Clackmannanshire, Birch Coppice in Warwickshire, Newton Hill in Yorkshire, or Grassmoor in the East Midlands Division. At Grassmoor, 'pit training' was offered in a realistic surface pit, as well as underground in the Grassmoor Colliery. At Newton Hill, the training pit was located a mere 14 ft underground. Other common facilities included lecture rooms, maintenance areas (where the 15-year-old and upwards trainees could disassemble and reassemble machines such as the Samson cutter), workshops, gymnasia, and outside sports fields and athletics grounds. An interior photograph taken in 1957 of the Grassmoor gymnasium shows a lofty space whose steel frame was realised in a thin-membered lattice structure which articulated both the walls and the ceiling, illuminated by an uninterrupted row of clerestory windows accompanied by other windows below at ground floor level.

Further training and learning opportunities for technical, administrative and managerial grades were often provided in off-site facilities, knitted within the educational institutions – including the universities – of coalfield towns and cities, or even further afield. These included a new five-storey building in the city centre for the first permanent home of University College, Cardiff's Mining Department. A flat-roofed 'reinforced concrete, steel and glass' building with a

relief sculpture in its foyer of miners 'hand-filling on to a chain scraper' (Anon. 1956a: p.5), it abutted its neighbour in a polite modernist style. Its first phase was finished in 1956 and the completed building opened by HRH Prince Philip in 1960.

The mobile X-ray and pneumoconiosis units offered another type of visibility within the public realm as they circulated from site to site. This would be greatly enhanced by a more generic fleet of vehicles belonging to the NCB. One of the organisation's files – now held within the National Archives at Kew – shows the evolution of the livery and lettering applied to these vehicles as they emerged as forms of advertising for both specific services, as well as the organisation's overall corporate brand. A photograph, presumably from the late 1940s, of a 'pilot tipper' – in this case a Bedford lorry designed specifically for the delivery of coke in the North Western Division – shows the legend NATIONAL COAL BOARD printed in caps in the same, simple sans-serif modern font that had graced the Vesting Day notices in 1947. Another photograph, possibly from 1960 in this undated series, is of a Morris lorry which has been converted to the more public-facing function of a 'Mobile Order Office' for the National Coal Board Retail Department. Designed to make the procuring of the fuel more convenient to the domestic customer, the vehicle has 'Coal at your Service' emblazoned across its top. Below, the three letters of NCB have been placed individually within three white hexagonal shapes – the ordinary molecular structure of carbon – and brought together to form a logo. But it is a series of photographs likely to have been taken some time in the late 1960s or early 1970s which are perhaps most significant. These show 'vehicles submitted for choice of new N.C.B. livery' (National Archives Coal 80) – to be specific, a Commer Walk-Thru type van, painted in different colours and colour combinations: yellow and grey; brown and yellow; orange and grey; and dark blue and yellow. The latter – perhaps echoing the famous 'warning yellow'

144
Mobile Pneumoconiosis Field Research unit

145
NCB van with final logo and colour scheme

panel that would announce the front and rear of British Railway locomotives after its introduction 1965 – would become the unique and distinctive colour scheme for all NCB vehicles and other graphics nationwide throughout the 1970s and 1980s. More importantly, however, is the presence of a new NCB logo. Effected in yellow on a dark blue background, or in dark blue/black on an orange background, this arrangement of the three capital letters of NCB – still sans serif but now fattened and pushed tightly together – would become one of the most defining and enduring expressions of the unified nature of the organisation. It would be seen everywhere there were NCB activities over the next decades: from transport and signage to letterheads and donkey jackets. Immediately recognisable as an icon for the nationalised industry, it was especially conspicuous – often as a talisman of controversy – within the infamous industrial unrest of the mid-1980s (FIG.145).

Other inter-colliery initiatives were less ephemeral. In 1947, the NCB inherited a series of facilities for the carbonisation or coking (heat applied in the absence of oxygen) of coal to generate fuels for specific purposes, including for the blast furnaces necessary for the making of steel. By 1957, ten years later, these had been subject to a rationalisation and expansion. Often attached to existing collieries, the programme for coking plants in some ways represented, at a less prolific scale, the plan and procedures in place for the development of collieries: the appraisal of the existing facilities, the identification and remodelling of those with the potential to be modernised, the closure of unfeasible plants, and the construction of new, state-of-the-art facilities where strategically appropriate.

Writing in *National Coal Board: The First Ten Years* – the *Colliery Guardian*'s appraisal of the first decade of the nationalised industry – the NCB's Director General of Carbonisation R. J. Morely gave an account of the situation. In the Southern Division on Vesting Day, for example, there had been four coke oven plants, all in South Wales. Bargoed, Tondu, Maritime and Coedely had been capable of carbonising a total of 490,000 tons of coal per annum. By 1958, only Coedely was left, and its total battery of 30 ovens replaced with new ones. A much-increased capacity of 1,210,000 tons per annum, however, was achieved by the addition of two completely new plants: at Nantgarw Colliery and at Cwm Colliery, which would ultimately come online in 1953 and 1958 respectively. At the time of its construction (there is a newsreel of its opening), Nantgarw was one of the most modern coking facilities in Europe. In addition to carbonising 1,500 tons of coal per day, it featured state of the art systems to deal with some of the various by-products that came with the process. As well as boasting benzole-refining facilities, for example, it captured 9 million cubic metres per day of ammonia gas. In the spirit of a new integrated industry, Nantgarw dealt not only with its own by-products, but also took crude material from other plants within the Division. Cwm, in addition, would also have the capability of producing coal tar. Meanwhile in the East Midlands Division by 1957 the coking plants at Grassmoor and Hardwick had been upgraded and a new plant at Avenue (in Chesterfield) – the NCB's 'most important single carbonisation project to date' – had been put into commission. This was a fully integrated coking and chemical plant covering over 188 acres in area (NCB 1957a: p.39) and capable of producing 790,000 tons of coke per annum while generating a series of other products such as 'smokeless fuels, sulphate of ammonia, coal tar chemical, pure benzole products and sulphuric acid' (Morley 1957: p.75). 'Secondary By-products' such as benzene, toluene and xylenes were also realised. Collectively, these formed raw materials for a series of recognisable everyday commodities such as some of those curated in the 'Home Life Enjoyment' section of the Miner Comes to Town Exhibition: plastics, dyes, explosives, paints, artificial fibres and so on.[13] Another coking plant was constructed at Manvers Main in Yorkshire for the NCB, while elsewhere, in Durham three new plants were constructed in the 1950s under private enterprise: at Fishburn, and Murton (built by the Woodall-Duckham Company), and at Lambton (built by the Coppee Company).

Relieved of the scale of workforce that might require the 'architecture' that Reid suggested as necessary for new and remodelled collieries, the forms of these coking complexes were generally unselfconscious industrial products, intimately responsive to the requirement and vicissitudes of the processes they contained: the flow of materials; the applications of heat and pressure; the containment and release of changes in the state of materials – the emissions of steam and smoke; rectification, and the distilled flow of new liquids, and so on. And yet, these series and networks of pipes, tanks, chimneys, gantries and cooling towers produced visually compelling forms. Perhaps the most spectacular sequence of these surrounded the process by which the coal was presented to – and passed through – the kilns. This involved the transportation of the mineral via long diagonal conveyors – perhaps seen most emphatically at Lambton – climbing to the top of a coal storage silo after it had been crushed and blended. From here it dropped into a large container which moved along rails to deposit the coal into the ovens below. After the baking process had been applied (and the gas or volatiles extracted), the coke was pushed out onto another receptacle on rails which took it to a cooling chamber where its temperature was lowered, and combustion prohibited through the application of water (and an accompanying dramatic release of steam). Finally, the cooled coke was discharged onto a coal wharf to be taken to be screened and used.

While these types and systems of forms would later be recognised – in photography such as that produced by Bernd and Hilla Becher from the 1960s onwards (see Becher and Becher 2010, for example), or in heritage sites such as the former steel works at Landschaftspark Duisburg-Nord in the late 1990s – as conspicuous, 20th-century examples of the architecture of the industrial sublime, perhaps the only aesthetically considered structure within the British coking plants at the time they were built was the coal silo. While still inevitably process-driven, their verticality made them starkly evident across landscapes and neighbourhoods. This was confirmed by the inclusion of the company

name, Dorman Long in large letters, on its coking tower built between 1953 and 1956 as part of the steel works at Redcar in Yorkshire. In the debates surrounding its controversial demolition in 2021, this building was termed an example of British industrial Brutalism (see, for example, Ing 2021; and Lloyd 2021), a description which can be extended to the other coking works towers discussed here. The examples at Avenue, Fishburn and Lambton all expressed a mass, articulated modernist concrete architectural form, which along with the chimneys that accompanied them, contrasted with the horizontal landscape of steel latticed gantries and tanks laid out in the rest of the plant beneath them (FIG.146). A further formal juxtaposition was provided by the lightweight tentacular structures of the conveyor belts that continually fed their solid forms pulverised coal. These conveyor structures clearly delineated in three dimensions the shortest and most efficient routes of a productive process. In the context of coal, they perhaps provide an inverse expression – a continuation above ground in space – of the new rationale being worked through the solid forms of the earth, in the technical modernisation of the country's collieries underground.

As of January 2022, the ruins of the coking works at Cym Colliery in Beddau are still extant. The tower forms the centre of a bilateral symmetrical arrangement of two batteries of ovens, which end in two chimneys. Other ancillary buildings are disposed asymmetrically around this composition. The tower itself emphasises its verticality in a series of three fins on each facade which travel from bottom to top before turning through 90 degrees to continue as horizontal beam-like elements on its roof. This sub-aesthetic order is echoed in the horizontal lines created by the pouring of the building's in-situ concrete structure. A dynamic diagonal mediation between the vertical and horizontal is provided by the concrete staircase – with thin steel balusters and handrails

146
Avenue Coking Plant

147
Coal preparation plant at Manvers Main Colliery

– which cantilevers from one of the facades. This is echoed in the arrival at the top of the building, on the opposite side, by the long tendril-like external conveyor belt whose cladding has, by design or otherwise, mostly been removed, making its underlying steel lattice structure apparent.

Another expression of a 'tentacular' architecture could be seen in the development of a 'major mining concentration scheme' at Manvers Main completed in the mid-1950s. This consisted not only of the colliery and coking plant – which when completed would be the largest operated by the NCB – but also a coal washery and preparation plant, also the largest in Britain.[14] Again, designed to supersede a series of older, outdated facilities and practices, it was capable of simultaneously treating three different types 'coking, gas and industrial coal at a rate of 1,320 tons per hour' (Grounds and Hirst 1957: p.66), from four neighbouring collieries, using a series of different methods. These included the German-invented and recently adopted Baum washery system. Like other new preparation plants, Manvers Main was also designed to operate on a closed circuit in an attempt to avoid 'tailings' and consequent river pollution (ibid.: p.66). Contemporary photographs taken from the air show an enormous slab of a building raised on *pilotis* over an array of railway lines (covering over 112 acres, the entire complex contained 30 miles of sidings). Punctured with linear patterns of horizontal windows (an arrangement also seen in, for example, Calverton and Westcoe – as well as at the starkly modern Mosley Common – preparation plants), it was apparently – and optimistically, given its purpose – white in colour. Indeed, from certain perspectives the building looked like a piece of International Style architecture from the late 1920s. *Coal* magazine described its concrete structure as 'gleaming' while commenting on its size in the article's title: 'Giant' (Payne 1957: p.13). The three sections for the different types of coal are clearly indicated, on one side, by the indented facade, and on the other by the three cylindrical and cubic washing plants. Also conspicuous, however, is the series of some 14 or 15 tendrils that not only connect this structure to the subordinate buildings that surround it, but also those buildings to each other. Like the coking plants, the arrangement of these buildings and their connections via the covered conveyor belts expresses in space the most efficient lines of production (FIG.147). But Manvers Main was perhaps also indicative of something more. Servicing a series of collieries and bringing together a range of functions onto one site, in its sleek white modernist forms and linear connecting elements suspended in space, it provides a synecdoche for the emerging, rationalised and newly networked coal industry.[15]

RECONSTRUCTED COLLIERIES AND SUPERPITS

The 'concentration scheme' at Manvers Mains involved the combining of three pits. This was achieved through a series of underground reconstructions and adjustments, including the creation of two new principal 'horizons' or roadways linking the three workings and the standardisation of their haulage systems. A fourth mine was connected directly to the preparation plant by one of the aerial conveyors on the surface. The presence of a power station completed this collection of mines, coking and preparation plants, the final element in a complex of 'modern industrial buildings of which South Yorkshire can be proud' (ibid.: p.13). There were, however, other examples in the 1950s of underground rationalisations and the driving of new tunnels to connect previously separate mines. These initiatives represented one means of responding to the prescriptions contained in the Reid Report – and the original 1950 *Plan for Coal* – of replacing smaller pits with larger entities. But, as at Manvers Main, they were often accompanied by significant consequences on the surface and, as such, became among the first physical architectural expressions of the new nationalised industry.

At Hafodyrynys in South Wales, for example, the three collieries of Hafodyrynys, Glyntillery and Tirpentwys were linked by a series of new underground roadways to form 'an integrated major production unit', with their collective produce treated at a new common preparation plant. Originally designed in 1953, but subjected to delays and changes, at its completion in 1960 the entire scheme was expected to double the output of the three collieries – and increase the OMS by 6 cwt. Rather like the MWC's nearby pithead baths building developed in the 1930s and discussed earlier, the visible architectural expression of the project – the unreservedly modernist and linear forms of the preparation buildings strewn along the narrow valley floor – contrasted dramatically with the confined and undulating Welsh topology in which it found itself. In fact, the site had to be widened to accommodate this surface complex, a process which involved the displacement of thousands of tons of earth and

148
Hafodyrynys coal preparation plant

rock, the culverting of a series of streams, and the construction of lengths of concrete retaining walls (White 1957: p.12). The coal arrived via an aerial conveyor to a poured concrete tower, which had high-level windows and rested on *pilotis*. From here it was dispatched by another conveyor to the washery, which ran transversely across the valley floor above the railway tracks. From photographs taken about the time of its completion, the building appears to be a concrete frame construction with semi-engaged columns whose vertical emphasis is picked up in the thin steel mullions of the glazing. Again, this provided a counterpoint to the otherwise horizontal linearity of the scheme. All of the buildings were flat roofed with the exception of the workshop (FIG.148). Arranged parallel to the railway lines, the roof of this building undulated in a series of thin concrete curves, not unlike the roofscape of the Thameside restaurant at the Festival of Britain, or perhaps the vaulted spaces of the Stockwell Bus Garage, which was also begun in 1951. While there are also similarities with other NCB buildings, such as the workshops of the Bold Colliery reconstruction, it is also possible that the roof was designed in sympathy with the slightly brooding presence of the curves of the hills seen

behind, whose darker tones served, in the photographs at least, to highlight the 'gleaming' qualities of the new structures.

Other 'concentration' or combining schemes included the connecting of two previously moribund collieries located in two different Welsh valleys and separated by a mountain: Mardy and Bwllfa. First proposed in 1949 and completed around 1960, this involved the driving of a 3,200-yard horizon underneath the mountain between the two sites to allow output to flow, firstly to Bwllfa and subsequently in the opposite direction when the extensive surface reconstructions at Mardy had been carried out (Anon. 1954b: pp 13–14). The latter included new workshops and a washery which were realised in a modular, reinforced concrete frame construction with brick infill and the frame exposed. This architecture perhaps bears some similarities to Mies van Rohe's steel-framed Metallurgical and Chemical Engineering Building at the Illinois Institute of Technology (begun in 1946), or even Alison and Peter Smithson's later cultural appraisal of – and paean to – industrial architecture and mass-produced ready-mades in their Hunstanton School in Norfolk (completed in 1960). Continuity and connection in the underground workings between the two mines were emphasised in the reuse of this architectural language, on the other side of the mountain, for the winding-house and workshops at Bwllfa. This was a nine by three bay modular block whose interiors were illuminated from above by a strip of rooflights, and steel windows which ran across the full width of its bays – the clerestory on its upper storey with conventional openings underneath. The ability of underground infrastructure to invisibly alter geography such as at this 'meeting of the valleys below' (ibid.) in South Wales, was also seen in Scotland in the linking of Kinneil and Valleyfield Collieries. These two mines were on the opposite sides of the Firth of Forth, Kinneil on the southern side (in Stirlingshire) and Valleyfield on the northern shores (in Fife). The connection of just under three and half miles deemed necessary to exploit more fully the 50 million tons or so of coal lying there, took place deep under the waters of the estuary.

149
Bwllfa headgear tower and winding house

But the interventions at Kinneil and Valleyfield had something else in common, in addition to their horizontal connections: both required new shafts to be sunk. The downwards verticality of this would have an upwards presence on the surface, in the new towers required to support their headgear. At Kinneil – although deploying advanced new Koepe winding technologies borrowed from Germany which incorporated endless rope and counterweighting systems – these headstocks were constructed in the familiar, latticed steel that had traditionally indicated the presence of coal mining in the British landscape.[16] At Valleyfield, however, the tower would be fabricated in prestressed concrete, a first in Scotland. In time, these types of structure would be among the most conspicuous icons of the new modernised landscape of coal mining, and the architectural expression that Reid had proposed was central to its psychological success. At Bwllfa, despite the fact that a new shaft had not been required, between 1947 and 1954, a new concrete headframe had been built over the existing shaft at the same time as the adjacent winding house. In some of its details the tower represented, perhaps, an old-fashioned type of architecture, indebted to the MWC pithead baths programme of the 1930s. These civic aspirations, present in the vertical composition of its windows and their articulation in the surrounding wall were, moreover, somewhat undermined by its finish in rough concrete. Yet, it was still an elegant building, one whose unexpectedly open-framed zenith gave it an almost ecclesiastical air – like a campanile – which was undisturbed by the visible presence of the winding wheel or, indeed, the concrete stairs with slender steel handrails that clung in cantilever to one of its facades (FIG.149). In contemporary photographs, moreover, its light colour appears to glow against its background, while its overall form – juxtaposing the apparently extendable modular, systemic building of the winding house next to it – seems to represent a singular, architectural object, one whose connectivity is both invisible and vertical.

The iridescent potential of this vertical architectural typology was emphasised in *Coal* magazine's coverage of the progress of another 'Three into One' scheme, published in February 1960. This project concerned concentrating the output of Sneyd and Hanley Deep Pit Collieries with that of Wolstanton in North Staffordshire. New Wolstanton required the usual underground reconstructions – the deepening of shafts, the driving of new connecting roadways, and so on – as well as the designed-in capacity to stow pit spoil permanently below the surface. Above, a new coal preparation plant would be built to accompany the adjacent steel works, where much of the pits' output would be consumed. But like at Kinneil and Valleyfield, the new Wolstanton complex also required the construction of a new coal-winding shaft. What was realised in its head tower was – echoing the coking towers – a more self-conscious appreciation of the aesthetic potential of rough, poured concrete. The hulking structure raised off the ground on four massive piers – articulated, on its surface by a series of small windows and the marks caused by the shuttering process, and in its overall form by the two massive cantilevers which stuck out like two great ears – can be described as Brutalist in its atmosphere, and indicative of a new sculptural sensibility in the architecture of the coalfields and its vertical expression above ground. This was iterated in the magazine's cover whose aerial photograph captured the vast scale of the surface reconstruction works at Wolstanton, where an entire landscape was being remade (FIG.150). Except for the tower, this landscape – including a disorderly collection of earlier mine buildings – has been rendered in sepia. Against this, the light-coloured, cubic forms of the tower is made to stand out, gleaming once again, like a sentinel for the new.

At the time of nationalisation, the NCB inherited plans 'for two new collieries, thirty major reconstructions, twenty partial reconstructions, and four new drift mines' which had been prepared by the former owners and sponsored by the Ministry of Fuel and Power (Ashworth 1986: p.197). By 1954, these number had been expanded to 12 new collieries and a total of 37 new shafts sunk, or in the process of being sunk (Anon. 1954a: p.18). In-situ concrete – as it would become elsewhere in 1950s and 1960s British architecture – was the defining material of the towers that would service this new generation of shafts. There were, however, some significant exceptions. These included the still-remaining structures at Clipstone Colliery near Mansfield (1953–4) whose slender steel forms, at 200 ft in height, were among the tallest in Britain (Harwood 2015: p.348). At Lea Hall (begun in 1954) in Staffordshire, there were two colossal, open-latticed steel A-frame structures. On the site of Barony Colliery near Auchinleck in Ayrshire a single, more muscular A-frame (begun in 1954) – the last survivor of an industrial complex which included a power station – can still be seen. The tower was like that at Hem Heath near Stoke-on-Trent, which was finished by 1960. Both structures were possibly indebted to a German doppelgänger, built about the same time in Dortmund, at the Germania Colliery.[17]

Of the concrete structures, the tower of Bradford Colliery was one of the most visibly conspicuous. This was partly a consequence of its location in the Clayton district of inner-city Manchester. Its thin elegant, light-coloured form, rising to 200ft from behind its colliery's wall and other buildings, offered a starkly modernist vision which contrasted not only with the dull urban landscape of brick houses and factories stretched out horizontally beneath it, but also with the brick verticality of the 19th-century chimneys with which it shared the skyline. Open on two sides near the top to reveal elements of the Koepe winding gear it accommodated, the adjacent headstock of the colliery's other shaft interrupted the views from the street of its lower reaches. Realised in a more traditional steel-lattice, this structure was, in fact, contemporaneous with its concrete partner – it had been built to replace an older version – but seemed to be of a different era.

Reconstruction works in collieries occurred at a series of scales. Some of the smallest represented mere fragments of a mine, while others were more comprehensive. Outside of the building of a completely new pit, Bold Colliery

150
Headgear tower
at Wolstanton

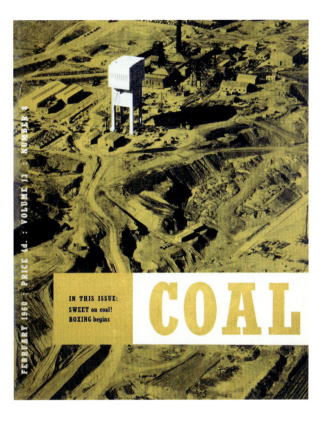

in the St Helens area of Lancashire was one of the largest and earliest reconstructed mines, essentially completed by 1956. The lower inclines and undulations of the seams at Bold, in comparison with other collieries in the St Helens area, had marked out its reconstruction as strategically the most viable means of accessing the 60 million tons of reserves in its vicinity. These would be extracted in tandem with a companion colliery. The iceberg-like structure of a coal mine inevitably meant that much of the modernising activity remained unseen below the surface. At Bold, in addition to the driving of two new intake tunnels, each a mile long, one of the key initiatives had been the accommodation and deployment of the Anderton shearer loader at the mine's Four Foot East coalface. As its name suggests, this machine – designed to run along the armoured flexible conveyer belt in the longwall system – mechanically combined previously separate manual activities. It could cut the 180 ft face in one and three quarter hours, extracting sections of coal 40 inches high and 18 inches wide, all the while suppressing the dust it produced though a series of high-pressure water jets aimed at its cutting disc. On the surface by 1956, however, the only remnants of the colliery's previous iterations were the spoil heap, the lamp cabin and the old screens which were about to be dismantled. The rest was essentially brand new (Anon. 1956b: p.11).

There were three head towers at Bold Colliery, all realised in reinforced in-situ concrete and perched over three shafts, which had been originally sunk in the 19th century. But unlike what would become a normative, solid form of enclosure (partly to facilitate consistency of air pressure in mines), Bold's three towers were all variations of an open-framed structure. The tallest (above No.1 shaft) at 170 ft high and visible for miles was particularly elegant in the way it held and presented, to the largely flat surrounding landscape, the Koepe winding gear that determined aspects of its form. The three towers sat close to each other at the epicentre of a complex which incorporated a coal preparation plant (just off the main London–Liverpool railway line) and a series of buildings containing pit offices, baths and a canteen, a medical centre,

151 and 152
Bold Colliery, and photograph of model

workshops and so on, within a landscape that also contained car parks, bicycle sheds and bus stops with shelters. In an architectural model of the new surface arrangements produced by the contractors and designers (Simon Carves Ltd, from Stockport) to advertise their services in *Coal* magazine, all of the buildings appear as if made from the same light-coloured material (FIG.151). In many ways, it represented an updated version of the model of Comrie Colliery which had provided a vision of the future a decade earlier. Gone is the latter's rigid Beaux-Arts-like symmetrical composition. Replacing it was an attempt at an ordered constellation of buildings, all dynamically linked by the aerial conveyors that – although not shown in the model – also connected the mining and preparation complex to the nearby (and since 1948 also nationalised) British Electricity Authority (BEA) power station. Its backdrop of concrete cooling towers would become ubiquitous and, like NCB collieries' concrete headframes, serve as occasional icons of Britain's industrial modernity (see, for example, Harwood 2015: pp 338–9).

As discussed, representations of the ideal – in model or other forms – had been central to the public-facing image of the nationalised coal industry as it waited for the ideas and strategies laid out in the *Plan for Coal* (1950) to be achieved in actual physical (and visible) forms. An artist's impression of the new coking works proposed for Nantgarw – which had also included reconstruction and reopening works on a moribund mine – had, for example, been published in *Coal* magazine in 1948. Other interventions were given similar treatment in the same journal and elsewhere. But while the model of Bold Colliery managed to convey a harmonious and composed image of modernity, the reality was more complex. Most of the buildings that surrounded the towers were, in fact, made from brick. Some had flat roofs and resembled aspects of the 1930s pithead baths architecture of the MWC.[18] Other roof forms included barrel vaults and the undulating curving pitches seen at Hafodyrynys. Contemporary photographs show a congestion of buildings that lack a coherent overall form, almost appearing to have been placed haphazardly upon a site which, despite its planning and contemporaneous construction, is reminiscent of the type of accreted developments seen in 19th-century collieries. The *Plan for Coal* had originally specified some 67 major and 192 minor reconstructions, by far the majority of the works which would be carried out under its rubric. While, unusually, Bold Colliery had managed to clear most of its site for reconstruction, it still had to shape the project around the three shafts it had inherited from the 19th century. Such constraints were shared by all the reconstruction projects which had, in varying degrees, to deal with the same issues of trying to apply 20th-century technologies, as well as an appropriate aesthetic, to a pre-existing infrastructure that could be many decades or even centuries old.

Accordingly, while the underground modernisations generally achieved significant increases in production and the all-important Output per Manshift at reconstructed pits – the 'streamlining' of the systems 'from face to pithead' at Bold increased its OMS from 21.5 tons in 1947, to 31.3 tons by early 1955 (Anon.

1956b: p.12) – coherent architectural expressions of this tended to be compromised or only achieved in isolated moments. The most significant and conspicuous of these fragments – as seen at Bradford, Wolstanton and Clipstone, as well as at countless other collieries – was in the headframe tower. It is tempting to consider these concrete structures – talismanic as they were of the NCB's modernising ambitions – as also relating, in their verticality, to the concrete tower blocks of housing which emerged at the same time, and which were also seen to symbolise, for good or for bad, a new modern Britain. Certainly, the towers were the most conspicuous and identifiable aesthetic features in the generation of large-scale, entirely *new* collieries prescribed in the *Plan for Coal* and begun in the 1950s and early 1960s. In England and Wales these included: Bevercotes, and Cotgrave in the East Midlands; Lea Hall in the West Midlands; Agecroft, and Parkside in Lancashire; Abernant and Cynheidre in South Wales; and Kellingley in North Yorkshire.

By 1963, the open-frame steel lattice towers at Lea Hall sat over a colliery layout that was defined in plan by a shifting axial relationship. This began in the entrance to the pithead baths and ended – after traversing a railway line with its coal preparation plant – in an aerial conveyor that fed the new power station of Rugeley. The latter was a joint venture by the NCB and the Central Electricity Generating Board, part of a series of initiatives embarked upon in the early 1960s by the NCB under its new chairman (Lord) Alfred Robens. These were designed to generate new – or develop existing – markets for coal. The *Plan for Coal* had initially overestimated the potential of its output. While the reconstruction and new works would ultimately realise greater efficiencies in the production of coal, their gains were offset by the simultaneous disappearance – the majority by closure, but some by merger – of between 350 and 400 collieries (Ashworth 1986: p.200). Despite the simultaneous opening of a series of new, smaller scale and shallower drift or adit mines[19] – which required less time and investment to build – to augment production, for most of the 1950s the industry was essentially running to stand still. The national output for 1957, for example, was 98 per cent of the output for 1952 (NCB 1957b: p.24). This shortfall was met by the importation of foreign coal, chiefly from the USA, France and Belgium, at a cost per ton that was more expensive than its domestic equivalent (Ashworth 1986: p.209). Ironically, by the time most of the new collieries and larger reconstruction works were coming online in the late 1950s, and promising and delivering greater outputs, efficiencies and increases in OMS statistics, another change had occurred. The *Plan for Coal* was designed to incorporate a 15-year period of increased production to meet demand until 1965, when it had been estimated that 240 million tons per annum would be both necessary and achievable. In 1957, however, under pressure from the increasing availability of oil for industrial, domestic, transport and energy-producing purposes, there was an unforeseen fall in coal consumption. This was the beginning of another long decline in the industry which would be exacerbated by the development of atomic energy and the harvesting of natural gas from the North Sea. From 1964–5 to 1970–71, for example, the consumption of coal would fall by 21.4 per cent to 151,300,00 tons (Ashworth 1986: p.238).

When it became clear that the consumption levels in 1957 were not an anomaly, the NCB embarked on several initiatives to actively reduce supply and cut costs. While this began with small steps, such as the stopping of Saturday working, the reduction of overtime, and a ban on recruitment unless in exceptional circumstances, and so on, further, more substantial contractions were necessary. And, for the first time in its history, in the 1960s the NCB began to close pits before their reserves were completely exhausted or became unworkable. After the *Revised Plan for Coal* (1959) predicted (erroneously) that demand and production in 1965 would still be between 200 million and 215 million tons a year, the NCB closed over 200 smaller collieries, mostly in northern England and Scotland, to address this drop (Hall 1981: pp 107–8). While the search for new ways to absorb output would involve increasing efforts to sell coal to industry (under the slogan 'progressive industry is going forward on coal' (Robens 1972: p.69), more emphasis was placed on the mass domestic and energy-producing markets: homes and power stations with the latter becoming its principal destination.

Yet, while in relative decline, coal remained the engine of Britain's modernisation throughout the 1960s. It was central to the prospects of a balanced economy involving both the production and consumption of goods within the State. While in 1950, 90 per cent of the nation's energy was produced by coal, by 1970 this still stood at 50 per cent.[20] The oil crisis of 1972 would also stimulate, at least temporarily, renewed interest in this indigenous fuel source in the 1970s. Under pressure from the convenience and costs of other types of fuel sources, new uses of coal were developed for the home. And coal – like oil and gas – participated in the making of a new domestic landscape of opportunities and freedom. These included the possibilities, offered by centrally heated space, of occupying every room (and consuming products within them). These new spatial patterns would both underpin and become enshrined in the space standards recommended for the future of the nation's social housing, which was defined in the Parker Morris report of 1961, and widely adopted until their abolition in 1980 (Boyd 2015: pp 38–48).

Attempts to consolidate or increase coal's share within the home heating market included the production of new, more convenient pre-packaged and branded coal products such as 'Sunbrite', 'Homefire' or 'Multiheat' which, in the wake of the Clean Air Act of 1956, had to be designed to be smokeless. By the 1960s, smokeless National Coal Board 'Nuggets' could be delivered to your home by NCB employees dressed – like milkmen – in white, to emphasise the cleanliness of the product. There was also the 'Fuelomatic' vending machines – placed in bus stations and other places of convenience – designed to allow a bag of fuel to be casually picked up on the way home (cited in Oglethorpe 2006: p.31). Newer means to consume both these and other more traditional products – such as the Parkray Coalmaster or the Rayburn CB.34, developed 'to burn normal bituminous coal smokelessly' (NCB 1971: unpaginated) – were often researched or prototyped in the NCB's Coal Research Establishment. Originally trialled at two housing estates owned by the NCB (one in Brimington near Chesterfield and one in Nottingham [Robens 1972: p.62]), these products and others like them were made available to the general public in high street showrooms, so-called 'Housewarming Centres'.[21] These new spaces both sold and publicised the 'benefits to be obtained from the attractive modern room-heaters' (NCB 1964: pp 7–8). The 1960s also saw the NCB experimenting with a series of about 'seventy coal-fired district heating schemes' scattered across the country (Roben 1972: p.70), which included a new modernist block in Paisley, Scotland (see NCB 1966: p.38.

In 1964, the 'Board's stand at the Ideal Home Exhibition at Olympia in March … received a good deal of publicity and thousands of inquiries' (NCB 1964: pp 7–8), while, throughout the 1960s and 1970s, there were advertising campaigns in both the local and national press, and elsewhere. Often nostalgically invoking the enjoyment of a real 'Living Fire', such adverts simultaneously suggested progress and convenience. An example from 1970 for the 'Parkray Coalmaster' – which incidentally could also power central heating – perhaps synopsises the type of lifestyle scenario that an updated use of coal could provide in your home. Far from the dirt and inconvenience of the past, it shows a couple in a modest but modern living room fitted with fashionable commodities – an abstract picture on the wall, a sofa and easy chair, a highly stylised electric lamp, a fitted carpet, and a cocktail tray complete with that paragon of 1970s drinking sophistication, a bottle of Martini Bianco, accompanied by a soda siphon (FIG.153). The comfortable heat – which has encouraged the woman to sit on the floor while her partner perches on the sofa facing her

153
Advertising photograph for the Parkray Coalmaster, 1970

– is provided by a slick, chrome-finished and futuristic-looking stove with an adjustment knob and dial. This device occupies the space of the traditional fireplace.[22] Such adverts continued a pattern, pursued since nationalisation, of placing coal within the public eye. Only here it was not the legitimisation of an industry in production, or a definition of its scope, reach and strategic importance – and, thereby, that of its workforce – that was being publicised. Rather it concerned the selling of coal products in new forms – products that in the past had never needed to be advertised, their use being taken for granted. In their search for convenience and branding, these expunged the messy environmental and social conditions of their making from the moment of their consumption. In the 1960s, domestic heating accounted for the absorption of approximately 30 million tons of coal per year (Robens 1972: p.61).

The new, consumer-led post-war epoch of British home life was obviously also hugely dependent upon the availability of electricity. The nationalised system of supply began on the 1st of April 1948. Attempts to continue and consolidate the position of coal as the fuel for its generation in the face of oil, nuclear and later gas, required both research and infrastructural development. A series of 80 new railway-mechanised coal depots across the country – including at West Drayton in Middlesex – had been built to bring greater logistical efficiencies to the market for domestic home fuels, while a new coal terminal at Immingham Dock in Lincolnshire would also be designed in the 1960s to facilitate potential export sales. In the electricity sector, a similar streamlining was developed using what were termed 'Merry-go-round' trains. These were permanently coupled entities of purpose-built wagons designed to make numerous daily trips directly between pits and power stations – sometimes a distance of 50 to 70 miles – without stopping. Creeping through newly created loading and unloading facilities – which charged them from new thin, vertical overhead bunkers at the pit, and discharged them into long hoppers beneath the rails at the power station – in many ways they mirrored, on the surface, the modernising attempts underground to approach an ideal of perpetual and frictionless motion in the moving of coal. Capable nationally of carrying 1 million tons of coal per week – and with a loading time for each train of just under an hour at the pit, and unloading in under 25 minutes at the power station – this new system, which eliminated the traditional waiting times associated with 'tippling' wagons, was an integrated national response involving the combined efforts of the NCB, the electricity boards and British Rail, to what was becoming an insatiable need for electricity.[23]

There were other innovations. Drawing upon earlier research – including that conducted by the pre-nationalisation Coal Utilisation Council into pulverisation exhibited at the Glasgow Empire Exhibition – new methods were developed and adopted to increase efficiencies in coal combustion. Coal powder or slurry was increasingly used in power stations in place of larger coals. Injected into the boilers of power stations, coal in this form would burn and behave much like it was a liquid. Meanwhile, these improvements were supported by much political lobbying on behalf of the industry by Lord Robens and others. Amongst other things, this resulted in a negotiated agreement between the NCB and the Central Electricity Generating Board (CEGB) to supply fuel from 1963 to 1966, and for the latter to defer its commissioning of new oil-fired power stations (Ashworth 1986: p.248). In addition, a new generation of coal-fuelled power stations would come on stream in the early 1960s. These included Drax in North Yorkshire under consideration in 1962, and two others – at Cottam in Nottinghamshire, and Fiddlers Ferry at Widnes, Lancashire – which were given consent to proceed by the Minster of Power in 1963 (Robens 1972: p.67).

Despite such efforts to uphold and develop its market and the sharp rise in demand for electricity experienced in the 1960s, a significant contraction of the coal industry became inevitable. The decline was only interrupted by the oil crisis of 1972, which prompted not only interventions such as the massive expansion of the Drax power station, but also the ambitious development of the Selby Superpit, an extensive underground complex. Emerging with some other major projects – such as the Betws Drift mine in South Wales – from another *Plan for Coal* published in 1974, Selby was designed to supply fuel exclusively for electricity production. It realised a series of new pitheads at Wistow, Stillingfleet, Riccall, North Selby, Whitemoor and Gascoigne Wood. All the coal was treated at the latter after being brought to the surface via a drift tunnel.[24]

Between 1957 and 1967, alongside the closures of many smaller and outmoded collieries, about 678,000 workers left the mining industry. Remarkably only 3.8 per cent of this number was due to redundancies but instead was mostly through natural wastage (Ashworth 1986: p.161). The contraction, however, also resulted in further concentrations of production. This happened geographically, mostly in the newer coalfield areas which had been outlined for expansion in the original *Plan for Coal*: Yorkshire, the East and West Midlands, Ayrshire, and Fife in Scotland, as well as in Lancashire and South Wales. There was also, however, an increased concentration within those pits that had been comprehensively reconstructed or begun anew in the 1950s, and whose share of overall output within the industry was now significantly greater. By the time this first and largest generation of superpits emerged in the late 1950s and early 1960s,[25] the conditions that had originally presupposed their existence had shifted or had begun to shift, irrevocably. But while coal was no longer the nation's prime mover for transport and its role in the production of gas and electricity – as well as fuel for industry and heating for homes – would become terminally compromised, these pits shaped, and would continue to shape, the modernisation of Britain. Emblematic of this, their architecture also simultaneously expressed the modernising transformations that had visited their own industry: the reinforced concrete and glass architecture with its poured sculptural fan house, axially arranged under the winding towers at Lea Hall (FIG.154); the rather prosaic sheet-metal clad towers of Bevercotes; the two nearly identical towers at Cotgrave (FIG.155), whose cantilevering projections (containing

154
Lea Hall Colliery

155
Cotgrave Colliery

elements of their Koepe winding gear) addressed each other almost melancholically in the flatness of the Nottinghamshire countryside across the void above their workers' car park; the grids of windows punched consistently into the two towers of unequal heights at Agecroft, whose pure geometric cubic

forms were articulated by equally cubic extractions and sat, like stranded pieces of future postmodernism, against the backdrop of cooling towers and, beyond this, the urban skyline of Salford and Manchester (FIG.156); their almost doppelgängers in the twin towers at Parkside, outside Warrington; the symmetrical composition of the towers at Abernant (FIG.157), whose projections turned away from each other in a hillside setting in South Wales; and the non-identical towers of Cynheidre, also South Wales, whose upper sections were clad in sheet-metal panels and whose lower sections were exposed to reveal the latticed steel frame beneath (FIG.158). All these conspicuous, heroic forms embodied the coming together of a series of – social, technological, economic, political, cultural and aesthetic – aspirations, factors and forces that had been decades in the making. These had been planned, promised, and discussed in texts, visual representations, exhibitions, films and other ephemeral media for years before finally emerging, above ground and within the public view – in its revolutionised and collective form as a nationalised industry, shaped and modernised under the *Plan for Coal* – as the architectural face of British coal. And yet, unlike the MWC pithead baths programme – and indeed unlike other aspects in the branding of the NCB – this architectural expression generally lacked an overall coherency. Despite the *tabla rasa* conditions available to brand new collieries, the possibility of harmonious layouts of modern aesthetics proposed by the Reid Report remained largely compromised and fragmentary.

156
Agecroft Colliery

157
Abernant Colliery

158
Cynheidre Colliery

This was perhaps partly to do with the position of the architect within the NCB. Whereas the Miners' Welfare Commission had given authority over regions and districts to individual teams, all these teams were located within the same centralised office in London, under a Chief Architect. No such structure existed with the NCB, and architectural works were devolved to Divisional level. Here, moreover, the architects seemed to have operated within an environment which was very much within the control of engineers, with architecture perhaps – and perhaps understandably – peripheral to a hierarchical command structure which (following recommendations in the Fleck Report) encompassed 'Chief Engineer at Headquarters, through the Divisional Engineer, the Area Engineer and the Group Engineer to the Colliery Engineer' (Metcalf 1957: pp 55–7). As B. L. Metcalf, Chief Engineer of the National Coal Board surmised in 1957, there was: 'No uniform pattern ... adopted as to the administrative level at which reconstruction work should be carried out ... in some cases the practice has been to make the engineer responsible for the whole surface layout' (ibid.: pp 55–7). In other cases, such as at Bold Colliery, it was the contractor who apparently took responsibility for the design of the surface layout. Finally, and also unlike the MWC, those architects who were involved tended to remain anonymised. There was, however, one significant exception to all of this.

ROTHES AND SCOTLAND

Not only did the Scottish Division build more superpits in the 1950s than any other in the NCB, but these new collieries were built in the context of the largest programme of concentration to take place within the British coalfields. While this was prescribed within the *Plan for Coal*, its origins lay in the *Report of the Scottish Coalfield Committee* which was published in 1944. This sought to switch production geographically from the outmoded, worked-out, uneconomical, and often heavily watered collieries of Lanarkshire and the central districts – where in 1949, for example, at least 19 pits were known to be operating at a significant loss of nine shillings per ton – to new developing mining zones in Ayrshire, Fife and the Lothians. Thus, the new collieries – Bilston Glen (begun 1952) and Monktonhall (begun 1954) in the Lothians; Killoch (1960) and the comprehensively reconstructed Barony (begun 1945) in Ayrshire; and Rothes (begun 1946) and Seafield (begun 1954) in Fife – would contribute not only to the reorganisation of Scottish mining, but also to the large-scale displacement and reorganisation of coalfield communities. Indeed, over the decade or so the programme would take to implement, aspects of social life within the Central Lowlands in general would be permanently altered. Despite there being a historic tradition of internal migration and movement between unproductive and productive coalfields and pits, Abe Moffat (the President of the Scottish NUM), writing in 1949 at the beginning of the initiative, still felt compelled to describe the complexities and sensitivities involved in a project of this scale: 'Concentration schemes bring with them social problems which must be treated with the greatest tact and humane consideration. Mass transfer of whole communities is something never previously tackled in the history of the mining industry, and from that aspect everything and everyone concerned must be taken into account – miners, families, background, ties' (Moffat 1949: p.18).

Whether they responded to the psychological need for architecture that Charles Carlow Reid had determined was necessary for the new industry, combined within the context of the largest and most radical of all resettlement schemes, the Scottish superpits were universally beautiful. Collectively, they were the responsibility of another designer who, like John H. Forshaw, deserves greater acknowledgement of his contributions to British architecture. His name was Egon Riss. In fact, Riss is renowned, but rather more as the creator of the iconic Penguin Donkey Bookrack which he designed in association with Jack Pritchard for the Isokon company. The Donkey – created to accommodate the inexpensive and popular Penguin paperbacks that had first arrived on the market in 1935 – used straight and curved sections of plywood to hold the books anthropometrically within reach above the ground, in a curved form supported by thin canted legs. Like other objects he produced for Isokon in plywood, such as the 'Gull' and the 'Bottleship', it was an efficient, economic and elegant piece of design which, according to Pritchard, exhibited 'great wit and charm' (Benton 1995: p.200).[26] Born in Vienna in 1901, Riss was a Jewish émigré architect who – following his training at the Vienna Technische Hochschule (between 1919–20 and 1923–4) – seems to have attended the Bauhaus in Weimar, where he knew modernist luminaries such as Oskar Kokoschka and Paul Klee. In Vienna, in association with another architect (Fritz Judtmann) he designed a series of buildings including a tuberculosis hospital, clinics and administrative buildings for different workers' groups, some individual houses, and some structures within the Silesian coalfields. A member of the Building Council of the League of Nations Sub-Committee for hospital buildings, he also produced an unimplemented plan for the centre of Vienna. In the context of all his other works including the Donkey, the latter suggests competencies across a series of scales – from the detailed design of objects to that of city planning – that would be confirmed in his work for the NCB. He moved, fleeing persecution, to London in 1938 where, like so many other modernist émigré architects (such as Walter Gropius and Marcel Breuer), he was accommodated by Pritchard and his wife Molly at the Lawn Road flats, apparently in return for stoking the boilers and doing other odd jobs. Serving in the British Army during the war, he joined the architects' department of the Miners' Welfare Commission sometime soon after the cessation of hostilities, before moving to Scotland to work for the NCB Scottish Division in 1949, as chief architect in charge of surface building and layouts (Benton 1995: pp 199–200; Dictionary of Scottish Architects 2016). This involved not only many small and large interventions into existing collieries as part of modernising reconstruction programmes,[27] but also producing designs for other aspects of the NCB's administration in Scotland including, for example, the offices at Lugar near Cumnock, not far from the Killoch and Barony Collieries in Ayrshire.

At the new colliery surface layouts Riss designed, he brought a consistency of approach, design quality and aesthetic presence that was unparalleled within the British coalfields. As part of the design process, he often made three-dimensional perspective drawings of the new schemes, reminiscent of some of the drawings produced in the 1930s by the MWC to describe and publicise the architecture of the pithead baths. Drawn from an aerial viewpoint, as if from an aeroplane or a helicopter, these drawings allowed the relationships between the buildings and the landscape they sat within to be appraised and tested. Characteristically what emerged in Riss's pits, was a harmonious integration of the horizontal elements – of offices, winding houses, workshops, baths, canteens, welfare facilities, and so on – with vertical towers that were often punctuated by large expanses of glass. An exception to the latter was provided at Bilston Glen (FIG.159). The first of the Scottish pits apart from Rothes, the two towers at Bilston Glen – visible for miles on the southern outskirts of Edinburgh – consisted of framed structures in poured concrete not unlike those seen at Bold Colliery. Each tower provided a slightly different iteration of the frame. The man-winding structure, located above the upcast shaft, was a semi-enclosed hybrid. The frame here seemed to buttress a solid rectangular box-like form, canting outwards as it descended from the roof where it outlined the winding wheel. The poured concrete was crisp and sharp. Indentations between frame and infill cast shadows, and the play of solid and void was accentuated by the diagonal presence of concrete cantilevered stairs that climbed the side of the tower. In a contemporary photograph taken during construction from the other tower, this, and the clear lines of the other buildings beneath – with their differing but coordinated types of glazing and window openings and flat roofs – can be seen against the backdrop of the Pentland Hills (FIG.160). Another contemporary photograph provides a romanticised rendering of the latter coal-winding tower. Taken at about ground level, it is perhaps also reminiscent of the earlier attempts taken to use photography to valorise the MWC's pithead baths. It places the tower – like a modernist campanile, complete with exposed winding gear and accompanied by elements from the complex's preparation plant including the tendrils of aerial conveyors – within a frame provided by natural vegetation: as if the rude interruption to the countryside traditionally associated with mining had somehow been resolved through these modernist forms (FIG.161).

Bilston Glen's companion in Midlothian was Monktonhall, located on the eastern periphery of Edinburgh. With shaft-sinking beginning in 1954 and construction continuing for the next 13 years, Monktonhall was the last of the Scottish superpits to be completed (Oglethorpe 2006: p.226). Like at Bilston Glen, the offices, canteens, baths, workshops, and so on, were formed into an articulated horizontal element consisting of individual parts made to coordinate with each other. The creation of a continuous datum in the roofline reinforced this, while its occasional breaking created a sense of formal hierarchy or even contextual response – such as at the end of the block where the roofline stepped up to resonate with the adjacent coal-winding tower. The

159
Bilston Glen Colliery with coal preparation plant

160
Bilston Glen Colliery, man-winding tower and landscape

horizontality of these buildings – reinforced in the counterpoint of the vertical towers – was further emphasised by the integration of a linear walking gantry on *pilotis* which, while linking two of the elements within the long front facade, also echoed the forms of the aerial coal conveyers located on the other side. Collectively, and like Bilston Glen and Riss's other pits, these buildings – the spaces in the mine most associated with human beings – did not look unlike a modern office or factory complex. As such they were expressive of the new technological, almost white-collar, reorientation of the industry that had been one of the tenets of the *Plan for Coal*. Yet inevitably it was the towers which held the most architectural drama. While both were enclosed with great expanses of glass curtain walling, it was the coal-winding (No.1 shaft) tower that was the more architecturally significant. An elevated glass box framed by concrete members, held aloft on two central piers and four elegantly attenuated columns, its beacon-like qualities across the surrounding landscape were accentuated by it proudly bearing the name, Monktonhall Colliery, in large letters on its zenith (FIGS 162 and 163).

Riss's perspective drawing of Killoch Colliery in Ayrshire (begun in 1953) gives a sense of the coordinated flow of men and coal – from the car park at the front of the site, through the series of flat-roofed buildings to the towers, and the preparation plants and railway sidings at the rear – contained within and facilitated by the surface spaces and, by extension, their unseen underground counterparts (FIG.164). As in some other modern pits, sometimes these flows

ROTHES AND SCOTLAND 261

161
Bilston Glen Colliery, coal-winding tower

162
Monktonhall Colliery

163
The towers at Monktonhall Colliery, coal-winding to the right

were connected, sometimes separate. Underground, Killoch's miners were provided with continually moving, step-on step-off 'man-riding' conveyor belts, to carry them frictionlessly from the pit-bottom to the face and back again. An NCB photograph taken in 1952, shows the site of the colliery before construction began. It is a beautifully bucolic scene – cows at pasture in a gently rolling landscape which includes a farmhouse nestled into a hill. While another photograph shows the presence of modernity in the form of mechanised bulldozers in acts of clearing the site, it is most emphatically demonstrated in the towers which are seen to emerge from and – at approximately 10 and 13 storeys high – abruptly confront this landscape (FIG.165). Their unrelenting block forms heightened this, rising from the ground as two pure cuboid volumes (the coal-winding tower longer and less tall than the other) with solid gables. The latter expressed the horizontal pour lines of the concrete. While their main facades were chiefly of glass, its framing and support was more present and robust than at, for example, the coal-winding tower of Monktonhall. Instead at Killoch, there was a measured interweave between the glazing system's concrete horizontal and vertical elements in a manner – reminiscent of some of Louis Sullivan's tall buildings – that emphasised the vertical. Yet, a more immediate architectural kinship was perhaps again within the new configurations of domestic space found in the concrete housing blocks that were proliferating throughout Scotland at the time of the colliery's completion in the early 1960s – and whose imposition on urban landscapes was often as uncanny as that of Killoch over its rural Ayrshire site.

Of the Scottish superpits, Seafield Colliery (which was begun in 1954 and commenced production in 1966–7) was perhaps the most spectacularly located. Designed to produce coal from under the seabed – whose extent had been measured and surveyed by an out-to-sea boring tower (Anon. 1955b: p.12) – the mine occupied a prominent raised site overlooking both the North Sea and the seaside town of Kirkcaldy upon whose southern edges it sat. Alongside Monktonhall, Seafield's towers were perhaps Riss's most sophisticated. The two forms were non-identical twins. While the man- and material-winding tower was taller and more slender than its coal-winding equivalent, otherwise they shared the same features: a blank concrete facade facing the sea, large vertical panels of glazing arrayed in a grid of thin steel square frames on the two side elevations; and a volume jutting from the top of the landward side centrally supported by a pier-like form carrying its load to the ground. As at Killoch and Rothes, Seafield's underground workings were ventilated by a fan house expressed within a sculptural concrete form. This wedged-shaped building both extracted pit air through the upcast shaft, and 'forced' nitrogen-laced air into the downcast shaft to alleviate problems with spontaneous combustion (Oglethorpe 2006: p.159). By the mid-1960s, Seafield's towers had found immediate local counterpoints in the series of multi-storeyed housing blocks also arranged along the shoreline at Kirkcaldy – the eight-storey buildings at Linktown and, more conspicuously, the 15-storey edifices at Pathhead built by Wimpey (1964 and 1965) (Glendinning and Muthesius 1994: p.213).

164
Egon Riss's drawing of Killoch Colliery

165
The towers in the landscape at Killoch Colliery

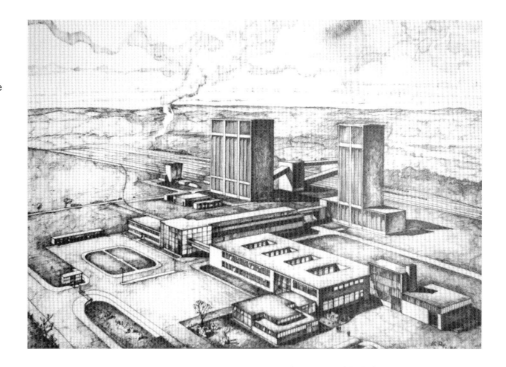

Together, they made an archipelago of totemic, vertical industrial and domestic modernist forms across the front of an otherwise traditional seaside town (FIG.166).

Notwithstanding aspects of some of these collieries' subsequent production and social histories – Killoch was, for example, the first pit in Scotland to produce over 1 million tons of coal per year, while Monktonhall briefly became a model for a new type of organisation in the early 1990s with its workers' take-over of the mine after its mothballing by the NCB in 1987 – the most culturally significant of all the Scottish superpits was the first: Rothes, which was located

in Fife, a few miles to the north of Kirkcaldy. It was also the most architecturally disciplined and rational. At Rothes, many of the colliery's horizontal surface elements – which tended to be articulated, cranked, or even isolated from one another in the other superpits – were pulled together and simplified into one long rectangular form. Both towers emerged from and were integrated with this, while other facilities including elements such as the elegant sculptural forms of the fan-house (which would be echoed at Killoch), were arranged perpendicularly or parallel to its dominant form (FIG.167). The towers – which also shared some characteristics with those at Killoch – were identical. Two sides of them contained the familiar large swathes of glazing which was given a dominant vertical emphasis by a series of concrete columns. This, however, was tempered by a single horizontal member in the same dimensions and material near the top of the tower, which economically rendered the upper row of glazing as a type of a cornice, and the whole elevation – again similar to some of Louis Sullivan's tall buildings – into a classical tripartite composition of solid base, glazed middle and glazed cornice. An acknowledgement of classical

166
Seafield Colliery, No.1 winding tower

167
Rothes Colliery
(photograph R. H. de B. Galwey, courtesy of RIBApix)

architecture was, perhaps, also present in the other two solid elevations of each tower which tapered gently outwards – like the entasis of a classical column – as they descended to the ground a few metres proud of the low, horizontal building that held them.

Part of Rothes' significance was due to its early arrival as a complete integrated piece of modernist architecture within the coalfields. Originally conceived pre-nationalisation by the Fife Coal Company, the colliery was already designed by Riss – operating within the nascent NCB – by 1948. Thus, preceding even the *Plan for Coal*, it became one of the first and most potent visualisations of the potential modernity of the new industry, finding expression in publications such as *Coal* magazine – where it appeared in model form in 1949 as an 'example of development plans' (Anon. 1949: p.17) (FIG168) – and depicted under construction in the *Colliery Guardian*'s retrospective of the National Coal Board's first ten years in operation (Metcalf 1957: p.57). Most emphatic, however, was its appearance on the cover of *Coal*, again in 1957.

PART III: ARCHITECTURE, PUBLICITY AND THE PLAN FOR COAL

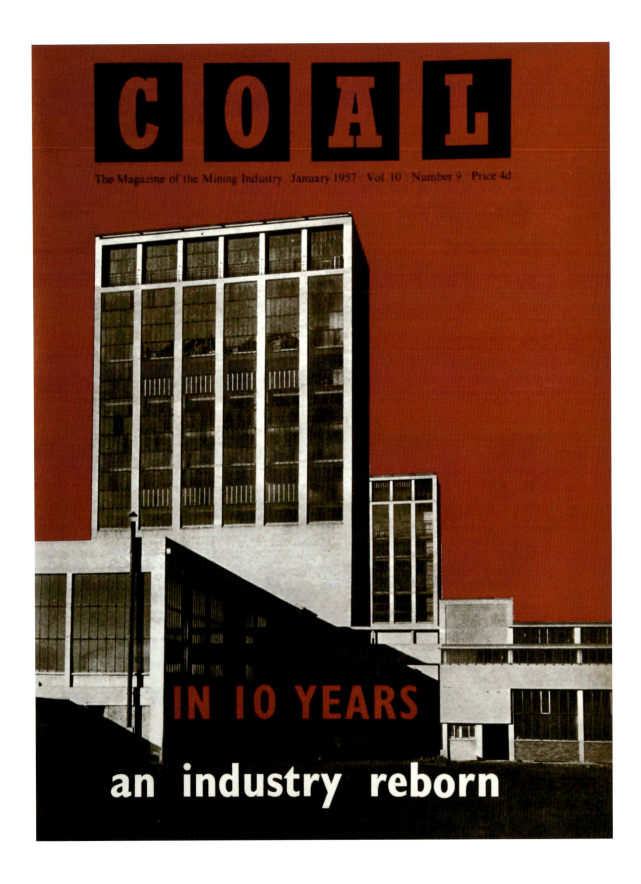

Here, the two towers and horizontal building are seen – against a background of deep red – above the affirming statement: 'in 10 years an industry reborn' (FIG.169). The colliery was opened, with much fanfare, on the 30th of June 1958 by HM Queen Elizabeth II, who descended underground to inspect its workings dressed in a white boilersuit.

Together, the Scottish superpits designed by Riss represented the most complete aesthetic apotheosis of the nationalised industry. They were worthy successors to the works carried out in the pithead baths programme, and provided a serial iteration of the ideal model pit and its integration of landscape exhibited in Glasgow in 1938, and built (with design advice from the MWC's architects' department) at full scale at Comrie in 1935. Indeed, it is remarkable to compare the latter – with its polite brick Dudokian forms and traditional steel winding towers – with the generation of emphatically iconic and modernist pits realised by Riss and introduced at Rothes, with their reinforced concrete and swathes of curtain wall glazing. They appear to be of a completely different epoch and agenda.

CODA: COAL AND THE NEW TOWNS

In fact, Rothes contained another layer of significance, one that connected it to a larger architectural and social context within British modernity and modernism. The colliery was not built in isolation, but instead was designed to exist as part of a larger, symbiotic planned unit of working and living: it was accompanied by the construction of that epitome of modernity and the post-war welfare state in Britain: the New Town. Rothes's colliers – many of whom would be transferred from the worked-out pits of Lanarkshire – would live in Glenrothes. Writing in 1943, John H. Forshaw had surmised:

168
Rothes Colliery on the cover of *Coal*, January 1957

169
Rothes Colliery in model form in *Coal*

> The provision of baths at the pithead, recreation grounds, village institute and health clinics, all excellent in themselves, remain in form *palliatives* [my emphasis] only, when the two essentials of home and workplace, are many years behind modern requirement. Before the war, few collieries in this country were equipped with modern mechanised coal getting and conveying plant, and other labour-saving devices. It seems a curious anomaly that the facilities for the proper use and enjoyment of leisure should tend only to emphasize to the individual miner the complete inadequacy of his house as 'a home to live in,' and inefficiencies of the mine as a 'place to work in'. There is no doubt that these unsatisfactory conditions could be removed under a national scheme of reconstruction applied to the coal industry.
>
> (Forshaw 1943: p.6)

The evolution of underground and surface space and architecture in post-war collieries found some equivalency within miners' domestic circumstances. While, along with most of the population, these generally improved in the post-war years, it was augmented by specific initiatives. For example, by 1952, 50,000 new homes had been built by the Government for miners. In addition, an NCB Housing Association had been set up in England and Wales, with the Scottish Housing Association taking responsibility on behalf of the NCB for building miners' houses in Scotland. By the 1960s, as the result of this, a series of new estates had been built, for example, at: Goodyers End Estate at Bedworth, Warwickshire; Cotgrave, Clipstone and Ollerton, all in Nottinghamshire; Kellingley in North Yorkshire, and Hamstead in South Staffordshire.

It was suggested in Part II that coal mining had a significance influence – especially through the theories, practices and projects of Raymond Unwin and Patrick Abercrombie – on the development, not only of Garden Cities, but also, by extension, the post-war New Towns movement. Described in 1966, as the 'greatest conscious programme of city building ever undertaken by any country in history' other, more recent, commentators have suggested it represented a broadening 'of the benefits of modernity to the working classes' (Leslie Lane, director of the Civic Trust, cited in Farmer and Pendlebury 2013: p.267). Unwin proposed as early as 1921 that London reduce its population by using a series of satellite towns. His viewpoint – along with others such as that of Frederic Osborn – was influential on the *Royal Commission on the Distribution of the Industrial Population* (the Barlow Report) (1937–40). The Commission – which included Abercrombie among its members – had concerned itself with two principal considerations: the population of older industrial areas within the coalfields and the population of London. Abercrombie's *Great London Plan* of 1944 – which built on and related to the *County of London Plan* that he co-authored with Forshaw – proposed the construction of eight to ten satellite towns to relieve the city. The report of the New Towns Committee (Reith Committee, chaired by Lord Reith creator of the BBC) in 1946 underpinned the

New Towns Act of the same year. This, along with the Town and Country Planning Act of 1947, realised the policy infrastructure necessary to allow the first generation of New Towns to proceed. However, in 1946 the Chancellor of the Exchequer, Hugh Dalton suggested to the rest of the Cabinet that, for economic reasons, the first phase of any New Town programme should be 'devoted to the mining industry' (Levitt 1997: p.230). Joseph Westwood, Secretary of State for Scotland also proposed large New Towns specifically for Scottish miners in the late 1940s (Smith 1989: p.77). In fact, of the 14 first designated New Towns, three were specifically concerned with mining: Glenrothes, Peterlee (Durham), and Cwmbran (South Wales). Of the others, eight related to the London overspill, one to the Glasgow overspill (Irvine, Ayrshire), one was for steel workers in Corby (Northamptonshire), and one concerned a new industrial base centred at Newton Aycliffe (Durham).

Outside the London overspill category, however, all these could be defined as being located geographically on the coalfields. Or, in the case of Corby, very close by and, moreover, closely related to coal mining by its principal industry. It is a pattern that is also apparent when extended across the total of the 27 New Towns constructed in Great Britain (excluding Northern Ireland) after 1946. Of these, a total of 13 were situated in coalfields or former coalfields – in addition to those cited above: Telford in Shropshire; Skelmersdale, and Runcorn, in Lancashire; Washington in County Durham; and Irvine, Cumbernauld, and Livingston in Scotland.[28] Of the three New Towns directly connected to coal mining designated in 1948, Cwmbran in South Wales was built to provide alternative sources of employment to mining within South Wales.[29] In fact, acknowledging the isolation and vulnerability of single industry settlements, Glenrothes was designed so that only one in eight of its inhabitants would be actually be engaged in mining. The rest would be involved in paper-making or other existing industries. This was echoed in the proposed diversification of industry and employment at Peterlee, which was intended partly to facilitate opportunities for women to work. Yet Glenrothes and Peterlee would still be associated with both mining and an idea of the future.

Of the two, Peterlee was more architecturally conspicuous, a proposed miners' citadel whose origins, uniquely, lay in bottom-up campaigning from the community itself (Farmer and Pendleton 2013: p.267), galvanised by the proposals by C. W. Clarke (Engineer and Surveyor to Easington Rural District Council) made during the war (Harwood 2008: p.91). The New Town of Peterlee was designated by Lewis Silkin, the Minister for Town and Country Planning in March 1948. Its original incarnation would combine the administrative talents of Monica Felton (Lady Chairman of Peterlee Development Corporation), the town manager A. V. Williams, and the creative genius of Berthold Lubetkin, within a design process that also involved the participation of local miners. Indeed, while Felton described the familiar traditional grid-iron local mining settlements as being not so much villages or towns in the traditional sense, but rather mining camps 'built with dreadful terrifying permanence', Lubetkin

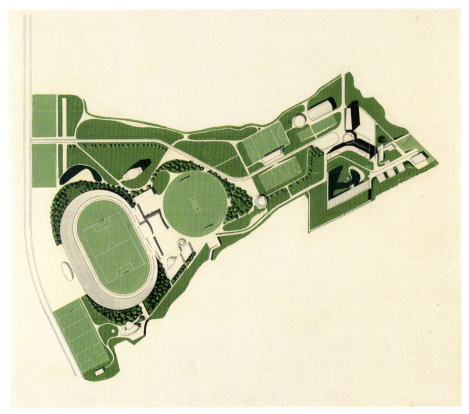

170
Unexecuted scheme for housing and sports facilities by Berthold Lubetkin, at Peterlee

171
Housing on Avon Road, Peterlee by Peter Daniel, F. G. Dixon, R. J. A. Gazzard, and Victor Pasmore

considered their terraced forms 'an expression of the individual cohesion of the whole community' (cited in Allan 2012: pp 454–5). For the local union leader Tommy Mulgrew, commenting on the first proposals in 1948,

> Peterlee appears to me to be one of the finest schemes this country has ever known. Whereas our present mining villages are right down in the dips built around the dust and filth of pit head pulley-wheels, we are going to build a town on top of a hill, away from the valleys of forgotten men. Instead of building housing higgledy-piggledy, as if they had been dropped from an aeroplane, we shall have a planned community. Peterlee will have its community halls, parks, gardens, shopping centres, quick bus services and every facility for harnessing the social and cultural talents which abound in mining villages.
>
> (quoted in Kelly 1948: p.10) (FIG.170)

As is well known, Lubetkin's 'vision of a new life', a 'miners' capital'– with its strikingly modernist composition and forms including multi-storey housing and an innovative town centre – ironically foundered upon the coal seams themselves (ibid.: p.10; and Lubetkin in Allan 2012: p.506).[30] The Designated Area of the town sat on top of some 34 million tons of coal, with an estimated

extraction time frame of 30 years. This process would cause considerable amounts of subsidence. The complex history of protracted negotiations and compromises between the NCB, the Development Corporation, other agencies and the design team, would prove incompatible with the 'type of town [Lubektin] had agreed to design'. His tenure as Architect-Planner for Peterlee ended two years after the New Town's designation, on the 31st of March 1950 (Allan 2012: p.466 and p.507).

His replacement, the firm of Grenfell-Baines and Hargreaves resorted to a more conventional and ultimately relentless ribbon development of semi-detached houses, described by the artist Victor Pasmore as spreading 'like a disease over the whole countryside, these masses of red brick houses with little holes for windows and a beastly little garden lining all these wiggly roads' (cited in Grieve 2010: p.94). Perhaps acknowledging the unimplemented ambition for the town among the miners and Lubetkin's previous project, Williams (who had worked with Charles Reilly on housing at Bilston near Wolverhampton) asked Pasmore to collaborate with the architects Franc Dixon and Peter Daniel on a more dynamic and innovative new scheme for the south-west of the town. They developed a system of cubic flat-roofed red brick houses built using cross-wall construction methods with white timber cladding and windows on the non-loadbearing walls (Harwood 2008: p.93), a structural module which allowed for 'both spatial expansion and freedom of movement between its intersections' (Pasmore in Grieve 2010: p.95) (FIG.171). This was combined with a judicious reading of existing topology and the separation of motorised traffic from pedestrians, to create a unity of 'housing and landscape [which was] most fully realised' in Sunny Blunts, the location for Pasmore's famous Apollo Pavilion (Harwood 2008: p.95).

After East Kilbride, Glenrothes was the second of Scotland's New Towns and was designed partly to address the rural-industrial sprawl of 'a chain of miserable little villages, surrounded by all the usual signs of the unplanned exploitation of coal' (Gardner-Medwin and Connell 1950: p.310). Its position to the north of Kircaldy between the two existing villages of Leslie and Markinch corresponded with that suggested in the influential *Regional Survey and Plan for Central and South-East Scotland* by Sir Frank Mears published in interim format in 1945 (and finally in 1948). While acutely aware of the need to both rehouse native Fife miners, whose domestic circumstances were poor – as well as settling new incomers from Lanarkshire and the older coalfields as proposed by the *Report of the Scottish Coalfield Committee* – Mears suggested that the exigencies of mining should not dominate the area. Rather, the opening up of the East Fife coalfield should be used to bring about a broad range of industrial interests, located in 'constellations' of smaller scale New Towns. While by 1950 a new mining village was being built at Kennoway, Mears's constellation idea was never implemented. Meanwhile, emerging out of the Clyde Region Valley Plan by Abercrombie, another mining New Town was being proposed for emigrant Lanarkshire miners at Coylton (just east of Ayr) in the modernising coalfield of Ayrshire. By 1946, Westwood, the Secretary of State for Scotland was considering two New Towns for miners in Fife, one for new miners to work at Rothes Colliery, the other between Lochgelly and Cowdenbeath, to resettle local miners. Locating the schemes in the context of approaching nationalisation, he described these projects as part of 'a forty-year dream about to be fulfilled' (Smith 1989: p.73). But this dream was also about the future: '(I) for one … will see that the building up of these communities is well balanced, without anything in the shape of the mining towns we have known in the past' (ibid.).

Despite Westwood's exhortations, Glenrothes perhaps had less of a burden of expectation and certainly less of an architectural pedigree than Peterlee. Neither of its Chief Architects – E. A. Ferriby, who was both appointed and resigned in 1950, nor Peter Tinto, who had experience in local housing and public architectural practice chiefly in Glasgow – had the reputation of Lubetkin or Pasmore.

Yet unlike Peterlee, which did not benefit from the creation of any new colliery, Glenrothes with Rothes embodied and expressed the coming together – within a single and integrated architectural space – of two of the most significant modernising initiatives to shape post-war Britain: the *Plan for Coal* and the

172
Plan diagram of Glenrothes New Town

New Towns programme. This can be seen in the outline plan for the town published in 1952 which shows its proposed residential and industrial areas, town and neighbourhood centres, all precisely planned between the two existing settlements of Leslie and Markinch. To the south and carefully connected to the new road system and its plethora of roundabouts, is an arrow describing the way to Rothes pit. Another adjacent dotted line indicates the limits of the coalfield, upon which the town was conceived below the surface (FIG.172).

It is also possible, however, to recognise in this plan some of the same imperatives that shaped the modernisation of the coal industry, both under and above ground. The insistence on the freeing up of motion in the development of means to encourage the frictionless movement of coal so necessary

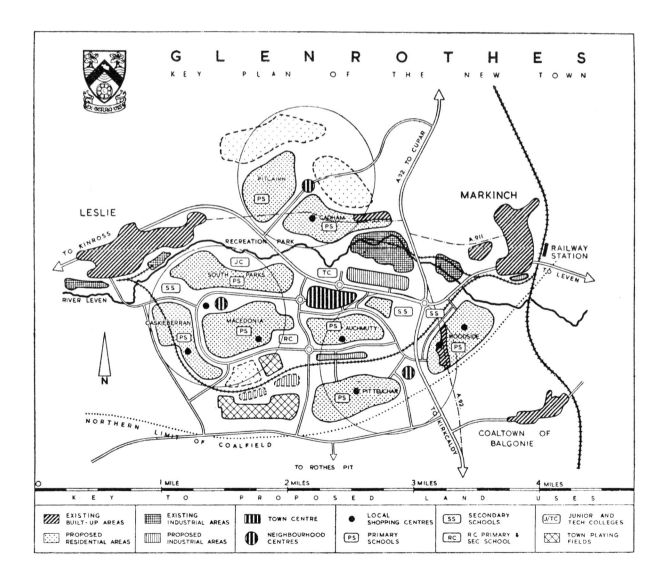

to the increasing of a colliery's production and distribution – armoured flexible conveyor belts, aerial conveyors, skips, and merry-go-round trains – seemed to find counterparts in the relief, ring and distributor roads which, with their roundabouts and separation of motor traffic from pedestrians, characterised not only Glenrothes, but most – if not all – of the New Towns. The continual flow of coal and men was paralleled by that of goods and people within a complimentary modernist approach to the management of time and space. Contemporary photographs of Glenrothes – with the distribution of horizontal and vertical elements and spaces of flow – bear some resemblance to the colliery surface layouts designed by Riss. Like all of the Scottish superpits designed by Riss, Rothes fulfilled Reid's idea of the functional, social and psychological needs for collieries to be realised with beautiful architecture, while both it and Glenrothes answered Forshaw's call for improved working and living environments. But in their provision of recreation, health, culture

173
Site of Castlebridge Colliery, 2020

and education to the working classes, Glenrothes and the New Towns in general, carried on an agenda and pattern first executed in the projects of the 'colossal social experiment taking architectural form' (Bertram 1938: pp 42–3) of the Miners' Welfare Commission's wider remit.

Rothes Colliery was not an economic success. Irresolvable flooding beset the mine almost from the very beginning. It closed in 1962, just four years after it was opened by HM Queen Elizabeth II. Of all the blowdowns of colliery architecture and head towers witnessed over the last decades as the coal industry inexorably dissolved, perhaps the most symbolic was that of Rothes in March 1993. Having lain moribund since 1962, and silently witnessed the Miners' Strike of 1984–5 and further contractions of the industry, this great icon of post-war modernisation – of integrated work and living environments; of planning and a balanced economy; of the public ownership of resources; of the interweaving of technological and social innovations and conditions; of unions and the visibility and dignity of workers – was demolished on the eve of the end of the National Coal Board, and the (re)privatisation of the industry under the Coal Industry Act 1994. It marked a pivotal moment, the eclipsing of the dream of nationalisation and confirmation of a future where Fife and the rest of the British coalfields would be without miners.[31]

The last deep colliery in Scotland, Castlebridge (Clackmannanshire) closed in 2002 (FIG.173); Tower, the last Welsh pit – which like Monktonhall had latterly been run as a workers' cooperative – was closed in 2008; and Kellingley (North Yorkshire), England's last deep mine, closed in 2015. Between 1995 and 2020, the UK imported approximately 340 million tons of coal.[32] Almost all of this was used to produce electricity.

INTRODUCTION

1. Indeed, its pervasiveness has partly been the source of recent ideas to use the frequently warm water found in abandoned, flooded coal mines as a means of providing carbon-neutral domestic heating.

PART ONE

1. The organisation was termed the Miners' Welfare Committee from 1921 until 1939 when it became the Miners' Welfare Commission under the Mining Industry (Welfare Fund) Act of 1939. For all of John Henry Forshaw's tenure as Chief Architect it was, therefore, the Miners' Welfare Committee. However, throughout this chapter and book, I use the abbreviation MWC for both its iterations.

2. Abercrombie mentions how well Forshaw was thought of by both himself and Reilly in a vote of thanks given to Forshaw on the occasion of his presenting a paper at the Royal Institute of British Architects in 1938 (see Forshaw 1938). Also significant is the fact that both Abercrombie and Reilly gave references for Forshaw in his application to become deputy chief architect of London County Council (Forshaw Papers, University of Liverpool).

3. One of his predecessors in the late 1920s was Raymond Unwin, see Part II, below.

4. Between 1948 and 1956, Forshaw published at least 16 articles on housing in various journals.

5. The undated but likely 1936 document titled Architects' Branch details the personnel involved. It lists a Miss Vaughan and Miss Mackenzie as Architectural Assistant II and III respectively. Vaughan started as a junior (architect?) on the 15th May 1928. Meanwhile, Cheryl Buckley describes the recruitment of young female architects based on personal correspondence with R. Bronwyn Thomas ARIBA in 1984 (cited in 2007: 237).

6. 'To be encouraged by a warmth and understanding; and to be depressed by indifference – these are the joys and burdens of a 'Reformer' and I have risen and fallen with these tides of interest and opinion' (Forshaw 1946).

7. That the annual report was published a year later than its title can cause confusion. Thus, for example, the seventh annual report for 1928 was, like all the rest, not published until a year later, in 1929.

8. As is well known, this would have become a general strike but for the last-minute rejection of industrial action by the two other members of the Triple Alliance of unions, the Transport Workers' Federation and the National Union of Railwayman. This event, known as Black Friday, was subsequently regarded in the Labour movement as a great betrayal, 'when not only was a general strike abandoned, the Triple Alliance ruined and the miners' sacrificed but the whole structure of working class resistance to an expected attack on wages and living standards was demolished at a blow' (Mowat 1987: 123.

9. They were Messrs W. Walker, Secretary of Mines; Frank Bain, coal owner, and Robert Smillie, the renowned trade unionist. Smillie also served on the Sankey Commission.

10. Nos 3 and 4 Pits Friedrich der Grosse, Herne; Ickern Mine, near Rauxel; Concordia, Nos 5 and 6 Pits, near Oberhausen (Germany); Colard Mine, Seraing; Six Bonnniers, Seraing; No.18 (Providence) 8 and 10 Pits Charleroi (Belgium); Dourges, 6 and 6 Bis; Nos 3 and 15 Pits Courrières; Lens, No.5 and 5 Bis, Nos 13 and 15 and 15 Bis (all Pas-de-Calais, France) (Home Office Committee Report 1913: p.2).

11. Forshaw would echo this view of the necessity of propaganda in 1938 at the end of his tenure as chief architect of the MWC in 'The Architectural Work of the Miners' Welfare Committee', an article he wrote for the *Journal of the Royal Institute of British Architects*.

12. This was in fact the second facility to be installed at Atherton, the first opened six weeks earlier on the 1st August 1913 (Chappell and Lovat-Fraser 1920: p.55).

13. José Luis Sert, Fernand Léger and Sigfried Giedion's manifesto (written in 1943) 'Nine Points on Monumentality' seems to offer a justification for Dudok's approach (as well as that of the expressionists) especially 'Point 7: The people want the buildings that represent their social and community life to give more than functional fulfilment. They want their aspiration for monumentality, joy, pride, and excitement to be satisfied' (cited in Ockman 1993: pp 29–30). Le Corbusier's concept of the mythical qualities of 'ineffable space' written three years later in 1946 also reinforces this.

14. Because of the economic problems of the 1930s, the levy of 1 penny per ton specified under the Mine Industry Act of 1920 was reduced to ½ pence per ton between 1932 and 1938.

15. A undated document presumably from 1936 contained in the Forshaw papers details the starting dates of all the current employees. No other appointment dates from 1925 or 1926.

16. South Yorkshire: Orgreave, Treeton, Barnsley Main, Tinsley Park, Robroyd, Maltby Main and Dodworth, Wath Main and Nunnery Collieries; Northumberland: Backworth, 2 Linton, Ellington, Newbiggin and Benwell Collieries – plus Bold Colliery in Durham; Harworth in Nottingham; and Chislet in Kent.

17. Also contained within this are two rooms denoted 'North Area' and 'South Area' on the plan, but whose exact purpose is unspecified (MWC 1927: Appendix X).

18. While women had not been able to go down the pits since the Mines and Collieries Act (1842), in certain areas such as Scotland, Lancashire and Cumbria, they still formed a significant workforce on the surface involved in cleaning and grading coal, and so on.

19. A sketch on the rear of a photograph in the National Archives makes it clear that, in section the lockers enjoyed cross ventilation in an arrangement similar to that famously used by Le Corbusier in the Unité d'Habitation in Marseille. This seems to date from the late 1940s about the same time as the Unité was being built (National Archives Coal 80/1147).

20 At the time of writing (2021), bars of pithead bath soap were available for purchase as collectables on eBay.

21 Aside from the output of buildings, there is evidence of a creative and close working culture in the menu cards produced for the MWC Architects' and Surveyors' annual dinners contained in Forshaw's paper in the University of Liverpool's archives. These are witty affairs, providing caricatures of the key architects or drawn depictions of their activities. One drawing shows the dinner served to an architect at his drawing board. Underneath the plate and tankard of beer one can see the familiar tripartite section of the experimental baths described above. The card for 1929 shows two cherubim pouring a basin of water behind a menu. At the bottom, a pair of legs from the knees down can be seen, evidently in a shower. On the right, a man in dirty work clothes is disappearing behind the menu and on the left another man emerges, spruce, clean and dapper.

22 The report for 1937, whose front cover was a beautiful black, red and blue rendering of the position of the coalfields in Great Britain, also contained on the rear inside cover an equally beautiful graphic icon of a pit's headgear whose winding wheel resonated with the roundness of the sun whose rays are shining down. Subtitled by the words Miners Welfare [sic], it can be interpreted in many ways but the presence of the sunlight whose yellow coats the industrial form it interacts with seems like a potent symbolism of the bringing of light, cleanliness, health, and so on, to the adverse conditions and life associated with mining.

23 In the 1930s alone, the form could be seen in pithead baths in collieries such as: Bestwood (Notts.), Silksworth (Durham) and Manor Powis (Lanarkshire) in 1932; Sherwood (including its swimming baths) (Notts.), Penallta and Oakdale (South Wales), Betteshanger (Kent), Aitken (Lothians), Thorne (S. Yorks.) in 1933; Glebe (N. Staffs.), Rothwell Haigh ('Fanny') (W. Yorks.), Cardowan (Lanarkshire), Manvers Main (S. Yorks.), Bentick (Notts.), Hatfield (S. Yorks.) in 1934; Michael Colliery (Fife), Castlehill (Lanarkshire), Bentley (S. Yorks.), Easington (Durham), Seven Sisters (S. Wales), Seghill (Northumberland), Whitfield and Madeley (both N. Staffs.), Astley Green (Lancs.) in 1935; Morton (Derbyshire), Pennyvenie (Ayrshire), Prosperous (Northumberland), Morrison Busty and Ryhope (both Durham) in 1936; Newtown (Lancs.), Hamstead (S. Staffs), Bedlington Doctor (Northumberland), Nook (Lancs.) in 1937; Hafod (N. Wales), Bowhill (Fife and Clackmannan), Newcraighall (Lothians), Newbiggin (Northumberland), Ravensworth ('Betty and Ann') and Dean and Chapter (Durham), Babbington (Notts.) in 1938; and Wester Auchengeich (Lanarkshire), Mauchline (Ayrshire), North Walbottle (Northumberland), Swanwick (Derbyshire), North Gawber (S. Yorks.), Sandhole and Lea Green (both Lancs.), Church Greasley (S. Derbyshire), Hucknall No.1 (Notts.), and Albion and Coegnant (both S. Wales) in 1939.

24 It has been suggested that these characteristics, and especially the use of white or cream render in these other buildings – such as at Pennyvenie Colliery (Ayrshire), Castlehill (Lanarkshire), Kames (Ayrshire), Polmaise (Stirlingshire), Whitehill (Lothians), and so on – represented a distinctive Scottish variant on the pithead baths types (McKean 1987: p.116). However, there were plenty of pithead baths buildings in Scotland finished in brick – such as Cardowan (Lanarkshire), Manor Powis (Stirlingshire), Aitken (Fife) and Tillicoultry (Clackmannanshire); and equally, many finished in light-coloured render in England and Wales – see, for example, Coventry Colliery (Warwickshire), Coegnant (South Wales), or Hafod (South Wales).

25 In fact, the scheme was a collaboration between Woodland and a local architect who designed the cottages and cycle store. According to the *Thirteenth* and *Fourteenth Annual Reports*, this was a Mr T. D. Griffiths of Coventry (1935: unpaginated and 1936: unpaginated, respectively). But as with some other design work which lay outside the exact remit of the MWC architects department – like, for example, the Forshaw's design for the model colliery of Comrie in Fife (1935) – it is likely that Woodland (possibly with other MWC colleagues) prepared the masterplan and advised the local architect.

26 I am indebted to Chloe Whittaker for drawing my attention to this article.

27 When I visited in 2018, it was boarded up.

28 'White brick, well grouped. The tower which is a functional necessity of a pithead baths has on one side a curved glass projection containing a spiral staircase' (Pevsner and Richmond 1957: p.136).

PART TWO

1 Forshaw's personal copy of this is in the Forshaw Papers in the University of Liverpool.

2 One method was 'arling', whereby after accumulating some debt, often through the provision of commodities, coal workers were obliged to bind their children to the colliery – '"legal slavery" was replaced by "debt slavery"' (Hassan 1980: p.77; see also Ashton and Sykes 1929).

3 By 1914, another school had been built to the east of the new village outside its curtilage and not conforming to any of its geometry. Across the road was a (Methodist?) church and beyond this, an orphanage. Another church, St. Winifred's Mission Church was located a short walk away. At some point in the twentieth century, the original axial school was demolished and now only the second school remains. See Ordnance survey map Derbyshire XXVI.6 (Bolsover), published 1918.

4 Subsequently a member of parliament, Houfton would be knighted 1929 for his services to politics and public life.

5 In Newbattle in Midlothian, in a colliery school supported by the local aristocracy, a dictation test included sentences such as 'I am grateful for all the benefits I have received' (cited in Hassan 1980: p.88).

6 The immense influence and contribution of Raymond Unwin to housing and planning was summarised at the presentation of the Ebenezer Howard Memorial Award to him in 1938, when the Minister of Health, Walter Elliot, suggested 'that to speak of planning was to speak of Unwin' (cited in Miller 1992: p.1).

7 The 'Sutton Hall' Unwin cites is actually Sutton Scarsdale Hall. Abercrombie would also mention a somewhat similar future for the manor house located at Woodlands in his article on Houfton's project, some 20 years later.

8 In fact, 'Down a Coal Pit' also contrasted with some of Unwin's own early polemical and more idealistic writing expressed within *Commonweal*.

9 Subsequently, the Industrial Housing Association (IHA) would build another settlement also called Poolsbrook adjacent to this one in the 1920s. Appropriately or perhaps paradoxically, the form of this later addition, sometimes called New Poolsbrook was influenced by the Garden City movement (see note 17 below).

10 This reference cited in Jackson 1982 was gleaned by Jackson from Raymond Unwin's cousin, Miss Christine Boot.

11 Certainly, the coal mining industry was not only well established within Bradford, but was also undergoing a process of consolidation and expansion: New Market pit opened in 1873, New Thornton in 1898 and New Mytholm in 1903. These augmented existing mines such as Norwood established in 1865 and remaining open until 1943, as well as future ones like Norwood Green which would open in 1929 and close 30 years later (Northern Mines Research Society 2021). Potential demand for housing would have been identified at the outset within the surveying of the coalfield and identification of the sites for new pits. The drawing does, however, specify that the houses were for artisanal workers, a description not normally applied to miners.

12 In one of his last commissions, shortly before his death in 1924, Houfton was involved in designing new offices for the Staveley Coal and Iron Company and designed an unbuilt scheme for the MWC-funded Derbyshire Miners' Convalescent Home at Skegness. Before this he had been consulting architect to Chesterfield Rural District Council, as well as having some involvement with the design of a series of 'open-air schools' along with the Derbyshire County Council's Chief Architect George H. Widdows. Widdows is credited as having designed schools at both New Bolsover and Creswell (Cousin 2021: p.2).

13 The nomenclature of 'Type D' etc. was devised by Mark Swenarton in his book *Homes Fit for Heroes* (1981) to distinguish between the different housing types presented in the Tudor Walters report.

14 Ultimately, owners would be required to submit a record of their workings to a registry of shafts kept by the Ministry of Mines.

15 Appendix on Coal Subsidence by Joseph Humble, a member of the Institute of Civil Engineers.

16 The Regional surveys were as follows: Doncaster, Bath and Bristol, East Kent, Middlesbrough and Teesside, Chester and Deeside, North Wales 1, North Wales 2, Cumberland, Gloucestershire, Wye Valley, East Suffolk, Oxfordshire, Thames Valley, North Riding, Lincolnshire (cited in Dix 1981: p.126).

17 There is some confusion about the total extent of the IHA's interventions. *The Building of Twelve Thousand Houses* lists a total of 28 settlements in the Yorkshire and East Midlands. However, more recent research by Hay and Fordham has suggested some of these are misnamed or mislocated on the Tudor Walters map. They give the following as a more definitive list in the form of a gazetteer: Nethertherpe, Hollingwood, Poolsbrook, Duckmanton, Newbold, Piccadilly, Langwith and Bramley Vale in Derbyshire; Skellow, Carcroft, Woodlands East, Armthorpe, Edlington, Wadworth, Highfields, Rossington, Thurnscoe, Cortonwood, Sunnyside, Maltby and Dinnington in South Yorkshire; Havercroft and Upton in West Yorkshire; Blidworth, Langold, Newstead and Warsop in Nottinghamshire (Hay and Fordham 2017: pp 65–127).

18 Richard Barry Parker had also designed an alternative scheme which proposed additional crescents and quadrangles around the original model settlement at New Rossington in 1919. While unimplemented, his proposal may have exerted some influence over the final layout as realised by the IHA. Perhaps ironically or possibly fittingly, the IHA also built a scheme adjacent to the original settlement at Poolsbrook that Raymond Unwin had been involved in designing some 20 years earlier, for the Staveley Company. Thus, Unwin's grid-iron village was directly confronted by a built consequence of his own critique of such housing, designed and built by someone else, wrought in curving streets, with short stepping blocks of houses, articulated here and there by elliptical or quadrangular spaces, and characterised overall by generous front and back gardens. Like most of the IHA villages, it still exists. Of Unwin's original scheme, sometimes called Old Poolsbrook, very little remains except for the Methodist Chapel (now converted to a private dwelling), and possibly the hotel. A flat-roofed newer school occupies the site of the previous one and the rows of streets of houses with back alleys are now perhaps fittingly a rectangular-shaped, open green space.

19 D. H. Lawrence also comments on this, albeit misogynistically, in his 1929 essay 'Nottingham and the Mining Countryside'.

20 Their observations went against popular opinion, and Parker and Unwin's Letchworth Garden City – as well as other schemes designed by them – and IHA settlements provided houses with parlours. It would be some decades before the popularity of the parlour ultimately waned.

21 How much women had an active role in influencing the actual planning and conceptualisation of these spaces – through, for example, the types of social pressure applied by collectivised organisations such as the Women's Co-operative Guild in South Wales in their campaign for pithead baths, or by other means – remains, as yet, unclear and under-investigated.

22. Under the leadership of George Spencer, the NMIU had emerged as a breakaway from the NMA in the aftermath of the General Strike of 1926. Despite the two unions subsequent merging into one as the Nottinghamshire Federated Union in 1936, the term 'Spencerism' remained a byword for betrayal and toadying practices among the labour movement for decades.

PART THREE

1. Hugh Dalton, Chancellor of the Exchequer was born and grew up in Neath, South Wales and Aneurin Bevan, Minister for Health was a former miner, also from South Wales. Wilson's *New Deal for Coal* was published in 1945.

2. The Ministry of Fuel and Power (MoFP) was established during the Second World War in 1942. Shinwell became Minister on the 3rd of August 1945, taking over the position from the previous and first Minister Gwilym Lloyd George who had served in the role under the wartime coalition.

3. The USA's performance was more or less discounted as it was recognised that, in general, American mining conditions were more favourable than European pits to the application of machinery.

4. Ultimately, the drive for recruitment would extend overseas and result in the immigration of miners from other countries, most conspicuously Hungary, Italy and Poland. Their integration was periodically a cause for comment within mining media – see, for example, *Mining Review 10/8: Hungarians in Britain*, or Chiami Giacomo! ('Call me Jack!') in *Coal: Magazine of the Mining Industry*. Giacamo/Jack was 19 years old from Rovigno near Venice, and in 1951, was being trained for the British pits in Maltby, South Yorkshire (Craig 1951: p.22).

5. An account of the modernised mine titled *The Layout and Equipment of Comrie Colliery in Fifeshire*, was written by Charles Carlow Reid's son – later Sir – William Reid. President of the Mining Institute of Scotland 1951–2 and President of the Institute of Mining Engineer 1956–7 he was, within his own right, an influential figure within British coal mining.

6. Spence had been assistant architect to Tait for the Empire Exhibition of 1938, and had designed three of its pavilions.

7. Of course, Alexey Stakhanov was a coal miner. He reputedly set a Soviet record of mining 227 tons of coal on a single shift, which led to the creation of the Stakhanovite movement to celebrate prodigious feats of production. He appeared on the cover of *Time* magazine in 1935.

8. The decision to create these units was solely that of the central Board – the Nationalization Act made no references to Areas, Divisions, and so on (Townshend-Rose 1951: p.57).

9. On an immediate practical level, this idea was implemented through the creation of a consultative committee at each colliery. This was made up of miners and management and met regularly to discuss ideas, and air grievances, on the running of the pit. As an innovation initiated in 1947, the NCB sponsored a 1950 film titled *Nines Was Standing* – with engaging issues of increasing productivity – to publicise its purposes and uses (see also Russell 2009: p.14).

10. In the section titled 'We won the war … we can win the coal' comparisons are made between the use of complex machines as weapons during the conflict and the potential to use them for peaceful, if strategic means afterwards (MoFP 1945: p.10)

11. The position of women in society in general was also approached in the same edition of *Coal*, in a much more significant and progressive article titled 'Wife or Wage Earner?' written by Jennie Lee (a Labour member of Parliament). This looked at the personal conflicts often experienced by women regarding the post-war workplace, discussing issues such as the gender pay-gap and women's rights to a sexual life (Lee 1947: p.8).

12. Marble Arch Colliery would have a more permanent West London iteration in the South Kensington Science Museum – another life-sized simulacra designed by Fred Lebeter, a former mine manager in Britain and India, and Keeper of the museum's Mining Collection. The 'mine' consisted of plaster coalfaces featuring scenarios of dramatic and everyday occurrences underground, including facework and a rescue. Old and new methods of extraction were contrasted both within the full-sized section, as well as in scale models (Anon. 1953b: p.8). Meanwhile, 1959 would see another major coal trade-related exhibition in London – the Mining Machinery Exhibition, sponsored by the Council of Underground Machinery Manufacturers, at the Grand Hall, Olympia from the 9th to the 18th of July.

13. Other by-products from coke included the development of a germicidal oil which, when mixed with an emulsifying agent, could be dissolved through any liquid. This became the 'active' ingredient in Izal Antiseptic Toilet Paper, the infamous shiny toilet paper found in many institutions and some homes (my grandparents' included) throughout the 20th and early 21st century, until production finally ceased in 2010 (Poole 2020).

14. It took over the position as the largest from the preparation plant at Lynemouth, which in 1955 could deal with 800 tons of coal an hour.

15. Another architecture of movement, on stilts and connecting through tentacles to other units, would be seen again in Ron Herron and Archigram's 'A Walking City' a few years later in 1964.

16. Latterly one of these towers would be enclosed in brick.

17. This structure is also still extant having been dismantled and reconstructed at the Deutsches Bergbau-Museum in Bochum.

18. The baths themselves at Bold displayed a very direct lineage to a 1930s MWC typology.

19. Forthbank Colliery, Alloa (1949) and the new surface mine Lady Helen, Dundonald (1953) represented two

20 Scottish examples of such drift mines (see Oglethorpe 2006: p.104 and p.148).

20 See, for example, https://ourworldindata.org/death-uk-coal.

21 'Housewarm' was the brand given to the type of coal which the Parkray or Rayburn could burn smokelessly.

22 The reconciliation of traditional comforts and modernity offered by these new products would, in later adverts, be augmented by attempts to express the orange flickering of flames. See, for example, the television advertisement 'Now you know what people see in a real fire' from the early 1980s, https://www.youtube.com/watch?v=xbFzZlfJaa0.

23 There is a very nice film of this by the NCB film unit titled *Merry-Go-Round* from 1979. Again, the film uses the motif of a past and present comparison to convey modernisation and the progress made.

24 With building work beginning in 1984 and coal production commencing in 1991, Asfordby – one of three collieries also proposed in the 1970s to develop the Leicestershire coalfield (the unbuilt others were at Hose and Saltby) – was the last deep pit in England to be developed (Thornes 1994: p.16). Its twin corrugated concrete towers dominated the Leicestershire countryside that surrounded it. It closed in 1997.

25 Later collieries would include Longannet (sinking commenced 1969), Castlebridge (sinking commenced in 1978) (see Oglethorpe 2006: pp 149–50 and p.102).

26 Outside a few scant sources, there is no significant writing on Riss. Almost all of the information on Riss detailed here derives from two very short pieces in Benton (1995), and the Dictionary of Scottish Architects, Architect Bibliography report http://www.scottisharchitects.org.uk/architect_full.php?id=207844, accessed 20th January 2022. Riss is also mentioned in Miles Glendinning's book, *Rebuilding Scotland: The Postwar Vision, 1945–75*.

27 See, for example, the still extant concrete aerial walkway or gantry he designed to convey miners to and from the pit top across the main public road to the pithead baths (also designed by Riss, but now demolished) at Lady Victoria Colliery (National Mining Museum Scotland) at Newbattle, Midlothian.

28 The original Skelmersdale was a mining village. It is perhaps fitting that John Henry Forshaw had been born and brought up in close proximity to what would become the site for the New Town.

29 Washington in County Durham, designated in 1964 and one of the later generations of New Towns, also had connections with coal mining.

30 See Chapter 10 in John Allen's excellent monograph on Lubetkin.

31 Fragments of the administration blocks designed by Riss at both Rothes and Killoch still exist (2022), as does the sculptural fan house and other parts of the administration structure at Rothes.

32 See https://www.statista.com/statistics/370921/united-kingdom-uk-mined-coal-trade/, accessed 26 January 2022.

Much of the material generated for this book emerged from engagement with a series of archival collections. The National Archives at Kew in London hold the papers of the National Coal Board and those of the Miners' Welfare Committee and Commission. This was the single most important source I accessed, a vast, largely untapped, treasure trove which has been exploited only to a small degree in the present volume. The photographs contained in the COAL/80 series of this collection were particularly useful in understanding the visual, spatial and material characteristics of the buildings described here. These were supplemented by some of the visual material pertaining to the Scottish pits held by the Royal Commission on the Ancient and Historical Monuments of Scotland (RCAHMS) accessible through its Canmore interface. The Royal Institute of British Architects (RIBA) and its ancillary RIBAPIX were also helpful in retrieving images of pithead baths, pits and new towns. The RIBA library also has a vast collection of journals where I was able to access early mid-century writings by Forshaw, and about Dudok and Abercrombie, and so on.

I was able to access pamphlets written by Katharine Bruce Glasier and others at the British Library.

The personal papers of both John Henry Forshaw and Patrick Abercrombie are held in the Special Collections and Archives of the University of Liverpool. These offer personal and often moving insights into the motivations of these two men. I was able to read the *Colliery Guardian* – which for over a century gave perspectives on the industry from a managerial and owners' point of view – at Trinity College, Dublin and the National Library of Scotland in Edinburgh. The Big Pit National Coal Museum in Wales was invaluable in its opportunity to experience the spaces, fixtures and fittings of a resurrected pithead baths building, as well as the sense of relief when coming to the surface after being underground. The National Mining Museum Scotland offered a similar physical experience in engaging with the surface buildings of a pit and the chance to view the overhead walkway designed by Egon Riss. Regretfully, because of Covid restrictions I was able to visit both sites only once each and did not have the chance to engage meaningfully with their archival holdings. A similar situation befell my interaction with the important holdings of the North of England Institute of Mining and Mechanical Engineers, and those of Woodhorn Museum.

The National Coal Mining Museum in Wakefield proved incredibly useful in their digitised online collection of *Coal: The NCB Magazine* which gave crucial information of all aspects of the industry in its critical years following nationalisation. Certain other publications also stand out as pivotal to the research contained here. These include the Miners' Welfare Fund's annual reports from 1922 to 1939, and the National Coal Board's Annual Reports from 1946 to 1982. While both are available in a range of institutions, the latter were made available to me at the library of the Institute for Social Movements, Ruhr University Bochum.

Of the vast amount of secondary sources on coal mining available, I found the five volumes of *The History of the British Coal Industry* published in the 1980s by the National Coal Board and Oxford University Press – especially when accompanied by its reference handbook *Bibliography of the British Coal Industry: Secondary Literature, Parliamentary and Departmental Papers, Mineral Maps and Plans and a Guide to Sources* – to be among the most useful. Outside this, Miles Oglethorpe's *Scottish Collieries* inventory is something anybody interested in the industry in Scotland should not be without.

Abercrombie, P. (1910) Modern Town Planning in England: A Comparative Review of 'Garden City' Schemes in England Part II, *The Town Planning Review*, vol.1, no.2, July, pp 111–28.

Abercrombie, P. (1918) The Basis for Reconstruction: The Need for a Regional Survey of National Resources, *Town Planning Review*, vol.VII, Nos 3–4, March, pp 203–10.

Abercrombie, P. (1924) *Sheffield: A Civic Survey*. Liverpool: University Press of Liverpool.

Abercrombie, P. (1931) The Kent Coalfields, *Journal of the Royal Society of Arts*, vol.79, no.4091, 17th April, pp 504–19.

Abercrombie, P. and Archibald, J. (1926) *East Kent Regional Planning Scheme: Preliminary Report*. Liverpool: University of Liverpool Press.

Abercrombie, P. and Archibald, J. (1928) *East Kent Regional Planning Scheme: Final Report*. Canterbury: Austens.

Abercrombie, P. and Brueton, B. F. (1930) *Bristol and Bath Planning Scheme*. Liverpool: University Press of Liverpool.

Abercrombie, P. and Johnson, T. H. (1922) *The Doncaster Regional Planning Scheme*. London: Hodder and Staunton.

Abercrombie, P. and Kelly, S. A. (1932) *Cumbrian Planning Scheme*. Liverpool: University Press of Liverpool.

Agricola, G. (trans. H. C. Hoover and L. H. Hoover) *De Re Metallica*. New York: Dover Publications.

Allan, J. (2007) Rediscovering Lubetkin, in *British Modern: Architecture and Design in the 1930s*, edited by S. Charlton, E. Harwood and A. Powers. London: Twentieth Century Society, pp 89–104.

Allan, J. (2012) *Berthold Lubetkin: Architecture and the Tradition of Progress*. London: Artifice.

Aldridge, M. (1979) *The British New Towns: A Programme without a Policy*. Abingdon: Routledge.

Alexander, A. (2009) *Britain's New Towns: Garden Cities to Sustainable Communities*. London: Routledge.

Allison, G. (1994) The Miners' Welfare

Commission and Pithead Baths in Scotland, *Twentieth Century Architecture*. no.1, pp 55–64.

Allsop, R. O. (1894) *Public Baths and Wash-Houses*. London: E. F. & N. Spon.

Anon. (undated) *Kells and District Community and Miners' Welfare Centre*. London and Hertford: Simon Shand, Ltd.

Anon. (1935) *Swedish Cooperative Wholesale Society's Architects' Office*. Stockholm: Kooperativa Förbundets Bokförlag.

Anon. (1935) *Coventry Colliery Coal*. Keresley: The Warwickshire Coal Company Limited.

Anon. (1937) Polkemmet Pithead Baths, Lanarkshire, Scotland, *Architect and Building News*, 4th June, pp 278–80.

Anon. (1938) *Empire Exhibition: Official Guide*. Glasgow: Empire Exhibition/Scottish Development Council.

Anon. (1941) News of the Week, *Architect and Building News*, 7th April, p.2.

Anon. (1947) "The Miner Comes to Town", *The Times*, 11th September, p.3.

Anon. (1949) Horizon Mining is Launched, *Coal: Magazine of the Mining Industry*, November, pp 5–6.

Anon. (1949) 1948: A Year of Profits, Settling Down, Advance, *Coal: The NCB Magazine*, July, pp 16–17.

Anon. (undated, early 1950s?) *Concrete in Colliery Work*. London: The Cement and Colliery Association.

Anon. (1950a) Through Ice to the Coal Face, *Coal: The NCB Magazine*, May, pp 10–13.

Anon. (1950b) *Pit Ventilation*. London: Industrial Training Branch of the National Coal Board.

Anon. (1951a) *Festival of Britain: Exhibition of Industrial Power, Kelvin Hall, Glasgow, May 28–August 18*. Exhibition brochure.

Anon. (1951b) Greatest Show on Earth, *Coal: The NCB Magazine*, June, pp 12–13.

Anon. (1952) *Coal: Its Origin and Occurrence*. London: Industrial Training Branch of the National Coal Board.

Anon. (1953a) Britain Looks In, *Coal: Magazine of the Mining Industry*, January, pp 5–7.

Anon. (1953b) Kensington Colliery (London Area), *Coal: Magazine of the Mining Industry*, January, p.8.

Anon. (1954a) New Pit Sinkings, *Coal: Magazine of the Mining Industry*, September, p.18.

Anon. (1954b) The Valleys Meeting Below, *Coal: Magazine of the Mining Industry*, September, pp 13–16.

Anon. (1954c) Architecture and the Coal Board, *The Architects' Journal*, 14th July, pp 41–2.

Anon. (1955a) Central Workshops, *Coal: Magazine of the Mining Industry*, May, pp 8–10.

Anon. (1955b) Through Seabed to Coal, *Coal: Magazine of the Mining Industry*, July, pp 12–16.

Anon. (1956a) For Mining and Research, *Coal: Magazine of the Mining Industry*, April, pp 5–7.

Anon. (1956b) The Bold Way: Part Two, *Coal: Magazine of the Mining Industry*, October, pp 11–13.

Anon. (1958) *Shaft Story*. London: Industrial Relations Training Branch National Coal Board.

Anon. (1959) *Moving Coal Underground*. London: Industrial Training Branch of the National Coal Board.

Anon. (1960) New Face of the Coalfields, *Coal: Magazine of the Mining Industry*, January, pp 11–13.

Anon. (1974) *Strata Control*. London: Industrial Training Branch of the National Coal Board.

Anon. (1973) John Henry Forshaw obituary, *Building*, 21st September, p.92.

Anon. (1974) *Coal: Its Origins and Occurrence*. London: Industrial Training Branch of the National Coal Board.

Anon. (1976a) *Transport Underground: Part 1 Moving Out the Coal*. London: Industrial Training Branch of the National Coal Board.

Anon. (1976b) *Transport Underground: Part 2 Moving Men and Supplies*. London: Industrial Training Branch of the National Coal Board.

Anon. (1982) *Armoured Flexible Conveyors*. London: Industrial Training Branch of the National Coal Board.

Architectural Review (1935) Pioneer Health Centre, Peckham; Architect: Sir E. Owen Williams, May, pp 203–16.

Ashton, T. S. and Sykes, J. (1929) *The Coal Industry of the Eighteenth Century*. Manchester: Manchester University Press.

Ashworth, W. (1954) *The Genesis of Modern British Town Planning*. London: Routledge and Kegan Paul.

Ashworth, W. (1986) *The History of the British Coal Industry, Volume 5: 1946–1982: The Nationalised Industry*. Oxford: Clarendon Press.

Bacon, M. (1985) *Ernest Flagg: Beaux-Arts Architect and Urban Reformer*. Cambridge, MA: MIT Press.

Ballantyne, H. (1918) *Report of the Royal Commission on the Housing of the Industrial Population of Scotland (Rural and Urban)*. London: HMSO.

Barlow, Sir M. (1940) *The Report of the Royal Commission on the Distribution of the Industrial Population*. London: HMSO

Barman, C. (1979) *The Man Who Built London Transport: A Biography of Frank Pick*. Newton Abbot: David and Charles.

Becher, B. and Becher, H. (2010) *Bergwerke und Hütten*. Munich: Schirmer/Mosel.

Bellamy, E. (1888) *Looking Backward 2000–1887*. Boston, MA: Ticknor.

Benevolo, L. (1971) *The Origins of Modern Town Planning*. Cambridge, MA: MIT Press.

Benson, J. (1980) *British Coalminers in the Nineteenth Century: A Social History*. New York, NY: Holmes and Meier.

Benson, J. and Neville, R. G. (eds) (1976) *Studies in the Yorkshire Coal Industry*. Manchester: Manchester University Press.

Benson, J., Neville, R. G. and Thompson, C. H. (eds) (1981) *Bibliography of the British Coal Industry: Secondary Literature, Parliamentary and Departmental Papers, Mineral Maps and Plans and a Guide to Sources*. Oxford:

Oxford University Press and the National Coal Board.

Benton, C. (1979a) Miner Improvements: The Architects to the Miners' Welfare Committee, *Architectural Review*, vol.166, pp 305–8.

Benton, C. (1995) *A Different World: Émigré Architects in Britain 1928–1958*. London RIBA.

Benton, C. and Benton, T. (1979b) Architecture: Contrasts of a Decade, in *Thirties: British Art and Design before the War*, edited by W. Feaver et al. London: Arts Council of Great Britain, pp 47–61.

Berger, S. and Alexander, P. (2020) *Making Sense of Mining History: Themes and Agendas*. London: Routledge.

Berger, S., Croll, A. and LaPorte, N. (2005) *Towards a Comparative History of Coalfield Societies*. Abingdon: Routledge.

Bertram, A. (1938) *Design*. London and New York, NY: Penguin.

Beveridge, W. (1942) *Social Insurance and Allied Services*. London: HMSO.

Boughton, J. (2018a) Aylesham and the Planning of the East Kent Coalfield, Part I. Available at: https://municipaldreams.wordpress.com/2018/02/06/aylesham-and-the-planning-of-the-east-kent-coalfield-part-i/, accessed 2nd June 2021.

Boughton, J. (2018b) Aylesham and the Planning of the East Kent Coalfield, Part II. Available at: https://municipaldreams.wordpress.com/2018/02/13/aylesham-and-the-planning-of-the-east-kent-coalfield-part-ii/, accessed 2nd June 2021.

Boulton, J. T. (ed.) (2004) *D. H. Lawrence: Late Essays and Articles*. Cambridge: Cambridge University Press.

Boyd, G. A. (2012) Designing Bare Essentials: Aldi and the Architectures of Cheapness, in *Peripheries: Edge Conditions in Architecture*, edited by R. Morrow and M. G. Abdelmonem. London: Taylor and Francis, pp 67–79.

Boyd, G. A. (2015) Parker Morris and the Economies of the Fordist House, in *Economy and Architecture*, edited by J. Odgers, M. McVicar and S. Kite. London: Routledge, pp 38–48.

Bradbury, D. (ed.) (2018) *Essential Modernism: Design between the World Wars*. New Haven, CT: Yale University Press.

British Film Institute (BFI) (2009) *National Coal Board Collection Volume 1: Portrait of a Miner*. London: BFI.

Brown, G. (1965) The National Plan for Economic Development, Department for Economic Affairs REM 13/274. The National Archives. Available at: https://www.nationalarchives.gov.uk/education/resources/sixties-britain/national-plan/, accessed 9th December 2021.

Bryan, A. (1976) Coal and Coalmining, in *Coal Technology for Britain's Future*, edited by J. Bugler. London: Macmillan, pp 29–51.

Buckley, C. (1984) Miners' Welfare: Progress by Pressure, *The Architects' Journal*, 13th June, pp 48–59.

Buckley, C. (2007) *Designing Modern Britain*. London: Reaktion Books.

Bullock, N. (2002) *Building the Post-War World*. Abingdon: Routledge.

Burnet, J. (1978) *A Social History of Housing 1815–1985*. London: Methuen.

Campbell, A. B. (1979) *The Lanarkshire Miners: A Social History of their Trade Unions, 1775–1874*. Edinburgh: John Donald.

Cantrill, T. C. (1913/2015) *Coal Mining*. London: Forgotten Books.

Casciato, M. (1996) *The Amsterdam School*. Rotterdam: 010 Uitgeverij.

Chadwick, E. (1843) *Report on the Sanitary Condition of the Labouring Population of Great Britain*. London: HMSO.

Chaplin, S. (1947) The Pit Comes to the Public, in *Coal: The NCB Magazine*, September, pp 5–7.

Chappell, E. L. and Lovat-Fraser, J. A. (1920) *Pithead and Factory Baths*. Cardiff: Welsh Housing and Development Association.

Charlton, S., Harwood, E. and Powers, A. (2007) *British Modern: Architecture and Design in the 1930s*. London: The Twentieth Century Society.

Cheap Cottages Exhibition (1905a) *The Book of the Cheap Cottages Exhibition, containing a complete catalogue, with plans, and an article on the origins of the exhibition, etc.* London.

Cheap Cottages Exhibition (1905b) *Supplement of the Cheap Cottages Exhibition*. London: The Country Gentleman & Land and Water Ltd. 16th September.

Cherry, G. E. (1981) *Pioneers in British Planning*. London: The Architectural Press.

Church, R. (1986) *The History of the British Coal Industry, Volume 3, 1830–1913: Victorian Pre-eminence*. Oxford: Clarendon Press.

Clark, G. (2020) Lancaster and Morecambe Regional Planning Scheme (1927), in *Contrebis*, vol.37.

Cole, G. D. H. (1948) *The National Coal Board: Its Tasks, Its Organisation, and its Prospects*. London: Fabian Society.

Colls, R. (1977) *The Collier's Rant*. London: Croom Helm.

Colls, R. (1987) *The Pitmen of the Northern Coalfield: Work, Culture and Protest, 1790–1850*. Manchester: Manchester University Press.

Colomina, B. (1997) The Medical Body in Modern Architecture, *Daidalos*. no.64. Berlin, pp 60–71.

Conekin, B. (2003) *'The autobiography of a nation': The 1951 Festival of Britain*. Manchester: Manchester University Press.

Coombes, B. L. (1939/2002) *These Poor Hands: An Autobiography of a Miner Working in South Wales*. Cardiff: University of Wales Press.

Court, W. H. B. (1951) *History of the Second World War: Coal*. London: HMSO.

Cousins, P. (2021) Biography of Percy Bond Houfton. Available at: https://www.victoriacountyhistory.ac.uk/explore/assets/biography-percy-bond-houfton, accessed 27th April 2021.

Cranston, R. (2009) Mining Review (1947–1983), *National Coal Board Collection Volume 1: Portrait of a Miner*. London: BFI.

Craig, B. (1951) Chiamo Giacomo! ('Call

Me Jack!'), *Coal: Magazine of the Mining Industry*, July, pp 22–3.

Cross, A. W. S. (1906) *Public Baths and Wash-Houses: A Treatise on Their Planning, Design, Arrangement, and Fitting, Having Special Regards to the Acts Arranging for Their Provision, With Chapters on Turkish, Russian, and Other Special Baths, Public Laundries, Engineering, Heating, Water Supply, Etc*. London: B. T. Batsford.

Darley, G. (2007) *Villages of Vision: A Study of Strange Utopias*. Nottingham: Fives Leaves Publications.

Daunton, M. J. (1980) Miners' Houses: South Wales and the Great Northern Coalfield, in *The International Review of Social History*, vol.25, no.2, pp 143–75.

Dehaene, M. (2005) A Conservative Framework for Rural Development: Abercrombie's Interwar Experiments in Regional Planning, in *Journal of Planning Education and Research*, vol.25, pp 131–48.

Dennis, N., Henriques, F., Slaughter, C. (1956/1976) *Coal is our Life*. London: Tavistock.

Dictionary of Scottish Architects (DSA). John Henry Forshaw. Available at: http://www.scottisharchitects.org.uk/architect_full.php?id=201268, accessed January 2018.

Dictionary of Scottish Architects (DSA) Egon Riss. Available at: http://www.scottisharchitects.org.uk/architect_full.php?id=207844, accessed 20th January 2022.

Dix, G. (1981) Patrick Abercrombie 1879–1957, in *Pioneers in British Planning*, edited by G. E. Cherry. London: The Architectural Press, pp 103–30.

Duckham, B. F. (1970) *A History of the Scottish Coal Industry, Volume 1: 1700–1815*. Newton Abbot: David and Charles.

Duncan, R. (2005) *The Mineworkers*. Edinburgh: Birlinn.

Ellis, L. (1955) *The Future for Miners*. London: The Communist Party.

Engels, F. and Marx, K. (1848/1978) 'Manifesto of the Communist Party', in *The Marx-Engels Reader*, edited by R. C. Tucker. New York, NY: Norton.

Esher, L. (1981) *A Broken Wave: The Rebuilding of England 1940–1980*. London: Penguin.

Evans, H. (ed.) (1972) *New Towns: The British Experience*. New York: John Wiley and Sons.

Evans, N. and Jones, D. (1994) 'A blessing for the miner's wife': The Campaign for Pithead Baths in the South Wales Coalfields, 1908–1950, *Llafur*, vol.6, pp 5–28.

Ewald, F. (2002) *Société assurentielle et solidarité*, interview with Olivier Mongrim and Joël Roman, *Esprit*, vol.288, October, pp 117–35.

Farmer, G. and Pendlebury, J. (2013) Conserving Dirty Concrete: The Decline and Rise of Pasmore's Apollo Pavilion, Peterlee, *Journal of Urban Design*, vol.18, no.2, pp 263–80.

Fawcett, C. B. (1924) New Plans for Industrial Development: Review, *The Town Planning Review*, vol.63, no.5, May, pp 440–42.

Feaver, W. et al. (eds) (1979) *Thirties: British Art and Design*. London: Victoria and Albert Museum.

Ferguson, K. (1973) *Glenrothes 1948–1973: The First Twenty-Five Years*. Dunfermline: Dunfermline Press.

Ferguson, K. (1982) *A History of Glenrothes*. Glenrothes: Glenrothes Development Corporation.

Flagg, E. (1894) The New York Tenement-House Evil and its Cure, *Scribner's Magazine*, July, pp 108–17.

Flagg, E. (1922) *Ernest Flagg's Small Houses: Their Economic Design and Construction*. New York: Dover Editions.

Fleck, A. (1955) *Report of Advisory Committee on Organisation*. London: National Coal Board.

Forshaw, J. H. (n.d.) Architects [*sic*] Department, unpublished document listing of MWC architectural personnel, D113 Forshaw papers, University of Liverpool.

Forshaw, J. H. (1922) High Buildings in New York and the Influence of Zoning Law upon their Design and Plan. Unpublished B.Arch thesis, D113 Forshaw papers, University of Liverpool.

Forshaw, J. H. (1923) Vauxhall Bridge, No.8 panels as above. Unpublished drawing, D113/8/1 Forshaw papers, University of Liverpool.

Forshaw, J. H. (1927) *Lancaster and Morecambe Regional Planning Scheme, prepared for the Joint Town Planning Committee of Local Authorities*. London: Hodder and Stoughton; Liverpool: University of Liverpool Press.

Forshaw, J. H. (1935) The Architectural Work of the Miners' Welfare Committee, *Journal of the Royal Institute of British Architects*, vol.42, Third Series, no.19, 7th September, pp 1077–90.

Forshaw, J. H. (1936) Manuscript headed 'Note by Mr Forshaw of Visit to the Pioneer Health Centre, Peckham 19.11.36', D113 Forshaw papers, University of Liverpool.

Forshaw, J. H. (1938) The Architectural Work of the Miner's Welfare Committee, *Journal of the Royal Institute of British Architects*, 7th March, pp 421–38.

Forshaw, J. H. (1939a) Memo to Miners' Welfare Committee (May), Agenda 177, Paper 6, Construction Work – Criticisms and Question of Decentralisation. Unpublished document, D113 Forshaw papers, University of Liverpool.

Forshaw, J. H. (1939b) Pithead Baths at Small Collieries: Memorandum by the Chief Architect concerning the design, construction and cost of small baths. Miners' Welfare Committee (May), Agenda 177, Paper 7. Unpublished document, Forshaw papers, University of Liverpool.

Forshaw, J. H. (1943) *Town Planning and Health: A Chadwick Public Lecture*. London: King and Staples Ltd.

Forshaw, J. H. (1946) Resignation speech. Unpublished, D113, Forshaw papers, University of Liverpool.

Forshaw, J. H. (1948) Housing and Town Development, *RIBA Journal*, April, pp 253–59.

Forshaw, J. H. (1951) Housing in Britain: A Mid-century Review, presentation to International Federation for Housing and Town Planning, 14–18th July.

Forshaw, J. H. (1954) Towards New Building. Presentation to the Modular Society, 5th May.

Forshaw, J. H. and Bevan, R. C. (1956) Russian architecture and building 1955: report of a recent tour, *RIBA Journal*, pp 182–9.

Forshaw, J. H. (undated) Heating in the United Kingdom – Present and Future. D-113/4/74a. Unpublished document, Forshaw papers, University of Liverpool.

Forshaw, J. H. and Abercrombie, P. (1943) *Country of London Plan*. London: Macmillan and Co. Limited.

Forty, A. (1976) Festival Politics, in *A Tonic to the Nation: The Festival of Britain 1951*, edited by M. Banham and B. Hillier. London: Thames and Hudson, pp 26–38.

Forty, A. (1986) *Objects of Desire: Design and Society since 1750*. London: Thames and Hudson.

Frampton, K. (1980/2020) *Modern Architecture: A Critical History*. London: Thames and Hudson.

Fraser, N. (2016) Contradictions of Capital and Care, *New Left Review*. no.100, pp 99–117.

Galloway, R. L. (1882) *A History of Coal Mining in Great Britain*. London: Forgotten Books.

Gardner-Medwin, R. and Connell, F. T. (1950) New Towns in Scotland, *The Town Planning Review*, vol.20, no.4 (January), pp 305–14.

Garside, W. R. (1971) *The Durham Miners 1919–1960*. London: George Allen & Unwin.

Gaskell, M. (1979) Model Industrial Villages in S. Yorkshire/N. Derbyshire and the Early Town Planning Movement, *The Town Planning Review*, vol.50, no.4, pp 437–58.

Gerhard, W. P. (1908) *Modern Baths and Bath Houses*. New York: John Wiley and Sons.

Giedion, S. (2014) *Mechanisation Takes Command: A Contribution to Anonymous History*. Minneapolis, MN: University of Minnesota Press.

Gilbert, D., Matless, D. and Short, B. (eds) (2003) *Geographies of British Modernity*. Oxford: Blackwell.

Glasier, K. B. and Richardson, T. (1912) *Baths at the Pithead and the Works*. London: The Women's Labour League.

Glendinning, M. (1998) *Rebuilding Scotland: The Postwar Vision 1945–1975*. Edinburgh: Tuckwell Press.

Glendinning, M. (2021) *Mass Housing: Modern Architecture and State Power*. London: Bloomsbury.

Glendinning, M. and Muthesius, S. (1994) *Tower Block: Modern Public Housing in England, Scotland, Wales and Northern Ireland*. London: Paul Mellon Centre for Studies in British Art.

Gold, J. R. (2013) *The Experience of Modernism: Modern Architects and the Future City, 1928–1953*. Abingdon: Routledge.

Graham, S. (2016) *Vertical: The City from Satellites to Bunkers*. London: Verso.

Graves, C. (1932) A Miner's Life Above the Ground, *The Sphere*, 23rd April.

Gray, D. (1982) *Coal: British Mining in Art 1680–1980*. London: Arts Council/British Coal Board.

Great British Commissioners for Inquiring into the Employment and Condition of Children in Mines and Manufactories (1842) *The Condition and Treatment of the Children employed in the Mines and Collieries of the United Kingdom Carefully compiled from the appendix to the first report of the Commissioners With copious extracts from the evidence, and illustrative engravings*. London: William Strange.

Green, O. (2013) *Frank Pick's London: Art, Design and the Modern City*. London: V&A Publishing.

Gregory, R. (1968) *The Miners and British Politics: 1906–1914*. Oxford: Oxford University Press.

Grieve, A. (ed.) (2010) *Victor Pasmore*. London: Tate.

Griffin, A. (1962) *The Miners of Nottinghamshire: A History of the Nottinghamshire Miners' Union*. London: George Allen & Unwin.

Griffin, A. (1977) *The British Coal-Mining Industry: Retrospect and Prospect*. London: Moorland.

Grounds, A. and Hirst, A. (1957), 'Coal Preparation', *National Coal Board: The first ten years*, G. Nott-Bower and R. Walkerine (eds). London: National Coal Board.

Guillen, M. F. (2006) *The Taylorised Beauty of the Mechanical: Scientific Management and the Rise of Modernist Architecture*. New Jersey: Princeton University Press.

Hall, P. (2014) The Birthplace of Garden Cities, in Planning – Planning Resource: independent intelligence for planning professionals. Available at: https://www.planningresource.co.uk/article/1292986/birthplace-garden-cities-sir-peter-hall, accessed 8th April 2021.

Hall, T. (1981) *King Coal: Miners, Coal and Britain's Industrial Future*. London: Penguin.

Hannavy, J. (2013) *Edwardian Mining in Old Postcards*. Wellington: PiXZ Books.

Harris, B. (2004) *The Origins of the British Welfare State: Social Welfare in England and Wales, 1800–1945*. London: Palgrave Macmillan.

Harrison, R. (ed.) *Independent Collier: The Coal Miner as Archetypal Proletarian Reconsidered*. New York, NY: St Martin's Press.

Harwood, E. (2008) Neurath, Riley and Bilston, Pasmore and Peterlee, in *Housing the Twentieth Century Nation* (Twentieth Century Architecture 9), edited by E. Harwood and A. Powers. London: The Twentieth Century Society, pp 83–96.

Harwood, E. (2015) *Space, Hope and Brutalism: English Architecture 1945–1975*. New Haven, CT: Yale University Press.

Harwood, E. (2019) *Art Deco Britain: Buildings of the Interwar Years*. London: Twentieth Century Society.

Harwood, E. and Powers, A. (eds) (2001) *Festival of Britain* (Twentieth Century Architecture 5). London: Twentieth Century Society.

Hassan, J. (1980) The Landed Estate, Paternalism and the Coal Industry in Midlothian, 1800–1880, *The Scottish Historical Review*, vol.59, no.167, Part 1, April, pp 73–91.

Hawkes, D. (ed.) (1986) *Modern Country Homes in England: The Arts and Crafts Architecture of Barry Parker*. Cambridge: Cambridge University Press.

Hawkes, D. and Taylor, N. (1980) *Barry Parker and Raymond Unwin: Architects*. London: Architectural Association Publications.

Hay, H. and Fordham, D. (2017) *New Coalfields New Housing: Reviewing the Achievements of the Industrial Housing Association*. Doncaster: Fedj-el-Adoum Publishing.

Hayter, M. (2016) Home for Good: A History of Social Housing in North East Derbyshire: A Brief Overview of Developments. Available at: http://socialhousinghistory.org.uk/wp-content/uploads/2016/09/A-History-of-Social-Housing-Max-Hayter-March-2016, accessed 27th July 2020.

Hole, W. V., Adderson, I. M. and Pountney, M. T. (1979) *Washington New Town: The Early Years*. London: HMSO.

Holley, S. (1983) *Washington: Quicker by Quango: The History of Washington New Town 1964–1983*. Washington: Washington Development Council.

Holme, C. G. (ed.) (1935) *Industrial Architecture*. London: The Studio.

Home Office Report of the Departmental Committee (1913) *Washing and Drying Accommodation at Mines*. London: HMSO.

Howard, E. (1898) *To-morrow: A Peaceful Path to Real Reform*. London: Swan Sonnenschein and Co.

Howard, E. (1902) *Garden Cities of Tomorrow*. London: Swan Sonnenschein and Co.

Hughes, S., Malaws, B. Parry, M., Wakelin, P. (1994) *Collieries of Wales: Engineering and Architecture*. Aberystwyth: Royal Commission on the Ancient and Historical Monuments in Wales.

Hume, J. R. (1976) *The Industrial Archaeology of Scotland: 1. The Lowlands and Borders*. Frome: Butler and Tanner.

Hutton, G. (1999) *Fife: The Mining Kingdom*. Newtongrange: Scottish Mining Museum.

Hutton, G. (2000) *Mining: From Kirkintilloch to Clackmannan and Stirling to Slamannan*. Newtongrange: Scottish Mining Museum.

Hutton, G. (2001) *Scotland's Black Diamonds: Coal Mining in Scotland*. Newtongrange: Scottish Mining Museum.

Ing, W. (2021) Brutalist Teesside tower handed lifeline by Historic England listing, *Architects' Journal*. Available at: https://www.architectsjournal.co.uk/news/brutalist-teeside-tower-handed-lifeline-by-historic-england-listing, accessed 6th January 2022.

Jackson, A. (1970) *The Politics of Architecture: A History of Modern Architecture in Britain*. Toronto: University of Toronto Press.

Jackson, F. (1985) *Sir Raymond Unwin: Architect, Planner and Visionary*. London: Zemmer.

Jackson, M. P. (1974) *The Price of Coal*. London: Croom Helm.

James-Chakraborty, K. (2018) *Modernism as Memory: Building Identity in the Federal Republic of Germany*. Minneapolis, MN and London: University of Minnesota Press.

Jeremiah, D. (2000) *Architecture and Design for the Family in Britain, 1900–1970*. Manchester: Manchester University Press.

Jevons, H. S. (1915) *The British Coal Trade*. London: Kegan Paul, Trench, Trübner and Co.

John, A. V. (1980) *By the Sweat of their Brow: Women Workers at Victorian Coal Mines*. London: Croom Helm.

Johnson, B. (2014) *Carbon Nation: Fossil Fuels in the Making of American Culture*. Lawrence, KA: University Press of Kansas.

Jones, I. (1957) Research, in *National Coal Board: The First Ten Years*, edited by G. Nott-Bower and R. H. Walkerdine. London: National Coal Board, pp 83–90.

Kelf-Cohen, R. (1973) *British Nationalisation 1945–1973*. London: Macmillan.

Kelly, A. (1948) Vision of a New Life, *Coal: The NCB Magazine*, February, pp 10–11.

Kemp, C. G. (1940) Architecture of State IV: Buildings for Miners' Welfare, *Architecture, Design and Construction*, July, pp 156–66.

Knight, D. and Sabey, A. (1984) *The Lion Roars at Wembley: The British Empire Exhibition 1924–1925*. London: Don R. Knight.

Knox, W. W. (1999) *Industrial Nation: Work Culture and Society in Scotland, 1800–Present*. Edinburgh: Edinburgh University Press.

Kynaston, D. (2007) *Austerity Britain: 1945–1951*. London: Bloomsbury.

Lang, R. (2014) Architects Take Command: The LCC Architects' Department, *Volume #41: How to Build a Nation*, no.3, pp 32–6.

Langmead, D. (1996) *Willem Marinus Dudok, A Dutch Modernist: A Bio-Bibliography*. London: Greenwood Press.

Lawrence, D. H. (1913/2012) *Sons and Lovers*. London: Penguin.

Lawrence, D. H. (1929) Nottingham and the Mining Countryside, in *D. H. Lawrence: Late Essays and Articles*, edited by J. T. Boulton (2004). Cambridge: Cambridge University Press, pp 285–94.

Lawrence, R. (2018) *Bradwell's Images of Coal Mining in South Wales*. Sheffield: Bradwell Books.

Lee, J. (1947) Wife or Wage Earner?, *Coal: The NCB Magazine*, May, p.8.

Legg, S. (producer) (1952) *Plan for Coal*. Data Film Productions.

Levitt, I. (1997) New Towns, New Scotland, New Ideology, *The Scottish Historical Review*, vol.76, no.202, Part 2, October, pp 222–38.

Linehan, D. (2001) Bodywash: The Rise and Fall of pithead baths and other washing machines in the 20th Century. Unpublished conference paper presented IBG Conference, Brighton.

Linehan, D. (2003) A New England: Landscape, Exhibition and Remaking Industrial Space in the 1930s, in *Geographies of British Modernity*, edited by G. Gilbert, D. Matless and B. Short. Oxford: Blackwell, pp 132–50.

Lloyd, N. (2021) Nadine Dorries clears way for brutalist Dorman Long tower to be toppled, *The Times*, 17th September. Available at: https://www.thetimes.co.uk/article/nadine-dorries-clears-way-for-brutalist-dorman-long-tower-to-be-toppled-bq0nwx35c, accessed 6th January 2022.

Lock, K. and Ellis, H. (2020) *New Towns: The Rise, Fall, and Rebirth*. London: RIBA.

Lockard, D. (1998) *Coal: A Memoir and Critique*. London: University Press of Virginia.

Long, V. (2011) Industrial Homes, Domestic Factories: The Convergence of Private and Public Space in Interwar Britain, *Journal of British Studies*, vol.50, no.2 (Autumn), pp 434–64.

Machin, F. (1958) *The Yorkshire Miners: A History. Volume 1*. Huddersfield: National Union of Mineworkers (Yorkshire Area).

Malm, A. (2016) *Fossil Capital: The Rise of Steam Power and the Roots of Global Warming*. London: Verso.

Manning, R. D. (1938) Official Departments V: Miners' Welfare Committee Architects' Department, *The Architects' Journal*, 14th July, pp 63–4.

Mason, P. F. (2012) *The Pitsinkers of Northumberland and Durham*. Stroud: The History Press.

McKean, C. (1987) *The Scottish Thirties: An Architectural Introduction*. Edinburgh: Scottish Academic Press.

Mears, F. C. (1948) *A Regional Survey and Plan for Central and South-East Scotland, prepared for the Central and South East Scotland Regional Planning Advisory Committee*. London: HMSO.

Metcalf, B. L. (1957) The Place of the Engineer in Coal, in *National Coal Board: The First Ten Years*, edited by G. Nott-Bower and R. H. Walkerdine. London: National Coal Board, pp 53–7.

Miller, M. (1992) *Raymond Unwin: Garden Cities and Town Planning*. Leicester: Leicester University Press.

Mines Department, Departmental Committee of Inquiry (1931) *Report to the Secretary of Mines*, Cmd 4236. London: HMSO.

Miners' Welfare Commission (MWC) (1940) *Miners' Welfare 1939: Annual Report of the Miners' Welfare Commission*. London: HMSO.

Miners' Welfare Commission (MWC) (1945) *Mining People: Miner's Welfare Commission 1920–1945*. London: HMSO.

Miners' Welfare Commission (MWC) (1946) *Miners' Welfare in War-time: Report of the Miners' Welfare Commission for 6 ½ years to June 30th 1946*. Ashtead, Surrey: Miners' Welfare Commission.

Miners' Welfare Committee (MWC) (1923) *Miners' Welfare Fund: First Report of the Committee Appointed by The Board of Trade to Allocate the Fund 1921–1922*. London: HMSO.

Miners' Welfare Committee (MWC) (1924) *Miners' Welfare Fund: Second Report of the Committee Appointed by The Board of Trade to Allocate the Fund 1923*. London: HMSO.

Miners' Welfare Committee (MWC) (1925) *Miners' Welfare Fund: Third Report of the Committee Appointed by The Board of Trade to Allocate the Fund 1924*. London: HMSO.

Miners' Welfare Committee (MWC) (1926) *Miners' Welfare Fund: Fourth Report of the Committee Appointed by The Board of Trade to Allocate the Fund 1925*. London: HMSO.

Miners' Welfare Committee (MWC) (1927) *Miners' Welfare Fund: Fifth Report of the Committee Appointed by The Board of Trade to Allocate the Fund 1926*. London: HMSO.

Miners' Welfare Committee (MWC) (1928) *Miners' Welfare Fund: Sixth Report of the Committee Appointed by The Board of Trade to Allocate the Fund 1927*. London: HMSO.

Miners' Welfare Committee (MWC) (1929) *Miners' Welfare Fund: Seventh Report of the Committee Appointed by The Board of Trade to Allocate the Fund 1928*. London: HMSO.

Miners' Welfare Committee (MWC) (1930) *Miners' Welfare Fund: Eighth Report of the Committee Appointed by The Board of Trade to Allocate the Fund 1929*. London: HMSO.

Miners' Welfare Committee (MWC) (1931) *Miners' Welfare Fund: Ninth Report of the Committee Appointed by The Board of Trade to Allocate the Fund 1930*. London: HMSO.

Miners' Welfare Committee (MWC) (1932) *Miners' Welfare Fund: Tenth Report of the Committee Appointed by The Board of Trade to Allocate the Fund 1931*. London: HMSO.

Miners' Welfare Committee (MWC) (1933) *Miners' Welfare Fund: Eleventh Annual Report of the Miners' Welfare Committee for the Year 1932*. London: HMSO.

Miners' Welfare Committee (MWC) (1934) *Miners' Welfare Fund: Twelfth Annual Report of the Miners' Welfare Committee for the Year 1933*. London: HMSO.

Miners' Welfare Committee (MWC) (1935) *Miners' Welfare Fund: Thirteenth Annual Report of the Miners' Welfare Committee for the Year 1934*. London: HMSO.

Miners' Welfare Committee (MWC) (1936) *Miners' Welfare Fund: Fourteenth Annual Report of the Miners' Welfare Committee for the Year 1935*. London: HMSO.

Miners' Welfare Committee (MWC) (1937) *Miners' Welfare Fund: Fifteenth Annual Report of the Miners' Welfare Committee for the Year 1936*. London: HMSO.

Miners' Welfare Committee (MWC) (1938) *Miners' Welfare Fund: Sixteenth Annual Report of the Miners' Welfare Committee for the Year 1937*. London: HMSO.

Miners' Welfare Committee (1939) *Miners' Welfare 1938: Annual Report of the Miners' Welfare Committee*. London: HMSO.

Mining Association of Great Britain (MAGB) (1938) *The Model Coal Mine: Exhibited by the Mining Association of Great Britain at the Empire Exhibition, Scotland 1938*. D113/2/7 Special Collections, Glasgow University.

Mining Industry Act (1920) 10 & 11 Geo. 5. Ch. 50. Section 50.

Ministry of Fuel and Power (MoFP) (1945) *The Future of the Coal Miner: How Coming Changes Mean a New Deal and New Opportunities for All who Work in the Coal Industry – A Brief Explanation Based on the Reid Report*. London: HMSO.

Mitchell, T. (2013) *Carbon Democracy Political Power in the Age of Oil*. London: Verso.

Moffat, A. (1949) What I Think of Migration, *Coal: The NCB Magazine*, February, p.18.

Morgan, W. J. (1990) The Miners' Welfare Fund in Britain 1920–1952, *Social Policy & Administration*, vol.24, no.3, November, pp 199–211.

Morley, R. J. (1957) Coal Carbonisation and Other Treatments, in *National Coal Board: The First Ten Years*, edited by G. Nott-Bower and R. H. Walkerdine. London: The Colliery Guardian, pp 73–9.

Morris, W. (1890/1993) *News from Nowhere*. London: Penguin.

Mowat, C. L. (1955/1987) *Britain Between the Wars: 1918–1940*. London: Methuen & Co.

Mumford, L. (1934/2020) *Technics and Civilisation*. Chicago, IL: University of Chicago Press.

M'Vail, J. C. (1911) *Housing of Scottish Miners: Report on the Housing of Miners in Stirlingshire and Dunbartonshire*. Glasgow: Robert Maclehose and Co. Ltd.

Myles-Wright, H. (1954) The Work of the Miners' Welfare Committee, *The Architects' Journal*, 14th January, pp 42–8.

Nairn, G. (2016) *Durham Collieries on Old Picture Postcards*. Keyworth: Reflections of a Bygone Age.

Nairn, G. (2018) *Northumberland Collieries on Old Picture Postcards*. Keyworth: Reflections of a Bygone Age.

National Archives ADM 196/45/180 Executive Officers' Services Record, Commander Bernard Trotter Coote.

National Archives Coal 80/378 (Easington Colliery).

National Coal Board (1947) *Annual Report and Statement of Accounts for the Year Ended 31st December 1946*. London: HMSO.

National Coal Board (NCB) (1948) *Annual Report and Statement of Accounts for the Year Ended 31st December 1947*. London: HMSO.

National Coal Board (NCB) (1950) *Plan for Coal: The National Coal Board's Proposals*. London: National Coal Board.

National Coal Board (NCB) (1956) *Investing in Coal: Progress and Prospects under the Plan for Coal*. London: National Coal Board.

National Coal Board (NCB) (1957a) *British Coal: The Rebirth of an Industry – Published on the completion of the first ten years of public ownership*. London: National Coal Board.

National Coal Board (NCB) (1957b) *Annual Report and Accounts 1957*. London: HMSO.

National Coal Board (NCB) (1959) *Revised Plan for Coal: Progress of Reconstruction and Revised Estimates of Demand*. London: National Coal Board.

National Coal Board (NCB) (1964) *Report and Accounts 1964: Volume 1*. London: HMSO.

National Coal Board (NCB) (1966) *Report and Accounts 1965–1966: Volume 1*. London: HMSO.

National Coal Board (NCB) (1971) *Report and Account 1970–1971: Volume 1 Report*. London: HMSO.

Nef, J. U. (1932/2016) *The Rise of the British Coal Industry*. Abingdon: Routledge.

Noel-Baker, P. (1951) Seven Point Plan to Beat the Crisis, *Coal: The NCB Magazine*, pp 10–11.

Northern Mines Research Society (2021). Available at: https://www.nmrs.org.uk/assets/mines/coal/yorkshire/1854/N.html, accessed 12th April 2021.

Nott-Bower, G. and Walkerdine, R. H. (1957) *National Coal Board: The First Ten Years*. London: The Colliery Guardian.

Ockman, J. (1993) *Architecture Culture 1943–1968: A Documentary Anthology*. New York, NY: Rizzoli.

Oglethorpe, M. (2006) *Scottish Collieries: An Inventory of the Scottish Coal Industry in the Nationalised Era*. Edinburgh: Royal Commission on the Ancient and Historical Monuments of Scotland.

Orwell, G. (1937/1977) *The Road to Wigan Pier*. London: Victor Gollancz/London: Penguin.

Orwell, G. (1937/1989) *The Road to Wigan Pier*. London: Victor Gollancz/London: Penguin.

'Our Woman Correspondent' (1947) Power behind the Skeins, *Coal: The N.C.B. Magazine* (May), pp 12–13.

Overy, P. (2008) *Light, Air and Openness: Modern Architecture between the Wars*. London: Thames and Hudson.

Page Arnot, R. (1949) *The Miners: A History of the Miners' Federation of Great Britain, 1889–1910*. London: George Allen & Unwin.

Page Arnot, R. (1953) *The Miners: Years of Struggle; A History of the Miners' Federation of Great Britain (From 1910 Onwards)*. London: George Allen & Unwin.

Page Arnot, R. (1955) *A History of the Scottish Miners From the Earliest Times*. London: George Allen & Unwin.

Page Arnot, R. (1961) *The Miners in Crisis and War: A History of the Miners' Federation of Great Britain From 1930 Onwards*. London: George Allen & Unwin.

Page Arnot, R. (1967) *South Wales Miners: A History of the South Wales Miners' Federation, 1898–1914*. London: George Allen & Unwin.

Pavitt, K. (ed) (1980) *Technical Innovation and British Economic Performance*. London: Macmillan.

Payne, G. C. (1957) Giant Part 1, *Coal: The Magazine of the Mining Industry*. September (5), pp 13–18.

Paynter, W. (1958) *Outlook for Mining*. London: The Communist Party.

Peto, J. and Loveday, D. (1999) *Modern Britain 1929–1939*. London: Design Museum.

Pevsner, N. (1953) *County Durham*. London: Penguin.

Pevsner, N. (1959) *Yorkshire: West Riding* (The Buildings of England). London: Penguin.

Pevsner, N. and Richmond, I. A. (1957) *Northumberland* (The Buildings of England). London: Penguin.

Phillips, J. (2019) *Scottish Coalminers in the Twentieth Century*. Edinburgh: Edinburgh University Press.

Poole, D. (2020) Izal: 'The invisible guardian against risks to health', 2nd April. Available at: https://sheffielder.net/2020/04/02/izal-the-invisible-guardian-against-risks-to-health/, accessed 6th January 2022.

Powers, A. (1996) Liverpool and Architectural Education in the Early Twentieth Century in *Charles Reilly and the Liverpool School of Architecture*, edited by J. Sharples, A. Powers and M. Shippobottom. Liverpool: Liverpool University Press, pp 1–24.

Powers, A. (2005) *Modern: The Modern Movement in Britain*. New York: Merrell.

Ravetz, A. (2001) *Council Housing and Culture: The History of a Social Experiment*. Abingdon: Routledge.

Raynes, J. R. (1928) *Coal and its Conflicts*. London: Ernest Benn.

Reid, C. C. (1945) *Coal Mining: Report of the Technical Advisory Committee*. London: HMSO.

Reid, W. (1939) *The Layout and Equipment of Comrie Colliery in Fifeshire*. Cardiff: Institute of Mining Engineers.

Rich, L. (2003) Pithead baths of former Princess Royal Colliery. Twentieth Century Society. Available at: https://c20society.org.uk/casework/pithead-baths-of-former-princess-royal-colliery, accessed January 2022.

Richards, J. M. (1935) The Idea behind the Idea, *Architectural Review*, May, pp 7–9.

Ritchey, H. (2019) The Death of UK Coal in Five Charts, in Our World in Data. Available at: https://ourworldindata.org/death-uk-coal, accessed May 2022.

Robens, A. (1972) *Ten Year Stint*. London: Cassell.

Roberts, H. (1957) Health and Safety, in *National Coal Board: The First Ten Years*, edited by G. Nott-Bower and R. H. Walkerdine. London: The Colliery Guardian, pp 45–53.

Rogan, J. M. (1957) Medical Development and Medical Problems, in *National Coal Board: The First Ten Years*, edited by G. Nott-Bower and R. H. Walkerdine. London: The Colliery Guardian, pp 95–100.

Rowe, P. (1995) *Modernity and Housing*. Cambridge, MA: MIT Press.

Royal Commission on Mines (1909) *Second Report of the Royal Commission on Mines*. London: HMSO.

Russell, P. (2009) Nines Was Standing, in *National Coal Board Collection Volume 1: Portrait of a Miner*. London: BFI, pp 14–15.

Saint, A. (2013) John Henry Forshaw, in *Oxford Dictionary of National Biography*. Available at: www.oxforddnb-com, accessed January 2018.

Sales, W. H. (1956) Human Relations and Welfare, in *National Coal Board: The First Ten Years*, edited by G. Nott-Bower and R. H. Walkerdine. London: The Colliery Guardian, pp 101–6.

Salway, G. (1998) *The Architecture of Cleanliness: Miners' Welfare and the Pithead Baths at Penallta Colliery*. Caerphilly: Groundwork.

Sankey, J. (1919a) Coal Industry Commission, Vol.1, Reports and Minutes of Evidence on the First Stage of the Inquiry Cmd 359. House of Commons Parliamentary Papers online, accessed 1st July 2019.

Sankey, J. (1919b) Coal Industry Commission, Vol.2, Reports and Minutes of Evidence on the First Stage of the Inquiry Cmd 360. House of Commons Parliamentary Papers online, accessed 1st July 2019.

Sankey, J. (1919c) Coal Industry Commission, Vol.3, Appendices, Charts and Indexes Cmd 361. House of Commons Parliamentary Papers online, accessed 1st July 2019.

Schaffer, F. (1970) *The New Town Story*. London: MacGibbon & Kee.

Scott-James, R. A. (1924) 'Housing Conditions in Mining Areas', in *Coal and Power: The Report of an Inquiry Presided Over by the Right Hon. D. Lloyd George*.

Scottish Home Department (1944) *Scottish Coalfield, Reports of the Scottish Coalfields Committee*, Cmd 6575. Edinburgh: HMSO.

Searing, H. (1978) With Red Flags: Housing in Amsterdam 1915–23, in *Art and Architecture in the Service of Politics*, edited by H. A. Millon and L. Nochlin. Cambridge, MA: MIT Press, pp 230–269.

Sharples, J. (1996) Reilly and his Students, in *Charles Reilly and the Liverpool School of Architecture*, edited by J. Sharples, A. Powers and M. Shippobottom. Liverpool: Liverpool University Press, pp 25–42.

Sharples, J. (2004) *Liverpool: Pevsner City Guide*. New Haven, CT: Yale University Press.

Shinwell, E. (1957) The Purpose of Nationalisation, in *National Coal Board: The First Ten Years*, edited by G. Nott-Bower and R. H. Walkerdine. London: The Colliery Guardian, pp 1–4.

Simpson, E. S. (1966) *Coal and the Power Industries in Postwar Britain*. London: Longmans.

Smart, R. C. (1931) Response to Patrick Abercrombie paper on the Kent coal fields, *Journal of the Royal Society of Arts*, vol. 79, no.4091, 17th April, p.518.

Smith, R. (1989) New Towns for Scottish Miners, *Scottish Economic & Social History*, vol.9, no.1, pp 71–9.

Stamp, G. (1997) Charles Reilly and the Liverpool School of Architecture, 1904–1933, *Journal of the Society of Architectural Historians*, vol.56, no.3, September, pp 345–8.

Statista (2020) Imports and exports of coal mined in the United Kingdom (UK) from 1970 to 2019. Available at: https://www.statista.com/statistics/370921/united-kingdom-uk-mined-coal-trade/, accessed 26 January 2022.

Stieber, N. (1998) *Housing Design and Society in Amsterdam: Reconfiguring the Urban Order and Identity*. Chicago, IL: University of Chicago Press.

St John Wilson, C. (2007) *The Other Tradition: The Uncompleted Project*. London: Black Dog.

Supple, B. (1987) *The History of the*

British Coal Industry, Volume 4: 1913–1946: The Political Economy of Decline. Oxford: Clarendon Press.

Swenarton, M. (1981) *Homes Fit for Heroes: The Politics and Architecture of Early State Housing in Britain*. London: Heinemann.

Swenarton, M. (2008) *Building the New Jerusalem: Architecture, Housing and Politics 1900–1930*. Bracknell: BRE Press.

Swenarton, M., Avermaete, T. and Van den Heuvel, D. (eds) (2015) *Architecture and the Welfare State*. London: Routledge, pp 1–2.

Sykes, Sir F. (1939) Unpublished Forshaw testimonial, 21st March. Forshaw archives, University of Liverpool.

Szeman, I. and Boyer, D. (2017) *Energy Humanities: An Anthology*. Baltimore, MD: Johns Hopkins University Press.

Tarn, J. N. (1971) *Working-class Housing in 19th Century Britain*. London: Lund Humphries.

Taut, B. (1919) *Die Stadtkrone*, translated by U. Altenmüller and M. Mindrup. Available at: http://socks-studio.com/2013/09/28/bruno-taut-the-city-crown-1919/, accessed 4th December 2020.

Tenfelde, K. (ed.) (1992) *Sozialgeschichte des Bergbaus im 19. Und 20 Jahrhundert*. München: Verlag C. H. Beck.

The Times (1951) *Festival of Britain Supplement* (8 May).

Thompson, L. (1923) The Doncaster Regional Planning Scheme, *The Town Planning Review*, vol.10, no.2, May, pp 134–8.

Thornes, R. (1994) *Images of Industry: Coal*. Royal Commission on the Historical Monuments of England, London: Her Majesty's Stationery Office.

Thorsheim, P. (2006) *Inventing Pollution: Coal, Smoke and Culture in Britain since 1800*. Athens, OH: Ohio University Press.

Tomlinson, R. C. (1971) *OR Comes of Age: A Review of the Operational Research Branch of the National Coal Board 1948–1969*. London: Tavistock Publications.

Townshend-Rose, H. (1951) *The British Coal Industry*. London: George Allen & Unwin.

Tremenheere, H. S. (1844–59) *Report into the State of the Population of the Mining Districts*. London: Her Majesty's Stationery Office.

Tudor Walters, Sir J. (1927) *The Building of Twelve Thousand Houses*. London: Ernest Benn Ltd.

Uncredited (dir.) (1957) *Hungarians in Britain*, Mining Review 10th Year No.8 (film). London: National Coal Board and Data Film Production.

Unwin, R. (1888) Socialism and Progress, *Commonweal*, 7th April, pp 108–9.

Unwin, R. (1889) Sutton Hall, *Commonweal*, 15th June, p.190.

Unwin, R. (1890) Down a Coal Pit, *Commonweal*, 7th June, pp 177–8 and 14th June, pp 188–9.

Unwin, R. (1901) Co-operation in Building, *The Art of Building a Home*. Project Gutenberg. Available at: https://www.gutenberg.org/files/63071/63071-h/63071-h.htm#LECTURE_VII, accessed 12th April 2021.

Unwin, R. (1902) *Cottage Plans and Common Sense*. Fabian Tract no. 109. London: The Fabian Society.

Unwin, R. (1921) Some Thoughts on the Development of London, in *London of the Future*, edited by Sir A. Webb. London: The London Society, pp 177–92.

Vielvoye, R. (ed) (1976) *Coal: Technology for Britain's Future*. London: Macmillan.

Waldron, T. (2017) Edgar Leigh Collis: Industrial Lung Disease and Ergonomics, *Journal of Medical Biography*, vol.28, no.3, 20th October, pp 157–62.

Wall, C. (2013) *An Architecture of Parts: Architects, Building Workers and Industrialisation in Britain 1940–1970*. Abingdon: Routledge.

Waller, R. J. (1983) *The Dukeries Transformed: The Social and Political Development of a Twentieth Century Coalfield*. Oxford: Clarendon Press.

Watkins, H. M. (1934) *Coal and Men: An Economic and Society Study of the British and American Coalfields*. London: George Allen & Unwin.

White, J. H. (1957) Three in One: Hafodyrynys New Mine, Part Two, *Coal: Magazine of the Mining Industry*, December, pp 11–12.

Wilk, C. (ed.) (2006) *Modernism 1914–1939: Designing a New World*. London: V&A.

Williams, R. (2008) *Notes on the Underground: An Essay on Technology, Society and the Imagination*. Cambridge, MA: MIT Press.

Wilson, H. (1945) *New Deal for Coal*. London: Contact Publications.

Wilson, I. (dir.) (1942) *The New Mine*. Gaumont-British Instructional.

Zola, E. (2008/1885) *Germinal*. Trans. P. Collier. Oxford: Oxford University Press.

Abercrombie, Patrick 23, 26, 33, *35*, 139, 179–86, 268, 272, 277 n.2
  and Doncaster regional plan 178, 179–180, 185, 186
  and East Kent regional plan 180–185, *182–3*, *185*, 193, 198
  and *Plan for London* 27–8, 29, 34, 35–6, *36*
  and Woodlands 163, 175, 192
Abernant Colliery (South Wales) 248, 254, *255*
Agecroft Colliery (Lancashire) 248, 253–4, *254*
Aitken Colliery (Lothians) *120*, 121, 278 n.23
Alexandra Colliery (Lancashire) 133–7, *134*
Allsop, Robert Owen 55, 59
Amsterdam School 64, 65, 67
Amthorpe (South Yorkshire) 189, *192*
Archibald, John 181, 182, *182–3*, 184, *185*
architects 23, 27, 34–5, 277 n.5
Architects' Journal 108, 121, 135, 139
architecture 24, 25, 26, 27–8, 35–7, 65, 163
  and monumentality 58, 62, 67, 72, 277 n.13
  and morality 63–4
  and social reform 23, 24, 25, 27, 28, 33, 146
Arley Mine, Atherton (Lancashire) *60*, 61
armoured flexible conveyor (AFC) 224, *230*, 231, 245, 274
Arniston Colliery (Midlothian) 127–130, *129*, *130*
Arts and Crafts style 160, 163, 164, 176, 195
Atherton (Lancashire) *60*, 61, 62, 75, 156, 277 n.12
Avenue coking plant (Chesterfield) 237, 238, *238*
Aylesham (Kent) 181, 183, 184–5, *185*, 198

Badhuis baths, Bostrift (Dudok, 1921) 67, 72–3, *72*
Baily, Basil 160, 172, 173
Bainbridge, Emerson Muschamp 161, 162
Barlow Commission (1940) 165, 179, 185, 268
Barnsdall 'Hollyhock' House (Wright, 1921) 114, *115*, 121
Barony Colliery (Ayrshire) 244, 256, 257
baths, public 55, 58–9, *58*, 63
Baths and Washhouses Act (1846) 55, 58
Bauhaus 68, 71, 257
Bavinckschool, Netherlands

(Dudok, 1921) 67, *68*, 69
Beaux Arts style 24, 26, 247
Becher, Bernd/Becher, Hilla 237
Belgium 47–9, 62, 91, 203, 248
Bertram, Anthony 14, 17, 19, 37
Bestwood Colliery (Nottinghamshire) *15*, 278 n.23
Betteshanger Colliery (Kent) 108–9, *108*, 139, 181, 182, 183, 278 n.23
Bevan, Aneurin 27, 226, 280 n.1
Bevercotes Colliery (East Midlands) 248, 252
Big Pit National Coal Museum (Wales) 137, *138*
Bilston Glen Colliery (Lothians) 256, 258, *259*, 260, *260*
Blackhall Colliery (Durham) 16, 117–118, *118*, 119, 122, 278 n.23
Blair Castle (Fife) 137
Blidworth (Nottinghamshire) 189, 195, 279 n.16
Bold Colliery (Lancashire) 241, 244–7, *246*, 256
Bolsover Colliery (Derbyshire) 159, 161, 162, 163, 196
Bournville (Birmingham) 156, 172
Bradford Colliery (Lancashire) 95–7, *96*, 244, 248
Bradford (West Yorkshire) 97, 171, 248, 279 n.11
Brewill, Arthur 160, 172, 173
Broomside Colliery (Motherwell) 80, 81, *82*, 83–4, *83*, 97
Brora Colliery (Sutherland) 10, 131, *131*
Bruay, Compagnie des mines de (France) 48, 49–50, *50*, 51, 62
Building of Twelve Thousand Houses, The (Tudor Walters) 187, 188–9, 190, 192, 193, 195
Bwllfa Colliery (South Wales) 242, *242*

Calverton Colliery (Nottinghamshire) 110–111, 208, *208*
canteens 21, 83, 90, 104, 109, 122, 143, *143*
Cardowan Colliery (Lanarkshire) 16, *18*, 106–8, *107*, 278 nn.23,24
Carpenter, Edward 165, 170, 198
Carron Iron Works (Falkirk) 51–2, *52*, 56
Castlebridge Colliery (Clackmannanshire) *274*, 275
Central Engineering Establishment (Bretby, Derbyshire) 232
Chappell, Edgar L. 57, 61, 62, 80, 93–4
Chesterfield (Derbyshire) 165, 166, 168–170

Chesters, Humshaugh (Shaw, 1891) 15, *16*
children 53–4, 142, 145, 153, 155
Chislet Colliery/village (Kent) 181, 183–4, 187, 208–9, *209*
Clean Air Act (1956) 249
Clipstone Colliery/New Town (Nottinghamshire) 176, 187, 195, 244, 248, 268
Clock Face Colliery (Lancashire) 109–114, *111*, *112*, 127, 131, 207
Coal (magazine) 220, 222–4, *222*, 233, 239, 243–4, 247, 265–7, *267*, 280 n.11
Coal: Its Origin and Occurrence (pamphlet) 231–2
coal industry
  contraction of 248–9, 252
  disappearance of 10, 12, 17, 137, 275
  expansion of 177–8, 187, 205
  importance/ubiquity of 10–11, 22, 40, 154–5, 216, 226
  labour intensivity of 22, 56–7, 148, 203–4
  location of collieries 11, 17, 63, 148, 157
  modernisation of 201–7, 208, 212, 221–2, 224, 227–30, *228*
  productivity of 203–4, 240, 247, 248
  see also nationalisation
Coal Industry Act (1994) 275
coal miners 9, 12, 22, 63, 207, 280 n.4
  and diseases 20, 37, 47, 63, 233–4
  hazards faced by 12, 37, 38, 153–4, 167, 233–4
  militancy of 154–5, 158
  and poverty 12, 37, 41
  wages of 37, 40, 41–2
Coal Mines Act (1911) 39, 60, 76, 130
coal preparation plants 205, 232, 239–240, *240*, *241*, 243, 246, *259*
coal products 11, 212, 237, 249–50, 280 n.13
Coal Research Establishment (Gloucestershire) 232, 250
Coal Utilisation Council (CUC) 212, 251
coking plants 236–9, *238*, 247
Colliery Guardian 186, 265
Commonweal 166, 168, 279 n.8
Comrie Colliery (Fife) 10, 12, 29, *29*, 206–8, 228, 247, 267, 278 n.25
  and propaganda 209–210, *210*, *221*, 225, 247
Connell, Amyas 19, 20
convalescent homes 37, 45–6, *46*
Coote, Bernard Trotter 75, 87, 93, 94, 111
Cotgrave Colliery/New Town (East Midlands) 248, 252–3, *253*, 268
Coventry Colliery (Warwickshire) 21, 114–115, *114*, *115*, 117, 119, 207, 278 n.24

Creswell (Derbyshire) 155, 159–160, 161, *161*, 162–3, 164, 172, 173, 174, 195, 196, 197, 198
Cross, Alfred William Stephens 55, 57–9, *58*
Cym Colliery (South Wales) 238–9
Cynheidre Colliery (South Wales) 248, 254, *255*

Dalton, Hugh 269, 280 n.1
Dalzell and Broomside Colliery *see* Broomside Colliery
Daniel, Peter 271, *271*
Dawdon Colliery (Durham) 15–16, 92–3, *92*, 94, 102, 122
Day, Robin 225, 226
de Klerk, Michel 64, 65, 68
Dempster, Jack 16, *18*, 29–30, 31, 94, 104, 106, 118, 121, 127, 139, 144
Denaby Main (South Yorkshire) *12*, 151, 153, 155, 157, 158, 159
Devon Colliery (Fife) 95, 97
Devonshire, Duke of 166, 168, 175–6
diseases 20, 37, 47, 63, 233–4
Dixon, Franc 271, *271*
Doncaster (South Yorkshire) 163, 178–9, 180, 185, 186, 187, 189
drift mines 244, 248, 252, 280 n.19
Dudok, Willem Marinus 24, 25, 65–73, 80, 127
  Badhuis baths (Hilversum) 67, 72–3, *72*, 122
  and Hilversum Town Hall 65–7, *66*, 103, 106, 210
  schools of 67–73, *68*, *70*, *71*, 95, 102, 103, 122, 127, 212–213
  see also under pithead baths
Dukeries coalfield/villages (Nottinghamshire) 195–8
Dullatur Colliery (Lanarkshire) 137, *138*

Easington Colliery (Durham) 122, *124*, 125
East Kent regional plan 178, 180–185, *182–3*, 193
East Kirby Miners' Institute (Derbyshire) 43–4, *44*, *45*
East Midlands coalfield 178, 187, *188*
educational facilities 37, 137, 143, 234–5
Edwinstowe (Nottinghamshire) 187, 195, 197
electricity generation
  see power stations
Elemore Colliery (Durham) 16, *23*, 122
Empire Exhibition (Glasgow, 1938) 105, 209–213, *210*, *211*, 251

INDEX

Empire Exhibition (London, 1924–5) 213, 216
Exhibition of Industrial Power (Glasgow, 1951) 214–216, *214, 215*
expressionism 64, 65, 67, 72, 80, 122, 125

factories 19, *31*, 75, 204
Festival of Britain (1951) 213–16, *214, 215*, 222, 225, 241
Fife Coal Company 203, 207, 265
First World War 23, 25, 33, 34, 39–40, 165, 202
Fishburn coking plant (Durham) 237, 238
Flagg, Ernest 24–5, 33
Forshaw, John Henry 23–9, *23*, 30, *35*, 69, 111, 267–8, 274, 277 nn.1,2,4,6,11, 281 n.28
  and Abercrombie 26–7, 33
  and Comrie Colliery 29, *29*, 207, 278 n.25
  and LCC 27, 28–9, *29*,32, 33, 34
  and MWC see under MWC
  and *Plan for London* 27–8, 29, 34, 35–6, *36*
  and social housing 25, 27, 28–9
  and town planning 26, 27–8, *29*
Fortissat Colliery (North Lanarkshire) 91
France 39, 47, 49–50, 51, 62, 151–2, 203, 248
Franks, Robert 149–150
Frizzell, Frederick G. 15–16, 29–30, 31, 73, 94, 95, 117, 121–5, *124*
Fry, Maxwell 24, 34
Future of the Coal Miner, The (pamphlet) 221–2, 227

Garden City movement 163, 164, 168, 175, 176, 179, 184, 186, 189, 195, 197, 268
Geddes, Patrick 35, 180
General Strike (1926) 37, 42, 60, 154, 279 n.21
Gerhard, William Paul 55, 56
Germany 42, 47, 49, 50, 51, 55, 59, 62, 71, 111, 114, 129, 203, 243, 244
Gewerkschaft Gottessegen (Germany) 47, *48*, 50, 62
Glasier, Katharine Bruce 54, 59, 61, 62, 105, 170
Glenrothes (Fife) 185, 268, 269, 272–5, *273*
Godin, Jean-Baptiste 159
Grange Ash Colliery (West Yorkshire) 132–3, *132*
Grassmoor (East Midlands) 234, 236–7
Great Northern Coalfield 148, 178
Gropius, Walter 19, 68, 69, 70, 129, 257

Hafod Colliery (North Wales) 98, 278 nn.23,24
Hafodyrynys Colliery (South Wales) 115–117, *116*, 240–242, *241*, 247
Haggerston Baths, Hackney (London, 1904) *58*, 59
Hampstead Garden Suburb Act (1906) 34
Harrington Colliery (Durham) 91
headframe towers *225*, 243, 247, 248
health and safety 24, 38, 39, 43, 143, 167
Heath Robinson, William 230, *231*
'High and Over', Amersham (Connell, 1928–9) 19–20
Hilversum (Netherlands) see Dudok, Willem Marinus
Holden, Charles 16, 17, 129
Homes for Heroes project (1918) 34, 39–40, 165
horizontal mining 227–8, *228*
Horner, Arthur 218, 223
hospitals/health centres 25, 37, 137, 142, 143, 144–5
Houfton, John Plowright 161, 163, 278 n.4
Houfton, Percy Bond 163, 164, *164*, 166, 172, 173–5, 176, *176*, 191, 279 n.12
housing 9, 11, 25, 27, 28–9, 40, 64–5, 249
  and byelaw legislation 158, 159, 168–9, 170, 172, 174
  and garden city movement 163, 164, 168
  and Homes for Heroes project (1918) 34, 39–40, 165
  and modernism 19–20, 176
  and social reform 24–5, 28, 34
  and Tudor Walters Report (1918) 34, 39–40, 165, 177, *177*
  and Unwin see Unwin, Raymond
  see also miners' housing
Housing Acts (1919/1923/1924) 186
housing associations 186–7, 268
  see also IHA
Housing and Town Planning Act (1909) 26, 34
Howard, Ebenezer 168
Huskar Colliery disaster (1838) 38, 153
hygiene/sanitation 19, 20–21, 22, 24, 28, 34, 37, 45, 54–5, 59, 63, 79, 147
Hyndley, The Lord 217, 222, 224

Industrial Housing Association (IHA) 187–96, *188*, 197
  layouts of schemes 189–91, *190, 191*, 279 n.17
  and Non-Parlour Three Bedroom House 191, 193–5, *194*
  and pithead baths 193, 194–5
  and representations of schemes 192–3, *192*
  settlements built by 279 n.16
Industrial Welfare Society (IWS) 43, 74–7, *76*, 87
industrialisation 19, 33–4, 59, 75, 155
International Style exhibition (1932) 19, 67
iron/steel works 51–2, 55, 166, 183, 200, 212, 236, 237, 238, 243, 269

Jack, Donald Denoon 29–30, 31, 32, 94, 118
Johannes Calvijnschool, Netherlands (Dudok, 1929) 69, *71*
Julianaschool en Catharina van Renesschool, Netherlands (Dudok, 1925–7) 68–9, *68*, 69, 212–213

Keay, Lancelot 25
Kellingley Colliery (North Yorkshire) 248, 268, 275
Kells Welfare and Community Centre (Cumberland) 144–6, *144, 145*
Kemp, Cecil George 29–30, 31–2, 94, 126, 139
Killoch Colliery (Ayrshire) 256, 257, 260–2, *263*, 264, 281 n.31
Kinniel Colliery (Stirlingshire) 242–3
Kirkmichael House (Ayrshire) 45–6, *46*, 137
Klein, Alexander 79

L-shape plan 103–114, 122, 278 n.23
Labour Party/Government 202, 213, 228
Lady Victoria Colliery (Midlothian) 139, 281 n.27
Lambton coking plant (Durham) 237, 238
Lancaster and Morecambe Regional Plan 26, *26*, 27
Langold (Nottinghamshire) 189–190, *190*, 195, 279 n.16
Lawrence, D.H. 150–151, 195, 279 n.18
Lawther, Will 222–3, 224
Le Corbusier 19, 20, 127, 277 nn.13,14
Lea Hall Colliery (Staffordshire) 244, 248, 252, *253*
leisure facilities see recreational facilities
Lens, Société des Mines (France) 47, *48*, 51, *51*
Letchworth (Hertfordshire) 164, 171, 173, 174, 175, 176, 279 n.19
Letham Colliery (Stirlingshire) 80
Lever, William Hesketh 26, 33, 156

libraries/reading rooms 37, 43, 44, 45, 142
Linton and Ellington Collieries (Northumberland) 74, 75
Liverpool 25–6, 27, 55
  School of Architecture 23, 24, 26, 29, 34
local authorities 34, 59, 133–5, 178, 186
London 28–9, 165, 179, 180, 185, 268–9
  public baths in 55, *58*, 59
London County Council (LCC) 27, 29, *29*, 32, 33, 277 n.2
London, Plan for (Forshaw/Abercrombie, 1943) 27–8, 29, 34, 35–6, *36*, 268
London, Survey of 35, 36
London Underground 16, 17, 19, 30
longwall system 206–7, 228–9, *230*, 245
Lorentzschool, Netherlands (Dudok, 1929–30) 69
Lovat-Fraser, J.A. 57, 61, 62, 80, 93–4
Lubetkin, Berthold 269–70, 272
Lugar Colliery (Ayrshire) 232–3, 257
Luma factory (Stockholm) 30, *31*
Lumphinnans (Fife) 151, *152*
Lynemouth Colliery (Northumberland) 122, 137, 280 n.14

Madeley Colliery (North Staffordshire) 125–6, 278 n.23
MAGB (Mining Association of Great Britain) 42, 209, 212, 213
Mainsforth Colliery (Durham) 80, 83, 84, 91
Maltby (South Yorkshire) 186, 190, 277 n.16, 279 n.16, 280 n.4
Manchester 35, 154, 165, 244, 254
Manvers Main Colliery (Yorkshire) 207, 239–240, *239*
Mardy Colliery (South Wales) 242
Markham family 163, 166, 176, 190
mass production 21, 28, 33, 50, 63, 87, 90, 98, 104, 133–140
May, Ernst 114, 176
Michael Colliery (Fife) 104, 278 n.23
Mies van der Rohe, Ludwig 68, 242
mine owners 21, 22, 37, 39, 41, 42, 60, 202
  and housing 148–9, 157–8, 165–6
'Miner comes to Town' exhibition (1947) 223–6, *225*, 237, 280 n.12
Miners' Federation of Great Britain (MFGB) 40, 42, 57, 198, 202, 213
miners' housing 9, 52–4, 135, *136*, 146–98, *147*
  19th century 149–150
  and Cheap Cottage 174–6, *174, 177*, 191, 195

council estates 163, 175
and Doncaster coalfield 178–9, 180
and Dukeries villages 195–7
and East Kent coalfield 180–185, *182–3*
and Garden City *see* Garden City movement
and housing associations *see* housing associations
model towns *see* model towns
and New Towns 165, 179, 181–2, 183–4, 185, 267–75
planned settlements/company towns 33, 158, 176, 196
row 150, *151*, 165, 168–9, 171
rural villages 17, 148, 149, 150–154, 186, 187–9
in Scotland 54, 146–8, *147*, 149–50, *151*, 156–7, 269, 272–5
and social control 156–7, 195–7
in South Wales 149, 150, 183, 187
tied 148–9, 157–8, 186, 196
Type D house plan *176*, 177, 191, 194
and Unwin *see* Unwin, Raymond
urban 154
miners' institutes 43–5, *44*, *45*
Miners' Strike (1984-5) 12
Miners' Welfare Act (1952) 139
Miners' Welfare Committee/Commission *see* MWC
Miners' Welfare Fund 16, 38–9, 41, 42–6, 69, 74, 104, 146, 155, 211
Mines and Collieries Act (1842) 38, 277 n.18
Mining Association of Great Britain (MAGB) 42, 209, 212, 213
mining communities 42, 44–5, 54, 57, 73, 99, 142, 144, 149, 151–4, 205
lawlessness in 152–3, 155
relocation of 256–7, 267–8, 272
Mining Industry Act (1920) 39, 41, 42, 142, 146, 277 n.14
Mining Industry Act (1926) 39, 73–4, 76
Mining People (pamphlet) 221, *221*
Mining Review (newsreel) 220, 222
'Model Coal Mine' (Empire Exhibition, 1938) 209–211, *211*, 225
model towns 155–6, 158–64, 190, 195, 196
modernism 19–21, 24, 32, 35, 201, 225, 257, 258, 265
and housing 19–20, 176, 267, 270, 274
and MWC publications 99–100, *100*, *101*
and pithead baths 9, 14, *15*, 19, 20–21, 59, 67, 68, 73–80, 87–90, 106, 125, 132–5

and social issues 7, 25, 28, 63–4, 267–8
see also Dudok, Willem Marinus
modernity 12, 20, 37, 57, 247, 265, 281 n.22
Moffat, Abe 256–7
Monceau-Fontaines Baths (Belgium) 47–9, *48*, 49, 50, 62, 75
Monktonhall Colliery (Lothians) 256, 258–260, *261*, 262, 263, 275
Moro, Peter 225, 226
Morris, William 33, 64, 75, 162, 165, 168, 169, 176, 198
Morrison Busty Colliery (Durham) 126, 278 n.23
Morton Colliery (Derbyshire) 126, 278 n.23
Mulgrew, Tommy 270
Mumford, Lewis 38
M'Vail, John C. 146–7, *147*
MWC (Miners' Welfare Committee/Commission) 10, 12, 189, 217, 233, 277 n.1
annual reports 41, 45, 75, 81–3, 84, 94–5, 99–102, *100*, *101*, 103, 113, 207–8, 277 n.7
dissolved (1952) 139
District/Local 22, 43, 75, 127
and miners' housing 193, 275
MWC Architects' Department 21, 29–37, 62, 116–117, 121–2
facilities created by 37, 142–6
and Forshaw 23, 25, 26, 27, 29–30, 31, 32–3, 75, 87, 93, 94, 98, 99, 116, 117, 139, 144, 145, 207, 257
and modernism 32, 69, 106
and pithead baths *see* pithead baths
structure/premises of 31–2, 256
and Swedish Cooperative Society 30
working culture of 94, *94*, 121, 278 n.21
Myles-Wright, Henry 139–140

Nantgarw Colliery (South Wales) 236, 247
National Coal Board *see* NCB
National Health Service 27, 226
National Plan (Brown) 226–7
National Union of Mineworkers (NUM) 157, 202, 227, 229
nationalisation (1947) 10, 38, 40, 41, 42, 79, 139, 201, 202, 216–219
and geographical Divisions 216–217
and miners' housing 148, 185, 272
problems with 218–219
NCB (National Coal Board) 21, 139, 148, 198, 201, 205, 212, 216
and central workshops/stores 232–3

and inter-colliery initiatives 232–240
logo/vehicle fleet of 235–6, *235*
and pit closures 249
and public relations 219–26, 227, 230–232, 249–51, *250*
and reconstructed collieries 244–8
and research establishments 232
and smokeless coal 249–250
structure of 217, 232, 256
and superpits 240–244, 252
Netherlands 23, 34, 64–73, 111, 203
see also Dudok, Willem Marinus
New Bolsover (Derbyshire) 155, 158, 159–62, *160*, 164, 172, 173, 174, 195, 196, 197, 198
New Earswick (North Yorkshire) 171, 175
New Mine, The (film, 1945) 206–7, 209
New Ollerton (Nottinghamshire) 196–7
New Rossington (South Yorkshire) 190–191, 279 nn.16,17
New Statesman 196, 197, 198
New Towns 165, 179, 181–2, 183–4, 185, 267–75
New Towns Act (1946) 179, 268–9
New York (US) 23, 24–5, 27, 33
Newstead Colliery (Nottinghamshire) 126, 279 n.16
Newton Colliery (Lancashire) *113*
Nienke van Hichtumschool, Netherlands (Dudok, 1929) 69, *70*
Non-Parlour Three Bedroom House 191, 193–5, *194*
North Walbottle Colliery (Durham) 15, *16*, 278 n.23
NUM (National Union of Mineworkers) 157, 202, 227, 229

Ocean Colliery (Wales) 61, *61*, 62
OMS (output per manshift) measurement 203, 204, 240, 247
Orwell, George 22, 154, 216

pamphlets 54, 55, 57, 221–2, 230–232
Park Pit (Wales) 80, 83, 91
Parker, Henry Perlee 153
Parker, Richard Barry 33, 164, 168, 173–4, 175, 186, 279 n.17
Parkside Colliery (Lancashire) 248, 254
Pasmore, Victor 271, *271*, 272
paternalism 10, 26, 33, 45, 59, 75, 156, 158, 197
Penallta Colliery (South Wales) 109, *110*, 115, 137, 278 n.23
Peterlee (Durham) 185, 269–72, *270*, *271*
Pevsner, Nikolaus 15–16, 17, 30, 67, 137, 163, 175, 278 n.28

Pick, Frank 16, 17, 19
Pioneer Health Centre (Peckham) 144–5, 146
Pit Ventilation (pamphlet) 230
pithead baths 14–23, *15*, 29, 38–9, 45, 46–62, 73–140, 155, 211, 258, 280 n.18
and aesthetics 58, 59, 62, 67, 84, 92–3, 95, 98, 99–102, 104–5, 125
basilica form 50, *50*, 62, 75
block form 121–5
boot-cleaning facilities 78, 81, 83, 87, 91
and canteens 21, 83, 90, 104, 109, 122, 143, *143*
circular form 127–130
clothes storage/washing/drying facilities 47, *48*, 49–50, 61, 77
and cubicles 50, 51, 61, 62
disappearance/conversion of 10, 16, 17–19, 137
and Dudok 16, 19, 20, 23, 67, 68–9, 73, 93, 103, 109, 122, 205
and Forshaw 23, 32, 33, 75
and health/hygiene 19, 20–21, 22, 52–5
and Home Office Committee 46–7, 49, 50, 51, 58, 62, 77
and IWS 74–7, *76*, 87
L-shape plan 103–114, 122, 278 n.23
and legislation 37, 39, 60
and linear plan 103, 114–121
lockers in 49–51, 77, 80, 81, 84–7, *84*, *86*, *88*, 91, 104, 109
and mass production 21, 28, 33, 50, 87, 90, 98, 104, 133–140
miners' objections to 57
and modernism
see under modernism
and MWC 9, 14, 16–17, 21–2, 23, 75, 77–80, *78*
number of facilities/miners served by 21, 90, 98, *99*, 135
and pitched roofs 125–7
precedents of 46–52, *48*, 55–6, 125, 137–9
prototype/experimental 80–84, *82*, 95
representations of 97, 102, *102*, *103*, 107–8, 110–113, 116–118, 192
and Samuel Commission (1925–6) 39, 42, 60–62, 77
and Sankey Commission (1919) 39–42, 52–4, 57, 60, 73
showers 47, *48*, 49, *52*, 55–6, 61, 75, 83, *89*, 91, 127–8
slipper 49, 51–2
in smaller collieries 130–137
and social reform 30, 54–5, 57
'Specimen Design' plan 77–8, *78*, 79–80, 81
and Swedish Cooperative Society 30

and Taylorist principles 78, 79, 90
typology of 16, 19
ventilation in 51, 61, 77, 91, 95
water towers 102, 103, 127
and women mineworkers 49, 81, 97, 109, 111, 113–114, *113*, 277 nn.5,18
see also specific collieries
Plan for Coal (document, 1950) 185, 200, 219, 227, 228, 240, 247, 248, 252, 254, 256, 260, 265, 272
Plan for Coal (document, 1974) 252
Plan for Coal (film, 1952) 200–201, 206, 221, 227
Pneumoconiosis Field Research units 233–4, *234*, 235
Polkemmet Colliery (Lanarkshire) 15, 104–6, *105*, *106*, 128
Pooley Hall (Warwickshire) 80, 81, *82*, 83
Poolsbrook (Derbyshire) 168, 169, *169*, 171, 172, 279 nn.16,17
Port Sunlight (Wirral) 26, 156, 158, 173
Portland, Duke of 159, 162
poverty 12, 37, 63, 148
power stations 240, 244, 247, 248, 249, 251–2
propaganda 41, 57, 61, 62, 80, 93, 201, 219–222, 277 n.11
public houses 44–5, 153, 169
Public Works Loans Act (1922) 186
Pugin, Augustus W.N. 160, 162

Raynes, J.R. 153
recreational facilities 37, 43, 99, 142–6, *142*, *144*, *145*
regional plans 26, *26*, 27, 178–85, *182–3*, 272
rehabilitation centres 45–6, 137, 166
Reid, Charles Carlow 23, 202, 203, 205, 207, 217, 218, 256, 274
Reid Report (1945) 202–6, 207, 208, 218, 219, 227, 228, 240, 254
Reilly, Charles Herbert 23, 24, 26, 34, 277 n.2
Rembrandtschool, Hilversum (Dudok, 197–20) 67, 95, 122
Revised Plan for Coal (1959) 219, 249
Riss, Egon 257–67, 274, 281 nn.26,31
Robens, Lord Alfred 248, 252
Rose Heyworth Colliery (Wales) 95, 97
Rothes Colliery (Fife) 256, 262, 263–8, *265*, *266*, *267*, 272, 273, 275, 281 n.31
Rowse, Herbert J. 24
Royal Commissions 37, 39, 47
Royal Institute of British Architects (RIBA) 27, 67, 277 n.2

Rufford Colliery (Nottinghamshire) 176, 186
Ruskin, John 58, 64, 75, 162, 165, 170, 176, 198
Ryhope Colliery (Durham) 122–5, *123*

Safety in Mines Research Establishment (Buxton/Sheffield) 233
Saise, Alfred John 16, *18*, 29–30, 31, 32, 94, 95, 109, 126
Samuel Commission (1925–6) 39, 42, 60–62, 73, 77
Sankey Commission (1919) 39–42, 52–4, 57, 60, 63, 146, 147, 194, 201–2, 204
schools 25, 135, 148, 158, 169
Dudok-designed 67–73, *68*, *70*, *71*, 72, 95, 102, 103, 127
and model towns 156, 159, 162, 163, 278 nn.3,5
scientific management 78, 79, 193
Seafield Colliery (Fife) 256, 262–3, *264*
Second World War 27, 202, 221
Selby Superpit (North Yorkshire) 252
Shafton Colliery (Yorkshire) 232, 233
Shaw, Norman 15, *16*
Sheffield 174, 180, 194
Sherwood Colliery (Nottinghamshire) 16, *19*, 278 n.23
Shinwell, Emmanuel 202, 217–218, 220, 222, 224, 280 n.2
Shirebrook Colliery (Derbyshire) 102, *102*, 176
Silverwood Colliery (South Yorkshire) 126, *126*
Skelmersdale (Lancashire) 23, 269, 281 n.28
Smith, H. 31, 32, 144
Smithson, Alison/Smithson, Peter 133, 242
smokeless coal 249–250, *250*
Snelliuschool, Netherlands (Dudok, 1930–32) 69, 70, *70*, 71
Snowdown Colliery (Kent) 139, 181, 182, 184, 185
social reform 23, 24, 25, 27, 28, 30, 33, 146, 146–7
and model towns 155–6, 159
socialism 30, 33, 65, 154, 156, 165, 166, 169–170
municipal 23, 25, 59
South Bantaskine Colliery (Stirlingshire) 137
Soviet Union 216, 222, 280 n.7
Spence, Basil 214, 215, 280 n.6
spoil heaps 10, 12, 149, 211, 228
sports facilities *see* recreational facilities

Stadtkrone 6, 63, 64, 65, 80
Staveley Coal and Iron Company 165, 166, 168, 171, 172, 175–6, 279 nn.12,17
strikes 12, 37, 40, 42, 154–5, 157, 236, 277 n.8
Sullivan, Louis 71, 95, 262, 264
Sunnyside (South Yorkshire) 189, 191–2, *191*, 279 n.16
superpits 240–244, 252, 256–67, 274
Swedish Cooperative Society 23, 30
Swenarton, Mark 170, 175
swimming pools 16, *18*, 25, 37, 59, 142, 145

Tait, Thomas S. 95, 211–212, 280 n.6
Taut, Bruno 63–4
Taylorist principles 78, 79, 90
Thorne Colliery (South Yorkshire) 102, *103*, 278 n.23
Tillicoultry Colliery (Clackmannanshire) 18, *20*, *132*, 133, 201, 278 n.24
Times, The 41, 149, 213, 224
Tirpentwys Colliery (South Wales) 127, *128*, 200
Town and Country Planning Act (1932) 180
Town and Country Planning Act (1947) 269
town planning 26, 27 0, 33, 168, 176
Town Planning Acts (1919/1925) 165, 180
trade unions 57, 198, 279–280 n.21
training facilities 234–5
Transport Underground (pamphlets) 231
Traylor, W. 31, 32, 94, 115
Tremenheere, Hugh Seymour 54, 147, 156
Truck Act (1872) 158
Tudor Walters, John 187, 188–9, 190
Tudor Walters Report (1918) 34, 39–40, 165, 177, *177*, 191, 194

U-shape plan 103, 111
United States (US) 23–4, 27, 33, 78, 79, 203, 248, 280 n.3
Unwin, Raymond 33, 34, 164–77, 179, 186, 188, 195, 197, 198, 268, 277 n.3, 279 n.17
and Letchworth 164, 171, 173, 174, 175
mining experience of 166–7, 168
and row housing 165, 168–9, 171
socialism of 165, 166, 169–170
Yorkshire Town scheme of 171–2, *172*

Viewpark Colliery (Lanark) 95, *96*, 97
Vondelschool, Netherlands (Dudok, 1929) 69, *71*

walkways/footbridges 81, 111, 127
Warsop Vale (Nottinghamshire) 172–3, *173*
Washing and Drying Accommodation Committee 46–7, 49, 51, 58, 62, 77
Washington (Durham) 185, 269, 281 n.29
Wattstown (South Wales) 90–91, *91*
Wearmouth Colliery (Durham) 95, *96*, 97
welfare of miners 22, 32, 54, 90, 137, 159
see also hospitals/health centres; recreational facilities
welfare state 10, 35, 54, 135, 143–4, 213, 226
Wellesley Colliery (Fife) 118–121, *120*
Wemyss Colliery/village (Fife) 61, 156
Wendingen (journal) 64, 65
Westwood, Joseph 269, 272
Whalen, Thomas 215, *215*, 216
Wharncliffe Silkstone Colliery (Yorkshire) 47, 61, 176
Wheldale Colliery (West Yorkshire) 127, *129*
Whitburn Colliery (Northumberland) 91
Williams, Owen 21, 144, 145
Wilson, Harold 202, 280 n.1
winding gear/houses 10, 99, 210, 215, 242, *242*, 243, 246, 253, 258, *259*, 260, *260*, 264–5, *264*, 267
Wolstanton Colliery (Staffordshire) 243–4, *245*, 248
women 49, 57, 81, 90, 97, 109, 113–114, *113*, 153, 155, 277 nn.5,18
and housing 192–3, 194–5, 279 n.20
and NCB publications 223, 226, 280 n.11
Women's Labour League 54, 55, 61
Woodland, W.A. 31, 32, 94, 114, 121, 126, 278 n.25
Wooodlands (Yorkshire) 163–4, *164*, 173–4, 175, 176, 186, 192, 279 n.7
Wright, Frank Lloyd 19, 65, 67, 71, 114, 115, 121, 127
Wyndham Colliery (South Wales) 118, *119*

Zola, Emile 151–2, 216

IMAGE CREDITS

Abercrombie and Archibald, 1928, *East Kent Regional Planning Scheme*: 124, 125, 126
Abercrombie and Forshaw, 1943, *County of London Plan*: 15
© Alamy: 147
Anon. (undated), *Kells and District Community and Miners' Welfare Centre*: 109
Architectural Press Archive, RIBA Collections: 140
Architecture and Building News, 1930: 36, 37
Architecture and Building News, 1937: 66
Architecture Design and Construction, 1945: 68
Architecture Review, 1941: 72
Author: 33, 34, 35, 86, 105, 173
Author, courtesy of Big Pit National Coal Museum: 103, 104
Bertram, 1938, *Design*: 2
Chappell and Lovat-Fraser, 1920, *Pithead and Factory Baths*: 21, 27, 28, 29
Colliery Guardian, 1930: 112
Cross, 1906, *Public Baths and Wash Houses*: 26
Ferguson, 1973, *Glenrothes 1948–1973*: 172
Forshaw, 1924, *Lancaster and Morecambe Regional Scheme*: 9
Forshaw, 1943, Chadwick Public Lecture: 11
© Historic Environment Scotland (Sir Basil Spence Collection): 135, 136, 137
© Courtesy of Historic Environment Scotland (*Annual Report of Miners' Welfare Fund*, 1937): 65
© Courtesy of Historic Environment Scotland: 67, 84
Holme, 1935, *Industrial Architecture*: 3, 5, 6
HP, 1913, Home Office Departmental Committee: 24, 25
Journal of British Architects, 1935: 78
Letchworth Garden City Heritage Foundation: 121
Mining Association of Great Britain, 1938, *The Model Coal Mine*: 133
M'Vail, 1911, *Housing of Miners*: 110, 111
MWC, 1923, *Miners' Welfare Fund – First report*: 16, 17, 18
MWC, 1924, *Miners' Welfare Fund – Second report*: 39, 40, 41
MWC, 1927, *Miners' Welfare Fund – Fifth report*: 42
MWC, 1928, *Miners' Welfare Fund – Sixth Report*: 43, 44
MWC, 1929, *Miners' Welfare Fund – Seventh report*: 45, 46
MWC, 1931, *Miners' Welfare Fund – Ninth Report*: 49, 53, 54
MWC, 1932, *Miners' Welfare Fund – Tenth report*: 56, 57, 58, 63, 64
MWC, 1934, *Miners' Welfare Fund – Twelfth report*: 70, 81, 85, 93, 94
MWC, 1935, *Miners' Welfare Fund – Thirteenth Report*: 90, 61
MWC, 1936, *Miners' Welfare Fund – Fourteenth report*: 62, 98
MWC, 1937, *Miners' Welfare Fund – Fifteenth report*: 96
MWC, 1938, *Miners' Welfare Fund – Sixteenth report*: 60
MWC, 1939, *Miners' Welfare Fund 1938*: 71, 91, 92, 134
MWC, 1940, *Miners' Welfare Fund 1939*: 106, 108
MWC, 1946, *Miners' Welfare in War-time*: 12, 132
NA Coal 80: 75, 76, 77, 79, 80, 82, 83, 87, 88, 89, 95, 97, 99, 100, 101, 102, 107, 113, 131, 145, 148, 150, 154–166
NA Coal 80/253: 73, 74
NA Coal 80/477: 59
NA Coal 80/971: 7
NA Coal 80/1147: 19, 20, 22, 23
NA Coal 80/1147/1-46: 47, 48, 50, 51, 52
NA Coal 80/2063: 114
NCB, 1946, annual report: 1
NCB, 1938, *Mining People*: 138
NCB, 1946, *The Future of the Coal Miner*: 141
NCB, 1958, *Shaft Story*: 143
NCB, 1972, *Annual Report*: 153
NCB, 1982, *Armoured flexible conveyors*: 142
National Coal Mining Museum, www.ncm.org.uk/library/digitised-coal-magazine: 139, 151, 152, 168, 169
National Library of Scotland: 115, 116, 117, 118, 120
Nott-Bower and Walkerdine, 1957, *National Coal Board: The First Ten Years*: 144, 146
Pevsner and Richmond, 1957, *The Buildings of England: Northumberland*: 4
Rhondda Cynon Taff Library Service: 149
RIBA Collections: 69, 167, 170, 171
Swedish Cooperative Wholesale Society's Architects' Office, 1935: 13
Swenarton, 1981, *Homes Fit for Heroes: The Politics and Architecture of Early State Housing in Britain*: 122
The Proud City: A Plan for London, 1946 film: 14
Tudor Walters Committee, 1918, report: 123
Tudor Walters, 1927, *The Building of Twelve Thousand Houses*: 126, 127, 128, 129, 130
University of Liverpool Archives; John Henry Forshaw Papers D113/8/1: 8, 10, 55
Unwin, 1901, *Art of Building a Home*: 119
Wendingen, 1925: 30, 31, 32, 38

Cover design by Stefi Orazi, based on graphic produced by the Miners' Welfare Committee for its *Sixteenth Annual Report*, 1938.